THE BATTERED CHILD
Selected Readings

THE BATTERED CHILD

SELECTED READINGS

Jerome E. Leavitt
California
State University,
Fresno

TO
CLARA MARIE LEAVITT

PREFACE

The last two decades have revealed some of the best and some of the worst situations in economics, government, education, and family relationships. Young children are affected by all of these, especially those children— the battered children—whose parents or other adults responsible for their care have not been able to adequately handle themselves in today's society.

On the negative side of the situation, we find adults who cannot adjust to the stresses and strains of our society or of child care, and consequently either physically or psychologically abuse their children, many times in ways beyond belief.

On the positive side, we find that medicine and psychiatry have developed to a point where there is hope that these adults can be helped. Also, within recent years laws have been instituted requiring that child abuse cases be reported. As a result of these laws and through the required use of X-ray in hospital admissions, cases of child abuse can be pin-pointed.

This book was written to make it possible for the reader to take a multi-disciplinary look at the problem of child abuse and at its possible solutions. As an example, we might use the analogy of viewing a house. From some angles the house has a garage; from others, the garage is not apparent. From a different angle, a fireplace might be seen. So it is with the study of the battered child. The medical people have an excellent view of the physical damage done to a child; the social science experts see the family complex and how each individual fits into the picture. The legal people see the problem from the point of view of the state and the rights of the individuals concerned; educators recognize the need to understand and strengthen these wounded children.

To bring the full picture into focus, we have gone to the disciplines representing these various viewpoints and have selected those articles judged to be most helpful to the reader regardless of his own discipline. Additionally, the articles range from the historical viewpoint to the viewpoint of detection and prevention. The reader will find repetition of many points as he goes from one section to another. This is as it should be, for as previously mentioned, these disciplines viewed separately do not help us understand or solve our problems; seen collectively, however, they enable us to widen our perspective of the situation, increase our understanding of the problem, and, hopefully, aid in the solution.

The message of this book is to be found in the selections by writers in various areas of expertise. For the convenience of the reader, these selections are listed in the table of contents and then given in the text as they originally appeared in various scholastic publications. The articles belonging to each discipline are contained within a chapter, which opens with an introduction to the topic and closes with a summary to pull it all together. The chapters conclude with a number of discussion questions and additional suggested readings related to each aspect of our general topic—the battered child.

Since this book uses an interdisciplinary approach to the subject of the battered child, it is recommended for courses in a number of disciplines that encompass the study of children. These courses pervade the undergraduate and graduate levels of junior colleges, colleges, and universities and may constitute a part of in-service or pre-service training programs. Such courses include, but are not limited to, Child Psychology, Child Development, Development and Learning, Psychology of the Criminal Human Behavior and Social Environment, Sociology of the Child, Medical Sociology, Social Psychology, Child and Family Living, Nursing of Children, Disaster Nursing, School Nursing, Early Childhood Education, and Corrective Law.

The author wishes to acknowledge the assistance of the University students Charlotte Novak Plougher, Rick Saxon, Mary E. Wright, Millie Largent, L. Holmes, Lupe Ramirez, David Sinner, and Robert A. Keosheyan who helped to evaluate the articles used. Thanks is given to Diana Baskett for her patience in assisting with the library research and in typing the manuscript. Appreciation is also expressed to Jon D. Haughton, Reference Librarian, San Joaquin Valley Information Service for an extensive search of the literature in the field. And the author thanks his wife, Florence Wilkins Leavitt, who helped with the editing and provided the author with encouragement throughout the entire project.

Jerome E. Leavitt

California State University, Fresno
January 1973

CONTENTS

10,000 CHILDREN BATTERED AND STARVED. HUNDREDS DIE:

Some Parents Admit Guilt — Intensive Two-Year Study of Battered and Maltreated Children Reveals the True Story Behind Abused Youngsters

by Howard G. Earl

Americans undoubtedly will be shocked to learn that perhaps even among those residing in their own neighborhood, maybe right next door to them, are men and women who willfully and intentionally batter, burn, and starve their children.

■ **THESE PARENTS** are numbered among the many throughout the nation who each year brutally maltreat upwards of 10,000 children with hundreds of the victims dying as a result of the abuse, or even worse, paralyzed, physically deformed, or mentally retarded for life. The condition has come to be known as the "battered child syndrome."

Examples of the brutality are not hard to come by. For instance, in Paterson, New Jersey, a severely beaten two-year-old boy died in Paterson General Hospital after the boy's father, according to police, walked the child to the hospital. Bleeding from the head and body, the youngster died in the emergency room 10 minutes after arrival.

Dr. George Sugent, assistant medical examiner for Passaic County, explained what many physicians are learning today. It was not the first time the boy had been battered. Doctor Sugent said that the child had suffered kidney damage. There were old wounds on the youngster's body indicating how the kidney damage had been inflicted.

In Washington, D.C., the same type of treatment is

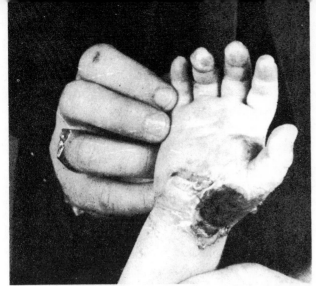

Mother beat boy for heating a pizza, then held his hand over gas flame after finding him trying to light cigarettes. She lost all her children after undergoing psychiatric study.

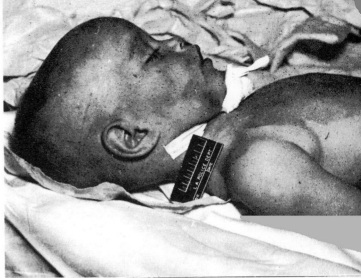

Photos: Los Angeles Police Department

A 13-month-old boy beaten by mother and stepfather had black and blue marks about eyes and cheeks, multiple hemorrhages inside right eye, and paralyzed right side. Died later. Mother sentenced to one year in jail, five years probation. Stepfather sentenced to six months to 10 years in county jail.

found to be inflicted upon children. There in the nation's capital, a blond, blue-eyed, four-year-old girl was admitted unconscious to one of the hospitals. An examination disclosed a fractured skull, and lacerations covered her back, face, arms, and legs. When questioned, she is reported to have told the doctors in her childish way:

"Mama kept hitting me with a big black stick."

It is not unusual for an infant, or a youngster up to the age of six and seven years old to be admitted to a hospital with face, legs, and arms, and other parts of the body swollen more than twice their normal size because of second-degree burns. Some parents have used their youngsters as human ash trays. Others have poured boiling water and other hot liquids over them, and even dunked them in scalding water.

In a Southwestern city a mother became indignant because her two-and-a-half-year-old daughter did not respond readily enough to toilet training. One day, in a fit of temper over the child's inability to control a bowel movement, the mother gave the youngster an enema with near scalding water. The doctor was forced to perform a colostomy to save the child's life.

Beatings and other abuse are said to cause more deaths among children than auto accidents, such diseases as leukemia, cystic fibrosis, and muscular dystrophy.

Mary Jean Clark, director of social work at Chicago's Children's Memorial Hospital, recently said that in a 24-month period at Children's Memorial there were 39 children from 38 families who were reported to the Department of Social Work by physicians who suspected or knew there had been physical abuse. Seventy-seven percent of the children were two years and younger, and 43 percent were under 12 months. Thirty-three percent of the children were brought in by one or both parents.

Abuse of nine of the children was admitted by a par-

ent. Two of the nine children suffered gunshot wounds inflicted by their fathers. But the majority of abuse cases are not reported and thus are not investigated.

The list could continue indefinitely, citing cases of children who have been beaten, burned with cigarettes, thrown downstairs, had their heads banged against walls and radiators, plunged into boiling water, suffocated, and otherwise tortured and starved—some to death—by parents who too often stubbornly refuse to admit guilt when confronted with the evidence contradicting their most vehement denials.

Wilson D. McKerrow, executive director of the Brooklyn Society for the Prevention of Cruelty to Children, reports:

"In my experience, in a great many instances, one parent has physically harmed a child. However, the other parent protected the one inflicting the harm, and there was no way to obtain proof."

McKerrow added that there have been additional instances where some children have appeared to be involved repeatedly in "accidents," and where it was suspected that the child had been maltreated. He also reported that the American Humane Society subscribed to a clipping service in the interest of obtaining information on the number of cases of seemingly child abuse. The service clipped from the nation's newspapers all accounts of seeming child abuse between January 1 and October 1 of 1962. The accounts were taken from newspapers in 48 states.

There were 662 children involved and, of these, 109 died.

"When one considers that many cases were published in the newspapers," said McKerrow, "one can surmise that several times that number of abuses actually occur but remain unpublished."

Last year Katherine Bain, M.D., deputy chief of the nation's Children's Bureau, released a paragraph of a letter from the director of a state crime prevention bureau. The paragraph read:

"The awful part of the death of the boy, under two years old, was that when admitted to the hospital, where he died after surgery that took four hours, he still had a cast on his left arm. It had been put there 10 days previously by the same hospital people—and abuse had been the cause of that broken arm."

The American Humane Society found that one of the horrible facts learned from newspaper clippings is that parents beat, burn, drown, stab, and suffocate their children with weapons ranging from baseball bats to plastic bags. Most of the victims are under four years of age and about one-quarter of them die.

A Denver study showed that of 302 cases of child abuse, 85 percent suffered permanent brain injury. And the Cook County (Illinois) Family Court, according to the *New York Times*, reported recently it is receiving 100 abused-children cases a month. The same situation exists in many areas of the country.

What would cause a parent to beat a child until permanent injury, often death, resulted?

The question was asked Mrs. Edith Lee, supervising probation officer of the San Francisco Juvenile Court. She replied:

"First, I think you must recognize the type of child who is abused before you determine the type of parent doing the abusing. You might say there is a correlation here."

The conversation went into more or less of an interview which developed the following points:

What kind of children are battered?

We frequently find where there is an illegitimate child in the family, the first one is born out of wedlock and the mother later marries the father. This child will receive the full force of the mother's fury. Again, it may be the child born while the husband is overseas with the armed forces. He returns home, accepts the child, but there is that feeling.

Does the child who causes economic problems receive similar treatment?

Yes. For example, the mother is contented and happy with two children who now may be in school. Then a third child comes along. She can no longer go out during the afternoon or continue her position if she happens to be working. She can't bring in that extra money, or enjoy that freedom that once was hers because of the new baby. This is the child who gets battered.

Again, a great many parents are horrified when they first learn they're about to have a child, or going to have their fifth one. Four was all they wanted. They're sensible, loving parents—or have been to the other four. But the fifth one is too much of an adjustment for them

to make. Arguments ensue and the fifth, or unwanted, child suffers the brunt of the parents' pent-up anger. This happens among parents too immature to adjust to another child who tips the economic and emotional cart.

Do you know of any cases, Mrs. Lee, where a deficiency in the child would account for abuse?

Quite a few. These are the children who fail parental expectations. Now this is apt to happen in the home of the striving parent, who, for example, wants the offspring to do very well in school. The child is in a very fine private school, and this is a status symbol for the parent. When the child fails, then the parent or parents become infuriated. The youngster is jeopardizing their status in the community. The child is abused for his inability to make the necessary high scholastic grades to remain in school. We find these types of cases in the upper-middle class and occasionally in the striving minority.

It has been said that sometimes a child will become the target of parental abuse because he resembles either the father or mother. Have you found this to be true?

Unfortunately, too often. The mother is in conflict with the father, and the child resembles the disliked parent. So, the mother really is going to take it out on 'that child every time she looks at him. Because she sees in him the father, whom she hates. She can't batter the father, so the child gets it.

Then again, the battered child may be the pawn between conflicting parents. They hate one another. They're fighting one another. If the child seems to be backing the father, then the mother batters and abuses the youngster. And if there seems to be a change in affections toward the mother then the father is the abuser. The child as a pawn between fighting adults happens more often than most people realize.

This 22-month-old youngster suffered with severe malnutrition, dehydration, and congested lungs. Maggots were in his eyes, nose, and mouth. Mother given 30-day jail sentence.

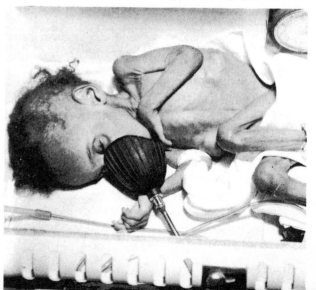

Is there any case you know about where the child is battered or maltreated in some way for no particular reason?

We find in most cases that there is some sort of a conflict, even though it may be beneath the surface. The mother or father hates the child for some reason, although they're not certain why. In cases of this type, the punishment is even worse than the brutality inflicted by a merely confused parent.

I've seen cases where the mother is a wonderful housekeeper and does everything well. But her little boy bangs on things. This upsets his mother and she lets him have what she believes he rightly deserves. The only problem is that her feelings run away with her and she becomes violent. Brutal batterings or other forms of violent punishment result.

And lastly, the one that really tugs at my heartstrings is the battered mentally defective or brain-damaged child. One or both of the parents cannot accept the fact that their child isn't quite right mentally. They argue: "Of course, he's all right. He's just as bright as any other child. He's just stubborn and won't do it." And with this kind of attitude, the poor little fellow really gets walloped. And you know where those blows usually fall? On the head!

You have named several types of children representative of those who are battered and abused. What type of parents do the abusing?

There are a number of types. Perhaps foremost is the parent who is so emotionally or mentally involved with his own problems that it's a flagrant error for the child to try to break through to that parent. When an attempt is made it calls for some type of punishment, usually very bizarre. This is the child who will come into the hospital covered with cigarette burns.

Now, the mentally ill mother inflicts all kinds of punishment such as cigarette and strap burns, broken arms and legs, fractured ribs, ducking in a tub of hot water, throwing the child down a flight of stairs, banging its head against a radiator, and laying the little one on its back or stomach on a hot radiator. Nothing seems too bizarre or too cruel. It's a sadistic desire to inflict harm upon someone. Since an infant or youngster is helpless to put up any kind of defense, the brutality is inflicted with ease and probably satisfaction.

Does the alcoholic parent pose a problem so far as child abuse is concerned?

In most instances we find the alcoholic parent when sober is a very sweet, gentle, child-loving individual. But when under the influence of alcohol he becomes an entirely different personality. The alcoholic does all kinds of things. He batters his children, rapes his daughters, and beats his wife, too.

Treatment of children often tells you something about the parent. The alcoholic parent, the very rigid parent, the parent who knows exactly what he wants from his child and is inflexible in his demands; these are the types of parents who are liable to beat their children with electric cords, a coat hanger, and any other implement readily available.

Wouldn't the striving parent you mentioned earlier come under one of the categories you just mentioned?

Yes, we touched upon the striving parent when we talked about the child who fails parental expectations. There also is the deviant parent, one who deforms a child. He is deviant because he is deviating from the conventional pattern. We find that this parent fits in among a number of the type patterns, including the socially deviating parent.

By socially deviating I mean the mother or father who has a paramour. The child by the former marriage is interfering with the affair between this man and woman. In the first place, the affair is morally wrong. Both know it and their sense of guilt adds to the fury when the child is abused.

Is there any particular age bracket in which children are abused. Or, does it occur from infancy, until they are able to defend themselves or leave home?

Battered and abused children range in age from a couple of months to 16 years or older. Recently a case was brought to my attention which involved an infant who was beaten so severely by retarded parents that brain damage resulted. They beat the child when she cried. One day the parents beat her so severely they thought they had killed her, and rushed her to a hospital. She was so badly battered the doctors referred her to us. When the little one was able to leave the hospital, she was sent to a very special type of foster home.

Another case involved the three-year-old daughter of a mentally ill father who had been left a considerable sum of money. He spent most of his time in a bar. The next-door neighbor in the apartment house thought she heard the child crying a great deal. Then the crying grad-

Mother of 29-month-old boy claimed he was behavior problem. She beat him with stick and screwdriver handle, dropped him on the floor, and beat his head on wall or threw him against it. She choked him to force his mouth open to eat. One day she banged his head against wall and next day found him dead in bed. He had burn marks on face and injuries on face and head, badly burned and blistered hands, and numerous old lacerations all over body. Mother pleaded guilty to murder.

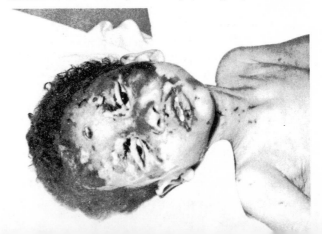

ually lessened and finally, there was only a whine or moan. Then there was no sound.

The neighbor became concerned, went to the landlady, who entered the apartment with a passkey. She found the little girl lying on the bed where her father left her constantly, giving her no care. The mother had died a few months previously. The girl was so badly malnourished that it took weeks of hospitalization to return her to a healthy physical condition. There was, of course, some risk of retardation because of the child's prolonged deprivation. However, wealthy relatives of the dead mother were located and they adopted the child, willing to cope with this retardation problem should it arise.

Six-year-old Mike presented quite a different case. He was in one accident after another. His mother was always present but she inevitably gave the same reasons. He fell downstairs, off a chair, climbed up on the table and rolled off, or fell out of bed.

Mrs. Lee filed a petition in Juvenile Court stating that any mother who was in the home and allowed these accidents to happen to her children was guilty of neglect and the child no longer should be entrusted to her care. The judge disagreed on the basis that the mother's culpability could not be proved, and refused to grant the petition to have the child removed from the mother's custody. The case was dismissed.

Three weeks later the child was referred once more to Mrs. Lee, this time by the hospital. He had been brought in again, not only beaten but ruptured. How did it happen? The mother blamed a fall down the stairs in the home. However, under probing, she admitted that the day before she spanked him because he complained of a pain.

A petition was again brought before the court. This time the hospital doctors were able to submit professional opinions linking the mother to the child's condition, which was in the medical opinions the result of abuse. On the basis of the medical findings, the judge removed the boy from his mother. The action was not taken because it had been proved that the mother did anything wrong but, in the light of the repetitive circumstances, the judge said, "The child needed protection."

There are cases when action comes too late. An example is a two-year-old girl whose father reported the child's mother was living with another man. He wasn't objecting to the mother's immoral behavior. He was protesting that the $125 a month sent the mother for care of the child was being spent to keep the other man and herself. Just 11 days after the father filed the report, the mother's boy friend beat the little girl to death.

One of the odd findings in national studies of child brutality is that usually one child is singled out for the abuse and battering. It is unusual for more than one offspring of the same family to suffer a similar fate. Time was when it was next to impossible to obtain medical evidence indicating a child had been repeatedly beat-

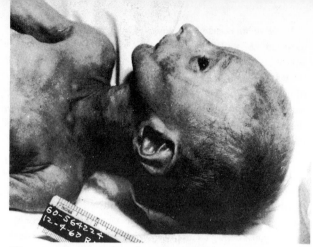

Three-month-old victim taken to hospital in advanced stage of dehydration and malnutrition. He weighed only five pounds and had severe bedsores. After death of child the parents were taken into custody. Father received 180-day suspended jail sentence and three-year probation. Later committed. Mother received suspended 180-day sentence and put on probation.

en or maltreated by a parent, parent's mate, or an amour.

Drs. Linwood J. Rayford, Marion Mann, Richard L. Whelton, and Jorge B. Morales of Howard University College of Medicine, Washington, D.C., point out that the first step in the diagnosis of a "battered child syndrome" is physical manifestations. These may vary from skin abrasions and bruises to ruptured organs in the head, thorax, abdomen, or pelvis. Doctors also should look for suspicious lesions which are in various stages of healing, soft tissue swelling, fracture of any bone, failure to thrive, and sudden death.

Dr. Vincent J. Fontana, chief of pediatrics at New York's St. Vincent's Hospital, believes child abuse can be spotted long before it reaches the critical stage. He says the maltreated child frequently exhibits signs of malnutrition, vitamin deficiency, and obvious physical neglect long before he is physically abused.

Radiology has become a valuable aid in detecting the abused or battered child. X-rays make it possible for doctors to determine how and when bones are broken. The x-rays provide a tool to determine with almost complete certainty whether injuries are due to abuse or accident. They also disclose when earlier fractures in various stages of healing are present. This is a major aid in deciding between willful abuse and accidents because experience has proved that child beating invariably is a repetitious process.

One of the problems confronting physicians is that the "battered child syndrome"—willful trauma to young children or syndrome of unsuspected trauma in infancy— is difficult at times to diagnose. One reason for the difficulty lies in clinical signs and symptoms which vary greatly according to the children involved.

It has been explained by a number of physicians that in battered children any or all signs of soft-tissue and **bone injury or disease may be present: petechia (a minute, rounded spot of hemorrhage on a surface such as skin,** mucous membrane, or a cross-sectional surface of an organ); abrasions; contusions on the head, trunk, joints, or limbs; pain or tenderness in the limbs with decreased voluntary movement, or even pseudoparalysis. Other common signs are irritability and absence of appetite. Among other things denoting the "battered child syndrome" may be blood in the urine, shock, vomiting, incoordination of muscular action, or impaired vision.

Whenever a child with broken bones is brought into a hospital, physicians are becoming suspicious of foul play if multiple bruises are seen, or if the reported cause of injury is inconsistent with the extent of the injury. Becoming better apprised of the number of children willfully beaten by a parent or parents, pediatric workers are beginning to ask more often than they once did, "What lies below the surface of those bruises?" Or, "What bestiality has occurred here?"

In Chicago, the juvenile agencies and the police department say some cases are referred to them for investigation. The referrals come from the Board of Education. However, there are many authorities who believe that the most severe injuries are inflicted on children from six months to six years old. The parents know that there is less likelihood of discovering these injuries, especially by school authorities because they wouldn't be likely to see children of pre-school age.

Unfortunately, up until the full force of publicity had been thrown upon this whole sordid picture of the "battered child syndrome," willful trauma was considered very seldom in the differential diagnosis. The physician's reluctance to believe it, even when suspected, delayed the necessary measures which would bring out the truth and ensure remedial measures.

Once a child is suspected of being maltreated by a parent or parents, physicians now are being urged to put forth every means at their disposal to prevent further injury—and possible death—because repeated trauma does occur more often than in a single isolated event.

Too often the lack of witnesses and the absence of the child's own testimony—many children are too young to testify in their own behalf—make it difficult for a physician to procure legal intervention for a child's protection. The doctor must make his own choice as to whether he will insist on a complete investigation of the home situation by proper authorities.

One of the problems in combating the "battered child syndrome" is reporting of incidents to the proper authorities. Dr. Ralph V. Platou, professor and head of pediatrics at Tulane University, and his associates called upon physicians to play an active role in detecting and preventing the abuse of children. However, doctors and hospitals are reluctant to report what they believe to be abuse of children. Why? There always is the possibility of getting into legal entanglements, and very few individuals, doctors or others, are eager to become involved with the law. Doctors fear slander suits if they tip off the police and the charge fails to hold up under investigation.

The U.S. Children's Bureau, to meet this problem, has drawn up what has been termed a model state law requiring all doctors and hospitals to report suspected child beatings immediately to the police. It would be considered a misdemeanor not to make such a report orally or in writing as soon as such treatment is suspected.

The law grants immunity from criminal or civil liability to anyone reporting in good faith. At least 38 of the states have enacted a law which conforms in some respects to the one suggested by the Children's Bureau.

"California has a special law on the abuse of children," explained Mrs. Lee. "It states that in any case in which a minor is brought to a physician for diagnosis and treatment, or is under his charge and care, and he suspects the minor to be a victim of abuse, the physician shall report the facts by telephone and write in to the police department of the city. The report should state, if known, the name of the patient, his whereabouts, and the character and extent of injury."

Mrs. Lee pointed out that she has spent considerable time explaining the law to health departments, various medical centers, and medical societies. She feels the physicians and others connected with the medical profession understand the law and know that reporting a case of child abuse is mandatory and that failure to do so is a misdemeanor. She thinks the number of cases uncovered has been on the increase since doctors and others are protected by the California law when reporting.

The office of the general counsel of the American Medical Association wisely summed up the situation in the *Journal of the AMA* with an editorial which stated:

"Statutes should be enacted which define child abuse in its several forms, and consideration should be given to the means of protecting the child. Since the problem is social as well as medical, the limited nature of presently proposed legislation should be questioned. No evidence has been presented, and none is known to exist, which establishes that mandatory reporting in and of itself will eradicate undesirable social conduct."

The editorial concludes that it would seem more desirable to devise a program of legislation which would confer immunity from litigation and damages on physicians, lawyers, nurses, social workers, and other professional people who, in good faith and on reasonable evidence, seek to protect abused children by reporting in confidence suspected problems to the proper designated authority.

"This legislation," says the editorial, "should relate not only to reporting abuse but also to providing protection for the child and his siblings. It is unwise to draft and adopt statutes which fail to come to grips with the entire problem. The legislative approaches should be thoroughly studied and laws devised which will be most effective in eliminating the battered child syndrome in all its forms." END

I
Who Are the Battered Children?

INTRODUCTION

There are varying estimates of the number of children who are mistreated—that is, "battered,"—in the United States each year. One source puts it at 50,000 to 75,000 children mistreated each year with one out of every four cases ending in the child's death. Another estimates at least 60,000 cases of children willfully beaten, burned, smothered, or starved every year. More children under five years of age die from mistreatment by parents than from tuberculosis, whooping cough, polio, measles, diabetes, rheumatic fever and appendicitis combined. The articles that follow provide greater detail on the subject and a divergence of opinion on the amount and kind of abuse.

Professionals both in individual disciplines and those in related disciplines disagree as to what is considered child abuse and what defines a battered child. Some say that physical abuse is all with which we need be concerned. Others maintain that psychological abuse can be equally damaging. However, the physical abuse of a child usually provides the only tangible evidence that we have.

It is a common misconception that so-called lower class people are the chief child abusers. This is not true. People from all strata of our society are abusers and each stratum abuses to nearly an equal degree. This misconception of greater abuse in the lower class probably results from the fact that the middle and upper class parents are in a better position to conceal the abuse.

Abusive parents usually do fit into one of three patterns. They are either sadistic in their tendencies and have a definite urge to kill the child; or they are often under unusual stress or suffer family discord; or they have been abused at the hands of their own parents and thus see this as the normal way to react in a given situation.

The articles that follow describe in detail who the battered children are, who batter them, and how they are battered.

The Battered-Child Syndrome

C. Henry Kempe, M.D., Denver, Frederic N. Silverman, M.D., Cincinnati, Brandt F. Steele, M.D.,

William Droegemueller, M.D., and Henry K. Silver, M.D., Denver

The battered-child syndrome, a clinical condition in young children who have received serious physical abuse, is a frequent cause of permanent injury or death. The syndrome should be considered in any child exhibiting evidence of fracture of any bone, subdural hematoma, failure to thrive, soft tissue swellings or skin bruising, in any child who dies suddenly, or where the degree and type of injury is at variance with the history given regarding the occurrence of the trauma. Psychiatric factors are probably of prime importance in the pathogenesis of the disorder, but knowledge of these factors is limited. Physicians have a duty and responsibility to the child to require a full evaluation of the problem and to guarantee that no expected repetition of trauma will be permitted to occur.

THE BATTERED-CHILD SYNDROME is a term used by us to characterize a clinical condition in young children who have received serious physical abuse, generally from a parent or foster parent. The condition has also been described as "unrecognized trauma" by radiologists, orthopedists, pediatricians, and social service workers. It is a significant cause of childhood disability and death. Unfortunately, it is frequently not recognized or, if diagnosed, is inadequately handled by the physician because of hesitation to bring the case to the attention of the proper authorities.

Incidence

In an attempt to collect data on the incidence of this problem, we undertook a nation-wide survey of hospitals which were asked to indicate the incidence of this syndrome in a one-year period. Among 71 hospitals replying, 302 such cases were reported to have occurred; 33 of the children died; and 85 suffered permanent brain injury. In one-third of the cases proper medical diagnosis was followed by some type of legal action. We also surveyed 77 District Attorneys who reported that they had knowledge of 447 cases in a similar one-year period. Of these, 45 died, and 29 suffered permanent brain damage; court action was initiated in 46% of this group. This condition has been a particularly common problem in our hospitals; on a single day, in November, 1961, the Pediatric Service of the Colorado General Hospital was caring for 4 infants suffering from the parent-inflicted battered-child syndrome. Two of the 4 died of their central nervous system trauma; 1 subsequently died suddenly in an unexplained manner 4 weeks after discharge from the hospital while under the care of its parents, while the fourth is still enjoying good health.

Clinical Manifestations

The clinical manifestations of the battered-child syndrome vary widely from those cases in which the trauma is very mild and is often unsuspected and unrecognized, to those who exhibit the most florid evidence of injury to the soft tissues and skeleton. In the former group, the patients' signs and symptoms may be considered to have resulted from failure to thrive from some other cause or to have been produced by a metabolic disorder, an infectious process, or some other disturbance. In these patients specific findings of trauma such as bruises or characteristic roentgenographic changes as described below may be misinterpreted and their significance not recognized.

The battered-child syndrome may occur at any age, but, in general, the affected children are younger than 3 years. In some instances the clinical manifestations are limited to those resulting from a single episode of trauma, but more often the child's general health is below par, and he shows evidence of neglect including poor skin hygiene, multiple soft tissue injuries, and malnutrition. One often obtains a history of previous episodes suggestive of parental neglect or trauma. A marked discrepancy between clinical findings and historical data as supplied by the parents is a major diagnostic feature of the battered-child syndrome. The fact that no new lesions, either of the soft tissue or of the bone, occur while the child is in the hospital or in a protected environment lends added weight to the diagnosis and tends to exclude many diseases of the skeletal or hemopoietic systems in which lesions may occur spontaneously or after minor trauma. Subdural hematoma, with or without fracture of the skull, is, in our experience, an extremely frequent finding even in the absence of

Professor and Chairman (Dr. Kempe) and Professor of Pediatrics (Dr. Silver), Department of Pediatrics; Associate Professor of Psychiatry (Dr. Steele), and Assistant Resident in Obstetrics and Gynecology (Dr. Droegemueller), University of Colorado School of Medicine; and Director, Division of Roentgenology, Children's Hospital (Dr. Silverman).

fractures of the long bones. In an occasional case the parent or parent-substitute may also have assaulted the child by administering an overdose of a drug or by exposing the child to natural gas or other toxic substances. The characteristic distribution of these multiple fractures and the observation that the lesions are in different stages of healing are of additional value in making the diagnosis.

In most instances, the diagnostic bone lesions are observed incidental to examination for purposes other than evaluation for possible abuse. Occasionally, examination following known injury discloses signs of other, unsuspected, skeletal involvement. When parental assault is under consideration, radiologic examination of the entire skeleton may provide objective confirmation. Following diagnosis, radiologic examination can document the healing of lesions and reveal the appearance of new lesions if additional trauma has been inflicted.

The radiologic manifestations of trauma to growing skeletal structures are the same whether or not there is a history of injury. Yet there is reluctance on the part of many physicians to accept the radiologic signs as indications of repetitive trauma and possible abuse. This reluctance stems from the emotional unwillingness of the physician to consider abuse as the cause of the child's difficulty and also because of unfamiliarity with certain aspects of fracture healing so that he is unsure of the significance of the lesions that are present. To the informed physician, the bones tell a story the child is too young or too frightened to tell.

Psychiatric Aspects

Psychiatric knowledge pertaining to the problem of the battered child is meager, and the literature on the subject is almost nonexistent. The type and degree of physical attack varies greatly. At one extreme, there is direct murder of children. This is usually done by a parent or other close relative, and, in these individuals, a frank psychosis is usually readily apparent. At the other extreme are those cases where no overt harm has occurred, and one parent, more often the mother, comes to the psychiatrist for help, filled with anxiety and guilt related to fantasies of hurting the child. Occasionally the disorder has gone beyond the point of fantasy and has resulted in severe slapping or spanking. In such cases the adult is usually responsive to treatment; it is not known whether or not the disturbance in these adults would progress to the point where they would inflict significant trauma on the child.

Between these 2 extremes are a large number of battered children with mild to severe injury which may clear completely or result in permanent damage or even death after repeated attack. Descriptions of such children have been published by numerous investigators including radiologists, orthopedists, and social workers. The latter have reported on their studies of investigations of families in which children have been beaten and of their work in effecting satisfactory placement for the protection of the child. In some of these published reports the parents, or at least the parent who inflicted the abuse, have been found to be of low intelligence. Often, they are described as psychopathic or sociopathic characters. Alcoholism, sexual promiscuity, unstable marriages, and minor criminal activities are reportedly common amongst them. They are immature, impulsive, self-centered, hypersensitive, and quick to react with poorly controlled aggression. Data in some cases indicate that such attacking parents had themselves been subject to some degree of attack from their parents in their own childhood.

Beating of children, however, is not confined to people with a psychopathic personality or of borderline socioeconomic status. It also occurs among people with good education and stable financial and social background. However, from the scant data that are available, it would appear that in these cases, too, there is a defect in character structure which allows aggressive impulses to be expressed too freely. There is also some suggestion that the attacking parent was subjected to similar abuse in childhood. It would appear that one of the most important factors to be found in families where parental assault occurs is "to do unto others as you have been done by." This is not surprising; it has long been recognized by psychologists and social anthropologists that patterns of child rearing, both good and bad, are passed from one generation to the next in relatively unchanged form. Psychologically, one could describe this phenomenon as an identification with the aggressive parent, this identification occurring despite strong wishes of the person to be different. Not infrequently the beaten infant is a product of an unwanted pregnancy, a pregnancy which began before marriage, too soon after marriage, or at some other time felt to be extremely inconvenient. Sometimes several children in one family have been beaten; at other times one child is singled out for attack while others are treated quite lovingly. We have also seen instances in which the sex of the child who is severely attacked is related to very specific factors in the context of the abusive parent's neurosis.

It is often difficult to obtain the information that a child has been attacked by its parent. To be sure, some of the extremely sociopathic characters will say, "Yeah, Johnny would not stop crying so I hit him. So what? He cried harder so I hit him harder."

Sometimes one spouse will indicate that the other was the attacking person, but more often there is complete denial of any knowledge of injury to the child and the maintenance of an attitude of complete innocence on the part of both parents. Such attitudes are maintained despite the fact that evidence of physical attack is obvious and that the trauma could not have happened in any other way. Denial by the parents of any involvement in the abusive episode may, at times, be a conscious, protective device, but in other instances it may be a denial based upon psychological repression. Thus, one mother who seemed to have been the one who injured her baby had complete amnesia for the episodes in which her aggression burst forth so strikingly.

In addition to the reluctance of the parents to give information regarding the attacks on their children, there is another factor which is of great importance and extreme interest as it relates to the difficulty in delving into the problem of parental neglect and abuse. This is the fact that physicians have great difficulty both in believing that parents could have attacked their children and in undertaking the essential questioning of parents on this subject. Many physicians find it hard to believe that such an attack could have occurred and they attempt to obliterate such suspicions from their minds, even in the face of obvious circumstantial evidence. The reason for this is not clearly understood. One possibility is that the arousal of the physician's antipathy in response to such situations is so great that it is easier for the physician to deny the possibility of such attack than to have to deal with the excessive anger which surges up in him when he realizes the truth of the situation. Furthermore, the physician's training and personality usually makes it quite difficult for him to assume the role of policeman or district attorney and start questioning patients as if he were investigating a crime. The humanitarian-minded physician finds it most difficult to proceed when he is met with protestations of innocence from the aggressive parent, especially when the battered child was brought to him voluntarily.

Although the technique wherein the physician obtains the necessary information in cases of child beating is not adequately solved, certain routes of questioning have been particularly fruitful in some cases. One spouse may be asked about the other spouse in relation to unusual or curious behavior or for direct description of dealings with the baby. Clues to the parents' character and pattern of response may be obtained by asking questions about sources of worry and tension. Revealing answers may be brought out by questions concerning the baby such as, "Does he cry a lot? Is he stubborn? Does he obey well? Does he eat well? Do you have problems in controlling him?" A few general questions concerning the parents' own ideas of how they themselves were brought up may bring forth illuminating answers; interviews with grandparents or other relatives may elicit additional suggestive data. In some cases, psychological tests may disclose strong aggressive tendencies, impulsive behavior, and lack of adequate mechanisms of controlling impulsive behavior. In other cases only prolonged contact in a psychotherapeutic milieu will lead to a complete understanding of the background and circumstances surrounding the parental attack. Observation by nurses or other ancillary personnel of the behavior of the parents in relation to the hospitalized infant is often extremely valuable.

The following 2 condensed case histories depict some of the problems encountered in dealing with the battered-child syndrome.

Report of Cases

CASE 1.—The patient was brought to the hospital at the age of 3 months because of enlargement of the head, convulsions, and spells of unconsciousness. Examination revealed bilateral subdural hematomas, which were later operated upon with great improvement in physical status. There had been a hospital admission at the age of one month because of a fracture of the right femur, sustained "when the baby turned over in the crib and caught its leg in the slats." There was no history of any head trauma except "when the baby was in the other hospital a child threw a little toy at her and hit her in the head." The father had never been alone with the baby, and the symptoms of difficulty appeared to have begun when the mother had been caring for the baby. Both parents showed concern and requested the best possible care for their infant. The father, a graduate engineer, related instances of impulsive behavior, but these did not appear to be particularly abnormal, and he showed appropriate emotional concern over the baby's appearance and impending operation. The mother, aged 21, a high school graduate, was very warm, friendly, and gave all the appearance of having endeavored to be a good mother. However, it was noted by both nurses and physicians that she did not react as appropriately or seem as upset about the baby's appearance as did her husband. From interviews with the father and later with the mother, it became apparent that she had occasionally shown very impulsive, angry behavior, sometimes acting rather strangely and doing bizarre things which she could not explain nor remember. This was their first child and had resulted from an unwanted pregnancy which had occurred almost immediately after marriage and before the parents were ready for it. Early in pregnancy the mother had made statements about giving the baby away, but by the time of delivery she was apparently delighted with the baby and seemed to be quite fond of it. After many interviews, it became apparent that the mother had identified herself with her own mother who had also been unhappy with her first pregnancy and had frequently beaten her children. Despite very strong conscious wishes to be a kind, good mother, the mother of our patient was evidently repeating the behavior of her own mother toward herself. Although an admission of guilt was not obtained, it seemed likely that the mother was the one responsible for attacking the child; only after several months of treatment did the amnesia for the aggressive outbursts begin to lift. She responded well to treatment, but for a prolonged period after the infant left the hospital the mother was not allowed alone with her.

CASE 2.—This patient was admitted to the hospital at the age of 13 months with signs of central nervous system damage and was found to have a fractured skull. The parents were questioned closely, but no history of trauma could be elicited. After one week in the hospital no further treatment was deemed necessary, so the infant was discharged home in the care of her mother, only to return a few hours later with hemiparesis, a defect in vision, and a new depressed skull fracture on the other side of the head. There was no satisfactory explanation for the new skull fracture, but the mother denied having been involved in causing the injury, even though the history revealed that the child had changed markedly during the hour when the mother had been alone with her. The parents of this child were a young, middle-class couple who, in less than 2 years of marriage, had been separated, divorced, and remarried. Both felt that the infant had been unwanted and had come too soon in the marriage. The mother gave a history of having had a "nervous breakdown" during her teens. She had received psychiatric assistance because she had been markedly upset early in the pregnancy. Following an uneventful delivery, she had been depressed and had received further psychiatric aid and 4 electroshock treatments. The mother tended to gloss over the unhappiness during the pregnancy and stated that she was quite delighted when the baby was born. It is interesting to note that the baby's first symptoms of difficulty began the first day after its first birthday, suggesting an "anniversary reaction." On psychological and neurological examination, this mother showed definite signs of organic brain damage probably of lifelong duration and possibly related to her own prematurity. Apparently her significant intellectual defects had been camouflaged by an attitude of coy, naïve, cooperative sweetness which distracted attention from her deficits. It was noteworthy that she had managed to complete a year of college work despite a borderline I.Q. It appeared that the impairment in mental functioning was probably the prime factor associated with poor control of aggressive impulses. It is known that some individuals may react with aggressive attack or psychosis when faced with demands beyond their intellectual capacity. This mother was not allowed to have unsupervised care of her child.

Up to the present time, therapeutic experience with the parents of battered children is minimal. Counseling carried on in social agencies has been far from successful or rewarding. We know of no reports of successful psychotherapy in such cases. In general, psychiatrists feel that treatment of the so-called psychopath or sociopath is rarely successful. Further psychological investigation of the character structure of attacking parents is sorely needed. Hopefully, better understanding of the mechanisms involved in the control and release of aggressive impulses will aid in the earlier diagnosis, prevention of attack, and treatment of parents, as well as give us better ability to predict the likelihood of further attack in the future. At present, there is no safe remedy in the situation except the separation of battered children from their insufficiently protective parents.

Techniques of Evaluation

A physician needs to have a high initial level of suspicion of the diagnosis of the battered-child syndrome in instances of subdural hematoma, multiple unexplained fractures at different stages of healing, failure to thrive, when soft tissue swellings or skin bruising are present, or in any other situation where the degree and type of injury is at variance with the history given regarding its occurrence or in any child who dies suddenly. Where the problem of parental abuse comes up for consideration, the physician should tell the parents that it is his opinion that the injury should not occur if the child were adequately protected, and he should indicate that he would welcome the parents giving him the full story so that he might be able to give greater assistance to them to prevent similar occurrences from taking place in the future. The idea that they can now help the child by giving a very complete history of circumstances surrounding the injury sometimes helps the parents feel that they are atoning for the wrong that they have done. But in many instances, regardless of the approach used in attempting to elicit a full story of the abusive incident(s), the parents will continue to deny that they were guilty of any wrongdoing. In talking with the parents, the physician may sometimes obtain added information by showing that he understands their problem and that he wishes to be of aid to them as well as to the child. He may help them reveal the circumstances of the injuries by pointing out reasons that they may use to explain their action. If it is suggested that "new parents sometimes lose their tempers and are a little too forceful in their actions," the parents may grasp such a statement as the excuse for their actions. Interrogation should not be angry or hostile but should be sympathetic and quiet with the physician indicating his assurance that the diagnosis is well established on the basis of objective findings and that all parties, including the parents, have an obligation to avoid a repetition of the circumstances leading to the trauma. The doctor should recognize that bringing the child for medical attention in itself does not necessarily indicate that the parents were innocent of wrongdoing and are showing proper concern; trauma may have been inflicted during times of uncontrollable temporary rage.

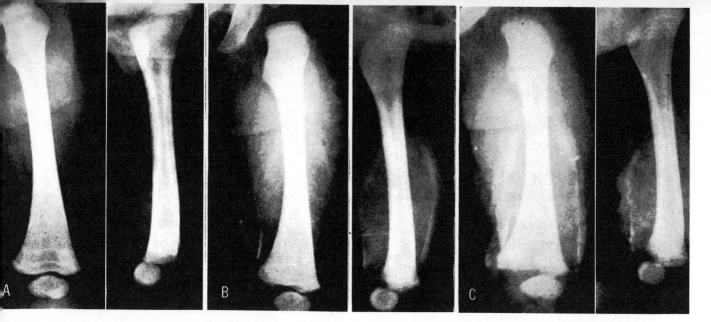

Fig. 1.—Male, 5 months: *a*, Initial films taken 3 to 4 days after onset of knee swelling. Epiphyseal separation shown in lateral projection with small metaphyseal chip shown in frontal projection; *b*, Five days later, there was beginning reparative change; *c*, Twelve days later (16 days after onset), there was extensive reparative change, history of injury unknown, but parents were attempting to teach child to walk at 5 months.

Regardless of the physician's personal reluctance to become involved, complete investigation is necessary for the child's protection so that a decision can be made as to the necessity of placing the child away from the parents until matters are fully clarified.

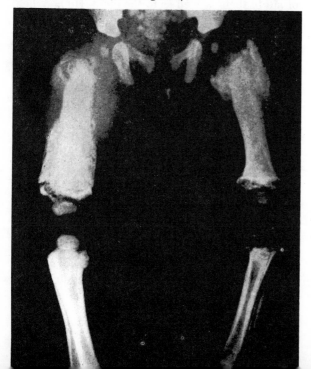

Fig. 2.—Female, 7½ months with a history of recurring abuse, including being shaken while held by legs 4-6 weeks prior to film. Note recent (2-3 weeks) metaphyseal fragmentation, older (4-6 weeks) periosteal reaction, and remote (2-4 months) external cortical thickening. Note also normal osseous structure of uninjured pelvic bones. (By permission of *Amer J. Roentgenol.*)

Often, the guilty parent is the one who gives the impression of being the more normal. In 2 recent instances young physicians have assumed that the mother was at fault because she was unkempt and depressed while the father, in each case a military man with good grooming and polite manners, turned out to be the psychopathic member of the family. In these instances it became apparent that the mother had good reason to be depressed.

Radiologic Features

Radiologic examination plays 2 main roles in the problem of child-abuse. Initially, it is a tool for case finding, and, subsequently, it is useful as a guide in management.

The diagnostic signs result from a combination of circumstances: age of the patient, nature of the injury, the time that has elapsed before the examination is carried out, and whether the traumatic episode was repeated or occurred only once.

Age.—As a general rule, the children are under 3 years of age; most, in fact are infants. In this age group the relative amount of radiolucent cartilage is great; therefore, anatomical disruptions of cartilage without gross deformity are radiologically invisible or difficult to demonstrate (Fig. 1a). Since the periosteum of infants is less securely attached to the underlying bone than in older children and adults, it is more easily and extensively stripped from the shaft by hemorrhage than in older patients. In infancy massive subperiosteal hematomas may follow injury and elevate the active periosteum so that new bone formation can take place around and remote from the parent shaft (Figs. 1c and 2).

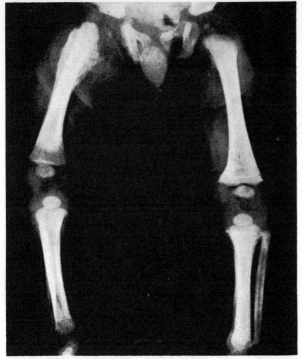

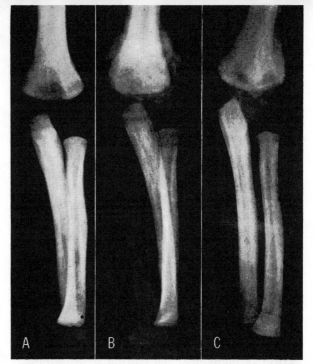

Fig. 3.—Male, 5 months, pulled by legs from collapsing bathinette 6 weeks earlier. Epiphyseal separation, right hip, shown by position of capital ossification center. Healing subperiosteal hematoma adjacent to it. Healing metaphyseal lesions in left knee, healing periosteal reactions (mild) in left tibia. No signs of systemic disease. (By permission of *Amer J Roentgenol.*)

Fig. 4.—Female 7½ months: *a*, Elbow injured 30 hours before, except for thickened cortex from previous healed reactions, no radiologic signs of injury; *b*, Fifteen days after injury, irregular productive reaction, clinically normal joint; *c*, Three weeks after *b*, organization and healing progressing nicely. (By permission of *Amer J Roentgenol.*)

Nature of Injury.—The ease and frequency with which a child is seized by his arms or legs make injuries to the appendicular skeleton the most common in this syndrome. Even when bony injuries are present elsewhere, e.g., skull, spine, or ribs, signs of injuries to the extremities are usually present. The extremities are the "handles" for rough handling, whether the arm is pulled to bring a reluctant child to his feet or to speed his ascent upstairs or whether the legs are held while swinging the tiny body in a punitive way or in an attempt to enforce corrective measures. The forces applied by an adult hand in grasping and seizing usually involve traction and torsion; these are the forces most likely to produce epiphyseal separations and periosteal shearing (Figs. 1 and 3). Shaft fractures result from direct blows or from bending and compression forces.

Time After Injury That the X-Ray Examination Is Made.—This is important in evaluating known or suspected cases of child-abuse. Unless gross fractures, dislocations, or epiphyseal separations were produced, no signs of bone injury are found during the first week after a specific injury. Reparative changes may first become manifest about 12 to 14 days after the injury and can increase over the subsequent weeks depending on the extent of initial injury and the degree of repetition (Fig. 4). Reparative changes are more active in the growing bones of children than in adults and are reflected radiologically in the excessive new bone reaction. Histologically, the reaction has been confused with neoplastic change by those unfamiliar with the vigorous reactions of young growing tissue.

Repetition of Injury.—This is probably the most important factor in producing diagnostic radiologic signs of the syndrome. The findings may depend on diminished immobilization of an injured bone leading to recurring macro- and microtrauma in the area of injury and healing, with accompanying excessive local reaction and hemorrhage, and ultimately, exaggerated repair. Secondly, repetitive injury may produce bone lesions in one area at one time, and in another area at another, producing lesions in several areas and in different stages of healing (Fig. 3).

Thus, the classical radiologic features of the battered-child syndrome are usually found in the appendicular skeleton in very young children. There may be irregularities of mineralization in the metaphyses of some of the major tubular bones with slight malalignment of the adjacent epiphyseal ossification center. An overt fracture may be present in another bone. Elsewhere, there may be abundant and active but well-calcified subperiosteal reaction with widening from the shaft toward one end of the bone. One or more bones may demonstrate distinctly thickened cortices, residuals of previously healed periosteal reactions. In addition, the radiographic features of a subdural hematoma with or without obvious skull fracture may be present.

Differential Diagnosis.—The radiologic features are so distinct that other diseases generally are considered only because of the reluctance to accept the implications of the bony lesions. Unless certain aspects of bone healing are considered, the pertinent findings may be missed. In many cases roentgenographic examination is only undertaken soon after known injury; if a fracture is found, reexamination is done after reduction and immobilization; and, if satisfactory positioning has been obtained, the next examination is usually not carried out for a period of 6 weeks when the cast is removed. Any interval films that may have been taken prior to this time probably would have been unsatisfactory since the fine details of the bony lesions would have been obscured by the cast. If fragmentation and bone production are seen, they are considered to be evidence of repair rather than manifestations of multiple or repetitive trauma. If obvious fracture or the knowledge of injury is absent, the bony changes may be considered to be the result of scurvy, syphilis, infantile cortical hyperostoses, or other conditions. The distribution of lesions in the abused child is unrelated to rates of growth; moreover, an extensive lesion may be present at the slow-growing end of a bone which otherwise is normally mineralized and shows no evidence of metabolic disorder at its rapidly growing end.

Scurvy is commonly suggested as an alternative diagnosis, since it also produces large calcifying subperiosteal hemorrhages due to trauma and local exaggerations most marked in areas of rapid growth. However, scurvy is a systemic disease in which all of the bones show the generalized osteoporosis associated with the disease. The dietary histories of most children with recognized trauma have not been grossly abnormal, and whenever the vitamin C content of the blood has been determined, it has been normal.

In the first months of life *syphilis* can result in metaphyseal and periosteal lesions similar to those under discussion. However, the bone lesions of syphilis tend to be symmetrical and are usually accompanied by other stigmata of the disease. Serological tests should be obtained in questionable cases.

Osteogenesis imperfecta also has bony changes which may be confused with those due to trauma, but it too is a generalized disease, and evidence of the disorder should be present in the bones which are not involved in the disruptive-productive reaction. Even when skull fractures are present, the mosaic ossification pattern of the cranial vault, characteristic of osteogenesis imperfecta, is not seen in the battered-child syndrome. Fractures in osteogenesis imperfecta are commonly of the shafts; they usually occur in the metaphyseal regions in the battered-child syndrome. Blue sclerae,

skeletal deformities, and a family history of similar abnormalities were absent in reported instances of children with unrecognized trauma.

Productive diaphyseal lesions may occur in *infantile cortical hyperostosis,* but the metaphyseal lesions of unrecognized trauma easily serve to differentiate the 2 conditions. The characteristic mandibular involvement of infantile cortical hyperostosis does not occur following trauma although obvious mandibular fracture may be produced.

Evidence that repetitive unrecognized trauma is the cause of the bony changes found in the battered-child syndrome is, in part, derived from the finding that similar roentgenographic findings are present in *paraplegic patients with sensory deficit* and in patients with *congenital indifference to pain;* in both of whom similar pathogenic mechanisms operate. In paraplegic children unappreciated injuries have resulted in radiologic pictures with irregular metaphyseal rarefactions, exaggerated subperiosteal new bone formation, and ultimate healing with residual external cortical thickening comparable to those in the battered-child syndrome. In paraplegic adults, excessive callus may form as a consequence of the lack of immobilization, and the lesion may be erroneously diagnosed as osteogenic sarcoma. In children with congenital indifference (or insensitivity) to pain, identical radiologic manifestations may be found.

To summarize, the radiologic manifestations of trauma are specific, and the metaphyseal lesions in particular occur in no other disease of which we are aware. The findings permit a radiologic diagnosis even when the clinical history seems to refute the possibility of trauma. Under such circumstances, the history must be reviewed, and the child's environment, carefully investigated.

Management

The principal concern of the physician should be to make the correct diagnosis so that he can institute proper therapy and make certain that a similar event will not occur again. He should report possible willful trauma to the police department or any special children's protective service that operates in his community. The report that he makes should be restricted to the objective findings which can be verified and, where possible, should be supported by photographs and roentgenograms. For hospitalized patients, the hospital director and the social service department should be notified. In many states the hospital is also required to report any case of possible unexplained injury to the proper authorities. The physician should acquaint himself with the facilities available in private and public agencies that provide protective services for children. These include children's humane societies, divisions of welfare departments, and societies for the prevention of cruelty to children. These, as well as the police department, maintain a close association with the juvenile court. Any of these agencies may be of assistance in bringing the case before the court which alone has the legal power to sustain a dependency petition for temporary or permanent separation of the child from the parents' custody. In addition to the legal investigation, it is usually helpful to have an evaluation of the psychological and social factors in the case; this should be started while the child is still in the hospital. If necessary, a court order should be obtained so that such investigation may be performed.

In many instances the prompt return of the child to the home is contraindicated because of the threat that additional trauma offers to the child's health and life. Temporary placement with relatives or in a well-supervised foster home is often indicated in order to prevent further tragic injury or death to a child who is returned too soon to the original dangerous environment. All too often, despite the apparent cooperativeness of the parents and their apparent desire to have the child with them, the child returns to his home only to be assaulted again and suffer permanent brain damage or death. Therefore, the bias should be in favor of the child's safety; everything should be done to prevent repeated trauma, and the physician should not be satisfied to return the child to an environment where even a moderate risk of repetition exists.

Summary

The battered-child syndrome, a clinical condition in young children who have received serious physical abuse, is a frequent cause of permanent injury or death. Although the findings are quite variable, the syndrome should be considered in any child exhibiting evidence of possible trauma or neglect (fracture of any bone, subdural hematoma, multiple soft tissue injuries, poor skin hygiene, or malnutrition) or where there is a marked discrepancy between the clinical findings and the historical data as supplied by the parents. In cases where a history of specific injury is not available, or in any child who dies suddenly, roentgenograms of the entire skeleton should still be obtained in order to ascertain the presence of characteristic multiple bony lesions in various stages of healing.

Psychiatric factors are probably of prime importance in the pathogenesis of the disorder, but our knowledge of these factors is limited. Parents who inflict abuse on their children do not necessarily have psychopathic or sociopathic personalities or come from borderline socioeconomic groups, although most published cases have been in these categories. In most cases some defect in character structure is probably present; often parents may be repeating the type of child care practiced on them in their childhood.

Physicians, because of their own feelings and their difficulty in playing a role that they find hard to assume, may have great reluctance in believing that parents were guilty of abuse. They may also find it difficult to initiate proper investigation so as to assure adequate management of the case. Above all, the physician's duty and responsibility to the child requires a full evaluation of the problem and a guarantee that the expected repetition of trauma will not be permitted to occur.

4200 E. 9th Ave., Denver 20 (Dr. Kempe).

References

1. Snedecor, S. T.; Knapp, R. E.; and Wilson, H. B.: Traumatic Ossifying Periostitis of Newborn, *Surg Gynec Obstet* **61**:385-387, 1935.

2. Caffey, J.: Multiple Fractures in Long Bones of Infants Suffering from Chronic Subdural Hematoma, *Amer J Roentgenol* **56**:163-173 (Aug.) 1946.

3. Snedecor, S. T., and Wilson, H. B.: Some Obstetrical Injuries to Long Bones, *J Bone Joint Surg* **31A**:378-384 (April) 1949.

4. Smith, M. J.: Subdural Hematoma with Multiple Fractures, *Amer J Roentgenol* **63**:342-344 (March) 1950.

5. Frauenberger, G. S., and Lis, E. F.: Multiple Fractures Associated with Subdural Hematoma in Infancy, *Pediatrics* **6**:890-892 (Dec.) 1950.

6. Barmeyer, G. H.; Alderson, L. R.; and Cox, W. B.: Traumatic Periostitis in Young Children, *J Pediat* **38**:184-190 (Feb.) 1951.

7. Silverman, F.: Roentgen Manifestations of Unrecognized Skeletal Trauma in Infants, *Amer J Roentgenol* **69**:413-426 (March) 1953.

8. Woolley, P. V., Jr., and Evans, W. A., Jr.: Significance of Skeletal Lesions in Infants Resembling Those of Traumatic Origin, *JAMA* **158**:539-543 (June) 1955.

9. Bakwin, H.: Multiple Skeletal Lesions in Young Children Due to Trauma, *J Pediat* **49**:7-15 (July) 1956.

10. Caffey, J.: Some Traumatic Lesions in Growing Bones Other Than Fractures and Dislocations: Clinical and Radiological Features, *Brit J Radiol* **30**:225-238 (May) 1957.

11. Weston, W. J.: Metaphyseal Fractures in Infancy, *J Bone Joint Surg (Brit)* (no. 4) **39B**:694-700 (Nov.) 1957.

12. Fisher, S. H.: Skeletal Manifestations of Parent-Induced Trauma in Infants and Children, *Southern Med J* **51**:956-960 (Aug.) 1958.

13. Miller, D. S.: Fractures Among Children, *Minnesota Med* **42**:1209-1213 (Sept.) 1959; **42**:1414-1425 (Oct.) 1959.

14. Silver, H. K., and Kempe, C. H.: Problem of Parental Criminal Neglect and Severe Physical Abuse of Children, *J Dis Child* **95**:528, 1959.

15. Altman, D. H., and Smith, R. L.: Unrecognized Trauma in Infants and Children, *J Bone Joint Surg (Amer)* **42A**:407-413 (April) 1960.

16. Elmer, E.: Abused Young Children Seen in Hospitals, *Soc Work* (no. 4) **5**:98-102 (Oct.) 1960.

17. Gwinn, J. L.; Lewin, K. W.; and Peterson, H. G., Jr.: Roentgenographic Manifestations of Unsuspected Trauma in Infancy, *JAMA* **176**:926-929 (June 17) 1961.

18. Boardman, H. E.: Project to Rescue Children from Inflicted Injuries, *Soc Work* (no. 1) **7**:43 (Jan.) 1962.

UNSUSPECTED TRAUMA WITH MULTIPLE SKELETAL INJURIES DURING INFANCY AND CHILDHOOD

Thomas McHenry, M.D., Bertram R. Girdany, M.D., and Elizabeth Elmer, M.S.S.

Departments of Pediatrics, Radiology and Social Service, Children's Hospital of Pittsburgh, Pittsburgh 13, Pennsylvania

D URING the past decade, reports concerning unsuspected and repeated trauma to the skeletons of infants and children have appeared in the pediatric literature; the condition has been given such descriptive titles as traumatic periostitis, the battered child syndrome, and unsuspected multiple trauma to the skeleton. These articles have been concerned with relatively small numbers of patients, 20 being the largest number included in any single report.[1] This paper documents the experience at the Children's Hospital of Pittsburgh with 50 children who had unsuspected traumata with multiple injuries to the skeleton. It emphasizes the age distribution in this group of patients and the variety of presenting complaints. It also offers observations on the family backgrounds from the preliminary studies made by the social service department.

Caffey,[2,3] Silverman,[4] and Gwinn et al.[5] described the roentgenographic manifestations of trauma to the skeleton. Clearly defined roentgenographic evidence of recent and old injury to the skeleton was found in each of the patients in this report. The findings included recent and old fractures of the skull, ribs, clavicles, long bones, and spine, as well as subperiosteal new bone formation and multiple small infractions of the metaphyses of the long bones (Fig. 1).

This report does not concern newly born infants with skeletal trauma associated with delivery. Snedecor et al.[6] described subperiosteal new bone formation and metaphysical infractions of the femurs of infants delivered by breech extraction. Bakwin[7] and Caffey[3] published additional evidence to confirm this occurrence. There are no roentgenographic differences in the individual lesions which distinguish multiple skeletal injuries of the newborn from unsuspected multiple skeletal injuries in later infancy and childhood. Unsuspected multiple traumata usually causes changes in the bones of different age of origin and in different stages of healing.

CASE MATERIAL

The films of 50 children with evidence of multiple skeletal traumata were seen at the Children's Hospital of Pittsburgh during the 10-year period from 1951 through 1960. Forty-four children were treated as inpatients and six were outpatients. Forty-four were from the clinic population; six were patients of attending private physicians. Thirty-three children were seen initially on the medical, 13 on the orthopedic, and 4 on the neurosurgical services, respectively. Twenty-four were male and 26 were female infants. Thirty-six infants were white and 14 were Negro, a distribution reflecting the clinic population.

Physical abnormalities were commonly observed on admission. Injured extremities were most frequent. Dehydration, macrocephaly, bruising, petechial hemorrhages, and pallor were common. Significant retardation in growth and development was observed in 40%, or 20, of the patients. In most instances the diagnosis of unsuspected multiple traumata was not initially entertained,

(Submitted May 21, 1962; accepted June 27, 1962.)

That portion of this paper that discusses "families" was included as part of the symposium on "The Battered Child" at the meeting of the Academy of Pediatrics in Chicago, October, 1961.

ADDRESS (B.R.G.) 125 De Soto Street, Pittsburgh 13, Pennsylvania.

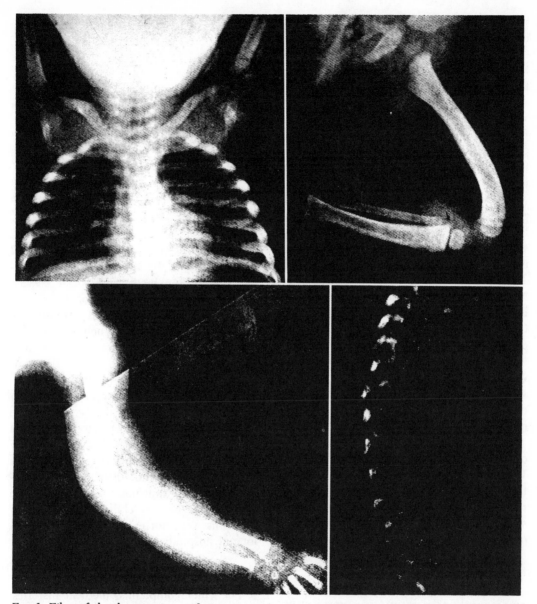

FIG. 1. Films of the thorax, spine, and extremities of a 7-month-old white male infant, showing evidence of old healing fractures of both clavicles, recent fracture through the proximal metaphysis of the left humerus, fractures of multiple vertebral bodies, and deformity of the distal portion of the femur. This infant was admitted for treatment of convulsions. He had bilateral subdural hematomas. Chest x-ray examination showed changes in the clavicles and humeruses as well as fractures of the vertebral bodies. In this instance etiology of the injuries was not determined.

and the children were admitted for diagnostic study (Table I). Clinical impressions on admission included rickets, scurvy, celiac disease, osteomyelitis, bone tumor, osteogenesis imperfecta, blood dyscrasias, congenital coxa vara, subdural hematoma, skull fracture, fracture of a long bone, meningitis, infectious diarrhea, purpura, and "failure to do well." In eight instances the diagnosis of multiple injuries to the skeleton was correctly suspected on admission.

Course in the Hospital

Roentgenographic examination of the skeleton established the diagnosis of skeletal injury. In some instances, x-ray films were made for evaluation of isolated fractures and showed evidence of unusual cortical thickening or injury to adjacent skeletal structures. In other instances, skeletal films for evaluation of bone age or for evidence of leukemia, rickets, or scurvy showed multiple skeletal injuries. Chest films occasionally revealed rib, clavicular, or humeral fractures. In one instance, the finding of fractured ribs on an excretory urogram prompted a skeletal survey.

Subdural hematomas were found in 14 patients; of these, 5 showed evidence of retarded growth and development; 5 others showed normal growth and development; in the remaining 4 instances, growth and development were not formally evaluated. Nine infants and children with subdural hematomas had histories of convulsions. Caffey[2] described the association of multiple skeletal injuries and subdural hematoma.

Twenty-four patients had hemoglobin values of 10 gm/100 ml or less on admission. Two infants had hemoglobin values of 4 gm/100 ml and required emergency medical management.

Three infants died in the hospital. Two of these were 2 months of age, and one was 1 month old on admission. Each of these three infants had bilateral subdural hematomas, multiple diastatic fractures of the skull, and evidence of injury to other areas of the skeleton.

TABLE I

SUMMARY OF CHIEF COMPLAINTS

Complaint	Number	Totals
Disability of an extremity		25
Injury to one extremity	12	
Weakness, pain or swelling of one extremity without history of injury	13	
Skin lesions		16
Bruises, petechial hemorrhages	12	
Impetigo	1	
"Lumps"	2	
Swelling of face	1	
Failure to do well (nonspecific)		12
Convulsions		12
Vomiting and diarrhea		4
Large head		3

TABLE II

KNOWN CAUSES OF MULTIPLE TRAUMATA

Cause	Cases (no.)
Parental assault	10
Minor injury or fall	5
Older sibling (history of assault by)	4
Older sibling, suspect	2
Abnormal physical restraints	1
Total	22

History of Trauma

A history of trauma was obtained in 22 of the patients. In 12 instances these histories were obtained after social service studies. The known stories of injury are listed in Table II. Parental assault was found most frequently. Included in this group were outright acts of brutality, drunkenness, and gross neglect. Four infants were traumatized by older siblings. The category of "minor injury or fall" in most instances did not entirely explain the multiplicity of skeletal changes. One child was emotionally disturbed and reportedly injured herself during fits of temper by throwing herself on the floor. It seemed unlikely that her tantrums were sufficient to account for her skeletal injuries. Temper tantrums were not evident during her prolonged hospitalization.

COMMENT

The chief complaints, medical histories, and physical examinations on admission frequently did not suggest multiple skeletal injuries (Table I). Often physical and developmental retardation were the indications for hospitalization. Several patients, because they were severely ill, required emergency treatment for dehydration, anemia, and convulsions.

Reference has been made to differential diagnoses. Syphilis, tuberculosis, blood dyscrasia, scurvy, rickets, congenital hip disease, neoplasm, osteomyelitis, infantile cortical hyperostosis, poliomyelitis, osteogenesis imperfecta, congenital bone defects, and

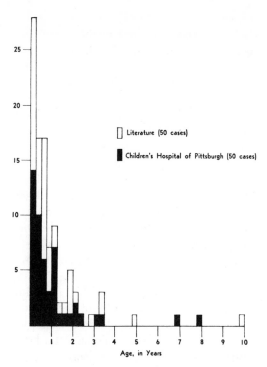

FIG. 2. Age distribution of patients with unsuspected multiple skeletal injuries.

meningitis were excluded by appropriate clinical, laboratory, and roentgenographic examinations.

Age of Patients

The age of the youngest patient in the group was 1 month; the oldest was 8 years. Thirty infants, or 60% of the group, were younger than 9 months. Ten infants were between 9 and 15 months of age.

Review of the literature[1-12] revealed 50 instances of unsuspected trauma in which the ages of the patients are recorded. The youngest child was 1 month of age, and the oldest was 10 years. Thirty-two infants (67%) were less than 9 months of age, and six infants (12%) were between the ages of 9 and 15 months. Figure 2 shows graphically the age distribution of these cases and of the 50 children reported here. The peak incidence is reached by 3 months of age, following which the curve of incidence decreases rapidly. This curve should be compared with the curve for childhood accidents in general, in which the peak is reached at 2 years of age and falls slowly in the years following.[13]

These statistics may seem surprising because early infancy is the age when parents are considered to be most protective of their offspring. Serious breakdowns in the parental capacity to provide normal infant care and protection must be responsible. Parents cannot be released from their responsibility to the infant even when sibling aggression is the cause of the multiple episodes of trauma. The paucity of reported cases in older children may be partly explained by the ability of the older child to remember episodes of trauma, to complain of bone pain, and within limitations, to prevent multiple episodes of injury.

Except for the work of Jones and Davis,[12] reports in the literature have not associated unsuspected injuries to the skeleton and retarded growth and development. In the experience reported here, growth and development were significantly retarded in 20 of the 30 children in whom accurate assessment of growth and development was recorded.

Twenty-four patients had hemoglobin values on admission which were abnormally low. The presence of anemia in a group of children presumably exposed to malnutrition and neglect is not surprising.

Five children died at home after they were discharged from the hospital. One 13-month-old infant was slain by her foster mother, who was later admitted to a state mental institution. A second 13-month-old infant died 10 days after discharge, presumably as the result of new injuries. The coroner's office officially stated that the cause of death was malnutrition.

All 50 infants and children reported here suffered traumatic injuries, proven roentgenographically "beyond a shadow of doubt." Much of the literature to date has summarized the sites of highest incidence of fracture or described the roentgenographic aspects of the fractures. It is the authors' conviction as well as that of others[4,7] that the types and distribution of the skeletal lesions are of secondary importance to the prevention of further injury or death. A confirmed history of trauma is not essential. The social aspects of the problem are paramount, for 10% of the patients reported here died after they were discharged, and other children sustained additional injuries following their release from the hospital. The prevention of further injury or death requires careful evaluation of the social and psychiatric backgrounds of the families. This is the responsibility of the attending physician, who may delegate part of the task to a psychiatrist, a social worker, or appropriate community agencies.

The Families

Several years elapsed after Caffey's original description before serious investigations of social factors which might have etiologic significance were undertaken. In 1955, Woolley and Evans[1] reported 20 instances of unsuspected multiple bone injuries and included detailed descriptions of 12 families. The particular families were described because they were thought to provide an environment conducive to injury. Unstable homes were the rule, and a high incidence of neurotic or psychotic behavior was observed in one or both parents.

Two years ago, a research project pertaining to patients with unsuspected multiple bone injuries and their families was begun at the Children's Hospital of Pittsburgh. Systematic review and analysis of data originally available showed that the pertinent facts were too sparse to permit generalizations of any kind about the families. Additional data obtained from several community social agencies gradually allowed a beginning picture of 15 of these families to be pieced together. This picture is tentative, since it is drawn from a small group of families, all of whom were involved with several social agencies as well as Children's Hospital. The families were characterized as follows: (1) The adults showed impulsive behavior in areas other than child care. For example, some had records of legal difficulties such as arrests, convictions, and imprisonments for the offenses of theft, assault, or rape. Impulsive behavior also appeared in the forms of excessive drinking and temper outbursts. (2) The parents demonstrated little guilt or anxiety about their children who had sustained the injuries. (3) The marital histories revealed an unusual degree of instability. Some parents had never been legally married; when a legal marriage had occurred, divorce or separation was common. If the parents remained together, their relationship was marked by frequent strife and violence. (4) In all instances where information was available, the adults had been subjected in early life to emotional deprivations, such as extreme rejection or overt hostility.

Other conditions which sometimes seemed to affect the ability of the adults to care adequately for the children were physical or mental illness, mental retardation, and/or environmental pressures such as marked poverty and substandard housing.

The generalizations derived from the study of the 15 families provided guidelines for subsequent work with other families. It often appeared that the parents were unusually ill-prepared for the pregnancy and anticipated birth of the infant. Their initial reactions to the pregnancy and their evolving ideas about parenthood were, in many instances, related to their youthfulness and psychic immaturity. The parents, after the birth of their infant and prior to the time of his injuries, often thought their offspring was unhealthy, defective, or unusually troublesome. If, coupled with these characteristics, there were environmental hardships, poor health, or if the pregnancy followed closely on another pregnancy, the stage seemed set for later tragedy.[14]

The experience gained by interviewing the adults involved with bone-injured patients showed that the clinician has a most difficult assignment. He must overcome personal feelings of shock and anger, must forego a judgmental attitude, and must find somewhere within himself a genuine interest in learning about the adults as individuals. If he can balance on this fine edge, he will be met by further frustrations, for the adults in these families are by no means anxious for his interest and help. They tend to say as little as possible, to make that little palatable to the interviewer, and to escape at the first opportunity. These parents have a pervading fear and distrust of authority, and become frightened and uncommunicative because they see in the hospital staff person a powerful figure of authority. This attitude may be related to their childhood disappointments with regard to the inadequacies of their own parents.

Some of the adults, when given appropriate help, may reveal a potential for providing adequate care of their children. Other adults who are unable to tolerate the strains of family life, may be willing to co-operate with the hospital in finding more suitable living arrangements for their children. The services of child-placement agencies may be well employed. In still other instances, it may be necessary to seek legal protection for the patient. Positive court action is easier to obtain when the petition is based on an objective evaluation of the family situation and its effect on the patient. When the petition is based solely on allegations of individual guilt with respect to the injuries, the case enters the realm of charge and countercharge, and the child's interest is frequently lost.

SUMMARY AND CONCLUSION

This report concerns the experience at the Children's Hospital of Pittsburgh with 50 children who had skeletal lesions considered to be the result of trauma. The peak age incidence was 3 months. The presenting complaints included disability of an extremity, skin lesions, failure to do well, convulsions, vomiting and diarrhea, and large head. The initial impressions of house officers ranged through the gamut of possible skeletal disorders and blood dyscrasias. Interviews with the parents indicated that the families of these injured children were characterized by parental failure, caused by immaturity, failure to accept responsibility, and other psychosocial afflictions. The seriousness of this disease is indicated by the deaths of five of the infants and the continued injury of others after their return home from the hospital.

REFERENCES

1. Wooley, P. V., Jr., and Evans, W. A., Jr.: Significance of skeletal lesions in infants resembling those of traumatic origin. J.A.M.A., **158**:539, 1955.
2. Caffey, J.: Multiple fractures in long bones of infants suffering from chronic subdural hematoma. Amer. J. Roentgenol., **56**:163, 1946.
3. Caffey, J.: Some traumatic lesions in growing bones other than fractures and dislocations: clinical and radiological fractures. Brit. J. Radiol., **30**:225, 1957.
4. Silverman, F. N.: The roentgen manifestations of unrecognized skeletal trauma in infants. Amer. J. Roentgenol., **69**:413, 1953.
5. Gwinn, J. L., et al. Roentgenographic manifestations of unsuspected trauma in infancy. J.A.M.A., **176**:926, 1961.
6. Snedecor, Spencer T., and Wilson, H. B.: Some obstetrical injuries to the long bones. J. Bone Joint Surg., **BI-A**:378, 1949.
7. Bakwin, H.: Roentgenologic changes in the bones following trauma in infants. J. Newark Beth Israel Hosp., **3**:17, 1952.
8. Lis, E. F., and Frauenberger, G. S.: Multiple fractures associated with subdural hematoma in infancy. PEDIATRICS, **6**:890, 1950.
9. Bormeyer, G. H., and Alderson, L. R.: Traumatic periostitis in young children. J. Pediat., **38**:184, 1951.
10. Friedman, M. S.: Traumatic periostitis in infants and children. J.A.M.A., **166**:1941, 1953.
11. Bakwin, H.: Multiple skeletal lesions due to trauma. J. Pediat., **47**:7, 1956.
12. Jones, H. H., and Davis, J. H.: Multiple traumatic lesions of the infant skeleton. Stanford Med. Bull., **15**:259, 1957.
13. Stallones, R. A., and Corsa, L., Jr.: Epidemiology of childhood accidents in two California counties. Pub. Health Reports, **76**:25, 1961.
14. Rose, J. A.: The prevention of mothering breakdown associated with physical abnormalities of the infant, in Prevention of Mental Disorders in Children, edited by Gerald Caplan. Basic Books, New York, 1961.

Denver's welfare department looks into the characteristics of . . .

INJURED
CHILDREN
and their PARENTS

BETTY JOHNSON ● HAROLD A. MORSE

The question of how to insure the day-to-day safety of children who have been injured by their parents if they remain at home or are returned to their parents after protective separation is always of major concern to persons responsible for protecting children, including child welfare workers, judges, physicians, and police officers. Before their services can be effective, the persons offering them must know what such children and their parents are like and what their problems are.

In June 1963, the Division of Services for Children and Youth of the Denver (Colo.) Department of Welfare began a study of its work with families in which a child or children had been injured by the parents to determine the characteristics of both.

The study included 101 children known to have been injured: 48 children in the division's caseload at the end of June 1963 and 53 children who were added between July 1963 and November 1964. These children represented 85 families with 268 children (167 of whom were not injured during the study period). The division identified all children in its caseload known to have been injured, without regard to the source of referral or the official action taken. A case was included if the child had been injured or mistreated by a parent or caretaker or if the injury occurred because of negligence. Instances of sexual abuse and malnutrition were excluded, as were cases involving children 14 years of age or over.

Since 1951, the division has participated in a Protective Service Program in cooperation with the Denver Juvenile Court, the Denver Police Department, and the Denver General Hospital. The purpose of the program is to help, not punish, parents who neglect or injure their children. The services the division offers include counseling, shelter care, homemaker service, foster boarding home care, tutoring for children, group care, assistance to parents in learning how to use community resources, and group activities for socially isolated parents.

The study schedule for each child was completed by the child welfare worker responsible for his case on the basis of case records and his knowledge, observations, and judgment. The tabulations and analysis were completed by the Research and Reports Unit of the Department of Welfare, in cooperation with the department's study committee.

The child welfare workers completed several schedules for each child: one for each incident of injury to describe the action taken by official agencies such as the police, the court, and the division; another on each injured child's development and ability to function at the time of the incident; another on his family; and one each for all other children in the family. These schedules provided material for evaluating the family at the time of the incident and at the time the case was closed or at the end of the study in July 1965. Child welfare workers conducted final studies from case records in December 1966.

Outcome, 1966

Of the original 101 children identified as having been injured by their parents or caretakers, 97 were alive and 27 were still receiving services from the division in December 1966. The child welfare workers felt that 19 of the children not being served were inadequately protected. One child was living with his mother awaiting institutional placement, but the cases of the other 18 had been closed and the division had no legal authority over them. In 12 cases, the families had left the State; in six, the families had refused further services.

One of the first matters of concern in a child abuse case is safety for the child in his home. If it appears that the child cannot remain safely in his home, at least temporarily, a dependency petition is filed with the juvenile court. During the study period, the court assigned custody of 45 children to the division; in December 1966, the division still held custody of 10 children. Of them, nine were in foster homes and one was living with his mother awaiting institutional placement.

During the period of service, 79 children were removed from their homes: 63 were removed as soon as the injury became known to the authorities; the others, after further work with the family or later court action. Most (53) were placed in receiving foster homes sponsored by the division; 10, with relatives. Sixty percent of the 79 children were placed at the parents' request and with their consent; the others, by court action. At the end of 1966, 97 children were living with their parents (65), with relatives (7), in foster homes (9), in adoptive homes (10), in group care sponsored by a private agency (3), in group care sponsored by a public agency (1), and in the State's training school for the retarded (2). The likelihood of removal, both temporary and permanent, and of immediate placement after the injury was higher when the mother rather than the father had inflicted the injury.

In a third of the cases, the cause of the injury was first reported as unknown or as having been inflicted by someone outside the family. However, the child welfare workers were usually able to determine who had inflicted the injury because parents or relatives frequently let them know, either directly or tacitly, who was responsible after a relationship of confidence had developed between them. On this basis, the work-

Betty Johnson and Harold A. Morse are both with the Denver (Colo.) Department of Welfare. Miss Johnson is supervisor of the Division of Services for Children and Youth, which has responsibility for protective services to children and their families. Mr. Morse is supervisor of the department's Research and Reports Unit.

ers decided that the injuries in question were inflicted by these persons: the mother in two-parent families (32), the father (or stepfather) in two-parent families (30), both parents (6), the mother in one-parent families (23), the mother's boyfriend (5), an adoptive parent (3), a brother (1), and an "undetermined" person (1).

Half the children were under 3 years of age at the time of injury; two-thirds were under 6. Almost a third were between 6 and 9. Only one or two were between 10 and 14. The parents on the whole were young; most were between 21 and 30 years old. About 45 percent of the families were Anglo-American; 35 percent, Spanish-American; 21 percent, Negro; and 1 percent, of other racial or national origin. About two-thirds of the families had three or fewer children. About 33 percent had four or more children. Two percent had eight or more.

A fifth of these families were already receiving services from the division because of child neglect at the time the injury was reported. The rest were referred as a direct result of the injury.

Classification of injuries

About two-thirds of the children were severely injured: 67 were seen by physicians, 45 of whom were hospitalized. As we have already mentioned, three were fatally injured and another died from gross neglect. As a result of injury, 11 children were physically impaired, six were mentally impaired, and nine were permanently disfigured. About a third of the children were not severely injured and were not seen by physicians.

Based on medical findings, the injuries were classified as skull fractures (8), subdural hematoma (5), limb fractures (11), wounds or punctures (27), burns or scalds (6), and bruises and welts (68). Some children sustained more than one kind of injury.

The injuring fathers were more likely to have inflicted injuries causing bruises and welts; the injuring mothers, wounds and fractures. In more than half the incidents, injury resulted from slapping, spanking, striking, yanking, throwing, or shoving. In a third, a belt, strap, or stick was the means of attack; in five, a bottle, club, hammer, or knife. Scalding water caused five children's injuries; a burning cigarette or match, another's.

Four of the parents who had inflicted injuries were considered to be psychotic on the basis of physicians' diagnoses made during the course of work with the family. In the opinion of child welfare workers, nine of the injuring parents were mentally retarded, 36 were mentally disturbed, and 16 apparently drank to excess.

The examinations of the 67 children seen by physicians indicated that the injuries in question were not the first: about 40 percent had sustained previous injuries. In these instances, the mother more typically than the father was the injuring person, whether or not the father was in the home. Twenty children suffered subsequent injuries from the same parent during the study period.

The community's response

Reports to the police of the first injuries came from several sources: landlords and neighbors (17), the child's mother (14), the child's father (1), other relatives (5), the Denver General Hospital (9), the Colorado General Hospital (1), the public schools (7), staff members of the division (13), a private physician (1), and a private hospital (1). (Since 1963, Colorado has required physicians and hospitals to report injuries of children appearing to be non-accidental to the police department and the division.)

Agents referring incidents to the division included the police (50), Denver General Hospital (13), the public schools (6), public assistance workers (5), the child's mother (6), the father (4), other relatives (5), the child himself (3), and a physician, a private hospital, and a private welfare agency (1 each).

Nearly three-fourths of the referrals to the division were made within a week after the incident. As the detective of the Juvenile Bureau of the Police Department is the liaison officer for protective services with the department and confers with the intake child welfare worker at the department daily about calls the police receive, all incidents of injury or neglect reported to the police are referred to the division within 24 hours. Thus, the child welfare worker usually becomes involved in a case at the time of crisis for the family.

Twenty-two arrests were made as a result of injuries to these children: 16 fathers, four mothers, and two other persons not related to the children. Both parents were arrested in two cases. At the end of the study, two cases were still pending and 11 had been dismissed. Nine parents had been convicted: three mothers, all of whom had been placed on probation; and five fathers, four of whom had been sentenced to imprisonment and one placed on probation.

By agreement between the police department and the division, the police file petitions for children removed from their homes because of immediate danger. The division files petitions only after having found through working with the family that court intervention is indicated.

Dependency petitions were filed in the juvenile court in behalf of 83 children. All but nine petitions were sustained. Custody was assigned to the division for 38 children after one hearing and for seven others after additional hearings. In three of these cases, the dependency petition was filed by the staff of the division based on subsequent information, not on the findings of the original investigation.

As a result of the first incident of injury, 63 children were removed from their homes either temporarily or permanently. Of them, 53 were placed by the division in child welfare receiving homes or foster homes and 10 with relatives. Twelve were placed outside the home voluntarily, without court involvement.

The injured children

A finding the division considers significant is that nearly 70 percent of the children had shown physical or developmental deviation before the injury was reported, perhaps caused by parental failure to meet the greater demands of some infants. Regardless of the etiology of the deviation, most of the children were hard to care for. They did not gratify the parents' self-image or were threatening to it because they failed to respond to care, to thrive, and to show normal growth and development. The child most likely to be abused was the one who was overly active or who was the most difficult to supervise and care for. The child welfare workers considered about 20 of the children to have been "uncontrollable" and subject to severe temper tantrums. In their opinion, about 19 were below normal in speech development; about 17 were mentally retarded; about 16 had toilet training problems; about 14 had feeding problems; eight had physical handicaps or deformities; and two suffered from brain damage.

The child welfare workers described the 52 children under 5 years of age as whiny, fussy, listless, chronically crying, restless, demanding, stubborn, resistive, negativistic, unresponsive, pallid, sickly, emaciated, fearful, panicky, unsmiling. They found that about 25 percent were below normal in language development; almost half showed signs of malnutrition, dehydration, arrested development, or failure to thrive; about a fourth of the girls were slow in learning to walk; about a fourth of the children had toilet training problems; about half had been bottle fed in infancy; about a half were born of unwanted pregnancies; and about a fourth had been born out of wedlock. In addition, the workers found, about half the children were not loved by their mothers and about the same proportion were not loved by their fathers.

The children 5 years old and over typically appeared to the child welfare workers as gloomy, unhappy, and depressed. They tended to be selfish and inconsiderate or unassertive and self-sacrificing. They were ingratiating or insincere. The girls tended to be flippant and impertinent. Nearly all the children were either hyperactive or listless, boisterous or silent. Other children usually bullied them, and they had few friends. They seldom took out their frustration through such acts as stealing or vandalism. They appeared to be deceitful, immature, and overly dependent for their ages. They were dissatisfied with home and school. They openly expressed disrespect toward their fathers, more so than most children, and were sullen or ingratiating toward their mothers. About 10 percent of the children were mistreated by their brothers and sisters, but about 20 percent mistreated their brothers and sisters.

Their brothers and sisters

Eleven of the 167 brothers and sisters of the 101 injured children in the study group were injured before the study period. Considering both groups, the older rather than the younger children were more likely to be the ones injured and the middle children, the least likely.

Half the children in both groups were boys, as in the general population. Thirty-six percent of the injured children and 40 percent of the uninjured children were born out of wedlock. But neither the child's sex nor the condition of his birth seemed to affect whether or not he was injured.

The children who had not been injured were generally healthier than those who had. The poor health of the injured children apparently was due in part to parental neglect.

Less than half the injured children showed satisfactory mental and emotional development. The uninjured children fared a little better, but both groups of injured and uninjured children tended to be shy, gloomy, and passive. All the children were generally deprived of parental care and affection. They were generally receiving less care than children in the aid to families with dependent children (AFDC) case-load, according to random samples made by the family service workers using the same schedules and instructions for evaluation.

The parents

The general incompetence of both parents, whether or not they injured their children, was noticeable to a marked degree, the child welfare workers found. They were beset by anxiety, hostility, and depression. They received little constructive support from relatives. They did not immediately trust offers of help and understanding from the child welfare workers, and they expected to be rejected. Their responses to events were inappropriate, impulsive, and excessive. They sometimes reversed roles with their children and sought the love, gratification, and fulfillment in their children they had not known in childhood. Very few enjoyed sound mental health or adequate social adjustment. Those who had inflicted injury were also those who most frequently exhibited anxiety, hostility, or depression. The others were more nearly adequate in mental health, but more than half of them were anxious, hostile, depressed, or lacked self-confidence, and more than a third appeared to be irresponsible or unreliable. A fourth of the fathers, but only a few of the mothers, drank to excess. The mothers more often than the fathers had appropriate social involvement.

The poor economic conditions of the parents matched the gloomy personal picture. Mobility in many families was limited, particularly in those without fathers. But even in two-parent families, only half had automobiles. Most of the families lived in the city's slums. Facilities and furnishings were inadequate for about half. Insufficient income or the misuse of what they had left most of the families in need; only about a third were managing on their income. About a third were receiving public assistance through the program of aid to families with dependent children.

Only about a half of the fathers were working at capacity, and only about a third had full-time employment. About 50 percent did skilled or semi-skilled work; about 30 percent, unskilled work; a few, professional or managerial work; and a few needed protected job placement.

Nearly two-thirds of the parents had not completed high school, though a few had a year or more of college. Some of the mothers could not read, write, or speak English; all of the fathers, however, could. The fathers who had not inflicted injury had the most education; the mothers in homes without fathers, the least.

The majority of the parents—over 70 percent—were going through severe marital conflict, particularly if the father had inflicted the injury.

The reports of the child welfare workers support the contention that parents who injure their children suffered from deprivation and defective parental care in childhood. Based on fragmentary information, almost a third of the parents in this group had been raised outside their own homes.

Poor housekeeping was usual in these families. They usually lived in rented, dilapidated houses, and they changed residences frequently. The patterns of their lives went back to their own parents. Both sets of the children's grandparents lacked education. Frequently, the grandfathers were unskilled laborers, and the grandmothers worked. Some of the grandfathers had drunk to excess, and many had tended to be harsh and strict as parents. Some of the grandmothers had been overprotective. Most were described as immature, impulsive, or self centered.

Family relationships

Interaction in these families was nonverbal except for lashing out in bickering, nagging, or berating. The parents often saw the child more as a burden and a source of irritation than as a source of satisfaction. They saw the child as a person who should love them, not as a person needing help and guidance.

In the opinion of the child welfare workers, the parents who had injured their children were rigid and domineering. The fathers were moralistic about parental authority and discipline and about child care. Both parents tended to expect behavior inappropriate to the child's age and ability. They seldom talked to their children except to lecture, criticize, tease, nag, or ridicule. They expressed the limits of their expectations by spur-of-the-moment outbursts of rage or despair. They often interpreted their children's behavior as "willful naughtiness," and were resentful and unforgiving. They frequently used corporal punishment, but more as an expression of agitation than as purposeful discipline. Many told the child welfare workers that the injury occurred when they tried to discipline the child, and many indicated that the child had antagonized or provoked them and did not love them.

Often, the parent who had injured his child saw himself as the only person in the family with a right to punish. The parent who had not inflicted injury was passive and ineffective in protecting the child from the injuring parent. The father who did not injure his child left all parental duties to the mother and tended to excuse or ignore his children's behavior. The mother who had not injured her child, however, tried to protect them. She was more flexible and reasonable in her expectations than her husband and tended to use rules for protecting and guiding her children. She blamed herself for her children's wrong-doing, and she relied less than the father on corporal punishment as discipline. Although she felt overwhelmed by family problems, she was congenial with her children at times. She tried to reassure, support, and explain matters to them.

The service

The child welfare worker's approach was to offer to help relieve stress and to recognize the parents as persons under overwhelming pressure who, because they had not experienced adequate parental care as children, were unable to love their own children. Through a stable and understanding relationship with the worker, many parents were able to reveal their fear of and dislike for parenthood and their anger toward their children. Some were able to ask to be permanently relieved of child care, not because they were unconcerned about their children, but because they recognized their inability to care for them.

Although the child welfare workers usually saw these families weekly or every other week, they were available daily for emergencies. The average length of time between the opening and the closing of a case was 27 months. Only nine cases were closed in 6 months.

By and large, the parents were evasive and resistant and found it difficult to accept help, perhaps because they were unaccustomed to being listened to and to discussing plans, attitudes, and relationships. Although the resistance to and the dependence on the workers had lessened by the end of the study period, the child welfare workers felt that fully constructive working relationships and full use of departmental services had been achieved with about a third of the parents. The mothers were more responsive than the fathers; the injuring father was the least responsive of all. Though significant improvement in ability to function and in ability to care for children occurred in many families, most were still at a low level of adequacy at the time the service was discontinued or at the end of the study.

Improvements, however, did take place. At the end

of the study, the child welfare workers reported that the mental health of a fifth of the injuring parents and that of a fourth of the other parents had apparently improved. But they also reported that about a third of the injuring parents and about a half of the others had adequate mental health. Home care had improved in 18 families; 62 percent of the families were functioning adequately in that respect. But the parents showed little improvement in educational attainment, occupational competency, stability at work, adequacy of housing, or marital adjustment. About 30 percent of the marriages ended in separation or divorce during the study period. The parents separated most often when the father had been the one who inflicted the injury. When the mother had been the parent inflicting the injury, the tendency was for the child to be removed from the home.

Child care had improved in 33 families by the end of the study. About 67 percent of the children were receiving adequate care, including children living with relatives, in foster homes, in group homes, and in adoptive homes, as well as those living with their parents.

The workers felt that about 80 percent of the children were no longer in danger of subsequent injury. However, they considered that 19 children, all living with the parents who had inflicted the injuries represented in the study, were inadequately protected.

The outlook

Programs developing today that are providing opportunities to low-income families for health care, job training, education, and good housing and job opportunities to young people may lessen the stress on parents, the child welfare workers believe. Certainly, the child welfare workers now have much more opportunity to demonstrate concretely to such parents their concern for them as individual persons as well as for their children when they can make a variety of services available when they are needed and wanted.

The incidence of child abuse in Denver may not be great when measured against the city's child population. Of the children studied, 33 were injured within a 12-month period (from July 1963 to June 1964), although the city had 135,000 children under 14 years of age at that time. However, the study shows that some injured children are in jeopardy of further injury unless effective treatment and services are provided by the community.

The following questions are some of those the division considers in determining whether a child can remain in or return to his home:

Has family stress been reduced to a tolerable extent?

Is the injuring parent aware of his behavior to the point that he can recognize potentially dangerous situations?

Is the other parent in the home sufficiently aware of what makes for dangerous situations? Can he or she care for the children in a time of stress for the other parent?

Are there other adults—friends or relatives—who can care for the children much of the day or who can be called on to help when a parent or parents are overwhelmed?

Has the child's "provocative" behavior been modified? Is he being helped to meet his physical and developmental problems?

Has the relationship between parents and child welfare worker developed to the point of trust and confidence? Can the parents use the relationship as a brake on their impulsive behavior?

The child welfare workers in reviewing the study have two basic recommendations to make concerning help for parents who deliberately injure their children.

First, the community must sanction a coordinated protective service program that can provide immediate foster care, counseling, and other child welfare services, medical care, and psychiatric care, and can bring the authority of the court into play as needed to help the injured child and his family. Second, the child welfare worker must reach out to these parents quickly and effectively to help relieve the major stress, which may have been created by such conditions as chronic or acute physical or mental illness or the child's "provoking" behavior, regardless of the etiology. He and the community must find ways to help families acquire adequate housing, education, income, knowledge of money management, and work skill and sufficient mobility so that they may have more choice about the way in which they live.

A followup study of children with multiple
bone injury provides clues to . . .

IDENTIFICATION OF ABUSED CHILDREN

ELIZABETH ELMER

Director, Fifty Families Project, Children's Hospital of Pittsburgh

THE AMOUNT of systematic research on the problem of child abuse and neglect is conspicuously scant. Abundant material is available about individual mistreated children and particular abusive families but data are lacking on comparable groups of children or families selected for study according to carefully defined criteria. This means that few objective guidelines for child protection have been firmly established; for example, little is known about the long-term effects of abuse on the child or about the nature of the factors which determine the outcome of rehabilitative efforts with the families.

Perhaps the chief reason for this state of affairs is the taboo in contemporary society regarding abuse and gross neglect.[1] The acute discomfort aroused by the topic leads to extremes of emotion and unquestionably accounts in part for the disregard of the subject by research workers. But practical difficulties also stand in the way of rigorous study. One imposing obstacle is the need to decide whether an abusive action has in fact occurred.

Few clinical symptoms can be directly correlated with the mistreatment of children. Abusive acts perpetrated by the children's own parents or substitute parents usually take place within the home where the sole witnesses are members of the imme-

diate family. Aware of society's standards, the abusers do not readily admit to abusive practices. If the child is too young to speak, there is no complainant; if the child is old enough to speak for himself, his listeners may come to conclusions based on subjective feelings instead of seeking the facts in the situation. The credibility of the child's story is also affected by the child's immaturity. Thus the principal basis for identifying the problem has had to be the judgment of the professional person. Judgment is an essential factor but it cannot substitute for objective criteria.

To help in the establishment of such criteria the Children's Hospital of Pittsburgh is carrying out a study of 50 former patients whose diagnoses included multiple bone injuries. A distinguishing feature of this condition is variation in stages of healing of several bone lesions, as shown on X-ray film. For example, a fresh fracture may be observed in one bone, signs of a healing fracture in a second bone, and signs of an old healed injury in still another. The variations in healing stages mean that the bone injuries had to be incurred at different times. This diagnosis has been chosen as the indicator of abuse or neglect in our study for two reasons: (1) multiple bone injuries in infants and young children have been documented in the medical literature as related to an environment dangerous for the child; and (2) experience in Children's Hospital has repeatedly illustrated the same connection.

In our study, abuse is defined as physical assault by an adult against a child; neglect is defined as the

This investigation is supported by a grant from the National Institute of Mental Health. Its codirectors are Drs. Thomas McHenry, Bertram R. Girdany, and John B. Reinhart.

chronic failure of the adult to protect the child from obvious physical danger. For the sake of simplicity in this paper, the term abuse will be used to cover either situation.

Recognition of the Problem

The development of pediatric X-ray diagnosis extended the possibility of medical identification of abused children. However, the tardy recognition of the problem in medical circles reflects society's discomfort in facing it. In 1946 Caffey reported his observation that subdural hematoma in infants was frequently accompanied by injuries to the long bones.[2] Implicit in this report was the possibility of inflicted trauma as the cause of the patients' injuries. However, the implications of the observation were not picked up by another writer until 1953 when Silverman described multiple bone injuries as "the most common bone 'disease' of infancy."[3] In various quarters efforts were made to pin the entity to organic disease, but these hypotheses gradually proved erroneous. Many reports published during the past 5 years have added to the weight of evidence that infants and young children may be brutalized or killed through the negligence or assault of their caretakers.[4-7]

Experience shows that new fractures are not incurred when the patient is separated from his usual surroundings; that is, when he is hospitalized.[7] In Los Angeles, it has been possible to trace the course of certain patients who returned home after being discharged from the hospital.[8] This has made painfully clear the vulnerability of these children to further traumatization when the environment is not constructively altered. Knowledgeable professional persons now believe that a child with multiple bone injuries has a 50-percent chance of being re-injured should he return to his usual habitat following hospitalization.

X-rays as a Starting Point

Multiple bone injuries have been well substantiated as an indicator of abusive treatment, but certain problems exist in the utilization of the indicator. Identification of the bone condition depends on X-ray film. Although this is an objective tool, it is an imperfect tool when used to define social problems. For example, bone changes, unless gross, do not appear on the film immediately after injury. Reparative changes first appear only 12 to 14 days after injury.[7] Thus, dependence on X-ray evidence as the chief criterion of abuse may result in noninclusion

of some children whose environments are dangerous. In this respect, the use of the clinical entity as indicator of abuse has the effect of limiting the size of any study group.

Another shortcoming of X-ray film in identifying abuse arises from the fact that film depicts only the condition of the bones; it cannot testify to other factors crucial to the study of child abuse. For example, the film does not contribute knowledge about the train of events leading to the child's injuries. Such information would throw light on the kind of daily care afforded the child, a factor intimately connected with the frequency and type of injuries to which the child is vulnerable.

Furthermore, important as it is as a clue to possible abuse, X-ray examination cannot identify the person who was responsible for the child at the times his injuries occurred. This may have been a sibling not much older than the patient. While the injury of a child by his sibling does not absolve the adult caretaker from his accountability, failure to prevent an injury caused by an immature sibling implies a different problem in child protection from that presented by adult assault against a child.

Finally, the film cannot define the motivation of the person responsible for the injuries. The intention which leads to an injury may have been laudable: for example, a parent may have grabbed at an infant who was about to roll off the bed. The parent's abrupt action may have resulted in a twisting injury typically found in abused children, but the obvious motivation of the parent was to protect the child. Although one occurrence of this kind is understandable, a series of injuries from such actions is unlikely to occur. Hospital experience shows that protective zeal is rarely a cause of multiple bone injuries.

All these limitations suggest that the radiologic report of multiple bone injuries is a firm starting point for exploration of social factors. Only when other data are added can the identification of abuse be validated. In undertaking research into the social factors associated with abuse, the merits of regarding multiple bone injuries as the first clue to possible mistreatment are:

1. The X-ray film provides a permanent record of the child's injuries. Such a record is less likely to be available when the diagnosis of the child's condition does not require X-ray examination. The diagnosis of simple malnutrition, for example, is not based on X-ray survey. After the signs of malnourishment disappear in response to adequate intake, there is

no objective record of the child's presenting condition, unless photographs were obtained.

2. The varied healing stages of bone lesions is irrefutable evidence that repeated injuries were incurred at different times.

While one injury may reasonably be attributed to a natural accident, it is less plausible to attribute a series of injuries to a series of accidents, especially in a very young child. Since the majority of children found to have evidence of multiple fractures are still infants, their injuries could not have resulted from unsure attempts to walk nor from climbing onto hazardous spots. An environmental factor has to be hypothesized.

3. The clinical nature of the bone findings releases professional persons from undue dependence on hearsay about the care of the child. Since children are frequently used as pawns in adults' quarrels, persons who work with children must contend with all manner of charges and innuendo against parents, often made by disgruntled relatives or neighbors who are retaliating for some grievance.

Few ways have been found to determine the real meaning of many conditions seen in children which may or may not be symptoms of abuse. However, multiple bone injuries, especially in a very young child, are now clinically recognized as a flagrant sign of danger in the child's environment. Without a glimpse of the family or a word of history, the clinician who is confronted with them knows that family factors are of primary importance for the understanding of the child and his injuries.

The Study

The present study grew out of several concerns about patients with such injuries: (1) The patient's physical symptoms often eclipse the acute social problems underlying his injuries, leading the hospital staff to concentrate on the physical injures at the expense of attention to his environment. (2) Hospital administrative policies in respect to these children and their families do not insure optimum management of the problem. (3) When abuse is suspected, few criteria exist for evaluating the family's adequacy for child care. (4) Community resources for abused children and their parents are frequently inadequate.

Our followup study of bone-injured children is designed to learn the present status of the former patients in respect to physical health, intellectual achievement, and social adjustment. Its second aim is to ascertain the kinds of families in which gross

neglect or abuse occurs. It is planned as a preliminary to a second study to be concerned with newly admitted patients and their families. In this second study, the operational definitions of abuse will be expanded and comparison groups will be employed. At the present time, the knowledge necessary for choosing appropriate comparison groups is not available.

The identification of the current study group was made by two of the codirectors of the project, a radiologist and a pediatrician, who reviewed the available X-ray films of all patients ever admitted to Children's Hospital. Other children were added to the study group as they were admitted and diagnosed. The criteria for selection were:

1. Multiple bone injuries as shown on X-ray film.
2. Absence of bone disease which might account for the injuries.
3. A history of neglect or assault, or the absence of a history which satisfactorily accounts for the injuries.

Fifty such patients were found.

Among the categories of patients rejected for the study were those whose injuries could be attributed to difficult births. There are no radiologic differences between bone injuries incurred during delivery and those resulting from trauma during infancy and later childhood. This is a clinical judgment based on the age of the patient, his birth history, and his course after discharge from the hospital.[9]

Also excluded were patients who were hospitalized more than once, each time for a different single fracture. For example, one infant had two admissions, the first at the age of 5 months because of a fractured leg, the other at 14 months because of an injured humerus. Staff opinion held that the indifference of his 17-year-old mother could have led to his injuries. However, this patient was excluded from the study group.

Patients with multiple fractures incurred in a single accident were also excluded, even though the accident might have stemmed from failure to provide adequate care for the child.

Strict adherence to the criteria insures that the study group is homogenous in an attribute of consequence: All the children had had repeated injuries, signs of which were discovered during a single hospitalization.

Half the patients were male; half female. Data showing the ordinal position of the patient in their families are so meager that no groupings are possible.

The age of the patients is by far the most striking item of information: the largest group, 17, was under 3 months of age when multiple bone injuries were found; the next largest group, 9, was from 3 to 6 months old. Groups decrease in size as age increases. This is in contrast to the curve for incidence of childhood accidents which shows that the incidence rate for accidents in children is minimal below the age of 9 months.[10] It then begins a sharp climb, reaching a peak between 2 and 3 years, when it begins to level off. This contrast would also seem to support the entity of multiple fractures as an indicator of abuse.

Detailed medical information about the condition of these children on admission has been reported elsewhere.[9] What has happened to them since is indicated by some of the followup data.

Followup Findings

The incidence of death among these children is high. Three infants died in the hospital. Each had multiple fractures of the skull in addition to other skeletal injuries. Four other children died following discharge from the hospital. Two of these four children were slain by their mothers. The third was brought dead to the hospital, and the cause of death was officially stated by the coroner's office as malnutrition. The fourth child, age 5 months, was returned from the hospital to her parents after the court denied a petition to place the child in a temporary foster home. Two weeks following hospitalization, the child died of causes unknown. Thus 14 percent of the 50 children are known to be deceased. Other deaths may have occurred without the fact becoming known to the hospital.

At least three other children sustained additional injury after discharge from the hospital. One had been sent home pending the completion of arrangements for temporary foster care. Within a month she was re-admitted to the hospital because of new injuries, including a fractured jaw. The second child later suffered enucleation of an eye which was injured in the course of a beating by her mother. The circumstances of the injury to the third child are not known.

Of the remaining 40 children, 8 have not returned to any department of the hospital since the discovery of multiple bone injuries, and we have no information about them. Of the 32 who have returned, either to the outpatient or inpatient departments, 19, on examination, showed no serious physical or intellectual problem. The information about the other 13 is

50 CHILDREN WITH MULTIPLE BONE INJURIES

History Since Admission
Children's Hospital of Pittsburgh

Current information	Number of children
Deceased in hospital	3
Deceased after hospitalization	4
Injured again after hospitalization	3
Physical defect	7
Petition filed for institutional care	3
Retarded mental development diagnosed in hospital	1
Rehospitalized for further treatment of condition associated with original injuries	2
No information of serious difficulties	27
Have returned to outpatient department 19	
Have not returned to outpatient department 8	
Total	50

This table of the history of children since the discovery of their multiple bone injuries through X-rays contains documented hospital data only, and is judged to be a minimum report of subsequent difficulties suffered by the children.

far from reassuring. Two were hospitalized again for prolonged treatment of chronic subdural hematomas associated with the bone injuries. Seven others had serious physical defects on their return to the hospital; four others were seriously retarded mentally.

Four of the seven children with serious physical defects were permanently crippled as a result of the old bone injuries; the conditions of the other three could not be clearly connected with their traumatic injuries. According to hospital records petitions for admission to State institutions for the mentally retarded were filed for three of the four children known to be mentally retarded. Each of the three was very retarded in development when the multiple bone injuries were discovered at the hospital at their respective ages of 5 months, 8 months, and 12 months. It is impossible to tell whether retardation preceded or followed the traumatic injuries. The other child regarded as mentally retarded had not yet been considered for institutionalization since she was still only 2 years old.

The foregoing account of these children is summarized in the table at the top of this page. Of the 42 patients on whom information is available, over half are deceased, handicapped, institutionalized, or have required rehospitalization.

The Families

Hospital data about the families of these 50 patients are sparse. Until recently, social factors were infrequently explored in respect to children with multiple bone injuries. This was especially true of patients admitted to the hospital 8 to 10 years ago, before the significance of the clinical findings was widely recognized. As the conviction grew that another person had caused the injuries of the child, the medical staff began to focus efforts on obtaining a history of the trauma. However, the relationships in the child's family were not yet recognized as a critical area for inquiry. The number of consultations requested by the medical staff from the social work or psychiatric staffs of the hospital is a rough measure of the importance placed by the medical staff on family factors in the child's condition. Our study shows requests for such consultations were infrequent: they occured for 22 of the 50 children, and most of them were made since 1957.

Several pilot studies have added to the information about some of the children's families who have extensive social agency records, but this subgroup is not considered representative of the group as a whole. One of the tasks of the present study will be to spell out the details of family structure and to learn whether abusive families show any significant configurations.

Our approach to the families is to explain the study as a study of former patients aimed at improving hospital services. Family relationships are being inspected through two structured interviews with the mother, one in the home and one in the hospital at the time of the child's examinations. Data about the children are being obtained from school reports, parents' reports, and appropriate outpatient examinations.

The passage of time since the injuries makes it difficult or impossible to learn much about the circumstances under which they occurred. Whether these families were abusive or neglectful is an un-answered question; but their pathogenic influence on their offspring appears clear in the data available about the children.

Multiple bone injuries will not be found, fortunately in the great majority of abused children. The entity reflects an extreme form of deviant child care. Its mere existence, however, implies a problem of some magnitude. For every child hospitalized with skeletal injuries, there are probably many more whose injuries heal without hospital care. Still others may be subjected to the same kinds of physical mistreatment but may escape injury. This study of bone-injured children and their families is expected to lead to new understanding about children whose abuse takes milder forms, and about families whose child-care practices are deviant, but not to such an extreme.

[1] Elmer, Elizabeth: Abused young children seen in hospitals. *Social Work*, October 1960.

[2] Caffey, J.: Multiple fractures in the long bones of infants suffering from chronic subdural hematoma. *American Journal of Roentgenology*, August 1946.

[3] Silverman, F. N.: The roentgen manifestations of unrecognized skeletal trauma in infants. *American Journal of Roentgenology, Radium Therapy, and Nuclear Medicine*, March 1953.

[4] Fisher, S. H.: Skeletal manifestations of parent-induced trauma in infants and children. *Southern Medical Journal*, August 1958.

[5] Miller, Donald S.: Fractures among children. *Minnesota Medicine*, September and October 1959.

[6] Gwinn, John L.; Lewin, Kenneth W.; Peterson, Herbert G., Jr.: Roentgenographic manifestations of unsuspected trauma in infancy. *Journal of the American Medical Association*, June 1961.

[7] Kempe, O. Henry; Silverman, Frederic N.; Steele, Brandt F.; Droegmueller, William; Silver, Henry K.: The battered-child syndrome. *Journal of the American Medical Association*, July 1962.

[8] Boardman, Helen E.: A project to rescue children from inflicted injuries. *Social Work*, January 1962.

[9] McHenry, Thomas; Girdany, Bertram R.; Elmer, Elizabeth: Unsuspected trauma with multiple skeletal injuries during infancy and childhood. *Pediatrics*, June 1963.

[10] Stallones, Renel A.; Corsa, Leslie, Jr.: Childhood accidents in two California counties. *Public Health Reports*, January 1961.

Hazards in Determining Child Abuse

This study of a carefully selected group of children assumed to have been abused makes apparent the necessity for painstaking social evaluation of the families suspected of abuse.

ELIZABETH ELMER

In a world full of uncertainties, child abuse may seem one obvious offense that everyone can agree upon and attempt to remedy. If this were true, dealing sensibly with the problem would be considerably easier than it is. The purpose of this paper is to point out some of the difficulties in determining *who* is abused. Although the difficulties described here were encountered in a study now being concluded, the same kinds of problems in evaluating abuse may well occur in the community at large. The mistreatment of children is by no means a black-or-white issue; instead, the most careful and thoughtful approach is required if we are to protect children adequately and, at the same time, treat the adult caretakers fairly.

Before presenting our experience, it may be useful to discuss certain background facts that have a bearing on the management and study of child abuse.

Problems in Defining Abuse

The investigator who wishes to study the problem of child abuse finds that the definition of abuse is by no means clear and commands no consensus—even among knowledgeable professional persons. Some claim that physical abuse is the only variety worth concern; others believe that, in the long run,

emotional trauma can be fully as damaging to the child.

If we concentrate on physical abuse, leaving out emotional trauma, a lack of consensus is still apparent. It is unclear, for instance, whether chronicity of mistreatment is a necessary condition to establishing abuse. In many families an isolated beating or hard spanking can be expected in the normal course of events. If this is so, how do we label the rare impulsive outburst that results in permanent injury to the child? Is this to be called abuse because of the damage to the child? Or is it to be called an accident, since it never occurred before? When the parent is filled with remorse, should this affect our judgment?

The visible effect on the child is often the criterion by which abuse is identified. For example, the doctor may immediately suspect abuse when an infant of ten months is presented for medical care because of third-degree burns of the buttocks. At first glance, this kind of injury in a baby appears impossible without a preconceived plan, and it is difficult to avoid prejudging the "perpetrator." Thus, the injuries of the child may lead to a ready-made judgment of the caretaker before the caretaker is even interviewed.

With the passage of time, most physical signs disappear and can no longer be used as benchmarks for abuse. For example, the signs of malnutrition recede with adequate

MISS ELMER *is Director, Fifty Families Study, Children's Hospital of Pittsburgh, Pennsylvania. This paper was presented at the CWLA Eastern Regional Conference, New York City, February 18, 1965. It is based on the study "Neglected and Abused Children and Their Families," supported by Public Health Service Research Grant No. MH-00880 R11 from the National Institute of Mental Health.*

intake. If there is no visible indication in the child, we find it difficult to believe that abuse could actually have occurred.

Finally, the ethnic or class identification of the family may determine the judgment about the caretaker's motivation. If the child is poorly dressed or has a skin color different from most of the population's, we may imagine that the caretakers are also different, perhaps abusive, in their child care practices. Not infrequently, one hears sophisticated social workers remark that certain parents could not have abused the child since they appear so beautifully dressed.

The criteria for designating abuse—chronicity, visible effects, and class identification—include a variety of unlike conditions. Since abuse undoubtedly results from a complex of pressures and reactions, it will never be simple to unravel. Nevertheless, the usual criteria seem inadequate and misleading.

Failure to agree on a common definition contributes to the lack of knowledge about the problem. Until very recently, systematic studies in this area have been sparse; little is known about the incidence of abuse, the characteristics of the families and of the children, the outlook for rehabilitation, and many other questions of importance. Another baffling aspect of the problem is the attitudes of professional persons confronted with suspected abuse. Aside from a few unusual individuals, they appear to divide into two general groups: first, those whose anger knows no bounds, who are spurred by fury to accuse and punish the parents and, second, those who shut their eyes and refuse to consider any evidence of mistreatment.

The array of emotional attitudes toward abuse, the sparseness (until recently) of descriptive literature, and the comparative absence of study all lead to the hypothesis of a societal taboo in this area. We middle-class professional people are made uncomfortable and anxious by signs of unbridled impulses in parents. We prefer to think of ourselves as civilized and immune to the same impulses. We resent the evidence that vindictive impulses exist in others and may, therefore, exist in ourselves. Hence, the "cloak of silence" and the determined actions to eliminate or disregard the evidence.

It may be pointed out, with accuracy, that the cloak of silence may have existed but is no longer important, that every month brings new publicity about abused children, that many states have passed laws requiring the reporting of abused children. All this is true; however, the focus of these efforts is instructive. With a few notable exceptions,[1] the chief objective, either latent or manifest, seems to be the punishment of abusive parents—parents judged guilty beforehand. An illustration is the use of the term "battered child." Several years ago, when the taboo was especially strong, the term served a useful purpose by dramatizing and calling attention to the existence of child abuse. It is less suitable today when the focus is on developing appropriate measures for management of the problem. The term "battered child" connotes willful assault, cruelty, even sadism; it leaves no room for the exploration of other etiological possibilities.

The continued widespread use of the term suggests that the taboo about child abuse is now appearing in reverse. The same aversion toward the phenomenon is currently expressed as a single-minded wish to punish parents, thereby getting rid of the abuse problem. No one can quarrel with the slogan "Protect the battered child." It accords with socially acceptable principles and satisfies the need to do something worthwhile. Concurrently, it raises a barrier against baffling and irritating questions that must be thought through if we are to achieve lasting solutions for these serious problems.

The Study Plan

The study to be discussed is one effort to shine light upon some of the murkiness about child abuse. With financial help from the National Institute of Mental Health, we examined a number of former patients of the Children's Hospital of Pittsburgh whose physical symptoms upon admission appeared to be caused by caretaker mistreatment. The first aim of the research was to evaluate the present status of the child as to physical

---

[1] See, for example, Edgar J. Merrill, "Physical Abuse of Children—An Agency Study," in *Protecting the Battered Child* (Denver: The American Humane Association, 1962), pp. 1–15.

health, intellectual functioning, and social adjustment. The second aim was to examine selected social, psychological, and demographic attributes of the families to see whether abusive families had characteristics in common. In this study, abuse was defined as adult assault against the child.

The patients selected for study had multiple bone injuries at the time of admission to the hospital. They had to be free of bone disease that might account for the bone condition, and they had to have a history of neglect or abuse, or a history inadequate to explain the injuries. A distinguishing feature of this condition is the variation in the healing stages of the bone lesions as shown on X-ray film. For example, a fresh fracture may be observed in one bone, signs of a healing fracture in a second bone, and signs of an old healed injury in still another bone. Such variations mean that the injuries had to be incurred at different times; thus, multiple bone injuries are considered by medical authorities as a potent indicator of abuse.[2]

This appears to be confirmed by the age distribution of the children at time of hospital admission: over half of them were under 9 months of age. The pronounced infancy means that the children were not usually walking and, therefore, were not apt to propel themselves into positions of danger. Their injuries as indicated by the various healing stages show that whatever happened to the children had to be a repetitive process rather than a one-time incident.

Based on the potency of the criteria, an assumption of consequence was that all the study children had been abused. We anticipated doing a simple, straightforward study of clearly abused children and clearly abusive

families. But, after intensive consideration of the available data, the research staff judged that not all the children had been abused; it was, therefore, necessary to alter the study procedures.

The original design called for two interviews with the mother: one in the home and one in the hospital. Following the hospital interview, three standardized questionnaires were administered. During the second interview with the mother, the child was evaluated in the outpatient clinics of the hospital. The child had a standard pediatric examination, psychological tests, a psychiatric interview, an X-ray survey of the skeleton, and a hearing test. A final visit was later made to the home to communicate the results to the family.

We also gathered pertinent collateral data —from social agencies, various institutions, police, and schools—that were useful primarily as a means of validating the information given by the parents. They also helped us to understand particularly difficult families.

The original study group numbered 50 former patients with multiple bone injuries; of these, 13 were either deceased or institutionalized at the time of the study (we did not gather data from their families), and 6 other families refused to participate. The final study group was made up of 33 children, including 3 sets of siblings (2 of these siblings entered the study at our request in view of history indicating that they also might have been abused). Twenty-eight mothers completed both the home and hospital interviews.

Difficulties Encountered in Study

Difficulties in determining abuse were mentioned earlier in this paper. The next few paragraphs will deal with the particular difficulties encountered in our study and how we attempted to solve them.

Upon the completion of hospital examinations, the interviewers and examiners met to clarify their clinical judgments about the children. They reviewed all the available medical data for each child, including prenatal, birth, and postnatal history; records from local doctors and other hospitals; data pertaining to the hospitalization for multiple

[2] See, for example: John Caffey, "Multiple Fractures in the Long Bones of Infants Suffering from Chronic Subdural Hematoma," *American Journal of Roentgenology*, LVI (1946), 163–173; F. N. Silverman, "The Roentgen Manifestations of Unrecognized Skeletal Trauma in Infants," *American Journal of Roentgenology*, LXIX (1953), 413–427; Donald S. Miller, "Fractures Among Children, I: Parental Assault as Causative Agent," *Minnesota Medicine*, XLII (1959), 1209–1213; C. Henry Kempe, Frederick N. Silverman, Brandt F. Steele, William Droegmueller, and Henry K. Silver, "The Battered-Child Syndrome," *Journal of the American Medical Association*, CLXXXI (1962), 17–24; and Thomas McHenry, Bertram R. Girdany, Elizabeth Elmer, "Unsuspected Trauma with Multiple Skeletal Injuries During Infancy and Childhood," *Pediatrics*, XXXI (1963), 903–908.

bone injuries; and available social data on earlier periods. The group then reviewed the data from the current research study, including the impressions and observations of the interviewers and examiners. The aim was to arrive at a consensus as to the current functioning of the child and to compare this with his past functioning.

The original plan purposely excluded any attempt to determine the circumstances of the child's old injuries; one reason was the assumption, basic to the study, that all study children had been abused. It was soon realized, however, that bone injuries incurred at different times are not necessarily evidence of mistreatment. For example, one infant had sustained injuries during a particularly traumatic birth. He was later involved in two consecutive accidents causing bone injuries that led, along with birth injuries, to his selection for this study. All injuries and their dates were verified by the family doctor; the research group therefore decided that there was no evidence of abuse in this case.

Once the original assumption of general abuse had been discarded as erroneous, the group decided to discuss fully the etiology of each child's old injuries. The following items were considered:

.. The caretaker's admission of assault.
.. The statement of a spouse concerning guilt of the other spouse.
.. A child's legal removal, based on alleged abuse, from the home in which the injuries had occurred.
.. Other reasonable causes of the injuries, including traumatic birth, sibling assault, or accident.
.. The general growth and development of the patient at time of hospital treatment for bone injuries.
.. Health history of siblings—reported neglect, abuse, injuries, or death.
.. Placement of patient or siblings away from home (along with reasons for such action).
.. Observations or verified reports of physical aggressions against others by adult family members.

Because some of these data were not directly measurable but depended for their validity on clinical judgment and experience, they were probabilistic rather than certain.

Also, not all the factors were of equal weight in the determination of abuse. Despite these difficulties, the judgments of the group were probably as satisfactory as could be made.

Classifications of Children

On the basis of the judgments made by the research staff as a group, the 33 children were divided into three hypothetical groups: abused children; nonabused children; and unclassified. Every effort was made to arrive at a conservative judgment.

The judgments concerning the abused and the nonabused children were unanimous; in fact, this was a requirement for placing a child in either category. Nonabused children were those whose earlier bone injuries had a plausible explanation other than adult assault. The unclassified category comprised children about whom there was disagreement among the clinicians and those children whose injuries could not be explained on any reasonable basis.

It is believed that some of the seven children in the unclassified category probably were injured through assault, but since there was no consensus among the research group, they were not included in the abused category. In one instance, a child was known to have had birth injuries; the X-ray film also showed fresh fractures when he was admitted to the hospital at the age of 3 months. But no report of accident was elicited, and exploration of family factors showed no reason to suspect mistreatment.

Advantages of Followup Study

In view of the powerful criteria for admission to the study, we anticipated a simple, straightforward study of clearly abused children and clearly abusive families. It was totally unexpected, therefore, to find so many children who were plainly not abused or whose injuries were caused by undetermined factors. Here certain characteristics of a followup study came to bear.

It is difficult, of course, to determine the etiology of injuries incurred a number of years before, but there are certain values to a retrospective look. The lapse of time means that records of various kinds are available for a larger proportion of the families.

Another value of the followup study is the absence of parental anxiety commonly aroused by a child's hospitalization. The child is at home with his parents, and real or fancied threats to remove him are no longer present. In all probability, these conditions contributed to the families' relaxed attitudes and their responsiveness. Indeed, some of the material divulged by certain parents may not have been within reach at the time of the children's hospitalization.

Still another benefit of a followup study is the relative calmness of professional feelings. The immediacy of the child's injuries and the acute necessity to make a decision about his welfare are no longer in the picture. All the professional persons involved can be deliberate and objective without the emotional turmoil often aroused by child abuse.

Comparisons of Evaluations

It is interesting to compare the research evaluation with the evaluation of these children at the time of hospital treatment for bone injuries. All but 5 of the 22 children that the researchers later evaluated as abused had also been judged as being abused at the time of hospitalization. In the other five instances, the families had not been interviewed concerning the origin of injury.

Among the four nonabusive families, two had not been questioned, indicating that the possible significance of the children's injuries was not picked up; in the remaining two nonabusive families, the parents were accused of having caused the children's injuries. In each instance, reliable information was available to clarify the problem, but the young medical resident was so determined to protect the children and his attitude was so negative toward the parents that he did not seek the facts.

In the unclassified category, three children were not identified at the time of admission as possibly abused; four children were. For these four, however, substantiating evidence was not available either way at the time of admission, a condition that prevailed throughout the study.

Some of the families suspected of abuse at the time of admission were referred for social evaluation. The social worker, however, was not always able to accept as valid the suspicions of the doctor. In still other instances, both physician and social worker could agree upon the danger to the child if he remained with the family judged as abusive. The court was then petitioned to remove the child from the home in which the injuries had occurred. Like the hospital, the court appeared to have no particular guidelines for decisions in these very difficult situations—the petition was denied in some cases and approved in others.

False Accusations and Stress Factors

In problems of suspected abuse the difficulties of doctors, social workers, and courts are very real. All professions are prone to serious errors resulting in grave danger for the child, who may be injured again and even killed, or leading to false accusations of the caretakers, which may cause serious psychological damage to both the child and his parents. It cannot be emphasized too strongly that false accusations of the parents can be harmful in the extreme. We saw an example of this during our study.

The mother willingly gave the first interview in the home. She was friendly and gave evidence of a good relationship with her husband and their three children. She did not appear eager to bring the child into the hospital for evaluation, however, and it was later learned that this was a result of her hospital experience when the infant was injured. She had been belligerently accused of beating him. She was most upset about this, went home and cried, and was determined not to come back. Nevertheless, she did return for a followup appointment—as ordered by the hospital physician. During the second appointment, the same accusations were made—this time in front of a waiting room full of people. She then resolved that she would never return to the hospital. When asked why she had not reported this event to the administration, the mother said that she did not wish to get into any trouble.

This same mother later gave an informative account of the circumstances surrounding the child's bone injuries and the hospital admission.

The patient was less than 1 year old when the mother again became pregnant. The family was living in cramped quarters; the independent business of the husband was not prospering;

and, following a brief illness, the mother's mother had suddenly died.

During this period of family stress, the mother occasionally left the baby with the landlady, who seemed to enjoy caring for him. This woman, however, was known as a belligerent, touchy person. Suddenly, the mother became aware that the landlady was handling the child with considerable roughness, and she withdrew the baby from the landlady's care. Later, when tenderness in one leg was noted, she took the child to the hospital where multiple bone injuries were discovered. But, instead of finding an interest and willingness to help, the mother received harsh accusations and humiliation in the eyes of the other parents. In addition to increasing the mother's burdens, the management of the situation did nothing to further the welfare of the patient.

We frequently found a pileup of environmental pressures at the time of the child's hospitalization—among both the abusive and nonabusive families under study. (Stress factors in many areas have also been found in another study of families whose children were hospitalized due to conditions of neglect or abuse.[3]) Stress factors in our study included a variety of circumstances such as illness or death of a parent, inadequate housing, an unwanted pregnancy, and a sick child. Characteristically, there was a multiplicity of environmental pressures. This leads to the hypothesis that the adequacy of child care may decline at times of family stress — as does the adequacy of other functions, such as job performance. When precipitate accusations are added to the picture, the parent's defenses are heightened, the true story is withheld, and the opportunity to protect the child by helping the parent is lost.

Remaining Questions

As this study has progressed, the necessity for painstaking social evaluation of the families suspected of abuse has become increasingly apparent. Areas for inquiry are the identity of the person responsible for the child; the ordinary patterns of child care; the variations in care that may occur and the reasons for them; and something of the history of the caretakers, to illustrate their prevailing behavior patterns. The final areas to be suggested for further study are the family events occurring at the time of the child's injuries and the typical reactions of family members to stress.

Only by means of evaluating such variables will it become possible in practice to separate the abusive from the nonabusive families. Certainly, premature or hostile accusations hold no promise for learning what has occurred; on the contrary, such behavior by responsible professional persons may well cause unnecessary psychological damage both to the parent and, through the parent, to the child.

It would be gratifying to be able to spell out the precise differences between abusive and nonabusive families; such differences would be useful in making predictions in practice. But predictors can be found only through patient and systematic study. This will eventually make possible a more rational approach to the problem by reducing the force of the hysteria surrounding child abuse in our society.

Only as this is dissipated will it become possible to view the problem objectively and to choose the type of action best suited to the needs of the particular situation. This, in turn, will lead to increased effectiveness in child protection, better selection of the adults who may be helped, and more adequate help for those adults who appear to have potential for better child rearing. Finally, as systematic studies accumulate and the findings are tested in practice, prospects for the prevention and reduction of abuse will become brighter.

RECEIVED MAY 20, 1965

---

[3] Eileen Branigan, *et al., An Exploratory Study of the Neglected-Battered Child Syndrome* (unpublished doctoral dissertation, Boston College School of Social Work, 1964).

Emergency Child Care Service:
The Evaluation of a Project

MERLE K. MILLER

HENRY J. FAY

In an effort to meet the needs of children abandoned or neglected during hours when most social welfare agencies were not operational (holidays, nights, and weekends), the Emergency Child Care Committee was formed in Springfield, Massachusetts. The Community Council (a coordinating and planning committee for all social welfare services in the Greater Springfield area) set up the emergency committee after the Police Department advised the council that it was receiving many telephone calls from citizens about neglected children at times when the social welfare agencies that normally would handle such situations were closed. There was no city facility that could provide such service. The Emergency Child Care Committee was to operate on a year's trial basis, and then make a report to the Community Council concerning the effectiveness and future of such a program.

This paper summarizes the results of the year's project. Since there was a relative lack of quantitative data in this area, procedures were instituted to collect from the caseworkers and the cooperating agencies complete case histories of each family serviced by the project.

At the start, five hypotheses were for-mulated as criteria against which to check data to determine whether the project should continue and to identify strengths and weaknesses.

Similar projects in other cities were studied and found to differ greatly; even the definitions of emergency care were dissimilar. Bernstein,[1] Hunt,[2] and Paget[3] each defined "emergency" in ways appropriate to the services their agencies provided. The Springfield committee decided that the project, rather than operate on a 24-hour basis, and thus duplicate the services of other agencies, would operate only when other agencies were not functioning. When the appropriate existing agency opened, it assumed the responsibility for any referrals. It was hypothesized (1) that a need for this service did exist in Springfield and (2) that the project would provide services that would have been provided if existing agencies had been open at the time of the emergency.

The kinds of services provided were selected on the basis of the reports on previous projects. Bernstein concluded from the Boston project that children were taken from their homes too often.[4]

Merle K. Miller, Ph.D., Acting Director, Division of Arts and Sciences, Springfield College, Springfield, Massachusetts, was Research Consultant to the Emergency Child Care Committee. Henry J. Fay was a Teaching Fellow and received his M.S. and Certificate of Advanced Study in Preclinical Psychology at Springfield College. The project was financed by the Dexter Fund. This paper is a condensation of a more extensive article, including tables, a copy of which may be obtained on request to the authors.

1. Rose Bernstein, "Emergency Care of Children—Necessary Evil or Meaningful Child Welfare Service?", Child Welfare, XLV, No. 6 (1966), 327.

2. Roberta Hunt, "Research Findings as a Base for Action in Child Welfare," Child Welfare, XLVI, No. 8 (1967), 456.

3. Norman W. Paget, Emergency Parent—A Protective Service to Children in Crisis," (Buffalo, New York: Children's Aid and S.P.C.C., 1967), p. 1.

4. Bernstein, op. cit., 75.

Paget maintained that only "emergency parents" (homemakers) were necessary to supervise abandoned children in Buffalo.[5] Hunt also emphasized the role of homemakers. In addition, she encouraged more extensive use of temporary foster homes.[6] In light of these findings, four levels of intervention were provided in the Springfield project. The first was direct intervention by a caseworker (recruited from existing agencies), whose initial effort involved location of parents, neighbors, or friends who could provide supervision for the children. Further action was taken by the caseworker via three available avenues—emergency homemakers, temporary foster homes, and hospital care—the action being determined by the individual situation.

Hypothesis 3 was that the kinds of intervention least disruptive to the children would be used most frequently. Hypothesis 4 was that there would be enough emergencies (involving subsequent referrals to daytime agencies) to make it worthwhile to have the caseworker on the scene of the emergency.

In the other programs the sources of referral, like the services provided, varied from city to city. The Buffalo project reported two referral sources, the police and the parent or neighbor. The Boston report listed eight referral sources, with the numbers from each source fairly even.[7] In the Springfield program an answering service was employed; it referred all inquiries to the caseworker on duty. Calls to the police were relayed to the answering service. Hypothesis 5 was that most calls would come from private citizens and the police.

Results

Analysis of the year's operation tended to support the five hypotheses, and to identify the strengths and weaknesses of the project.

Hypothesis 1: The Necessity for Emergency Child Care Exists in Springfield

A total of 46 requests was received from February 6, 1967, through February 5, 1968. Of these, four were not serviced because they were outside the scope of the project. There was no clear indication that requests were more numerous in any given month, but at least one-fourth of the requests were received on Saturdays, with the other requests spread out evenly over the other 6 days. Most requests came between 5 p.m. and midnight; thus, requests were most likely Saturdays from 5 p.m. to midnight.

The number of cases, of course, was only one criterion for evaluating the necessity of the project; severity of need was also a yardstick. A study of the kinds of situations requiring emergency service indicated the severity of the problems handled.

In 23 cases children were abandoned, in nine cases the mother was hospitalized as a result of an emergency, and in seven cases the mother was arrested. Of the total 42 cases, 39 involved children left unsupervised. (Child welfare literature has indicated that when children are abandoned or neglected at night, the possibility of injury increases. According to the National Fire Protection Association, in 1965 50,000 children left alone either died or suffered moderate to severe injury. The National Safety Council has stated that 25 percent of the children killed in home accidents were alone at the time.)[8]

Need for the emergency child care service was also demonstrated by the fact that 15 of the 42 referrals necessitated placement of the children in foster homes, although this measure was resorted to only after every effort to resolve the emergency in other ways had failed.

Hypothesis 2: The project's services would have been provided by existing agencies had they had been operational at the time.

In 33 of the 42 cases, previous contacts with one or more social welfare agencies had been established. Further, 41 cases were referred to other social welfare agencies for more intensive service following the emergency. These data support the hypothesis. If the services of the project had not been available, the emergencies would not have been handled by professional caseworkers and appropriate sup-

5. Paget, *op. cit.*, 11.

6. Hunt, *op. cit.*, 461-462.

7. Rose Bernstein, *Emergency Shelter Care for Children* (Boston: United Community Services, 1966), p. 20.

8. Shirley Camper Somon, "Emergency Parents," *Parade*, Jan. 29, 1967, p. 8.

portive services, such as foster homes and hospitals.

Hypothesis 3: The least disruptive forms of intervention would be used most frequently.

On the theory that the least intervention is the best intervention, caseworkers first attempted to handle the situations by telephone, enlisting cooperation of relatives and friends in supervising the children. Eight of the 42 cases were handled by telephone: the other 34 required that the caseworker personally visit the scene of the emergency.

It was found necessary to remove children from their homes on 15 occasions, despite efforts to contact relatives or family friends. In most cases few relatives or friends were available because of estrangement between them and the parent.

To overcome this difficulty, the Emergency Child Care Service sought homemakers to provide supervision in the homes of the abandoned children. The advantage of not removing children from their homes has been studied by Moss.[9] Brodsky has cited the use of homemakers even in slum sections of New York City.[10] The use of homemakers in this project was limited by two factors: (1) Recruitment was difficult, with those recruited available only from 5 p.m. to 6 a.m., and (2) the caseworker often thought a homemaker was not needed. There was some debate within the committee concerning more extensive use of homemakers, but policy was not defined. Further investigation is required, with attention to safeguarding the psychological well-being of the children.

In evaluating the 15 cases in which children were placed in foster homes, it was agreed that in only one situation could the child have been kept in the family home. Removal of the children presented a problem as to the legality of such action during hours when court officials ordinarily involved were not available. The caseworkers had a consent form that the parent was requested to sign if the children had to be removed. In only one case of the 12 where the parent was available did she refuse to sign the form. Court officials were cooperative, but the legality of the procedures employed remains to be clarified. The point must be resolved to safeguard the interests of the individuals involved—the policemen and the caseworkers.

Minor problems, such as purchasing food in the middle of the night, or getting prescriptions filled, were handled as they arose. Solution of each new problem established the procedure for recurrences. By the end of the 12 months techniques had been developed to handle efficiently most contingencies.

Hypothesis 4: The Presence of the Caseworker on the Emergency Scene Would Be Worthwhile

When a caseworker arrived at the scene of an emergency, her decision to remain until the situation was resolved was determined by two factors. The first was that if she left, and still another unfamiliar person came to stay with the children, their emotional strain would be heightened. The second was the caseworker's desire to talk with the parent when she returned home, and thus become better informed and able to make meaningful recommendations to the appropriate agencies (as noted, other agencies were involved in 41 of the 42 cases). In evaluation, the caseworker's presence at the scene of the emergency was considered one of the program's strengths.

Hypothesis 5: Most Requests Would Come from Citizens and the Police

Of the 42 requests, 32 were made by the Police Department. That there were few requests from agencies and private individuals perhaps reflected the lack of wide publicity for the program. Hypothesis 5 was thus confirmed in part, and it appeared that more adequate publicity might increase the number of requests made by individuals.

Conclusion

Evaluation of the first year's operation of the Springfield Emergency Child Care Committee demonstrated the importance of feedback information. The data have shown the value of such a program, and identified some of its strengths and weaknesses. ◆

9. Sidney Z. Moss, "How Children Feel About Being Placed Away From Home," Children, XIII, No. 4 (1966), 153-157.

10. Rose Brodsky, "Administrative Aspects of 24-Hour Homemaker Service," Child Welfare, XLV, No. 1 (1966), 35.

Preserving Family Life For Children

One major goal of child welfare is the prevention of the neglect and abuse of children—and that involves correcting family conditions that produce these problems. If family life is to be preserved, there must be a recognition of the parents' needs, and an extensive program of intervention and support.

CHARLOTTE L. HAMMELL

Under the 1962 amendments to the Social Security Act, child welfare services were redefined in a manner that specifically charges child welfare agencies with designing programs to prevent the neglect and abuse of children. The act now states: " 'Child welfare services' means public social services which supplement or substitute for parental care and supervision for the purpose of preventing or remedying or assisting in the solution of problems which may result in the neglect, abuse, exploitation, or delinquency of children."[1]

Prevention of neglect may require correction of conditions that produce it. Prevention at another level means detecting those parents most subject to being neglectful or abusive, and altering their personal adjustment or life circumstances. To date, we have accomplished only a kind of crisis psychology in which we pile up sandbags instead of redirecting the course of rivers.

We cannot prevent what we cannot comprehend. We resist facing the fact that one segment of our society consists of parents whose primary need is to be taken care of themselves. These childlike parents are becoming more visible in the literature, but are not identified as deserving and needing public support. To prevent is not the same as to stifle or ignore. We must find means to render less alien the people who neglect or abuse their children.

Development of the Delaware County (Pennsylvania) Child Care Service, which is publicly supported, has paralleled general trends in child welfare. Foster care, protective service, and adoption were established in the 1950s. Services added in the 1960s include homemaker ser-

Charlotte L. Hammell is Director, Child Care Service, Media, Pennsylvania. This paper was presented at the CWLA Eastern Regional Conference at Philadelphia in 1968.

1. Social Security Act, 1935, Title V, Part 3, Section 528.

vice, therapeutic nursery for preschool children, emergency shelter, and day care center. Psychiatric, psychological, and legal consultation services have been expanded. The new services have prevented placement of many children, but also have uncovered many families in need of supporting services. Protective service includes families reported for neglect and those who request specific services, such as homemaker, day care, or placement during a family crisis. Children served in their own homes now represent the largest number of children served by the Delaware County Child Care Service.

Most of the parents in the protective service are in the low-income group, employed in unskilled jobs or supported by public assistance. Although the family average is four children, there are many families with seven to 12. Many are one-parent families. Few are homeowners. Fewer than half are black. Two-thirds live in Chester, the largest urban center in the county.

The parents include many who are emotionally immature, chronically mentally ill, and mentally retarded. Some have psychopathic personalities and character disorders, and are social deviants. A significant number are products of a subculture. The girl who has her first illegitimate child in the years from 16 to 20, and who was one of several illegitimate children herself, follows a pattern learned from life and is more a faithful product of a subculture than a social deviant.

Our protective service focuses on these vulnerable families, many of which live in poverty, the adults straining to meet parental roles they are unable to fulfill. Our aim is to mobilize the strengths of the family and build in supports to offset parental weaknesses. Casework as the primary or exclusive means of help is irrelevant for some of the parents because it requires something more of them, when they already are traumatized by their own ungratified needs.

Examples of Vulnerable Families

D. Family

The D.s were an intact family "just making it" on the father's wages of $109 a week. There were already seven children. The parents were worried about the care of the children while Mrs. D. was to be in the hospital delivering the eighth child. The caseworker agreed to provide a homemaker who, out of medical orientation as a practical nurse, helped Mrs. D. resolve her conflict about a tubal ligation.

Homemaker service made it possible to help these parents without seizing the initiative from them. Did the mother feel free to talk over her fears of surgery with the homemaker because of their day-by-day relationship? What implication does this have for modification of the established way of helping?

J. Family

The J. family was referred by the hospital social service to get assistance in planning care for five children during the mother's imminent absence from the home for the birth of a sixth child. Heretofore, Mr. J. had taken care of the children during his wife's absences, but he was in jail. A homemaker stayed for a brief period while the father was absent. During the continuing casework support, Mr. and Mrs. J. were able to reestablish their relationship after the period of separation and to ask for help with their unhappy 7-year-old boy, who was resentful of the increasing number of babies. Mrs. J. was helped to give this child more attention when the agency provided day care for two of the younger children.

W. Family

Mrs. W., 28, is a chronic schizophrenic living with her mother. Three of her children were born out of wedlock, prior to her marriage to Mr. W. Two children were born of this stormy marriage. While she was living away from her mother with her husband, Mrs. W. suffered her first psychotic break. Although expressing great need for the children, Mrs. W. was clearly unable to carry a nurturing role for developing children. The grandmother's readiness and ability to nurture the children was not clear. Provision of day care for the two young children mitigated the situation, making it possible for the grandmother to continue care for the children.

The agency is watching closely, to help a durable plan evolve.

T. Family

This family was reported for neglect by neighbors. They said the mother put 4-year-old Billy on a ledge in the backyard, and spanked him with a wooden paddle if he got off. He was not allowed to play with other children. If an adult looked at him, he screamed. The parents were in their late 20s, with three children of preschool age. They were resentful of the neglect report, and fearful of the agency's intervention. The first indication of common concern was Mrs. T.'s expression of worry about Billy's retarded speech. She expressed a desire to have all three children in school, and spoke of needing some time away from them, because she got irritated and lost her patience.

The parents gradually learned to trust the caseworker enough to participate in an evaluation process consisting of interviews with a caseworker, and psychological, medical, and neurological examinations of the children. The caseworker provided transportation for the first trips. Study revealed all five members of the family as miserably troubled and unhappy. There was little communication between the parents, but a pathological bond operated to keep within the family any abuse of the children. All three children were functioning on a defective

level. Daytime group care in a school for retarded children was found for Billy. The 6-year-old was enrolled in the agency day care center and the youngest child in the therapeutic nursery. The parents participated in arranging and sustaining each plan.

In view of the long-standing deprivation and lack of parental nurture, a daytime program provided an experience for further evaluation of each child. Relief from daily care reduced stress for the parents. Mrs. T. said she was less irritable and better able to handle the children when they were home. Day care provided an experience for each child suited to his own needs, and opened the way for parents to recognize their problems in caring for children.

Ways of Aiding Parents

Homemaker service and day care, added to parent-focused placement services, are appropriate programs for reaching parents whose children are neglected or in danger of becoming so. They offer a specific service, for which it is acceptable to ask. Each offers support in different ways to the parents, and provides an experience through which the agency's intent to help may be tested. Both services provide a change in focus toward helping parents care for their children, rather than providing substitute parental care. They offer a reciprocal relationship through which parental capacity may be assessed.

Distinguishing between parents clearly unable to carry the parental role because of personality disturbances or deficit and those who can carry the role with help is of prime importance in a differential treatment approach. Responsibility to assess parental capacity is inescapable and is the core of professional knowledge. Many parents in neglect cases are not motivated to fill their role even partially and cannot be helped to become so. Their children have to be removed. We have acquired more skill in making such an assessment than courage and skill in acting upon it.

Sustaining agency service is appropriate for parents who are developmentally immature. The transition in role from marriage partner to parent may be blocked because of past or present experience. With removal of fears and anxieties, the person may grow in capacity for parenthood. Long-term support should be available. More than crisis intervention is required; supports throughout the child's growing years may be needed. Have we the courage to accept that many parents may need supplementary help for long periods or may need to return for aid several times during a span of 5, 10, or 15 years?

Child welfare has provided a multiplicity of services for children in foster care, somehow acquiring the money to pay for them. Have we the courage to insist that comparable funds be used for services for children in their own homes? I have noted that most of our agency's parents are struggling to maintain children on inadequate incomes, with all the implications of poor housing, underfeeding, inadequate clothing, lack of medical and recreational facilities, and—most serious of all—the defeat of the spirit. Many of these parents struggling with too many children might have had the strength to cope with two or three. Have we the courage to enlighten inadequate parents about the possibility of restricted reproduction, and to support sterilization programs for those who patently are unable to nurture the young?

Merger of Skills Needed

Only a massive program of support and intervention can develop a program designed to prevent neglect. Child welfare preventive work involves a fusion of skills and knowledge not at present possessed by any one profession. Possibilities for adaptation, innovation, and creative use of knowledge from outside social work must be pursued if we are to make maximum use of our skills. Collaborative efforts with physicians in detecting incipient neglect are vital in furthering early recognition, prompt referral, and treatment. A truly preventive program would provide skilled evaluation of capacity for parenthood in all social and medical facilities caring for women of childbearing age.

Adaptations of use of staff within our own services indicate selective use of skilled caseworkers for diagnosis and for sustained work with parents capable of developing their parental capacity. Casework is the vehicle for the delivery of services, and is the core service unifying the efforts of auxiliary helpers in other areas—transportation, clinic appointments, the marshaling of community resources, record-keeping—to name a few.

In the 1950s, the emphasis was on substitute parental care. In the 1960s, it has been on supplementing parental care. In the 1970s, our direction should be toward a comprehensive program geared to prevent breakdown and to preserve family life. Basic to this goal are vast programs to insure adequate standards of living for the disadvantaged segment of the population that produces the majority of neglected and dependent children: Guaranteed income, low-income housing, job training and opportunity, medical assistance, education suited to all levels of ability. Child welfare workers have as their professional responsibility the establishment of the causal relationship of social deprivation and child neglect. Only as all parents are supplied with these guaranteed supports for the essentials of life and childrearing can we hope to make a broad attack on the problem of neglected children. Prevention of neglect of children can be realized when parents are assured the essentials of childrearing, and child welfare is truly focused on helping parents care for their children. ◆

SUMMARY

The readings that we have concluded have most certainly been depressing. Unfortunately they are true and all of us must face up to the plight of the battered child.

As indicated, some of these children can be readily identified as their bruises or broken bones caused by gouging, beating, or burning are in many cases visible or observable as the child moves about. Teeth marks, whip marks, broken bones, burns, black eyes, and patches of hair missing are the most frequent identifying marks. When questioned as to what happened, the children's explanations will not justify the marks.

Battered children, as has been seen, usually have other problems. They are frequently malnourished because of the small amount of food given them or because the food they get is scraps. In this case it will often be said that the child is a finicky eater or the doctor does not know what is wrong with him. Very often these children will be given cast-off or dirty clothes to wear. If other children in the family are dressed in a better fashion, it may be a sign that this child is neglected.

Emotional factors sometimes help us to identify battered children. The abused child may not be harmed physically, but he may be abused through other means, such as fear, neglect, and various kinds of mental tortures. These children are often characterized as those who cry, suck thumbs, live in a world of fantasy, or are hostile towards others. Usually these children have a poor self-concept and develop peer relationships poorly. In addition, it is hard for them to accept the fact that someone may be interested in them.

Every person needs to be an observer in the effort to recognize and eventually help battered children. This is one area in which educators, social workers, medical workers, and all other professionals dealing with children need to work together. Even though more than half the time our suspicions will prove to be false, knowing the characteristics of a battered child and being willing to get involved in the life of a person who desperately needs our help may save a child from further abuse and help him on the way to emotional stability.

STUDY QUESTIONS

1. Which professional persons should become involved in a case of suspected child beating?

2. How does a false accusation affect a child and his family?

3. Why do battered children often want to go back to the same people who have so severely mistreated them?

4. Is a rare outburst of anger that does permanent physical damage to a child called child abuse?

5. To what age child does abuse occur most frequently? Why?

6. What are some of the conditions and characteristics that help to identify a battered child?

REFERENCES

A. Readings Included in This Text

Elmer, Elizabeth. "Hazards in Determining Child Abuse." *Child Welfare*, 45 (1966):28-33.

Elmer, Elizabeth. "Identification of Abused Children." *Children*, 10 (1963):180-184.

Hammell, Charlotte L. "Preserving Family Life for Our Children." *Child Welfare*, 48 (1966):591-594.

Johnson, Betty, and Morse, Harold A. "Injured Children and their Parents." *Children*, 15 (1968):147-152.

Kempe, Henry C.; Silverman, Frederick N.; Steele, Brandt F.; Droegemueller, William; and Silver, Henry K. "The Battered Child Syndrome." *Journal of American Medical Association*, 181 (1962):17-24.

McHenry, Thomas; Girdany, Bertram R.; and Elmer, Elizabeth. "Unsuspected Trauma With Multiple Skeletal Injuries During Infancy and Childhood." *Pediatrics*, 31 (1963): 903-908.

Miller, Merle K., and Fay, Henry J. "Emergency Child Care Service." *Child Welfare*, 48 (1969):496-499.

B. Suggested Additional Readings

"The Battered Child." *Newsweek*, 71 (1968):68-69.

"Battered Child Cases." *America*, 110 (1964):559.

"Battered Child Syndrome." *America*, 116 (1967):236.

"Battered Child Syndrome." *Time*, 80 (1962):60.

"Battered Parent: Battered Child Syndrome." *Time*, 94 (1969): 77.

Blumberg, Myrna. "When Parents Hit Out." *Twentieth Century*, 173 (1964-1965):39-44.

Earl, Howard G. "10,000 Children Battered and Starved." *Today's Health*, 43 (1965):27-31.

Fruchtl, Gertrude, and Brodeur, A. E. "The Battered Child, Know Enough to Care — Care Enough to Know," *The Catholic World*, 209 (1969):156-159.

Gardner, S. W. "Abused Child." *McCall's*, 94 (1967):96-97.

Giovannoni, Jeanne M., and Billingsley, Andrew. "Child Neglect Among the Poor: A Study of Parental Adequacy in Families of Three Ethnic Groups." *Child Welfare*, 49 (1970):196-204.

Greene, Nancy B. *Identifying the Battered or Molested Child.* Palo Alto Unified School District, January, 1972.

Helfer, Ray E., and Wheeler, John S. "Child Abuse and the Private Pediatrician." *Feelings*, 14 (1972):1-4.

Sauer, L. W. "Problems of Teen-age Parents." *PTA Magazine*, 59 (1964):27-28.

"Shelter: Children's Center Deluged with Child Abuse Cases." *New Yorker*, 45 (1969):21-22.

Thomas, Mason P. "Child Abuse Cases: A Complex Problem." *Popular Government*, 32 (1965):17-18.

Vaughn, M. "Hungry Children Scavenge in Portsmouth Dustbins." *British Medical Journal* 2911:3. March 5, 1971.

"When They're Angry." *Newsweek*, 59 (1962):74.

II

The Psychologist Takes a Look

INTRODUCTION

The articles that follow reveal the terrible tragedy of the battered child. Child beatings have been common for hundreds of years, but only in the last few decades has much attention been focused on the abused child and on his parents. As a result of this increased attention, the psychological problems of the battered child and his parents are now under investigation. One indication of these studies is that many of the abusing parents were themselves abused when they were children.

Of the greatest public concern is the probability that children so treated may become murderers or perpetrators of violent crimes—if they survive! This three-word phrase must always be kept in mind in comprehending the serious nature of child battering.

As this area is studied, psychological implications must also be kept in mind. Such a study is not as difficult as it might seem.

Attention needs to be given to the possible emotional and developmental problems of abused children who have not been able to mature under normal conditions. Many abusing parents also need psychiatric treatment, but in most cases, their problems are so severe that they cannot recognize their need for help. Others fear punitive consequences if they reveal their need for help.

The readings that follow present the problems of both the abused and the abuser. The case illustrations point up clearly the psychological aspects of the syndrome.

*A study classifying parental factors
behind abuse gives clues for . . .*

PROTECTIVE CASEWORK
FOR ABUSED CHILDREN

JAMES D. DELSORDO
Departmental Supervisor, Children's Protective Service
Pennsylvania Society To Protect Children From Cruelty, Philadelphia

IN AN EFFORT to classify types of cases involving physical abuse of children and how they are handled by a protective agency, a study was made in 1962 of 80 cases in which children had been severely abused by their parents or parent substitutes. The study was based on a sample of cases handled within the past 3 years by the Pennsylvania Society To Protect Children from Cruelty.

The study's definition of an abused child was: any child against whom bodily harm was done to such a degree that it came to the attention of the agency and resulted in the rendering of service to protect the child. Malnutrition, starvation, or sexual misuse in children were not included unless bodily damage was also done. Three major factors were considered: (1) degree of injury inflicted; (2) probability of the abuse recurring; and (3) physical and psychological availability of parents to casework help. The cases were categorized as involving abuse which results from: (1) parents' acute mental illness; (2) an overflow from the parents' aimless way of life; (3) a nonspecific disturbance in the parent resulting in severe battering of the child; (4) parents' harshness in disciplining children; (5) parents' misplaced conflicts.

Abuse by Mentally Ill Parents

In families where a mentally ill parent is physically abusing a child, the mental illness soon becomes so apparent and unpredictable that separation of abusive parent and child is imperative. If a spouse or other relative is available, the degree to which he can be of assistance in getting the abusive parent to a psychiatric resource needs to be quickly determined. If the case situation is essentially made up of mentally ill parent, abused child, and protective caseworker, the willingness of the parent to get needed treatment voluntarily or relinquish her child must be explored directly with her, for occasionally such parents recognize their own illness and give up the child. Should either approach fail and the child is obviously in immediate danger, the police are called on to transport the parent to a psychiatric facility. If the child does not seem to be in immediate danger, a petition in behalf of the child is filed with the appropriate court.

A withdrawn, 3-year-old child with an old and unsmiling face came to the attention of the protective service on a referral from a city hospital, where he had been treated for burned hands. Small scars were found on his entire body, some healed, some with scabs. His mother, a 22-year-old single woman, maintained that a caretaker had inflicted the damage to her son. An interview revealed that she felt "done in" by her parents who had given her as a baby to an aunt, by the aunt who had put her out when she became pregnant, by the father of the child who had deserted her, and now by her son who "wants things his own way." The caseworker, she said, could "take him away," but later she refused to give up her son for placement and it was necessary to file a petition with the juvenile court.

The mother failed to show up for a scheduled court hearing and had to be brought in later. A psychiatric examination resulted in the diagnosis "schizophrenic, paranoid type."

Of the 80 cases studied, 4 fell into the category of abuse by mentally ill parents. The focus of service was on how to most helpfully separate parent and child. In two of the four families, unwed mothers were the abusers. Both had histories of mental illness. The other two families had histories of severe marital conflict and mental illness in the fathers, the abusers. In all four families, the homes were above average in organization and cleanliness. In two of the four families, more than one child was abused. The method of inflicting abuse varied, but it always involved a ritual rather than an impulsive approach. The most common prelude was to devise a situation in which the child either became petrified with fear or was provoked into behavior which was unacceptable to the parent and thereby "justified" punishment.

Overflow Abuse

Overflow abuse includes parents whose claim to parenthood seems to be little more than biologic. Their lives are marked by illegitimacy, paramour relationships, misuse of income, repeated evictions, excessive use of alcohol, deplorable housing and housekeeping. They obviously cannot help themselves. The abuse of their children seems to be rooted in an overflow of their own frustration, irresponsibility, and lack of belief in themselves or anything else.

In such cases, the possibility of the family remaining intact is remote. The parents are generally vacuous, pleasure-seeking, and devoid of guilt, except for periods of extreme remorse and self-pity. They make promises easily and plead with the caseworker for "one more chance." Most such parents respond poorly to formal psychotherapy. They sometimes begin, but seldom sustain contact with alcoholic clinics. They rarely make meaningful use of casework help, except in short-lived spurts.

Life for the children of such parents is degrading and dangerous, especially for infants, who cannot run from indiscriminate parental behavior. Parental abuse is most commonly dealt to the older children, perhaps because older children are more likely to become aware of values different from their parents'. When the child rebels, the parents, lacking any responsible coping capacity, try to control his behavior with their hands. The casework focus in cases of this type is to test the parents fully, in the hope of finding a spark of strength. In some instances this testing arouses a parent enough to participate in placing the children with relatives or in foster care.

The agency received a report of three teenagers who were beaten by their parents and made to beg for money on threat of burning if they refused; the father was said to have made sexual advances toward the 13-year-old girl and beat her on the face and body with his fists. The report was verified. There seemed no possibility of making functioning parents out of the alcoholic father and mother, whose 17-year-old marriage had been marked by repeated separations. Since they were unable to recognize the adverse effects of their behavior, the children were committed to the care of interested relatives.

Of the 80 cases studied, 13 were categorized as overflow abuse. In more than half the families of this type the father was not in the home. In nine cases the abuser was the mother. In every case where there was a man in the home there was a history of severe marital conflict. In only two of the cases were the housing and furnishings adequate. In all but one case the income was from public funds, paramours, or relatives. All parents who were examined psychiatrically received diagnoses of "inadequate personality." Most of the abused children were over the age of 5. The beatings followed no pattern and were rarely directed to any one child. They were administered by fist or with a belt or strap, and were repetitive and prolonged. Five cases were handled on an emergency basis, four of which required immediate admission of the children to a shelter.

The Battered Child

The "battered child" syndrome takes its name from the fact that the child's injuries are the result of twisting, throwing, knocking around, or some other form of "battering" by the abusive person. The injuries include bruises, hematoma, and one or a combination of fractures of the arms, legs, skull, or ribs. In many instances poor skin hygiene and some degree of malnutrition are also evident. X-rays of the child often reveal other fractures in various stages of healing, indicating that such abuse has been repetitive. Abuse of this nature is most severe (sometimes fatal) and is most often inflicted on children who are too young to speak, thereby ruling out their explaining how the injuries occurred. While it is strongly suspected that the parents either inflicted the injury, or know how it happened, they are most reluctant to volunteer any information.

Accurate figures regarding incidence of this type of abuse are difficult to come by. Physicians' suspicions may not be aroused because parents may shop for medical care after each injury of their child from different hospitals and doctors, fail to get treatment at all, or fabricate stories to account for the injury, blaming an ex-caretaker, a relative, or a jealous sibling.

Fortunately, the recent investigations of Kempe

and associates have gone far to alert the medical and other professions to the phenomenon of the battered child.[1] As a result, an increasing number of "battered" children are likely to come to the attention of child welfare agencies.

The process of dealing with physical abuse by battering usually begins at a hospital. Due to the severity of injuries, the child is brought there for treatment even if seen initially by a private physician. In some hospitals, if parentally inflicted trauma is suspected, or if the child is suffering from malnutrition with no apparent medical cause, the child's entire skeletal system is scanned by X-ray. Discovery of internal injury strengthens the physician's suspicions that more than medical treatment is needed.

Whether or not the police are alerted to the situation, the attending physicians should be required to refer the case to the hospital's social service department. The medical facts, along with a social service study of the emotional factors behind the child's injury, should indicate whether the child is in need of protective service. If so, such information as regularity of parents' visits with the child, their attitude, demeanor, use of social service, if any, and pertinent medical facts should be included in a referral to the protective agency. The parents should, of course, be informed of the referral so that a contact from the protective caseworker will not be the first indication they have that something is amiss. This will not, however diminish the force of the initial impact of confrontation between the protective caseworker and the parents.

If the injured child has not been discharged from the hospital, the protective caseworker assesses the home situation, parental attitudes, the validity of the parents' explanation of how the injuries were incurred, and the strength of the conviction with which they express desire for the child's return. Should it be obvious from parental attitude or behavior that the child should not be returned home, alternate plans for his discharge from the hospital will be attempted, either with or without court action. If the caseworker sees no immediate danger for the child in the home, he may support the child's return on condition that the parents continue to use the agency's service. This involves risk, but it also involves an opportunity to assess the situation by observing the child in his customary environment including all the familial cross currents and especially the manner in which the parents and child interact.

A small infant's fear and withdrawal from an intimidating and abusive parent are hard to detect except by spending hours with the parent and child. Conversely, an abusive parent often acts out his or her conflict with the battered child in the presence of the protective caseworker. Although this is done in miniature and with a parental air of acceptance of the child, the rejection seeps through in manifestations of intolerance and aversion to the abused child, indicating that the injury was more than an accident or an isolated impulsive act. In such instances, a separation from the family needs to be seriously considered, either of the child or the abusive parent. I know of no case of classical child battering in which the child has been able to remain safely with the abusive parent. Even when the parent accepts psychiatric help, separation is called for during the course of treatment, and precipitate reunions must be guarded against.

A family consisting of a young commercial artist, his wife, and two children, aged 2½ years and 1 month, was referred to the protective agency by a city hospital when the older child was admitted with fractures of the left femur and multiple bruises. The parents gave vague and conflicting stories to account for the child's injuries. In a series of separate and joint interviews with the parents, the protective caseworker found that the father had a pattern of abusing the child. The child had been a year old when the parents were married and the parents had already been separated and reunited twice during the brief period of their marriage. In the interview, the mother vacillated between minimizing her husband's behavior and expressing doubt and fear of him. The father who was obviously immature and indecisive, though with strong feelings, acknowledged having some part in the injury, which happened while he was bathing the child.

The protective worker concluded that it would not be safe for the child to return to his father upon discharge from the hospital. The mother concurred, separated from her husband, and moved into the maternal grandmother's home with the children.

For the next 3 months the caseworker continued having interviews with both parents, mostly with the mother, for the father rarely kept appointments. The father agreed to accept referral for psychiatric treatment but never followed through. Meanwhile he kept asking his wife to return to him. She finally yielded to his pressure and informed the caseworker of her intention. Since the protective agency had no authority to keep the parents from reuniting but felt strongly that such a move would place the children in grave jeopardy, it filed a petition in juvenile court in their behalf. However, the court condoned the reunion of the entire family on condition that both parents receive psychiatric treatment. A few months later the abused child died as a result of a blow on the head from his father.

Of the 80 cases studied, 8 were classified as battered child abuse. In six families containing more than one child, only one of the children was abused. In one family containing two children, both were equally abused; and in another containing three children, all were abused.

In four of the eight cases, a parent admitted that he "might have" caused the injury, but professed no intent to hurt. In all cases there was long standing, severe interpersonal conflict, either between parents or between the abusive parent and a significant relative. Psychiatric evaluation failed to reveal discernible psychosis in any of the parents. The most salient personality trait of the abusive parent in adult relationships was dependency. The injured child was invariably seen by the abuser to be either a competitor or a burden which had to be destroyed or at least made to suffer.

As in the case presented here, the nonabusive parent often separates from the spouse in order to protect a battered child but a few months later becomes reconciled. It is this all-forgiving, naive attitude, plus the fact that the continuing physical and emotional danger to the child cannot be seen and verified, which plague the protective caseworker and the court attempting to deal with cases of battered children.

Disciplinary Abuse

The category of disciplinary abuse includes children who are physically abused either for failing to comply with a parental expectation, or for having committed some forbidden act. All but one were at least 7 years of age, the majority being adolescents. The abuser was usually rigid and unfeeling.

Because of the age of the child, the caseworker tries to draw him into an ongoing relationship, to help him determine whether he is contributing to his own abuse and if so to decide what he can do about it. Often the child will acknowledge that he has been less than fair-minded and pliable on many issues. The parent usually acknowledges the abuse but always minimizes it. The caseworker must walk a tight rope, for this type of parent is standing firmly on parental rights. The casework focus is basically one of accepting the parental intention, but consistently trying to help the parent to moderate his methods.

Use of casework service by such parents may be called excellent in near-term protection, but only occasionally satisfactory for long-range prevention. The paradox of these cases is that the parents are usually upstanding citizens in the community. The abuse comes to light only when some family member (usually the abused one) releases his pent up feelings beyond the family confines. Protective intervention is intolerable for the parents in most of these cases, and they graciously comply with the agency's expectations in order to get the caseworker out of their lives.

This continually forces the agency to take a policy stand—that a parent cannot choose to discontinue use of service simply because he or she has stopped beating the child and promises not to do it again. Therefore, *if the parental conflicts which have resulted in child abuse have not been substantially resolved when the parent wishes to discontinue service, legal action is usually initiated in behalf of the child.* Such action generally results in a court decision that the abusive parent seek psychiatric help, family counseling, or be supervised by the court, or a combination of these alternatives. Danger to the children is rarely sufficiently clear for the court to decree their removal from home. And the children seldom choose to leave. In these cases, agency service acts as a safety valve.

The police brought three children, boys age 14 and 12, and a girl age 10, to the protective service shelter. They had come home a little late and had been severely beaten with an extension cord by their father, a truck driver and lay minister. The mother had interceded by enlisting police help. A warm, outgoing woman she told the caseworker that the beatings occurred often and had grown more severe. She was agreeable to the children's admission to a shelter.

These parents of six children acknowledged marital conflict of long duration. The mother obviously loved her children deeply and regarded them as responsible and well-behaved. The father, a cold stiff man, exaggerated their misbehavior. He acknowledged the beating saying maybe this time he went a little too far. He said it was his right and responsibility, and he did it so the children would not get into trouble.

Within 2 weeks, the mother and father both maintained that things were straightened out at home and insisted that the children be returned. As much help as possible was given prior to the formal court hearing. The father said he had moderated his views somewhat, but a good bit of this was obviously just going along with what he felt was expected of him. A neuropsychiatric examination resulted in diagnosis of "schizophrenic reaction, paranoid type." The court ordered that the children remain with their parents under court supervision and that the father be referred for intensive psychotherapy.

Twelve of the 80 cases studied were classified in the category of disciplinary abuse. Included were all (5) in which the abusive person was a parent substitute, usually a person at least 50 years old who was caring for the children due to parental default rather than by choice. All homes but one were spotless. The abuse usually took the form of severe beatings on all parts of the child's body, usually with some implement—strap, rope, stick—rather than the bare hands or fists. Abuse was not centered on one particular child, but on any child who "broke" the rules of expected behavior. Marital conflict was more underground than blatant.

Misplaced Abuse

The category of misplaced abuse contains cases in which a parent's conflict is being projected onto the abused child. Routine case study invariably reveals an essential family unit with parents in varying degrees of marital conflict *and* some situations which prove to be at the core of the abusive behavior. These include:

1. Conception prior to marriage. Either parent may punish the child for forcing an unwanted marriage.

2. An illegitimate child (usually the woman's, sometimes adopted by the stepfather). The stepfather may beat the child as a bad part of the mother; or the mother may beat the child as a part of the bad man who "did this and ran," or as the "thing" which caused her to lose him.

3. A brain-damaged child viewed as willful by a parent, who tries to beat out the "badness."

4. A child who has had his mothering process interrupted by the birth of a sibling. His natural reaction against this imposition may be handled so inappropriately that he further reacts, receives punishment, reacts more, and gets more severe punishment.

5. A child who has become a pawn in the conflict between parents, or between a parent and relatives, a "defeatable" substitute for a formidable adversary.

6. A badly handled separation of a child from the family and his precipitate return.

While some cases of "battered children" also fit into this category, the similarity holds more in the assessment than in their management. In the battered child category, severe and even fatal injury to the child is not uncommon and must constantly be guarded against; the abusive parent seems unable to control his behavior or feel much guilt about it; and resolution of his disturbance is apparently not within the present competence of casework skill. The converse is true in cases of children being abused due to misplaced parental hostility. Such children, although in a damaging situation, are rarely in danger of death; the abusive parents frequently manifest deep guilt and are able to control their behavior. Of all the groupings, parents in this category have demonstrated the greatest capacity to engage in a casework relationship in an effort to resolve the problems underlying their abusive behavior.

This does not mean that protection is an easy matter in these cases. In addition to the usual client resistance, the caseworker must deal with unacceptable child care which cannot be blamed on the neighborhood, insufficient income, or inadequate community resources. The parent is directly involved through deliberate action rather than failure to act. The caseworker can count on no assistance from either parent, for the parents initially protect each other regardless of the intensity of their disdain for each other.

Of the many approaches to breaking through the parents' armor, two stand out: (1) When the parents deny the abuse and maintain that the child is lying, the caseworker engages them in a discussion of the significance of the child's need to lie to someone regarding such a serious matter as a beating by his parents. (2) When his suspicions are confirmed by observation of fear or acting-out behavior on the part of the child, he patiently calls this to the attention of the parents and appeals to them to join with him in an effort to help the child.

The caseworker lets persistence and discretion be his guiding principles. Almost without fail, the agency intervention acts as a brake on the behavior of abusive parents; so the caseworker may be content with a momentary impasse as a calculated risk toward demonstrating some trust in the parents to insure that he will be able to see them again. At this juncture he weighs the advisability of interviewing the abused child. If there seems to be danger, he will pull out all stops in behalf of the child. Otherwise, forcing an interview with the child may only aggravate matters. *The most important aspect of protecting the child is not to prove the parental abuse, but to make a reliable assessment of the apparent danger for the child and somehow elicit a commitment from the parents to further discussions.*

In subsequent interviews, the full extent of the problems in the home is invariably aired, thus making possible a thorough evaluation of the situation. Usually at this point either continued protective service is agreed upon, or the parents flatly refuse the agency service. In the kinds of cases included in this study, the abuse is so severe that parents' refusal of service necessitates initiation of court action.

Some children who have endured misplaced abuse are so emotionally disturbed by the time they come to the attention of the protective agency that psychiatric treatment is clearly indicated. Many abusive parents are also in need of psychiatric treatment, but most of them receive the suggestion as either a joke or an insult. However, some regard it as a magical means of achieving quick alleviation of their problems. Either view when not adequately handled before referral for psychiatric service leads to rejection by the psychiatrist because of "insufficient client motivation, home too unstable to warrant treatment, client inability to acknowledge problem."

Ever present in dealing with cases of misplaced abuse is the caseworker's awareness that the children are in danger of further damage as long as they remain incorporated in the parents' acting out of a marital conflict. In protective service such conflict is handled through employment of generic concepts of casework help, plus the extra leverage of authority, and a steady focus on relating parental attitude and behavior to its effects on the children. If this help brings about a healthier balance in the family, to the obvious benefit of the abused child, either termination of service or referral to a family service agency is considered.

Where the union between parents has never been anything more than legal, or not even that, separation of parents, or parents and child, may be necessary to protect the child. If parental separation is advisable, the father usually leaves the home, sometimes under court order. The need to separate a child from his family might be immediately apparent to the caseworker, or recognized only after months of service. In either case, the goal is the same—to determine whether long-term placement seems essential, or whether through skillful help, eventual reunion on a more satisfying level can be achieved.

A family of 2 parents and 11 children was referred by a neighbor, who said that the children were beaten. Investigation was difficult, with threats to the caseworker from both parents. Yet within a month the parents were keeping regular appointments with the caseworker, some in the office. What came to light was that there was violent conflict between the mother and the oldest boy, Joey, who had been conceived before the parents' marriage and had spent his first 7 years with his maternal grandmother. Since Joey was big and not inclined to yield to his controlling, moody mother's unreasonable demands, the task of discipline was forced on the father. The father said that he began beating Joey "normally," but when the boy laughed at him, became incensed and started beating him with his fists. He later expressed uncertainty regarding his having fathered Joey.

When it became obvious that the child could not stand any more beatings, yet the mother was continually provoking them, the three family members agreed with the worker that a separation was needed. While in temporary shelter, Joey was seen regularly by the same caseworker who was holding regular interviews with his parents. Weekly visits between parents and Joey were scheduled, which the parents always kept. Gradually all three family members learned to trust and express themselves with the caseworker, and then to give respect to each other.

Eventually parents and child were spontaneously embracing each other and expressing the hurt and loss that they had been feeling before and during the separation. Within 5 months all three were showing sustained improvement and

gratification in their relationship, and Joey pridefully returned home.

Of the 80 cases studied, 43 illustrated misplaced parental abuse. In homes where the father was present, he was most frequently the abuser. As in all categories, except overflow abuse, the homes were clean, orderly, and adequate. Only 4 of the 42 families were receiving public assistance. In 32, there was severe marital conflict, with much indication of mismatch between parents—mother quietly self-pitying, father explosive; mother pliable, father rigid; mother self-righteous, father fair-minded. The parents' family backgrounds included stress and disruption but not to an excessive degree.

In 29 cases the child was either illegitimate, conceived prior to marriage, cared for off and on by friends or relatives, or had been considered for foster placement at least once. In 33 cases, all multiple-child families, only 1 child in each family was being abused. The abuse usually was in the form of beatings with fists or a strap and was severe enough to cause bleeding, welts, bruises, police intervention, or need for medical care. In 34 of the homes, the beaten child was at least 5 years of age. Most of the abused children were manifesting internal turmoil by bed wetting, truanting, firesetting, or withdrawal.

Need for Joint Effort

While this study sheds some light on child abuse, it clearly indicates that much more needs to be known about the distorted views of abusive parents and the mechanisms which trigger their damaging behavior. To undertake a study of the entire problem of abused children is obviously bigger than any one profession. Satisfactory results may be obtained only through joint professional endeavor. Yet, knowing that physically abusive parents are resistive to seeking help voluntarily, additional knowledge about them will unquestionably have to come largely from some authoritative reaching-out source, such as a protective service.

[1] Kempe, C. Henry; Silverman, Frederic N.; Steele, Brandt F.; Droegmueller, William; Silver, Henry K.: The battered-child syndrome. *Journal of the American Medical Association*, July 7, 1962.

OBSERVATIONS ON CHILDREN WHO HAVE BEEN PHYSICALLY ABUSED AND THEIR PARENTS

RICHARD GALDSTON, M.D.

This report summarizes observations gathered over the past five years on young children who had been admitted to the Children's Hospital Medical Center, Boston, because of physical illness due to parental abuse. Psychiatric consultation, which was part of the management of these cases, afforded the opportunity to observe the responses of the children and to study the psychodynamics of their abusing parents. Interest in this syndrome stemmed from an earlier study of young children who displayed a failure to thrive in the absence of any demonstrable organic disease. Certain of these cases were subsequently admitted because of physical abuse.

This syndrome is but one of the several disorders of the function of parenthood. *Physical abuse* should be distinguished from *parental neglect*. Many abused children are well-fed and cared for. It is striking to see a young child, covered with welts and bruises, all decked out in a fresh pinafore. Similarly, these cases should be distinguished from those of *deliberate punishment* which occur in older children whose verbal and motor development afford a potential for the provocation of parental ire.

The abused children ranged in age from 3 months to 3-and-one-half years, with the largest group between 6 and 18 months of age. None of them had sufficient verbal or motor skills to be considered capable of realistically provocative behavior, to know the nature of their thoughts and acts.

An average of 12 patients per year has been so diagnosed. Doubtless this is a minimum figure. Physicians are reluctant to consider the diagnosis of parental abuse because it is personally abhorrent, it threat-

Read at the 121st annual meeting of the American Psychiatric Association, New York, N. Y., May 3-7, 1965.

Dr. Galdston is with the Department of Psychiatry, Children's Hospital Medical Center, 300 Longwood Avenue, Boston, Mass. He is also an Instructor in Psychiatry at the Harvard Medical School.

ens to burden them with the role of accuser, there is a fear of retaliatory litigation and there is a sense of great futility about the ultimate management of such cases.

Once considered, the diagnosis is relatively readily established. There are few other diseases that produce the clinical picture of fresh and old bruises with new and healed fractures. Bleeding disorders and disorders of bone metabolism can be easily ruled out. Furthermore, such disease processes are seldom associated with the marked decrease in appetitive behavior which the abused child usually displays.

In describing the clinical material a composite picture may be illustrative. A young child is brought to the emergency ward by both parents who provide a brief history of easy bruisability or trauma inflicted by a sibling. Depending upon the site of the signs the child is admitted to a medical, surgical or orthopedic ward with the admitting diagnosis of "Malabsorption Syndrome —Failure to Thrive," "Bleeding Disorder" or "Fracture due to Accident." The parents leave quickly and seldom visit the child.

Often the possibility of parental abuse is raised by the radiologist who reports old, healed fractures of the ribs, skull or head of the humerus as an incidental finding.

In its extreme forms the behavior these children display initially is fairly characteristic, a fact which can be helpful in establishing the diagnosis. Some children manifest extreme fright upon any and all contact, whimpering and attempting to hide under the sheets. Others show a profound apathy to the point of apparent stupor, although they do withdraw from tactile stimuli. These children resemble cases of "shell-shock" in adults. They display a profound blunting of all the external manifestations of inner life. They sit or lie motionless, devoid of facial expression and unresponsive to all attempts at evoking recognition of the external world. They differ markedly from the autistic or schizophrenic child, whose behavior is bizarre. It appears not so much that their inner psychic life is distorted or idiosyncratic, but rather that it has been completely suspended.

The treatment of these patients includes the initial management of their more pressing medical and surgical needs, while deferring all elective procedures. Infection and dehydration should be treated promptly and vigorously. The correction of malnutrition is dependent upon the nursing care they receive, for the blunting of appetite renders nutrition a major problem. No other patients demonstrate as dramatically as do these children the extent to which the expression of appetite can be influenced by the quality of relations with another human.

As in many hospitals, the relative shortage of nursing personnel has made the maintenance of a one-to-one relationship difficult. However, experience has suggested that with these children it is less important that the nursing care be constant than that it be provided by women who are comfortable in offering the type of contact which these children are able to utilize.

Initially the children are left unbothered on the ward. As they begin to indicate some awareness of the environment by means of facial expression and voice, some bodily contact is proffered. When the child responds, the nurse or aide offers more and for several days the child may be carried about the ward by one or another nurse who furnishes the maximum amount of bodily contact. The child will lie inertly in the nurse's arms as she goes about her business, occasionally humming or speaking to the child.

Gradually the child moves from total passivity to increasingly active behavior. It is at this stage that a change in personnel occasionally is indicated. Often the children are unappealing, and their early activity may be offensive. The nurse who is comfortable with an inert child is not necessarily comfortable with a child who tries to poke fingers up her nose or bites. The goal is to find a person who can adjust her own responses to the changing needs of the child as he moves from total passivity towards awkward activity. It is at this stage that the child begins to eat. The expression of appetite for food appears to be inextricably linked with an appetite for contact with the nurse, as though they were the same.

None of these children has been kept in the hospital for more than two months. Two died within two weeks of admission, having failed to make any improvement. One had been noted to have poked his finger into the stoma of his feeding gastrostomy shortly before his death, though no cause for death was determined at postmortem.

In recovery from the acute phase, some of the children continue to display extreme anxiety by clinging indiscriminately to any and all persons. Others show an improvement in their nutritional state coupled with striking growth of their ego skills such that they leave the hospital at a more mature level of development.

Others make a satisfactory physical recovery but continue to display a striking absence of appetitive behavior. They do not play with toys, initiate contacts or speak. It is not that they are unable to do so; with sufficient encouragement they do respond. Rather, it appears that these activities are devoid of pleasure for the child. The ego skill remains but the exercise of the particular function provides insufficient gratification to mobilize its spontaneous expression.

In summary, these observations suggest that the capacities of the various ego skills of early childhood present in accordance with a timetable that is relatively independent of experience. The exercise and development of these capacities are highly contingent upon the quantity and quality of gratification which the child can obtain from his experience, particularly with other humans.

When a child does not receive sufficient gratification from his experience over a prolonged period of time, he fails to exercise and develop the various specific ego skills. This can result in an atrophy of disuse whereby the capacity for the specific ego skill becomes irretrievably lost.

There is no particular ethnic, social or economic distribution to the case material of this study. In general the parents interviewed were young and of limited financial means and education. In only a few instances did gross poverty or ignorance appear, and in a few cases the parents were of upper middle-class background.

A major reversal in the traditional roles of the parents was a significant feature. Many of the fathers were unemployed or worked part-time, often alternating with their wives who also worked. The wife cared for the child part of the time and worked the rest, relegating the care of the child to the husband or a babysitter. In appearance and demeanor many of the women were quite masculine and their husbands correspondingly passive and retiring.

This trend can be understood as an attempt to cope with the psychological distress occasioned in the parent by the child. In a number of instances, the actual assault followed upon a breakdown in the arrangements. In one case the mother was forced to give up work as a result of another pregnancy and her husband's desire to return to school. She was forced into much closer contact with her ten-month-old son whom she subsequently beat because she experienced his cries as "so demanding."

It is in their choice of terms to describe the child that these parents most vividly illustrate their psychopathology. They speak of the child as if he were an adult with all the adult's capacity for deliberate, purposeful and organized behavior. Thus, one mother spoke of her three-year-old daughter, "Look at her give you the eye! That's how she picks up men—she's a regular sexpot." This woman brought in a photo of the girl at age two in which the child had been posed by the mother with her hands rigidly held in front to prevent masturbation.

A sergeant in the military police spoke of his nine-month-old son whose skull he had split, "He thinks he's boss—all the time trying to run things—but I showed him who is in charge around here!"

In these cases, as in most, the parents then proceeded to spontaneously associate their reactions to the child with personages and experiences from their own childhood. The mother told with great feeling of her loss through adoption of her only other daughter, born out of an illegitimate pregnancy when she was 16. Clearly she saw in the child she beat and accused of promiscuity all her own former guilt and loss.

The father told of his own alcoholic father who had beaten and tyrannized him in his childhood and who so dominated his mother that she took him and left the father whom he had never seen again. This man saw his son as the embodiment of his childhood relationship with his father.

In the extremity of their ambivalence, these parents perceive the child they assault as a hostile, persecutory adult. The child, by its presence alone, evokes affects in the parents which they find to be intolerable. Initially they attempt to deal with these emotions by withdrawing from the child and relegating its care to the other parent or someone else. It is usually upon the breakdown of this arrangement with the consequent confrontation of the parent with the child that the actual assault occurs.

Guilt and remorse often ensue, and there may be some intellectual awareness of the inappropriateness of the act. It is of little avail in constraining the parents, for the intensity of their ambivalence is such as to obscure the reality. The parents' normal narcissistic endowment of the child with the anticipated attributes of an adult is heavily contaminated with a residue of hostility from the past, distorting their perception of the child. Whereas most parents see their children *as if* they promised to reveal certain qualities in the future, these parents see the child as actually presenting these attributes of an adult here and now.

Thus the syndrome can be understood as the result of a transference psychosis in which there is a gross but circumscribed distortion in the perception of a particular child at a particular stage in its development. It should be emphasized that most of these parents are otherwise free from the major symptoms of psychotic illness.

Management of these cases requires early and active intervention, with emphasis upon the parents' misperception of the child. It has been found helpful to tell them initially and repeatedly that their perception has been erroneous and discolored by their own past experience, and to urge that they review their memories to ferret out any possible sources of such feelings. Such a recommendation serves to shift the focus of parental attention to their own unsettled past, where it properly belongs.

It is important to recognize the quality of their ambivalence. These are not simply rejecting or neglectful parents. None willingly placed an abused child for adoption, and a number vigorously opposed even the temporary removal of the child from the home. Often the child they beat was the object of great love as well as great hatred.

None of the children observed was schizophrenic or autistic. To whatever extent these conditions are determined by emotional climate, it appears that the developing ego is more likely to thrive in the warmth of wrath and to suffer blight in the chill of indifference.

DISCUSSION

HABIB NATHAN, M.D. (Gainesville, Fla.).—Abuse of children is as old as the history of man. It is said that about 10,000 children a year are being broken in body and spirit by parents and care-takers. It was not until 1961 that the medical profession initiated legal actions to prevent abuse of children. The symposium on "The Battered Child Syndrome" held at the American Academy of Pediatrics meeting brought into focus the increasing professional recognition of this old problem.

Studies carried out by distinguished investigators like H. Kempe and others in Denver, the staff of the Children's Division of the American Humane Society, Elizabeth Elmer at the Children's Hospital in Pittsburgh, Galdston's observations at the Children's Hospital Medical Center in Boston and others have increased our understanding of this phenomenon.

One of the immediate results of these efforts has been the adoption of legal actions against the abuse of children in about 15 states. It is very likely that other states will adopt similar resolutions before this decade comes to an end. But to what extent legal actions and immediate medical care will *prevent* further abuse of these and many other children cannot yet be estimated. We do not know how effective these approaches will be in the *treatment* of these children who are severely disturbed, feel rejected and tend to be impulsive. Furthermore, what are we doing to help these parents who are definitely psychotic or mentally defective or have severe maladjustment which accounts for their performing the way they do? These are the areas in which psychiatry should intervene and find a remedy.

Dr. Galdston's paper is one of the studies that answers such a call. For a period of five years he has studied abused children and their parents who were admitted to Children's Hospital Medical Center in Boston. His findings in regard to the age range of these children, reluctance of the physicians to make such a diagnosis and the denial of the parents are in full agreement with other investigators. However, his keen observations and introduction of a therapy program for these children and their parents while in the hospital are unique. He coordinates the medical treatment with psychotherapy in providing a trusting relationship between the child and his nurse. Possibly this is the first meaningful relationship between these children and an adult. While observing them he notices a shift from passivity to increasingly active behavior, which is difficult for the caretaker to accept. This he believes justifies a change in the caretaker. However, I wonder if these children are not testing this new relationship and such a change will not prove this concept of self as unwanted and nontrustworthy. After all, these children have suffered from a parental deprivation and are hesitant and tend to avoid human contact.

In regard to the results of the therapy, he notices two different responses—one of growth in ego skills by reaching at a more mature level of development and one of extreme anxiety by clinging to the personnel involved. This he relates to an insufficient gratification from previous experiences over a prolonged period of time, causing a failure to develop ego skills. It would have been extremely interesting had Dr. Galdston studied these two groups of reactors in terms of family interactions. This would have enabled us to learn why some children respond to therapy and some do not.

The second part of his research was devoted to the study of the parents. His observations of these families emphasize the following characteristics: reversal of parental role, father's unemployment, mother's masculinity and the occurrence of the actual assault following a breakdown of the former arrangements.

In regard to the treatment, instead of accusing these parents of cruelty, the author has tried to understand them. By telling them repeatedly that their perception of their child has been erroneous and discolored by their own experience, urging them to search their memories to find the possible source of such feelings, he shifts the focus of the parents to their own unsettled past, where it properly belongs. This approach is very different from that of society and the news media, which usually condemn these parents, increasing their despair and guilt feelings.

In conclusion it should be emphasized that the phenomenon of the "battered child" is a symptom, a symptom of social, familial and personal conflicts, one which is hard to treat. Dr. Galdston's paper paves the way for new efforts in eradicating this social tragedy.

The Parents' Center Project:
A Multiservice Approach
To the Prevention of Child Abuse

SHIRLEY L. BEAN

A group therapy program designed specifically to aid parents in families where patterns of child abuse were developing proved successful in improving service and in training personnel.

Work with families in which child abuse is a primary problem is difficult. Part of the difficulty stems from the fact that lack of coordination among a community's medical, legal and social welfare resources used in dealing with the problem often results in these families falling into a professional no-man's-land. "Pediatricians who encounter the physically abused child either fail to appreciate the diagnostic entity, or become preoccupied with the physical

sequelae or find themselves unable to contend with the complexities and demands of the psychological issues. Psychiatrists rarely see these cases because the parents do not initiate psychiatric contact. Social workers do not have the medical background to support them in the management of these cases and they lack the authority implicit in a hospital facility or explicit to the courts. Also, the personal demands of contending with child abuse are considerable. The ever-present potential for violence, the intensity of emotional exchange between parent and child and the responsibility for the child's health exact a heavy toll." *

This statement supports the notion that working with families that have abused their children demands a multi-faceted treatment approach, since these families suffer in all areas of life.

It was with this understanding of the

Shirley L. Bean, M.S.W., ACSW, is Project Coordinator, Parents' Center Project, Parents' and Children's Services, Boston.

* From unpublished material of Richard Gladston, M.D., Assistant Professor in Psychiatry, Harvard Medical School, and Principal Investigator of the Parents' Center Project for the Study and Prevention of Child Abuse.

problem that Parents' and Children's Services of the Children's Mission, Boston, a small, 120-year-old social agency with 12 full-time social workers, decided to sponsor the Parents' Center, a program devoted to the study and prevention of child abuse. This program was developed as an addition to the agency's regular parent-child counseling services.

The demonstration research project was made possible by the commitment of the agency's board and staff to develop innovative, preventive approaches in working with families of young children. For some time prior to the project's beginning in the fall of 1968, staff members reviewed cases, noting the group of children in families where abuse was suspected or a pattern of abuse appeared to be developing. These included situations of unusual punishment, deliberate deprivation of food, physical or medical care, and verbal expression of excessive anger. These cases had increased in numbers and, in reviewing the literature, the seriousness of the problem on a national level was well documented, with far-reaching implications. Discussions were held with representatives of the state agency responsible for intervening in these families once physical abuse was reported. The law requiring reporting of such cases to the state had been in effect since 1964. In the discussion with the director of the Battered-Child Unit of the Massachusetts Division of Child Guardianship, we reached agreement that new treatment techniques should be developed, and were encouraged to formulate a different approach.

Conception of Center

The center was conceived as a setting for both parents and children. Those to be considered were families in which the parents had serious personality defects, reflected in inappropriate behavior toward their children. In such families the children's needs could not be fully met in their own homes, yet the children would be harmed rather than helped by full-time placement. We visualized the setting as one where the activity and experience of both parents and children could be utilized for treatment purposes. The aim was to demonstrate ways of helping parents who were having difficulty controlling their behavior toward their children. The primary approach was to be group treatment, with a beginning group consisting of six couples meeting weekly, led by a male therapist and a female therapist, with individual counseling in emergencies best handled outside the group. Otherwise, primary responsibility was to rest with the cotherapists. We would provide supervised daytime care of an abused youngster during a period lasting at least 3 months. The agency's medical director would supervise medical care for the children, ranging in age from 6 months through 3 years. Criteria for selection of families included an incident of abuse or suspected abuse, intact families with both parents living in the home, and parents amenable to help, as well as those parents willing to attend the group meetings. The families also had to live near enough to the center for convenient transportation.

Before the new program became a reality, much work had to be done to convert a building owned by the agency (formerly used as a convalescent home for children) into a center for children and parents. The building is an old house set apart by its high ground and play area in a low-to-middle-income neighborhood of mixed apartment and single dwellings. The agency executive undertook to obtain permission of regulatory agencies. The complications were endless, since the project didn't fall into any existing category of licensed care.

Finally gaining legal permission to proceed by the spring of 1968, we held a series of meetings with representatives of agencies likely to come into contact with the families we wanted to identify. We were challenged at each meeting on our criteria of intact families, and were accused of being too exclusive. Concern was expressed as to whether environmental problems could be handled in the group. Did we have sufficient staff to cope with cases requiring immediate attention? What kind of policy agreement was there with the public agencies? How would we involve ourselves with families when there was massive denial? There were questions about our research focus. Intake for Parents' Center was slow over the summer, six cases being referred, but never materializing. In September the criteria were revised, and we mailed a statement to 35 doctors and 40 social service settings. Rather than emphasize those we would exclude (alcoholic or acutely psychotic parents, mentally retarded children, etc.), we indicated our willingness to consider any family in which physical abuse to children was a primary problem. In other words, we tried during the early stages of the program to "screen in" rather than "screen out." The only actual change in our criteria was to accept one-parent families rather than intact families only. In less than a month after the mailing of the statement, the first family of three children began attending the center.

Problems of Operation

During the initial year there was as much concern with the day-to-day operation of a center for children 6 months to age 4 as there was in learning how to work with parents. Staff consulted experts in child care and early childhood education in order to become equipped to run a program altogether new to the agency. One could not foresee all the difficulties that arose when the program was in actual operation. The problems of transportation were and continue to be major. Of great importance was finding child care workers who could be helped to respond without defensiveness and anger to testing-out on the part of parents. We were fortunate in being able to use one of our foster mothers with 15 years' experience, in a new capacity as chief child care worker. We experimented with a variety of aides and assistants. Housewives, college students and board members joined the program to act as drivers, child care workers, cook, and sometimes social workers, too. A stormy winter added to the trials of the first year. There was much juggling of schedules to permit medical and psychiatric coverage at the center. The agency's homemaker service was drawn into the program at points of crisis. We soon learned the importance of maintaining lines of communication among staff through regular meetings, and of coordinating work among agencies already involved with the families. Weekly psychiatric consultation meetings gave support.

In the project's first 22 months there were 72 inquiries because of child abuse. Forty-two of these families made initial application upon referral. Twenty-three of the families, with their 42 children, have been treated in the Parents' Center. None of the 42 children has been physically abused again since they entered the project.

Group Therapy as Method

Group therapy of the parents was the major treatment method chosen, since intense transference and countertransference in child abuse cases make these clients difficult to involve in individual treatment. An early finding was that many workers were reluctant to refer parents to the center because the referral required explicit discussion of the workers' concern about the possibility of abuse. Many times the referring workers' own conflicted feelings prevented them from bringing this out in the open. Our position from the beginning was that it gave the parents emotional relief to be able to discuss their tendencies toward abusiveness with a worker who expressed willingness to understand and asserted confidence in his ability to help.

The following report from an early group meeting at the center illustrates this approach:

Several days prior to this session, an article describing our center had appeared in the *News*, a publication for employees at a local hospital. One mother, Mrs. A, telephoned one of the group leaders to say that a relative who works at the hospital had seen the article, which described the center as a place for abused children. Mrs. A was angry, since she hadn't known it was "that kind of place," particularly since she didn't abuse her children. The leader reminded her of their initial interviews concerning her feelings about her child and her awareness that she gets so angry that sometimes she feels as if she might really hurt him. The leader encouraged Mrs. A to bring up her concerns at the next meeting.

At the beginning of that meeting, however, Mrs. A remained silent. Mrs. B began the meeting with a hostile question: "Why do the child care workers let my son sleep so long, since I am having such a hard time getting him to sleep at night?" Later she commented on how inadequate she felt and related this to her own upbringing. Her childhood was a nightmare, with a drunken stepfather abusing her. She had always felt picked on by men. When it appeared that Mrs. A, despite her discomfort, would not bring up her concerns, the leader brought the group up to date on Mrs. A's question and distributed copies of the article to the entire group. Mrs. C, who was usually inarticulate, flung her copy of the article on the table, stating "I don't abuse my kids." Mrs. D quickly agreed with her and flippantly said, "Only on Sundays!"

Mrs. E, who had taken an active role in the group, pointed out that they were reacting to the word "abuse" and that the headline said "prevention of abuse." She objected to the article because it said the children were deprived of love, and she felt she loved her children and sent them to the center because she loves them and is working on straightening out her problems so their lives will be better. She acknowledged that abuse is an accurate term for what might have happened if she hadn't asked for help. Mrs. D, like Mrs. E, made a fairly accurate assessment of the article. She read the first paragraph, thought at first it was accusatory and then realized it didn't really say that they necessarily did all those things to their children.

The parent most disturbed by the article was Mrs. B, who was most acutely experiencing difficulty with her impulses toward her child and who had most recently actually hurt him. At first she reacted to the article with annoyance, denying she abused her children; then she squirmed uncomfortably, giggled nervously and said, "Maybe, sometimes." She then emphasized her love for her children by describing her participation in getting her child to the hospital for attention after he cut himself at the center. She indicated what a hard time the doctors gave her and how she tried to explain she had nothing to do with his injury, since they suspected she had caused it.

The leader asked the mothers what they thought, and they decided that some people hurt their children and can't be worked with, and in these cases the children have to be placed. The meeting ended with the leader acknowledging their concern to be good mothers and their efforts to do so, as evidenced by their participation in the group. The center was described further as a place to help them, as well as us, learn.

Since this meeting, early in the project, the group discussions have included sharing of experiences about themselves, their children, their marriages, and their annoyances and gratifications in their relationship with the staff of the center.

Parent Participation

The provision of supervised daytime care for small children affords immediate relief from pressure to the parent, temporarily removes the child who is the target of hostility, and permits him to experience a more healthy quality of parenting. Since the goal was not to separate the child from his parent completely, the center staff invited participation of parents in a variety of activities. One mother, who had particular difficulty in separating from her youngster, participated by supervising a group of children as they were being transported to the center. Other mothers assisted in preparing and serving food, helped child care workers to lead activities or offered special talents in music, arts and crafts.

The following vignette gives the flavor of the children as a group soon after they began to attend the center:

In a small play area beside the center five adults are supervising the play activities of 14 children of varying sizes and skin tones. One youngster is playing alone with a busy-board, oblivious of those around her. Approached by another child, she goes off to another area, rather than protect her possession. One restless little boy is whining and striking out physically. A child care worker is nearby and is devoting all of her attention to this little charge. A little girl is being held in the arms of a young worker. Despite her smile she is tense and rigid, and the smile masks her fright. A sore is noticeable on the edge of her tongue, resulting from her biting. Two little sisters and a boy sit in a group listening intently to a story being read to them, until the boy spies his mother coming up the driveway; the mother, without acknowledging anyone, sits apart from the group and the boy joins her silently. Another parent arrives but goes directly inside the house, where the housemother-cook is preparing lunch for the children.

Within a few weeks these frightened children from disturbed families began to evidence social and emotional growth in response to constancy and age-appropriate expectations on the part of staff.

Research Objectives

Research at the center is planned with three objectives: (1) the development of new techniques to improve the service to young children who have been abused and to their parents, (2) the training of personnel to pursue studies of child abuse, and (3) study of the origins and effects of violence as a force within the family. The research staff has gathered data about behavioral characteristics of the children, their general physical state, and physical and verbal violence during their attendance at the center. The data are being correlated with the information about the parents gathered in group meetings. Students from child care programs, graduate schools of nursing and nursery school programs are involved in our training program as child care workers.

The Parents' Center Project has proved to be a costly undertaking, necessitating application for funds from public and private sources. To date, support has been received from the W. T. Grant Foundation and the Permanent Charity Fund of Boston, as well as private individual donations of a newly formed Friends of the Parents' Center Committee.

Since we believe we can best serve the welfare of the child by preserving the integrity of his family, we must find better ways of working with his family. To this end, the Parents' Center is dedicated. ◆

GROUP THERAPY FOR MOTHERS WITH INFANTICIDAL IMPULSES [1]

HOWARD M. FEINSTEIN, M.D.,[2] NORMAN PAUL, M.D., AND
PATTISON ESMIOL M.D.[3]

There has been a reawakening of interest in the "syndrome of the battered child"(1). As Stern demonstrated in his review of the subject of infanticide, child murder has been common practice in human history(2). Contemporary society views both the act of infanticide and the thought of the act to be a sign of illness. This paper addresses itself to the hypothesis that women who present infanticidal thoughts as a significant part of their psychopathology have biographical and other psychopathological characteristics in common though they vary widely in descriptive diagnosis. A second hypothesis of this study is that group psychotherapy is a technique with special advantages for treating women with the impulse to harm their children.

Literature : Euripides portrays Medea as a mother who kills her sons in order to punish their father for infidelity. Wittles used the term Medea complex to describe the murderous impulse of a mother toward a daughter whom she considers a rival(3). Stern takes issue with this use of the term and prefers to limit the meaning to death wishes for the child which are displaced from the father(4). Anthony described a group of mothers similar to the one that is the basis of this paper. He made no statements regarding the sex of the children involved or the possible dynamics behind the mother's selection of a particular child as the object of her aggressive impulses(5).

The Group : The data for this paper are drawn from case records and the first 80 hours of group therapy of 6 women selected from the waiting list of the Southard Clinic (Massachusetts Mental Health Center) in Boston, Massachusetts. The *only* criterion of selection was the presence of the impulse to harm their children as a major symptom in the clinical picture. The group met twice weekly for one hour. Both the group leader and observer were psychoanalytically oriented psychiatrists. Of the original sample one of the members left after several meetings and another withdrew in the second month of therapy when hospitalization was advised. All 6 cases are used for examining the biographical and psychopathological characteristics shared by the group members.

Biographical Characteristics : Most prominent in the history is a strong feeling of resentment toward their parents, particularly their mothers, for not meeting their dependency needs during childhood. For some, maternal deprivation took the form of actual desertion ; for others, it was psychotic withdrawal of the mother ; for others, competition with a large number of children for the mother's attention. In every instance, the feeling that one had not "gotten enough" as a child was repeatedly raised in the group.

Characteristically the group members had at least one parent or significant parental figure who had uncontrolled outbursts of temper during which they were the object of or witness to acts of violence. It appeared that it was the mothers of the more disturbed members of the group who indulged in such outbursts of aggression.

When home responsibilities overwhelmed her, Mrs. R.'s mother would return to live with her own mother. She was often gone for weeks at a time. At these times the patient had full responsibility for caring for 5 other children. If she didn't keep the house immaculate she was beaten by her father whom she looked upon as a "vulture." She feared that he would murder her in one of his explosive outbursts. When she told the group about this she next associated it to the time she saw her father drive a tractor over her brother, "accidentally" cutting off his leg.

The members of the group expressed intense hatred for men. Some related this to rivalry with male siblings. Others had been jealous of masculine prerogatives all of their lives. They were "tom boys" during

---

[1] Read at the 119th annual meeting of The American Psychiatric Association, St. Louis, Mo., May 6-10, 1963.

[2] Ithaca, New York.
[3] Boston, Mass.

latency who resented being girls because "boys had all of the fun" and girls had none. As adolescents and adults they arranged experiences for themselves which confirmed these feelings. They had premarital love affairs or made impulsive marriages which resulted in unwanted pregnancies and desertion or withdrawal of their mates. One patient interpreted her dismal experiences in wartime as a demonstration of woman's fate at the hands of the hated male.

Another biographical characteristic is the inclination to seek maternal care from their mates. They formed relationships with men who were overtly homosexual or sought marriages with men who willingly assumed the feminine role as their wives progressively abdicated their mothering responsibilities. When the mate that they selected did not fulfill their maternal yearning, it reinforced their hatred and disappointment. Thus they hated their men for seemingly contradictory reasons. On the one hand they were not womanly or motherly enough to satisfy their wives' regressive dependency needs. On the other hand, they were hated because they were men who could work away from the home without having to care for children and could desert their women without having to worry about being pregnant.

When she was 6, Mrs. J.'s father deserted the family. Her mother never "told" the patient that her father would not return. When she was 14, she learned that this was in fact so. When Mrs. J. became engaged, her mother developed a paranoid psychosis. Mr. J. is a high school teacher. In the early part of their marriage he treated his wife like a little princess. When their first son was born, the patient seemed helpless and unable to cope with the added work. Her husband came home after school and did her work for her. This pattern became even more prominent when their second child was born. At this point Mr. J. was studying in a training program to further his career. Though the patient said that she was in favor of this advancement, her symptoms interfered. She did less of her work and her husband had to take time away from his studies to do more. When his work called for him to be out of town, she was afraid to stay alone so he couldn't leave. In the group, she complained that her husband did not do enough for her. One of the group members observed that she seemed not to be trying very hard to do anything for herself. When her husband threatened divorce she saw this as proof of the fact that all men were unreliable and deserted their wives like her father did.

Psychopathology: Though they all presented the symptom of the impulse to harm their children, there was considerable variation in what Anthony calls the "psychological gap" between the impulse and the act. At one end of the continuum were the "nice" women to whom any aggressive thought was alien to their self concept. Diagnostically, they were called obsessional neurotics. At the other end of the scale were the women who were quite aware of their murderous urges and had even acted upon them. For example, one of the group members in this category had tried to strangle her children because they were making too much noise. At this end of the scale where the gap between the thought and the act was narrow, the patients often resorted to extremely primitive defenses of conscious denial, projection, and acting-out. Diagnostically, they were classified as impulsive character disorders or borderline psychotics.

Mrs. B told the group about the first time she had an epileptic seizure. She was 19 and lived alone in an apartment with her newborn son, having been deserted by her husband and disowned by her family. One night she awoke to feed her screaming, hungry baby. The feeding didn't stop the baby from crying and she became furious. "I could have killed him," she said. Suddenly, she stiffened and lost consciousness. The baby dropped from her hands to the floor where she found him still crying when she regained consciousness.

As might be anticipated from a knowledge of the group members' attitude toward men, the major focus of their murderous impulses was a male child. For some of the women, this was because they simply saw the child unrealistically as a grown man. Others transferred their unresolved sibling rivalry feelings from their brothers to their sons. The sons were said to "act just like" their hated brothers. For still others this involved a displacement of aggression from their husbands to their children as in the Medea myth.

Mrs K. burst into tears as she described her unsuccessful attempts to keep from beating her son. He was the only other person she had in her life and she could not understand why she would, with little provocation, have a "spell." During the "spells" she shrieked curses at her son in her native tongue and beat him mercilessly. On one occasion he developed a facial tic after such a beating. Mrs. K. was so frightened that she vowed not to hit him again.

However, she could not restrain herself. She admitted to the group that she really wished that her son would remain a baby. When she looked at him she thought that she would soon have a loathsome man living with her instead of a little boy.

The group members all suffered from multiple phobias. They soon discovered their common fears. They were afraid to be alone. They were afraid to ride on the street car or bus. They were afraid to be out of doors. They were afraid to drive automobiles. There was wide variation in the effectiveness of the phobic symptom as a defense. As might be anticipated, the "nice" women experienced these phobias as irrational and unrelated to their own wishes or feelings. Those women with more primitive personality organization related the phobias more closely to the conscious impulse. They were afraid to be alone with their children for fear that they would kill them. They didn't dare drive a car for fear that they would kill someone. For all of the members of the group, the phobias were crippling symptoms which resulted in withdrawal from social contact. In addition to multiple phobias and infanticidal impulses, all complained of chronic depression, suicidal preoccupation, and intermittent or chronic frigidity.

The Children: Their children were reported to have a wide variety of difficulties which could be related to their mothers' psychopathology. These difficulties included learning inhibition, school phobia, accident proneness, allergies, and a high susceptibility to infection. Maternal aggression was not only expressed in physical abuse or neglect. Some of the mothers subtly encouraged their children to self-destructive acts as well.

Mrs. B. told the group that her son Phillip had gotten into trouble again. She had read an article in the newspaper about a freak accident in which a child touched his tongue to a metal pipe in freezing weather and had to be cut loose. A few days later her children were preparing to leave for school. She summoned Phillip and not the others and told him about the accident. She warned him to be sure that he did not do anything like that himself. As she described this part of the story to the group, she had a smile on her face and her tone of voice betrayed obvious pleasure. That afternoon her son returned home with his tongue lacerated.

Group Therapy: The following discussion focuses on unique aspects of work in a therapeutic group which seemed particu-

larly useful to these women. The group situation corrected the impression that their murderous impulses were unique. The women studied felt isolated with their "unmotherly" type thoughts. They were afraid to discuss them with anyone and it was only under the pressure of severe anxiety and depression that they were motivated to talk about them with a psychiatrist. Furthermore the support that the members provided for each other was instrumental in enabling some to overcome their phobic symptoms. For example, 3 of the women were afraid to ride on public transportation. One day Mrs. R. marched into the meeting smiling triumphantly. She announced to the group that her husband couldn't bring her that afternoon so she came on the bus by herself. She said that she was frightened but she kept thinking that she had to do it because she did not want to miss the group. The others admired her courage. One woman said that she was very glad that Mrs. R. had come because she was an important part of the group. From that time forward Mrs. R. came by public transportation. Soon after the two other members who had the same phobia had to make a similar choice. The group urged them to face their fear. They decided that if Mrs. R. could do it so could they. They did. Though symptom relief of this sort did not stem from working through of underlying conflicts, the symptom itself was such a burden to the patient and the family that giving it up brought considerable relief.

The opportunity for consensual validation in the group setting seemed important to the course of therapy. This was graphically seen in the correction of transference distortions. On one occasion Mrs. K. turned to the observer and said that she had a strong urge to sock him for making fun of her that way. The leader asked the other group members how they thought the observer was looking at Mrs. K. None felt he was making fun of Mrs. K. Mrs. K. then admitted that she had been irritated by him ever since the group began. She could not understand why she wanted to hit him. It occurred to her later in the meeting that he reminded her of her dead husband. While it would have been possible for the therapist to clarify the distortion in this situation, peer observations were less likely to be interpreted as criticisms. This was also true of dynamic interpretations made by peers.

During the course of the group a mixing of defensive patterns took place. The obsessional members were confronted repeatedly with direct expression of murderous aggressive feelings by the more impulsive members of the group. They learned to express their own feelings more openly from them. The more impulsive members were able to learn from the obsessional members as well. They had repeated opportunities to observe that one did not have to act on intense impulses. The one group member who held tenaciously to the paranoid position benefited from constant reality testing by the other members. Though she had some difficulty interpreting reality, she was most acute in her perception of the issues the group was trying to avoid and spoke up openly about them in a way which stimulated the group work.

Finally, the group helped satisfy the social hunger of its members. They had all withdrawn from social contact outside of the family. For some this meant complete absence of any social experience with another adult. The twice weekly group meetings mobilized them from their homes and brought them into close contact with other people.

SUMMARY

This study reports on the clinical experience with a group of mothers with infanticidal impulses. The 4 shared, biographical characteristics found were: 1. They have strong feelings of resentment toward their parents for not fulfilling their dependency needs during childhood. 2. One or both of the parents or a significant parental figure was subject to uncontrolled temper outbursts during which the patient was the object of or witness to acts of violence. 3. They had lifelong feelings of rivalry with and hatred for men. Many trace this feeling to intense sibling rivalry with their brothers during childhood. 4. They seek motherly type men for husbands.

Clinically they range from obsessional neurotics to borderline psychotics. Though there is this wide variation in diagnosis, there are a number of symptoms held in common: 1. They have disturbing thoughts about harming their children. The major focus of this aggression is a male child. The gap between the impulse and the act is on a continuum which parallels the diagnostic range. At the obsessional end of the scale the gap is wide and the impulse is alien to the concept of self. At the other end the impulse is felt in full intensity and primitive defenses are used to keep from committing infanticide. 2. They have multiple phobias. Here, too, the adequacy of the phobia as a defense varies on a scale parallel with the diagnostic range. At one extreme, the phobias, like the obsessional thoughts, effectively screen the rejected impulse from consciousness. At the other end of the scale the phobia is related in consciousness to the impulse which it is used to defend against. Throughout the entire range the phobias were crippling symptoms which encouraged progressive withdrawal from social contact. 3. They were depressed. Here too there is a range from vague feelings of hopelessness with unexplained episodes of tearfulness to psychotic depression with marked feelings of guilt, self-depreciatory ideas and retardation. 4. They were disturbed by suicidal impulses. 5. They were intermittently or chronically frigid.

Group psychotherapy offered a number of therapeutic advantages. 1. The group situation corrected the impression that the murderous impulses that they experienced were unique. 2. The patients encouraged and supported each other in their efforts to overcome common symptoms such as phobias about riding public transportation. 3. Consensual validation by the group members was helpful in correcting transference distortions. Such observations by group members were less likely to be interpreted as criticisms to be defended against than were observations by the therapist. 4. A mixing of defenses took place. The group members were able to learn different methods of adaptation from each other and to try them out in the group setting. 5. The group meetings provided a meaningful social experience for otherwise isolated people.

BIBLIOGRAPHY

1. Kempe, Henry C., *et al.*: J.A.M.A., **181**: 1.

2. Stern, Edward S.: J. Ment. Sci., **94**: 321, 1948.

3. Wittles, F.: *In*: Psychoanalysis Today. London: Lorand, 1933.

4. Stern: *Op. cit.*

5. Anthony, E. J.: Acta Psychother., **7** (Suppl.): 1.

PRACTICE FORUM

Verbal Accessibility
In the Treatment of Child Neglect

Helping the verbally inaccessible client to talk is treatment.

NORMAN A. POLANSKY
ROBERT D. BORGMAN
CHRISTINE DE SAIX
SHLOMO SHARLIN

For the last five years, the authors have been engaged in a program of research on child neglect in the mountains of Southern Appalachia. The area may be the exotic land of Daisy Mae, but it also is a setting for the practice of rural child welfare. A major focus of the research was suggested by those to whom we talked before designing the program. They described a type of woman who almost invariably defeated their best child welfare efforts, and then asked, "What would *you* do with such a person?" Of course, we did not know either. So, we have been studying what to do about personality problems of the mothers involved in rural child neglect, with special attention to what we call "the apathy-futility syndrome."

This paper is not intended as a presentation of research results. Some of the results have already been reported elsewhere.[1] This is a review of the studies and an examination of the implications they have for training and supervising the rural social worker who deals with the mother of children receiving poor care.

In most rural counties, the person directly in contact with the typical neglect situation is a welfare worker. She is likely to be fairly experienced, since staff turnover is not nearly so great as in urban departments. However, the worker usually has little or no formal training in the practice of casework. Supervision varies from shrewd and supportive to nonexistent. Many of the clients have such pathology and so little motivation to change that they would tax the most

This paper is adapted from a presentation at the CWLA Southern Regional Conference at Gatlinburg, Tennessee, 1970. The research was supported by a grant from the Children's Bureau, U.S. Department of Health, Education and Welfare, to the University of Georgia School of Social Work, Athens, Georgia. Norman A. Polansky, Ph.D., is Professor of Social Work and Sociology at the school, and Christine De Saix, ACSW, and Shlomo Sharlin, M.S.W., are Research Associates at the school's Child Research Field Station at Asheville, North Carolina. Robert D. Borgman was a Research Associate at the Field Station at the time of the presentation. He is now Clinical Psychologist, North Carolina State Department of Social Services, Raleigh.

knowledgeable among us. Moreover, there is often no other resource to whom to refer such a case if it is beyond the worker. She is the county's child welfare resource.

There are, of course, actions a worker can take. She can have a dream of large-scale social reform. "Comes the revolution" all mothers will be good mothers. Or, if faced with four to eight mal-nourished, unkempt, ill and recurrently deserted youngsters, she can try to have them removed if foster homes can be found and financed, except that such placements are almost always only temporary.

Another alternative is to try to help the mother through talking with her, through social casework. But when it comes to treating these women through the interview, the average worker is at a loss. Too many interviews with neglect-ful mothers lack the sense of direction that all interpersonal influence requires, and involve only a threat or a pleading offer of help. They are placebo inter-views. Beyond the broad prospectus of treatment, the worker needs a theory of how to interview, and with what im-mediate goals.

In the research we thought that the concept of *verbal accessibility*, utilized in previous research and used by the senior author in individual treatment, was ap-plicable. We believed interviews became more meaningful to the worker and more effective with the mother if attention was focused on the client's verbal accessibil-ity.

What is meant by this term? Verbal accessibility (VA) is defined as the readi-ness of the client to talk directly about her important attitudes and feelings, and to discuss them with the worker. This dimension of a mother's personality is well worth attending to in assessing her overall level of functioning. Beyond this, the concept offers a concrete goal to be pursued in any interview, even with per-sons having severe emotional problems. The principle is this: *Any move the worker can make that helps the client verbalize her important feelings and at-titudes and to stand behind her words will be a step in the direction of her integration and cure.* In other words, a worthwhile aim in any interview is to raise the level of the client's verbal acces-sibility.

This concept, which is derived from Kaiser, has both diagnostic and thera-peutic significance, not only with mid-dle-class neurotics but with women who are disorganized and living in poverty. The ideal, of course, has been to find a theory for the interview that can be read-ily transmitted to a welfare worker with suitable gifts but little training. At the same time, the approach should not be watered down; it should be sound and acceptable to the most sophisticated. The hope is that such a theory can be erected around the concept of verbal accessibility.

Verbal Accessibility As a Diagnostic Sign

Let us start examining the role of VA in treatment by fixing its place in diag-nosis. Nothing is more important in the process of an interview than the client's openness. One client proceeds quickly to the point, talking directly and with ap-propriate feeling. Another is inarticulate, or passive or evasive.

The worker usually responds to the in-accessible client by trying to help him express himself more freely. In effect, the nonverbalism is treated as a technical ob-stacle and a test of the worker's inter-viewing skill—which it is, of course. But one should pause to mark the pattern well, before moving to overcome the difficulty. This seemingly incidental challenge to technique may have more to do with pervasive patterns in the client than is generally realized.

Any concept can have alternative operational definitions. Verbal accessibility has been measured in various ways, depending on the circumstances of the study being carried out.[2] We utilized a scale designed to assess a client's spontaneity in the interview. The aim was not to measure verbosity or circumstantiality, but readiness to talk meaningfully about feelings. The scale range is: (1) Spontaneous verbalization. (2) Spontaneous with caseworker's explicit encouragement. (3) Responsive; equal give and take with the caseworker. (4) Receptive; little give, lots of take. (5) Unresponsive; complete lack of response despite explicit encouragement. (6) Avoidance or evasion of verbal expression.

This scale was applied to the total contacts with the client, whether in one interview or several. It has demonstrated construct validity both in judgments of case records, and in ratings by workers of their own cases. On one occasion when the same women were seen by two research caseworkers, there was satisfactory inter-rater reliability.[3]

Data from ratings by AFDC workers on 91 of their own clients give some idea of how one may expect scores to distribute on the spontaneity scale. Two-fifths of the clients were rated either spontaneous or very spontaneous, and another quarter as engaging in give and take (a score of 3.). Although we think that the ratings erred on the generous side, they serve to remind us that a majority of low-income rural women talk willingly to their workers. Often, too, they talk to the point and they mean what they say. As a matter of statistics, extreme reticence and eva-

siveness toward the helping person are atypical. If a mother is rated 4 or lower on the scale, she is verbally inaccessible, and this has ominous implications for the outcome of the case.

From studies in disparate settings, ranging from treatment institutions in Cleveland to farming counties in the mountains, the evidence is consistent. Verbal inaccessibility is associated with poor ego integration and low general competence in the personality.

This paper deals with child neglect, so it is germane to ask how a woman's VA related to her performance as a mother. To objectify measurement of child caring, we developed a checklist scale of about 150 items that we term the Childhood Level of Living Scale. The areas rated include such basics as housing, food and medical care, but there are also sections having to do with emotional security and cognitive stimulation. In two independent studies we found that children enjoying a relatively higher standard of living are likely to have mothers who prove more open in the interview. It was striking to find this relationship, because in each instance we were studying children who were near, or below, the poverty level economically. And there are sequelae in the children. At age 4 or 5, there is a significant positive association: the higher the maternal VA, the higher the child's IQ.

In one study of rural women, psychological tests were administered, including the Thematic Apperception Test. Our psychologist, Borgman, devised a way of scoring stories about the pictures to identify expressions of loneliness. It was intriguing to find that the women who were generally least articulate brought out significantly more material reflecting primitive loneliness of the sort associated with the forlorn, deprived child. Also, they seemed to form clinging but superficial object relationships; this was apparent in their use of fewer terms that specify kinships, especially such words as "mother" or "husband and wife."

Social histories of the same group of women indicated there had been little evidence of ego strength, even in adolescence. The inaccessible mothers, as compared with the accessible, had achieved less in school, were less likely to have held employment outside the home before or after marriage, and had less premarital dating experience. It would be easy to attribute these differences to cultural backgrounds, but the women involved all came from the same low-income segment of a single county in western North Carolina.

Structurally, inaccessibility may reflect psychological immaturity or primitiveness. Dynamically, in better-developed personalities it seems to reflect the invasion of the speech function by neurosis. Just as repression uses up psychic energy, so does a stubborn inexpressiveness. The refusal to let one's feelings come out may be as draining as the dramatizing of feelings one does not really have. Kaiser declared the inability to stand behind one's words to be the universal symptom of neurosis.[4]

A worker who encounters a markedly verbally inaccessible woman should be alert to four possibilities, not mutually exclusive. The woman may be intellectually dull (e.g., IQ of 80 or below), or extremely immature, both of which are structural deficiencies. Also, she may be neurotically blocked or seriously disturbed, which would represent dynamic interferences with speech. One cannot immediately distinguish which of these factors is causing the inaccessibility simply from the quality of the speech. But there are cues to bear in mind.

If a woman is verbose, while still saying little of consequence, you can assess the range and appropriateness of her vocabulary in ruling retardation in or out. Gross immaturity shows up in the mother who, despite evidently normal intelligence, shows a lack of judgment in what she says. Perhaps the best way to determine whether unreadiness to talk is due to dynamic interferences is to try to induce readiness. This can come about through reassurance about talking, or by gentle penetration of surface defenses through discussion of why it is hard for her to verbalize her feelings. Whenever a sharp increase in verbal accessibility is encountered, we know that it was being deterred by emotional inhibition (or cultural sanctions) rather than structural limitations. Our observations indicate that far more nonverbalism of welfare mothers is due to restraints against self-expression than to dullness, lack of vocabulary or the like, although these may also be present.

It may be concluded that verbal inaccessibility is a potentially ominous diagnostic sign, even if not a specific one. The contrary is also true; verbal accessibility is usually a hopeful feature in the client, both with respect to current level of functioning and prognosis for treatment, and this is also true of women whose children have been receiving poor care.

VA has one major advantage for diagnosis: It requires no special procedure in order to assess it. We simply have to learn to sharpen a set of impressions we form anyhow in talking with the client.

Workers' Reactions To the Inaccessible Client

We have urged that the worker pause to note the level of VA he is encountering, rather than plunge ahead. Let us look at how one group of 17 AFDC workers we studied responded to the shut-in mothers on their caseloads.

Originally, we had been curious to learn which of their efforts to get the women to open up proved most successful, but this aspect of the study did not work out. The worker seldom had a conscious plan for dealing with her client's nonverbalism. Therefore, the correlations obtained between the mothers' VA and the workers' behavior tell more about how workers react to such clients than they do about how workers get mothers to respond to them.

Data were collected by reading the case record first. Then there was an interview with the worker to fill in things she knew but had not recorded, as well as our impressions of how she felt about the case. It was of interest that in this study, as in an earlier one, the more verbally accessible mothers also rated higher on the Childhood Level of Living Scale. In other words, this correlation holds even within the constricted economic range of life on AFDC. For this study, the association meant that when an AFDC worker was dealing with an inaccessible woman, she was also usually responding to one involved in marginal child care or child neglect.

There is no question that noncommunicative women generate frustration and feelings of rejection in those assigned to help them. A fairly typical sequence is growing impatience, followed by a flurry of activity either to reach the mother verbally or to offer concrete services, and ending with concentration on questions of eligibility and with infrequent visiting. Initial eagerness gives way to frustration and resolves into detachment, with the worker "throwing in the towel."

Thus, there were repeated complaints of the mother's failure to comply with reasonable requests, general disapproval of her behavior, and eventually guarded expression of anger toward her. The emotional withdrawal from such clients is even more insidious; one way it may show itself is in worker uncertainty about how many children are in the household. The passive aggressiveness endemic among these inaccessible women seduces unwary workers into acting the same way.

All this is in contrast to responses to the women high on VA. Workers are enthusiastic about mothers' hobbies and skills; warmth and empathy are much in evidence; there is free exchange of feelings; indeed, a young worker may show impressive courage in helping the mother cope with fears and anxieties. Whereas the motivations of the inaccessible woman appear, if at all, in the record as if "from the outside," those of the mother with VA are portrayed as she herself might put them. The nonverbal client often is seen out of a sense of duty; the woman high on VA is liked, and visited with pleasure. In fact, there is danger that the young worker, encouraged by the mother's ability to relate, will be sanguine, and show a disregard for pathology in these women. Since the whole level of treatment seems to be higher and more organized, the optimism may generate a self-fulfilling prophecy.

We have identified the outlines of a role complementation that is complex, but clearly discernible. The mother's nonresponsiveness pushes the worker away, and if that is her intent, it succeeds. But the picture is complicated by the fact that some of the worker's reaction does have a basis in reality. Unless they can be changed, noncommunicative clients have poorer prognoses. Therefore, in perhaps a majority of cases of marginal child care, *a key symptom that is urgently in need of treatment ends by defeating the casework.*

The Clinical Rationale For Treating Verbal Accessibility

In the talking, as fellow practitioners, about the role of VA in the casework process, we are confronted with a paradox. On the one hand, a person's level of VA is a character trait, with the adumbrations of stability and resistance to change that this implies.[5] On the other hand, it is often desirable—indeed, it may be essential—to try to raise the level of VA.

Let us take full cognizance of the impact of verbal reticence on treatment. It is a serious deterrent to any attempt at a detailed understanding of dynamics in making a diagnosis. A woman low in VA is also deprived of many of the functions speech can subserve in advancing casework treatment or psychotherapy.[6] She cannot get relief from tension through ventilation, or substitute "talking it out for acting it out." Neither can she arrive at the kind of clarification that results from objectifying ideas and attitudes by telling them to another person. An early discovery in casework was that if some clients are offered a sympathetic hearing, they often resolve their woes in presenting them. In our experience, this element of casework is useful with most women from low-income families, just as with the educated middle-class. A high degree of VA is essential to the self-healing of psychic wounds.

The paradox, then, stems from the fact that a relatively stable feature of the personality may have to be changed if treatment is not to be defeated. Verbal accessibility is potentially a powerful ally in treatment; its absence can impede or prevent successful casework.

In this situation, some have concluded that efforts at "talking treatment" with low-VA women might as well be abandoned. Yet, if VA could be heightened, many of these clients would be highly accessible to a traditional casework approach. Further, there is reason to believe that although inability to talk about one's attitudes and feelings may reflect ego weakness, a positive change in VA leads to an overall improvement in competence. In other words, work on facilitating VA is not only preliminary to casework; it has curative value in itself; it *is* treatment.

Techniques for Facilitating Verbal Accessibility

The women in greatest need of help is typically concerned about concrete things. She worries about food, clothing and shelter for herself and her children. She is chronically lonely, and clings to her children and her husband because these are the only sources of human warmth she ever expects to have. She is extremely hesitant to chance attaching herself to a caseworker who may, as she sees it, abandon her at any time. Moreover, so far as she is concerned, never in her life has talking solved a problem. An additional handicap is her restricted vocabulary. If she were aware of nuances in her feelings, she would be at a loss to put them into words.

Following is a set of guidelines for relevance to working with rural women involved in marginal child caring.

(1) *The first necessity is a willingness to talk.* It has been emphasized that not all verbalizing is indicative of verbal accessibility. A mother may use rapid

speech in order to avoid speaking about what matters most to her. This mechanism is found sometimes among the women being considered here. After having been drowned in a long tale of woes with the kitchen stove, the worker may emerge knowing no more about what the mother thinks about anything of importance than she did before. Still, women who talk are the more likely to be accessible. The first step, therefore, may be to encourage conversation with the client, no matter the topic. It may be enough to start with.

(2) *First topics should be concrete, external and superficial.* Since so many of these women are concrete-minded, this must be taken into account. When we read in a record, *"Explained* the policy to Mrs. B.,'' it drives us to distraction. Very often Mrs. B. cannot grasp the rationale for agency policy; it will be enough if she can learn what the policy is. Her acceptance of the policy has little to do with understanding it, and the attempt to make her understand is self-indulgence on the part of the worker. The provision of concrete services is a good place to begin before tackling abstract needs. There is much concern at present about separation of service from financial aid. A latch on the door to treatment long used by astute caseworkers is being removed, in the name of client's rights but in the service of expediency. It is from the discussion of the external that entree to feelings may be gained. Rebudgeting to accommodate a daughter's illegitimate baby may easily lead to a flood of feelings of remorse and concern about her pregnancy.

(3) *Security encourages expansiveness.* The deprivation of emotional support in the lives of many of these mothers is almost unbelievable. Many blossomed under the simple attention of having their life histories taken for research purposes. In general, ego support through improving the client's self-image is conducive to VA. If a woman raises succulent October beans, makes good biscuits or irons well, praise and a desire to learn from her form ways of conveying admiration, and freedom to talk about attitudes rises.

(4) *Feelings have names.* A woman might blurt out, "I could murder my husband," but this might not be what she really means. The lack of words such as "irritated, provoked, sore" can handicap a woman in expressing feelings. So sometimes she says nothing. One service to the client trying to describe important attitudes is to teach her verbal symbols that express what she wants to say. This may be especially important in a lower-class milieu, where expression of nuances is not encouraged, and the common vocabulary is constricted.

(5) *Opportunities pass.* In reassuring young workers that "all roads lead to Rome" and that errors of technique can be corrected, we may go too far. A wasted chance to deepen the level of communication may not recur. If a worker shrinks back or is unable to share a mother's grief in a moment of crisis, she heightens the barrier. If one cannot stand to talk about the mother's anger toward the agency or toward oneself, that has a similar effect. Some opportunities are less dramatic, but still important. A worker may take a mother to the clinic, spending 2 or 3 hours in the privacy of the auto without the distractions to conversation encountered on a home visit. And what does she have to record about this chance to increase intimacy? Nothing, perhaps.

(6) *Talk has a background and repercussions.* In the subculture under study,

there is an injunction against discussing "family troubles" outside the family. In fact, they usually are not verbalized inside the home, either. Hence, a woman who describes her troubles with her own mother or with a child is—in effect—violating her own culture. Similarly, guilt may follow a verbal outburst against someone who is loved, so that the woman who fills the agency office with recriminations in a first interview may never appear for a second. The rural worker must be sensitized to these potential repercussions within the client who breaks through her usual inhibitions, and be taught to allow time in the interview for reassurance about these aftereffects. Otherwise, there will be even greater resistance the next time. Blame for what the mother expressed may even be projected onto the worker who encouraged her to speak out.

(7) *Honesty is the only policy.* If a caseworker prattles about an AFDC mother's going to work while knowing well that the mother has no intention of doing so, though she gives lip service to the idea, it is a mutually corrupting experience. It hardly bespeaks a relationship in which VA will flourish. Similarly, a worker who feels she must defend an irrational and meager food budget while simultaneously pretending not to notice the mess the house is in, is hardly encouraging an atmosphere of frank talk about attitudes.

(8) *How verbally accessible are you?* Finally, there is the worker's own readiness to act both as listener and role-model in helping the mother become more verbally accessible. We do not mean

that the worker must tell the mother all about herself in the hope of inducing her to do likewise. But it is appropriate, from time to time, to share immediate feelings. Social caseworkers who have trouble talking about their own feelings are most unlikely to be able to help marginal mothers stand behind their words. To encourage another to discuss important attitudes, it is first necessary to be able to bear hearing them. And to bear another's angry, despairing—or soft, loving—feelings, one must be comfortable with one's own, and able to voice them.   ◆

References

1. See Norman A. Polansky, Christine De Saix, Mary Lou Wing and John D. Patton, "Child Neglect in a Rural Community," *Social Casework*, XLIX, No. 2 (1968), 467-474; Polansky, Robert D. Borgman, De Saix and Betty Jane Smith, "Verbal Accessibility of the Appalachian Mother," *Social Work Practice, 1969* (New York: Columbia University Press, 1969); Polansky, Borgman, De Saix and Smith, "Two Modes of Maternal Immaturity and Their Consequences," *Child Welfare*, XLIX, No. 6 (1970), 312-323.

2. Norman A. Polansky, "The Concept of Verbal Accessibility," *Smith College Studies in Social Work*, XXXVI, No. 1 (1965), 1-48.

3. Shlomo Sharlin, "Infantilization: A Study of Intrafamilial Communication," unpublished Ph.D. dissertation, University of Georgia, 1971, 67.

4. Hellmuth Kaiser, "The Problem of Responsibility in Psychotherapy," *Psychiatry*, XVIII (1955), 205-211; Louis B. Fierman, ed., *Effective Psychotherapy: The Contribution of Hellmuth Kaiser* (New York: Free Press, 1965).

5. Norman A. Polansky, *Ego Psychology and Communication* (New York: Atherton, 1971).

6. Avery D. Weisman, "Silence and Psychotherapy," *Psychiatry*, XVIII (1955), 241-260.

CLINICAL NOTES

*(The Clinical Notes report the findings of the authors and
do not necessarily represent the opinions of the Journal.)*

VIOLENCE BREEDS VIOLENCE – PERHAPS ?

GEORGE C. CURTIS, M.D.[1]

Both the medical profession and the public are exhibiting growing awareness of and concern over what has been called "the battered child syndrome," *i.e.*, injuries to children as a result of excessive beatings, usually by a parent. An article on the topic has appeared recently in *Life* magazine(5). Bakwin(1), a pediatrician, stresses the difficulty of determining the true incidence of such parental brutality, the difficulty of obtaining an accurate history in a particular case, the ease with which the true nature of injuries may be overlooked, and the value of the x-ray in pointing to the correct diagnosis. He presents the case of a 4½-month-old boy brought to the hospital with a tender, swollen right shoulder, poor appetite, and a firm mass on his chest. The differential diagnosis included malignancy, metabolic disturbances, and leukemia. However x-rays revealed widespread traumatic changes in the bones, stripping and tearing of the periosteum of the right humerus, recent fractures of five ribs, and a healed fracture of yet another rib, which accounted for the the firm mass on the chest wall. It then became apparent that beatings by the parents were the cause. It is repeatedly stressed that these cases are not rare, and indeed the growing awareness of the unsuspected frequency is apparently one reason for the well-justified public concern.

It is important that the psychological implications of such extreme treatment of children be kept in mind. One might expect that the sequelae would be varied and difficult to study if one should attempt to trace out all their ramifications. However it may be useful to re-emphasize one possible consequence which is overt, obvious, and of great public concern and social consequence in its own right; namely, the proba-ble tendency of children so treated to become tomorrow's murderers and perpetrators of other crimes of violence, if they survive.

This assertion is based both on theoretical and empirical grounds. Theoretically a child so treated should have an unusual degree of hostility toward the parents and toward the world in general. The control and channelling of this hostility into non-destructive avenues of release would pose a problem both for the child and for society. In addition, the child would be presented with parental objects for identification who provided an example of the destructive and relatively uncontrolled release of hostile aggression. The vernacular expression "monkey see, monkey do" expresses the same idea in terms understandable to everyone.

Although the empirical grounds for the above assertion are not conclusive, the pilot work has been done and points strongly in the direction indicated. In 1940 Bender and Curran(2) published a brief review of the literature on children and adolescents who kill and presented a number of clinical vignettes from their experience with children who had committed unsuccessful murderous aggression. They suggested the following categories of etiological factors : intensification of a family rivalry situation, foster home situations in which the feelings of love were insufficient to curb aggressive tendencies, organic inferiority, educational difficulties and "the child's tendency to identify himself with aggressive parents and pattern after their behavior." The last category included children from all the others. One example came to light only after extensive questioning of the stepmother as to why the boy had cauliflower ears. The authors state "it has been our experience

---

[1] Eastern Pennsylvania Psychiatric Institute, Philadelphia, Pa.

that children who were treated with violence which cannot always be anticipated react with blind violence which is an expression of their fearful insecurity." In 1958 Duncan, *et al.*(3), published a report of a preliminary study of 6 male adult prisoners convicted of first degree murder. All were from middle class families of good social standing. The most striking feature of 4 of these case histories was continuous remorseless brutality suffered during childhood at the hands of one parent in the face of compliant acquiescence of the other. The remaining 2 prisoners were overtly psychotic and no such childhood history was obtained in their cases. The authors comment that intervention by a physician in a sadistic family pattern may avert a later violent crime. In 1961 Easson and Steinhilber(4) published brief clinical accounts of 8 boys who had made murderous assaults, one of them successful. All were from socially acceptable "normal" families. In 2 of these cases there was a clear history of habitual brutal beating by a parent, and the histories of 3 others contained remarks which lead one to wonder if brutality to the child were being concealed. Court action was pending in the case of the boy who had committed successful murder, and repeated interviews yielded only vague hints as to the family dynamics.

It is, of course, highly unlikely that there is any one-to-one relationship between child abuse and later crimes of violence. Important psychological differences probably underline, for example, the murder of an unfaithful lover and murder associated with armed robbery, murders which are and are not concealed, *etc.* It is also improbable that all physically abused children later commit crimes of violence. The child's reaction and adaptation to abuse probably vary with many other aspects of his life and circumstances. These limitations on the hypothesis raise additional challenging problems. It is often pointed out that sadistic parents are likely to be repeating a pattern which they experienced with their own parents. How and why do these patterns originate? What factors influence them to wax and wane from one generation to the next? Under what circumstances does criminal violence overflow from the family into society?

Psychiatrists may now have the opportunity to perform an invaluable service by holding the implications of child abuse steadily before the public's attention and by contributing valuable new observations and insights toward the understanding and solution of these important problems.

BIBLIOGRAPHY

1. Bakwin, H.: Consultant (SKF), May 1963.
2. Bender, L., and Curran, F. J.: J. Crim. Psychopath., **1**: 297, 1940.
3. Duncan, G. M., *et al.*: J.A.M.A., **168**: 1755, 1958.

4. Easson, W. M., and Steinhilber, R. N.: Arch. Gen. Psychiat., **4**: 27, 1961.
5. Life: June 14, 1963.

SUMMARY

Children who are abused psychologically are, in many cases, just as damaged as those who receive broken bones. Many end up psychologically crippled. It is common for these children to have learning inhibitions and disabilities, school phobia, be accident prone, develop allergies, and have a high susceptibility to infection. Some people have had such hostility instilled in them as children that they take it out on society. Others take it out on their own children.

The parents of battered children, in many cases, come from homes in which they were abused, or that were psychologically unstable, or very poor environmentally. Often their parents were immature, impulsive, self-centered, hypersensitive, or aggressive.

Studies indicate that the homes of these children tend to include alcoholism, sexual promiscuity, unstable marriages, and, most of all, a total void of any feelings of love.

Public and private agencies are just now starting to develop programs to help the children and their parents through psychological understanding and support. The role of these agencies is moving increasingly toward creating change in the individuals rather than being confined to the more limited role they had previously held of changing the environment of the child to a more protected and healthfully nurturing one.

STUDY QUESTIONS

1. What psychological damage is done to children by the abusing parents?

2. Do schools and other agencies contribute to psychological abuse of children? Do any social values contribute to this?

3. What psychological services are available to deter parents from abusing their children?

4. What is the relationship between physical and psychological battering?

5. What psychological services are available for children who have been abused?

6. What are some of the causes that produce parents who psychologically abuse children?

REFERENCES

A. Readings Included in This Text

Bean, Shirley L. "The Parents' Center Project: A Multiservice Approach to the Prevention of Child Abuse." *Child Welfare,* 50 (1971):277-282.

Curtis, George C. "Violence Breeds Violence—Perhaps?" *The American Journal of Psychiatry,* 120 (1963):386-387.

Delsordo, James D. "Protective Casework for Abused Children." *Children,* 10 (1963):213-218.

Feinstein, Howard M.; Paul, Norman; and Esmiol, Pattison. "Group Therapy for Mothers With Infanticidal Impulses." *The American Journal of Psychiatry,* 120 (1964):882-886.

Galdston, Richard. "Observations on Children Who Have Been Physically Abused by Their Parents." *The American Journal of Psychiatry,* 122 (1965):440-443.

Polansky, Norman A.; Borgman, Robert D.; De Saix, Christine; and Sharlin, Shlomo. "Verbal Accessibility in the Treatment of Child Neglect." *Child Welfare,* 50 (1971):349-356.

B. Suggested Additional Readings

Clarke, A. D. B., and Koluchova, J. "Severe Deprivation in Twins: A Case Study." *Journal of Child Psychology and Psychiatry,* 13 (1972):103-114.

David, Lester. "The Shocking Price of Parental Anger." *Good Housekeeping,* 158 (1964):87, 184, 186-87, 195-197.

DeFrancis, Vincent. "Parents Who Abuse Children." *The PTA Magazine,* 58 (1963):16-18.

Fruchtl, Gertrude, and Brodeur, A. E. "The Battered Child, Know Enough to Care — Care Enough to Know." *The Catholic World,* 209 (1969):156-159.

Fulk, Delores Leusby. "The Battered Child." *Nursing Forum,* 3 (1964):10-26.

Kaufman, Irving; Frank, Thomas; Heims, Lora; Herrick, Joan; and Willer, Lee. "Four Types of Defense in Mothers and Fathers of Schizophrenic Children." *American Journal of Orthopsychiatry,* 29 (1959):460-472.

Kempe, Henry C.; Silverman, Frederic N.; Steele, Brandt F.; Droegemueller, William; and Silver, Henry K. "The Battered-Child Syndrome." *Journal of American Medical Association,* 181 (1962):105-112.

McHenry, Thomas; Girdany, Bertram R.; and Elmer, Elizabeth. "Unsuspected Trauma With Multiple Skeletal Injuries During Infancy and Childhood." *Pediatrics,* 31 (1963):903-908.

Oettinger, Katherine B. "The Abused Child." *Childhood Education,* 41 (1965):235-237.

Page, Miriam O. "Cohesion, Dignity, and Hope for Multiproblem Families." *Children,* 8 (1961):63-68.

Sattin, Dana B.; and Miller, John K. "The Ecology of Child Abuse Within A Military Community." *American Journal of Orthopsychiatry,* 41 (1971):675-678.

Walton, Cynthia. "The Battered Baby Syndrome." *New Statesman,* 72 (1966):348.

III

The Criminologist Takes a Look

INTRODUCTION

A child abuse case usually cannot be handled adequately if it is not brought to the attention of the proper authority. Legislation for reporting child abuse cases was first passed in 1963, and by 1965 most states had adopted legislation that made reporting mandatory and provided immunity from suit. Only a few states do not have a mandatory reporting law, but even these states offer immunity if a case is reported.

The role of the criminologist in the disposition of child abuse cases is one of law enforcement, investigation, referral, and rehabilitation. Although every state advocates its own system for child abuse cases, the general rule is for police services to handle them. The detailed procedures used are presented in the readings that follow.

If the child is to be placed in the custody of the court, the law provides that the police have the responsibility and authority to take immediate custody of a child in danger of violence or serious injury. In order to remove a child from his home environment, sufficient grounds must exist and the desirability of removal must be thought through carefully.

In every state, statutory provisions give juvenile courts power over neglected children. The focus in the different states may be largely involved with specifics such as cruelty, environment, or physical abuse. The individual state codes dictate the evidence required for court decisions. The law enforcement agencies have serious problems and limitations in providing a well-rounded program for child abuse cases, and although these programs are not perfect, they are improving.

Illustrations of the dispositions of specific court cases and the strengths and weaknesses of the various child abuse protection programs are given in the following articles.

A Lawyer's View of Child Abuse

SAMUEL FELDER

During the past decade the phenomenon of child abuse has been given public acknowledgment. But to protect children who are mistreated by their parents is a difficult task. It is only when these children are brought to the attention of neighbors, teachers, policemen, doctors, and lawyers, who can and will become their advocates, that they can be saved from irreparable physical and emotional damage. Mr. Felder presented this paper at the Third National Conference, American Association of Public Welfare Attorneys, last August in Portland, Maine, when this group, which is a section in APWA's Division on Administration held its annual meeting. Since 1969 Mr. Felder has been Consultant on Social Policy, Federation of Protestant Welfare Agencies, New York, N.Y. He was formerly Counsel to the Department of Social Services of the City of New York.

My topic is the helpless child, abused physically and mentally by the very person who has given him life. This is the story of parents who discharge their responsibility for devoted concern toward their children in a manner that is terrifyingly warped and inhuman.

Within the past few years, physicians, social workers, judges and other court personnel, legislators, welfare administrators, the press, and the public generally have become keenly aware of the problem of children abused by their parents; whether deliberately or inadvertently, there is very little, if any, difference in the extent of the damage to the child.

Because of the abhorrent nature of the subject, there had been a reluctance to accept the actuality that such a large number of parents are capable of seriously mistreating their own children. Yet, according to Katherine B. Oettinger, formerly Chief of the Children's Bureau, Department of Health, Education, and Welfare, the fact is that there are people of every socio-economic, educational, religious, and geographical background who abuse their children. In recent years there has been a tremendous increase in aware-

ness of the widespread nature of child abuse. She points out that all 50 states have passed laws providing for mandatory reporting of suspected cases of child abuse, but that mere reporting is not enough; that the need for community follow-up services is great. When a doctor reports a suspected instance of child abuse, he is simply stating the case. It is up to the individual communities to resolve the problem and prevent repetition. Children who have been abused require protection and rehabilitation. Their abusers, generally the parents, need professional guidance to help them understand, accept, and cope with their parental roles.

The solution requires, in addition, the existence of sufficient facilities, such as adequately staffed institutions, the cooperation of many disciplines — the pediatrician, psychiatrist, social worker, children's court with its staff of judges and probation officers, as well as lawyers representing the interests of the child, the parent, and the community.

A tentative definition of child abuse was developed from a Brandeis University study as, "nonaccidental physical attack or physical injury, including minimal as well as fatal injury, inflicted upon children by persons caring for them."[1] This tentative definition, though quite sound, is nevertheless somewhat unsatisfactory for describing real-life situations because of the inherent ambiguity of the term "nonaccidental," and the vagueness of the boundary between the phenomena of neglect and abuse. As a matter of fact, new legislation, enacted in New York in 1970, repealed a child abuse act enacted less than a year previously. It also repealed Family Court Act provisions dealing with neglect proceedings and replaced them with an act which consolidated abuse and neglect proceedings. Although the act does provide separate definitions of an abused child and a neglected child, at times there is such overlapping that the distinction is not clear.

Causes of Parents' Behavior

As lawyers, and as members of one of the disciplines whose cooperation is needed to help in the solution of the problem, we need to understand some of its underlying causes. We need to understand, for example, how such behavior is related to the life experiences of the abusers themselves. Drs. Brant F. Steele and Carl B. Pollack, both professors of psychiatry, in their "Psychiatric Study of Parents Who Abuse Infants and Small Children," said,

> Without exception in our study group of abusing parents, there is a history of having been raised in the same style which they have recreated in the pattern of rearing their own children. Several had experienced severe abuse in the form of physical beatings from either mother or father. A few reported never having had a hand laid on them. All had experienced, however, a sense of intense, pervasive, continuous demand from their parents. This demand was in the form of expectations of good, submissive behavior, prompt obedience, never making mistakes, sympathetic comforting of parental distress, and showing approval and help for parental actions. Performance was expected before the child was able to fully comprehend what was expected or how to accomplish it. Accompanying the parental demand was a sense of constant parental criticism.[2]

The following are examples of this high parental demand combined with disregard of the in-

fant's capacity. *Mr. J.*, in speaking of his 16-month-old son, said, "He knows what I mean and understands it when I say come here. If he doesn't come immediately, I go and give him a gentle tug on the ear to remind him of what he is supposed to do." In the hospital, it was found that Johnny's ear was lacerated and partially torn away from his head.

Kathy, a young mother, made this statement: "I have never really felt loved all my life. When the baby was born, I thought he would love me; but when he cried all the time, it meant he didn't love me, so I hit him." Kenny, age 3 weeks, was hospitalized with bilateral subdural hematomas.

Implied in the above vignettes and clearly evident in the tone of voice of the parents as they told these stories, is a curious freedom from guilt and a sense of righteousness. From early infancy, the children of abusing parents are expected to show exemplary behavior and a respectful, submissive, thoughtful attitude toward adult authority and society.

Common parental expressions, prevalent in our culture, which express essentially acceptable ideals of child rearing are, "If you give in to kids, they'll be spoiled rotten," "You have to teach children to obey authority," "I don't want my kids to grow up to be delinquents," "Children have to be taught proper respect for their parents." The difference between the nonabusing and the abusing parent is that the latter implements such standards with exaggerated intensity, and most important, at an inappropriately early age. Related to the child beatings is the conviction that infants and children exist primarily to satisfy parental needs; that infants' and children's needs are unimportant and should be disregarded; and that children who do not fulfill these requirements deserve punishment.

Child battering, says Dr. Lester Breslow, President of the American Public Health Association, is a major element in the argument for repeal of all abortion laws. "Can anyone estimate," he asks, "how much physical harm to children is a byproduct of our rigid abortion laws? The unwanted child, resulting from contraceptive failure or failure to abort, may be born only to be victimized by hostile parents. Both fathers and mothers are assaulters and the number of recognized cases nationwide is causing justifiable alarm

---

1 David G. Gil and John H. Noble, "Public Knowledge, Attitudes and Opinions About Physical Child Abuse in the United States, No. 14, *Papers in Social Welfare* (Waltham, Massachusetts: Brandeis University, Florence Heller Graduate School for Advanced Studies in Social Welfare), p. 3.

2 R. E. Helfer and C. H. Kemp, *The Battered Child* (Chicago: University of Chicago Press, 1968), p. 111.

among physicians, police, and others. The consequences are profound. Not only are battered children sometimes killed and often disabled, but they are usually psychologically distorted. An enlightened policy on abortion would prevent much of this callous pain and waste."[3]

THE ROLE OF THE LAWYER IN CHILD ABUSE CASES

The understanding of the life styles of the abusors themselves should provide us with more insight into the lawyer's role, which is protection of the rights of all the parties in an abuse proceeding—those of the child, the community, and even the respondent. A court operates at optimum efficiency when all sides are adequately represented by counsel. Conversely, in the absence of attorneys, effective presentations and proper applications are not made, and errors are more likely to occur. In his essay entitled, "Justice For The Child," Dean Monrad Paulsen, of the Law School of the University of Virginia, commented that one of the criticisms of the New York law is that, although provision is made for legal representation of the child, the parents are not offered counsel. He adds that one cannot emphasize too strongly the need for lawyers in such cases.[4]

In this connection, Thomas T. Becker, Executive Director of The Society for the Prevention of Cruelty to Children, predicted that, whether by legislative action, court fiat, or the voluntary action of professional organizations, legal representation of respondents will be the rule rather than the exception in the foreseeable future.[5] The success of court action may depend largely upon the parents' acceptance and their cooperation in plans during the dispositional phase. Here the parents' attorney can play an important role. His interpretation of the court order and the parents' responsibility in its implementation will be more readily accepted than that of others, including court personnel.

Dr. David G. Gil, of the Florence Heller Graduate School for Advanced Studies of Brandeis University, who directed the nationwide study of child abuse in 1966, stated that it is somewhat discouraging to find that little is known about the incidence rates and distribution patterns of child abuse, so that opinions presented concerning the volume of child abuse in the United States and selected characteristics of people involved in incidents of child abuse must be viewed as educated guesses and not as definitive facts.[6] I strongly suspect, from the relative paucity of statistical information within the past few years, that this is still true. What is known, however, is that the incidence rates are such, and are so distributed, that every state and territory in the nation has, in the five-year period from 1963 through 1967, seen fit to enact legislation designed to curb and control this practice.

THE HISTORY OF CHILD ABUSE LEGISLATION

A review of the history of child abuse legislation discloses, according to Dr. Samuel X. Radbill, a lecturer on the history of pediatrics at the American Academy of Pediatrics, that abuse of children has excited periods of great sympathy, each rising to a high pitch, and then curiously subsiding until the next period of excitation.[7]

For example, a period of excitation that lasted for several years began in 1946 and was caused by the relatively new discipline of pediatric radiology. At about that time, radiologists began reporting observations regarding the common association of subdural hematoma and abnormal X-ray changes in the long bones. A few years later, the findings clearly defined the traumatic nature of the lesions. The startling fact of the willful infliction of the trauma was established by the X-rays and the documentation, in the early sixties, of the large number of children admitted to pediatric services suffering from non-accidental injury.

Another period of excitation was stimulated in 1961, when, in an effort to obtain a more accurate picture of the true incidence of the problem of child abuse, the American Academy of Pediatrics conducted a symposium on child abuse under the direction of Dr. C. Henry Kempe. In order to direct attention to the seriousness of the

[3] Speech presented at First National Conference on Abortion Laws, Chicago, February 15, 1969.

[4] Monrad Paulsen, "The Delinquency, Neglect and Dependency Jurisdiction of the Juvenile Court," *Justice for the Child*, Edited by Margaret K. Rosenheim (New York: Free Press, 1962).

[5] Thomas T. Becker, "Child Protective Services and the Law," 95th Annual Forum, National Conference on Social Welfare 1968, unpublished paper, p. 25.

[6] David G. Gil, "Incidence of Child Abuse and Demographic Characteristics of Persons Involved," *The Battered Child, op. cit.*, p. 19.

[7] Samuel X. Radbill, "A History of Child Abuse and Infanticide," *The Battered Child, op. cit.*, pp. 15, 16.

problem, he proposed the term, "the battered child syndrome."[8] At about this time, evidence of child abuse began to pour into the Children's Bureau at DHEW, which awarded grants for the study of the problem. In a single year the American Humane Society uncovered 662 cases in which every state and every social class were represented. Of these cases, 27 percent represented fatalities. A large percentage also represented cases of children with serious and permanent physical injuries, including permanent brain damage.[9]

In January 1962, the Children's Bureau of DHEW invited a group of consultants to meet and consider what could be done. One of the steps suggested was a "model law" for the various states. The Children's Bureau followed through by calling together a small technical group, largely from the legal profession, to discuss and develop specifications for such legislation, the sole purpose of which was to protect the child. It was designed to identify the child in hazard, so that he would be protected from further abuse and provided with a safe and wholesome environment denied him by his rightful and natural protectors—his parents. The proposed model law suggested language for state legislatures, which were becoming increasingly aware of and sensitive to the need for legislation mandating the reporting of physically abused children.[10] I believe it is safe to state that the activity of the Children's Bureau, as I have briefly outlined it, was largely responsible for the upsurge in legislative activity. During the five-year period from 1963 through 1967, all states, the District of Columbia, and the Virgin Islands enacted legislation mandating in various degrees the reporting and validating of cases of abuse, and the provision of protective services.

THE CASE OF ROXANNE FELUMERO IN NEW YORK STATE

Widespread excitation, which triggered legislative activity on a broad scale, also stimulated some states—because of the events that occurred within their own borders and the resultant no-

toriety—into taking hasty, drastic action on the legislative, judicial, and community fronts with dramatic results. An example of such legislative activity occurred in New York State. On March 25, 1969, the body of *Roxanne Felumero,* a three-year-old girl, was found in the East River in New York City. The event received such wide news coverage that its impact was felt throughout the nation.

A barrage of publicity followed the discovery that a neglect petition charging the child's mother with assault had been instituted in the Family Court several weeks prior to the child's death. Included in the publicity were statements charging mishandling of the proceedings by two Family Court judges. This led to a referral to a committee by the Appellate Division of the Supreme Court of New York to make a complete investigation and to report its findings. After extensive hearings and review of records of the court and the agencies involved, the conclusion was reached that if the Family Court and the complex of public and private agencies had functioned more efficiently, Roxanne probably would not have met her tragic death.[11]

It was the aim of the committee to lay a foundation for changes which would enhance the efficiency of the court and its auxiliary services and prevent such tragedies in the future.

Under the law existing at the time of the *Felumero* proceedings, allegations of physical abuse of a child were determined in neglect proceedings. After the furor raised by the publicity following the discovery of Roxanne's body, under a new law, hastily enacted, and effective June 1, 1969, a separate Child Abuse Part was created in the Family Court with jurisdiction over all allegations of physical and mental abuse of children. Provisions were also made for legal representation of the child during all stages of the proceedings, by a police attorney in New York City and by the district attorney in counties outside of New York City. In addition, the court was empowered to order the person charged with child abuse to be examined by a physician, psychiatrist, or psychologist and, during or after a hearing, to remand such person for a period not exceeding 30 days to a city, county, or state maintained hospital, or to a duly qualified private in-

8 *Supra.*
9 *Supra.*
10 *Principles and Suggested Language for Legislation on Reporting of the Physically Abused Child,* Children's Bureau (Washington, D.C.: Department of Health, Education, and Welfare, 1963).

11 Report of the Judiciary Relations Committee to the Appellate Division of the Supreme Court, State of New York, June 19, 1969, p. 2.

stitution designated by rule of the court.

Included in the definition of an abused child was one in the care and custody of a parent or other person who had been adjudicated a narcotic addict, without regard as to whether the child was injured by reason of being under such care.[12]

THE NEW YORK LAW IN 1969

The new act became effective June 1, 1969. However, before this date it was apparent that substantial changes would have to be made. A series of workshops were held throughout the state, attended by legislators, judges, public and private social agency administrators, and representatives of the medical and legal professions. All came up with proposals for change. As Mrs. Mary B. Tarcher, assistant attorney in charge of the Legal Aid Society, Brooklyn, stated in testimony before a subcommittee of the New York State Senate Committee on the Judiciary, "We urge the repeal of the child abuse law of 1969— it simply falls all over itself in its well-intentioned purpose of coming to the rescue of the abused child—it should be repealed and, if replaced by another, should take heed, at every step, of the complex issues involved: and any new law should also provide the financial resources needed to carry it out."[13]

The definition of an abused child was criticized as too limited in some respects and too broad in others; for example: the inclusion of uninjured children of adjudicated drug addicts. The substitution providing, instead of law guardians, police attorneys in New York City and district attorneys in other counties as legal representatives of the children was also viewed as inappropriate. As a matter of fact, this substitution did not happen in New York City: no police attorneys were made available by the Police Department. In some cases, this role was assumed by the Corporation Counsel of the City of New York and by lawyers assigned by the New York City Department of Social Services.

In any event, it is difficult to understand why the substitution was made. The legislature had been appropriating the funds needed for financ-ing the law guardians in the Family Court. The change represented the elimination of an important role in the area of child abuse proceedings. Fortunately, this was corrected the following year.

CORRECTION OF THE 1969 LAW

Credit is due to a legislative body for its recognition of the need for speedy action to correct a law that it had placed on the books less than one year previously, as well as to the organizations, agencies, public officials and interested citizens for the part they played in the enactment of the corrective measure. In Chapter 962 of the laws of 1970,[14] a few highlights are worthy of note:

1. The formerly separate proceedings of neglect and child abuse have been consolidated, so that the same judge sitting in a child abuse part will also hear issues of neglect concerning the abused child or his siblings.

2. Provision for law guardians, who will represent neither the petitioner nor the respondent but be concerned solely with the child's interests and will represent the abused child. In New York City, the Corporation Counsel, acting for the most part through the legal staff of the New York City Department of Social Services, will be a necessary party and, unless the petitioner is otherwise represented, will represent the petitioner.

3. An important feature, designed to prevent or reduce the likelihood of serious injury, is that part of the definition of an abused child which contemplates a situation in which the child escaped serious physical injury, although the parent subjected him to highly dangerous circumstances. An example of such a situation might be one in which the abuser fires a gun or swings a bat at the child but misses or causes little or no physical injury; or where the parent created or knowingly and willfully disregarded the presence of a hazardous condition in the home, such as the storage of explosives or highly flammable materials; or maintaining heating and lighting devices which are in themselves fire risks, or other threats to the health of the child.

4. Another type of abuse without actual injury specified in the law clarifies the former law to the extent that now an abused child is one whose parent or other person responsible for his care commits or permits to be committed an act of sexual abuse against the child, so that it is no longer necessary to prove penetration or other injury.

5. One other improvement relates to the expedition of removal of the child from the custody of the abus-

---

[12] Family Court Act, Article 10, "Proceedings Concerning Abused Children," added Laws of 1969, Chapter 264, repealed by Laws of 1970, Chapter 962.

[13] Written statement dated December 19, 1969 submitted at public hearing held same date.

[14] Family Court Act, Article 10, "Child Protective Proceedings" added Laws of 1970, chapter 962.

ing parent. This may be done even without the consent of such parent, and in emergency situations without court orders, with provision for immunity from civil or criminal prosecution for persons acting in good faith. This power of removal is extended not only to peace officers, but to agents of duly incorporated societies for the prevention of cruelty to children or designated employees of public departments of social services.

With all this, the statute recognizes the constitutional provisions regarding due process and provides:

1. For prompt notice to the parents of the facility to which the child is taken,

2. That the child be taken there promptly,

3. For prompt return of the child in cases involving neglect, but not abuse, if it is determined there is no imminent risk to his health in so doing,

4. Or if it is decided not to return the child, for the filing of a petition forthwith or as soon as possible if the removal occurred during a time the court is not open.

CRIMINAL PROSECUTIONS IN CHILD ABUSE CASES

Another type of legal procedure directly related to child abuse occurs in provisions of the criminal law. The major problem concerns the care and custody of the child; the child abuse problem does not require new criminal legislation, despite the pressure toward that end exerted on legislators by sensational cases. Today, state criminal codes in every state identify homicide and assault, even when committed by parents, as punishable crimes.

In any event, criminal sanctions are a poor means of preventing child abuse. Day-to-day family life, charged with the most intimate emotions, is not an area of life easily ruled by threat of fine or imprisonment. A criminal proceeding is more likely to divide than to unite a family— it cannot preserve or rebuild a child's family relationships. It is more likely to destroy them.

Criminal proceedings in cases of this type can be clumsy affairs. Convictions are difficult to obtain because guilt is hard to prove. An abuser rarely performs in the presence of witnesses who will testify—and guilt must be established beyond a reasonable doubt.

Dean Paulsen, in his paper entitled, "Legal Protections Against Child Abuse," based on a study conducted with the support of a research grant from the Children's Bureau, concludes, "the beginning of a prosecution is likely to be the end of a chance to improve a child's home situation. Parents are nearly always resentful of the proceeding. The hostility engendered makes casework with the child's family all but impossible if the offending parent is still in the home. All in all, criminal sanctions can do little to help a child."[15]

NEED FOR ADDITIONAL PROTECTIVE SERVICES

What are child protective services? In its report of a nationwide survey conducted in 1967 to assess the status and availability of such services, the American Humane Association came up with the following definition, "It is a program which seeks to prevent neglect, abuse and exploitation of children by reaching out with social services to stabilize family life. It seeks to stabilize the family unit by strengthening parental capacity and ability to provide good child care. Its special attention is focused on families whose unresolved problems have produced visible signs of neglect and abuse and the home situation presents actual and potentially great hazard to the physical or emotional well-being of children."[16]

In many states, the law has provided for protective services as a part of a public program of comprehensive child welfare services. In some states charters have been granted to voluntary agencies to carry out protective services. For example, in three of New York City's five counties (New York, Kings, and Queens), in addition to the protective services provided by the New York City Department of Social Services, the Societies for Prevention of Cruelty to Children offer such services. In the city of Buffalo, the SPCC of Erie County and the Children's Aid Society also offer protective services. Another state, Pennsylvania, purchases protective service from voluntary agencies. However, on a national basis, provision of child protective services under voluntary agency auspices is slowly fading away. Only the more highly motivated, the more highly financed, and the more adequate in terms of quality of service have survived. Again in New York State, the Westchester and Rochester SPCC's turned over

---

15 *Children* 42 (March-April 1966).

16 Report of Survey of American Humane Association, conducted in 1967.

their programs to the counties. Why?—the issue was: who was to pay the costs of the program? In at least one state the feeling that protective services could be more effectively provided by the public sector prevailed to the extent that all such services were transferred for that reason. From 1956 to 1967 the number of states in which private agency auspices for protective services existed dropped from 16 to 10.

It might be of interest to note that in New York City the only resource available in 1874 to provide protective services to rescue a grossly abused child was the Society for the Prevention of Cruelty to Animals. This agency stepped in for the first time on the theory that the child, *Mary Ellen,* was a member of the animal kingdom. This may have been the earliest recognition of the need for services to protect children from abuse.[17]

The service is usually initiated on a "complaint," report, or referral from a source outside the family. Sometimes, but not usually, one parent may report the conditions of neglect resulting from the other parent's behavior; or an older sibling, other relatives, or even a neighbor or other observer may report the neglect or abuse. A key point is that parents most in need of assistance do not seek such help voluntarily.

The protective agency, depending on the particular state law, is authorized or mandated to provide service when needed. The agency carries responsibility for maintaining services until the conditions are treated and neglect is eliminated. It has the additional obligation to involve the authority of the Juvenile Court or Family Court when such action is necessary to secure protection, care, and treatment of children whose parents are unable or unwilling to use the help offered by the agency.

Whether establishment of protective services should be required, or authorized, or merely permissive is a subject of much controversy, as is the question of whether reporting by physicians should be mandatory. Some physicians have objected to mandatory reporting on the ground that it would deprive them of making the judgment not to report in a given case where sound

medical reasons exist for that decision. Indeed, the 1963 California version of the California Reporting Law expressly authorized this use of a physician's discretion: It read in part, "The physician and surgeon shall not be required to report as provided herein if in his opinion it would not be consistent with the health, care, or treatment of the minor."[18]

The fact that subsequently mandatory reporting was injected into the law does not necessarily alter the fact of legitimate difference of opinion.[19]

However, the case for mandatory reporting appears to enjoy the support of the consensus of legislative judgment. It is thought better, as a matter of social policy, that all cases of suspected child abuse should be investigated by a social service agency carrying the function of protecting children. It would seem, then, that mandated reporting should be followed by mandated protective services. Moreover, the 1962 amendments to the Social Security Act included a new definition of child welfare services, stating in part, "Child Welfare services means public social services which supplement, or substitute for, parental care and supervision for the purpose of —preventing or remedying, or assisting in the solution of problems which may result in the neglect, abuse, exploitation, or delinquency of children . . ."[20]

Thus, for the first time, child protection is identified as a national concern and as part of all public child welfare. Under this definition, even if a state were to lack more specific authorization for providing child protective services, it would have undeniable responsibility for it, if the state uses Federal funds to support its child welfare program.

MUCH MORE STILL TO BE DONE

How are the states carrying out this responsibility? A single statistic may provide the answer to the question. In New York City, in the one year period from May 1969, to May 1970, the number of children under care in its public shelters rose from about 2,450 to 3,970, an increase

[17] Robert M. Mulford, "Development of Child Protective Services in the United States, *In the Interest of Children,* presented at a session of the 90th Annual Convention of the American Humane Association on October 11, 1966 in New York City (Denver Colorado: The American Humane Association, Children's Division, 1967).

[18] Ch. 576, Sec. 1 (1963) Cal. Stats 1454.

[19] Ch. 1171, Sec. 2 (1965) Cal. Stats 2971.

[20] Social Security Act, Title V, Part 3, Sec. 528 (Title V of the Social Security Act appears in the United States Code as subchapter V of Title 42).

of over 1,500, or about 60 percent.[21] This has resulted in almost inhuman overcrowding of these facilities, and the Commissioner of Social Services, in appealing to the voluntary agencies to increase the acceptance rate of these children to their shelters, has indicated that he expects the burden on his overtaxed facilities to rise.

The *New York Daily News,* in an editorial dated July 27, 1970, while hailing the new child abuse law as a bill of rights for youngsters brutalized by their parents, excoriated the legislature for its failure to make proper provision for the care of the children, stating, "unfortunately these waifs have been rescued from one form of cruelty only to be subjected to deplorable living conditions in the city's overcrowded children's shelters.—Albany must provide a long range answer by funding a major increase in the city's child care."

I have little doubt that the same situation exists in many other states and localities throughout the nation. And this national problem must be solved not only in the states but in Washington as well. On the floor of the House, on July 22, 1970, Congressman James A. Burke of Massachusetts said, in discussing an amendment to a DHEW appropriation bill to increase child welfare services, that while the Federal government contributes 75 percent to 83 percent of the cost of the care of AFDC, it contributes practically nothing for the care of children whose parents cannot or will not take care of them. "They are just shuffled around and completely forgotten. They are youngsters without political muscle. This Federal government of ours has spent billions of dollars for lesser causes."[22]

And I say, "Amen." A government that spends countless billions for death and destruction in Indo-China, and can blithely write off additional millions in oil depletion allowances, farm subsidies, and other loopholes, can surely spend a small fraction of these monies for life and health for its children.

---

[21] *New York Daily News* Editorial, "Out of the Frying Pan," July 27, 1970.

[22] *Congressional Record,* July 22, 1970, p. H7035.

ARTICLES

THE PHYSICIAN, THE BATTERED CHILD, AND THE LAW

Fowler V. Harper, M.A., S.J.D.

Yale University, New Haven, Connecticut

THE PROBLEM of physical and mental injuries inflicted on infants and small children has increasingly attracted the attention of physicians and welfare workers within the past few years. A bibliography prepared by the Children's Bureau in August of last year compiled a substantial number of scholarly articles in scientific journals dealing with abused children. Careful case studies reveal the seriousness of the problem, and several surveys, its extent. What informed persons have suspected and what many doctors and social workers have believed, has been demonstrated, viz., that parents too often are their children's worst enemies. It may be because one or more parent is psychotic, of extremely low intelligence, of uncontrollable temper, or was himself an abused child with serious psychiatric after-effects. The assumption that, generally, a child is "better off" in the home, surrounded by the loving care of his parents is no doubt sound enough, but the exceptions are sufficiently numerous to warrant more attention by appropriate agencies and professional individuals, public and private, than they have received.

The Children's Bureau held two conferences devoted to this matter during the year 1962. Participants included well-qualified pediatricians, social workers, psychiatrists, lawyers, judges, juvenile court staff personnel, administrative and professional hospital staff members, and others concerned with child health and welfare. There was general agreement that the physician is perhaps the first person who will obtain knowledge of a situation involving inflicted injuries on a child, that he should report his findings to an appropriate investigating authority for further action, and that state legislation is necessary to impose a legal obligation on the physician in this regard.

In every state, the type of physical abuse we are here concerned with is a violation of the criminal law. It will constitute a battery, an aggravated assault, cruelty to children, or, if death ensued, as it too often does, murder. There was unanimous agreement by all conference participants that the primary purpose of the proposed reporting procedure is for the protection of the child, although a collateral result may be a criminal prosecution of a parent or other caretaker. It will often happen, however, that injunctions, restraining orders, immediate change of custodial care, or other legal measures will be indicated even though no criminal action is ultimately taken.

Purposeful physical abuse by a parent, guardian, or other person having permanent or temporary custody of a child will ordinarily be committed under circumstances when there are no witnesses. If the injury is serious enough to require hospitalization or medical care in the physician's office or in the child's home, it will almost always be the doctor who, through diagnosis and case history, first obtains knowledge of the type of trauma involved and some basis for an opinion as to its

Dr. Harper is Visiting Professor of Law, University of Miami, 1963.
ADDRESS: (F.V.H.) University of Miami, School of Law, P.O. Box 8087, Coral Gables, Florida.

possible cause. For example, the May 25th conference in Washington defined two such situations, and the pediatrician can no doubt think of others: (1) a series of injuries not accounted for by some physical incapacity of the child, (2) injuries which obviously could not be accounted for on the basis of the history given by the adult bringing the child for care.

In these and other situations suggesting purposefully inflicted injuries, it is clear that society should take action to protect the child even if the deterring effect of the criminal law eventually is invoked. It is equally clear that society can act effectively in such cases only through the state in the discharge of its role as *parens patria*. As a practical matter, it is the physician, whether as a private practitioner or as hospital staff doctor, who is most often in a position to set the machinery of government into action.

It could well be argued that the physician should report such cases to the appropriate authority as a matter of professional ethics. Every citizen has a civic duty to co-operate with law enforcement authorities and to report any criminal conduct coming to his attention. Indeed he has common law authority to arrest any person whom he has reasonable grounds to believe has committed a felony, with the qualification that the felony for which he makes the arrest must, in fact, have been committed by somebody. While most of us do not fancy the role of informer and certainly decline to report trifling misdemeanors, few would hesitate to notify the police of serious assaults upon a child whether by a parent or other person having its custody. But the physician is in a more significant position than a causal observer or neighbor. The victim is his patient, not the parent. It may be that his professional obligations go further than immediate medical care—some duty to afford protection from repeated future abuse.

It appears that California is the only state to enact legislation imposing a legal duty on the physician in this connection. The statute was not directed primarily to reporting injuries inflicted on infants or children but is part of a general reporting requirement. A section of the Penal Code makes it a felony for any person wilfully to inflict "upon any child any cruel or inhuman corporal punishment or injury resulting in a traumatic condition." Another section of the Code requires reports to the police by hospital authorities of "cases where injuries have been inflicted upon any person in violation of any penal law" and still another section calls for reports from physicians or surgeons who have in their care victims of such abuses.

As explained to the May 25th conference by a Los Angeles probation officer and a captain of the Los Angeles police department, Juvenile Division, the law, as applied to children's injuries, was of little effect until recent years when new diagnostic techniques have made it possible to discover a series of injuries in various stages of resolution. For the past several years, they report excellent co-operation from hospital authorities and from the medical profession.

As a result of the two Children's Bureau conferences, a tentative draft* of proposed state legislation has been prepared. It is still subject to revision, but the substance will not be subject to change. It provides for mandatory reporting by physicians "having cause to believe that a child under (a specific age) brought to him or coming before him for examination, care or treatment has had physical injury or injuries inflicted upon him other than by accidental means by a parent or caretaker."

This provision has two phrases which require some explanation. The first is "having cause to believe." These words are the equivalent of the legal formula "probable cause," used in various contexts. For example, a magistrate may issue a warrant for arrest or a search warrant authorizing police to invade private premises on "probable cause," that the person to be arrested has committed a criminal offense or that stolen goods or other evidence of crime are hidden on the premises to be searched. "Probable cause" in the case of search warrants was regarded by the Founders of this nation as so important to protect the right of privacy of the people in their homes that it was written into the Fourth Amendment to the Constitution.

Actually, "having cause to *believe*" is a bit misleading. "Belief" connotes a degree of mental certainty that is not required. When analyzed in its various legal contexts, it comes down here to something like "reasonable cause to suspect" that the child "may have been" the victim of inflicted injury. The physician does not have to "believe" or even have "cause to believe." He should report if a reasonable doctor would think that the child may have been abused.

Now just what is it that he must have "cause to believe"? It is that the child has had physical injuries inflicted upon him "other than by accidental means." This part of the proposed law also requires some explanation. If the injury was not "accidental," it was, in the law, the result of a voluntary act done for the purpose of causing injury. It is not only that the act was done purposefully. There is the further question, what was the purpose? It is not necessary that the actor intended to cause a bone fracture, other serious injury, or death. It is enough that he intended to inflict physical pain to an unreasonable degree or by unreasonable means. For example, parental "discipline," even by means of corporal "punishment" is recognized by the law. But if the baby cries, is it legal to spank him? How hard? The doctor is not called upon to make nice decisions on such matters. He will use common sense, derived from his professional experience as to whether his patient—and he should never forget that it is the *child* who is his patient and to whom he owes his first and foremost obligation—has been injured by the intentional and unreasonable behavior of the person responsible for its injuries. Reasonable parents do not attempt to discipline a 6-week-old infant by "punishment." Nor do they try to "condition" it by the use of force sufficient to cause a bone fracture or a serious lesion of the soft tissue.

It should be stressed that the physician is required to do no more than report the facts to the "appropriate law enforcement authority," if the matter comes to his attention in his capacity as a private practitioner. If the child is brought to him as a member of a hospital staff, it is necessary only for him to make his findings known to the administrator in charge of the institution or the person designated by him. Thus, the physician is not an investigator or a prosecutor. These functions are left to the appropriate state officials. It is also for them to determine whether court action should be sought and what other agencies, if any, should be brought into the case.

The proposed bill requires that the report include the names and addresses of the child and its parents or caretakers, if known, the child's age, the nature and extent of its injuries, including any evidence of previous injuries, and "any other information that the physician believes might be helpful in establishing the cause of the injuries and the identity of the perpetrator."

Another provision of the bill declares that the physician-patient privilege "shall not be a ground for excluding evidence regarding a child's injuries or the cause thereof," in any court action which results from the report. There are only a few states which recognize the physician-patient testimonial privilege. In any event, it is unlikely that it would be applicable in a criminal prosecution of a parent or other person who unlawfully inflicted the injuries. Where the privilege is recognized, it is by reason of the confidential relationship between the doctor and his patient and is for the benefit of the patient. It is true, that if the privilege applies unless waived, the infant has no capacity to waive it and if the natural guardian (the parent) is the accused, it would be against his interest to do so. By the usual rule of evidence prevailing in most of our states, the privilege is not available unless invoked by the patient. Inasmuch as the patient is not a party to the litigation, no issue of privilege should arise. Under the proposed legislation, however, there can be no doubt. It makes doubly sure that there will be no legal road-block to the physician's testimony.

To afford complete assurance that the physician or hospital administrator making the report will incur no personal liability, it is expressly provided that "anyone participating in making a report pursuant to this Act or participating in a judicial proceeding resulting therefrom shall in so doing be immune from any liability, civil or criminal, that might otherwise be incurred or imposed."

Here again, the protection is probably unnecessary but wisely included out of an abundance of caution. The only liability which "might otherwise be incurred or imposed" would be for defamation of character or, conceivably, for malicious prosecution. In either case it would be necessary to establish a malicious motive on the part of the physician, the chances of which would almost certainly be negligible. Nevertheless, it is well that the doctor be protected against the risk of a vascillating verdict of the jury. Moreover, he is entitled to protection against even successful litigation, the expense of which may be no trivial matter. Again, the effect of such litigation may be detrimental to his professional reputation in the community, notwithstanding he is exonerated of any wrongdoing. Many persons will read or hear that he has been sued but will not learn of the result. Against such possibilities he is given maximum protection.

It is to be hoped that the medical profession will recognize the serious nature of the problem of the physically abused child of such tender age as not to be able to protect itself even by telling what happened. Without the approval and co-operation of physicians, organizationally and individually, little improvement can be expected.

EDITOR'S NOTE:

Since Professor Harper's article was written, a revised draft of the Children's Bureau's Suggested Legislative Language has been received (see p. 897). Instead of requiring the reporting physician to have "cause to believe," the degree of mental certainty has been reduced to "reasonable cause to suspect." This appears to be consonant with Professor Harper's construction of the former draft and serves to make more clear the policy and intent of the proposed legislation.

LEGAL PROTECTIONS

In recent years, reports of shocking instances of child abuse in court records, professional literature, and the daily press have prompted an outraged public to demand that "something be done." Many States have responded with constructive measures to provide greater protection for children. Sometimes, however, the pressure has been for additional punitive laws, with little attention to the broader legal framework required for effective child protection. It seems pertinent, therefore, to review the general legal framework in which the problem of child abuse is being dealt with in this country and some of the legal and social issues involved.

In the United States, raising children is the business of parents, not of government. Hence, the law normally gives the custody of children to parents, counting on parental love to call forth the care and protection a child requires. The law in every State, however, has provided for intervention by society when parental care is dangerously faulty or insufficient.

Four sets of legal provisions are directly related to child abuse:

1. Provisions of the criminal law, which can be invoked to punish persons who have inflicted harm upon children.

2. Juvenile court acts, which universally provide that when there is evidence of abuse parents or other caretakers may be found to have "neglected" a child; and that in such instances the court may institute protective supervision of the child or order his removal from the home.

3. Legislation, in many States, authorizing or establishing "protective services" for abused and neglected children as a part of a comprehensive program of public child welfare services.

4. Child abuse reporting laws, now existing in almost every State, which encourage the reporting of suspected child abuse so that the other provisions for the protection of children can be called into play.

The criminal law

The child abuse problem does not require new criminal legislation though legislatures are often led to forget that fact by sensational cases. Murder, mayhem, assault, and battery, even when committed by parents, are punishable crimes in every State criminal code. Furthermore, existing criminal laws expressly forbid "cruelty to children" in those very words or in a similar phrase. However, State legislatures often forget these facts when the public, stirred up by newspaper reports of sensational cases demands new, but unnecessary, punitive laws.

In any event, criminal sanctions are a poor means of preventing child abuse. Day-to-day family life, charged with the most intimate emotions, is not likely to be an area of life easily ruled by the threat of fines or imprisonment. A criminal proceeding may punish an offender who deserves punishment but it may also divide rather than unite a family. The criminal law can destroy a child's family relationships; it cannot preserve or rebuild them. The most severe cases of child abuse may call for prosecution, but the prosecutors are not able to arrange for the care a child needs.

A criminal prosecution is a clumsy affair. The

An instructor in family law, criminal law, and criminal procedure at the Columbia University School of Law, **Monrad G. Paulsen** is conducting a study of the legal aspects of child abuse under a grant from the Children's Bureau. He is chairman of the Advisory Committee to the Welfare Law Testing Resource of the Columbia University School of Social Work and of the Legal Advisory Committee to the Legal Services Unit, Mobilization for Youth, New York City.

Based on a study conducted by the author with the support of a research grant from the Children's Bureau. A full report of the project is in preparation.

AGAINST CHILD ABUSE
MONRAD G. PAULSEN

proceedings take a great deal of time—for the prosecutor to prepare his case, for postponements to serve the convenience of the defense, the judge, or the witnesses. Guilt must be established beyond a reasonable doubt. Convictions are not easy to obtain because guilt is hard to prove, particularly in child abuse cases since the abuse usually takes place in the absence of witnesses who will testify.

The beginning of a prosecution is likely to be the end of a chance to improve a child's home situation. Parents are nearly always resentful of the proceeding. The hostility engendered makes casework with the child's family all but impossible if the offending parent is still in the home.

All in all, criminal sanctions can do little to help a child. The major problems concern his care and custody.

The juvenile court

In every State, statutory provisions give juvenile courts power over "neglected" children. And in every State, irrespective of the particular legislative language of the juvenile court act, a parent's physical mistreatment of a child is legally a form of "neglect." The neglect provisions, however, vary. Some of the States focus on the behavior of the caretaker: a neglected child is one whose parents "subjected him to cruelty or depravity." Other States stress the child's surroundings: "A neglected child is one who is not provided with a home or suitable place of abode, or whose home is unfit for him by reason of neglect, cruelty or depravity of either of his parents. . . ." Some States simply draw attention to the child himself: A neglected child is one "who is subject to cruel and inhuman treatment and shows the effect of being physically mistreated."

The differences in statutory language are important. The words tell us precisely what evidence is necessary to make out a case of neglect. In States which define neglect in terms of the misconduct of parents, a neglect case can be proved only by adducing evidence of parental involvement. In these States neglect adjudications are not possible in some cases because the injuries cannot be tied to the conduct of the parents, even though juvenile courts in most States only require proof by a preponderance of the evidence, not proof beyond a reasonable doubt. Even in the States requiring only a preponderance of evidence, this must be forthcoming. Situations about which objective items of proof cannot be produced, cannot be remedied in court.

In many cases, however, the judges are overly timid in how they view the evidence. Adjudications of neglect can properly rest on circumstantial evidence. Inferences of parental fault can properly be drawn, for example, from (1) the young age of the victim, (2) the number and nature of the injuries, (3) the place where they were incurred, (4) unconvincing parental explanations, and (5) the fact that the parents were the injured child's custodians and hence in proximity to him most of the time. Not every legal remedy need rest on the testimony of an eyewitness.

A recent opinion of Judge Harold A. Felix of the Family Court of the State of New York is especially significant because he permitted circumstantial evidence to put a burden of "satisfactory explanation" on the child's parents. Denying a motion to dismiss a neglect petition, Judge Felix wrote that the:

> . . . proceeding . . . was initiated undoubtedly by a consensus of view, medical and social agency, that the child Freddie, only a month old, presented a case of a battered child syndrome. Proof of abuse by a parent or parents is difficult because such actions ordinarily occur in the privacy of the home without outside witnesses. Objective study of the problem of the battered child which has become an increasingly critical one has pointed up a number of propositions, among them, that usually it is only one child in the family who is the victim; that parents tend to protect each other and resist outside inquiry and interference; and that the adult who has injured a child tends to repeat such action and suffers no remorse for his conduct.
>
> Therefore in this type of proceedings affecting a battered child syndrome, I am borrowing from the evidentiary law of negligency the principle of "res ipsa loquitur" and accepting the proposition that the condition of the child speaks for itself, thus permitting an inference of neglect to be drawn from proof of the child's age and condition, and that the latter is such as in the ordinary course of things does not happen if the parent who has the responsibility and control of an infant is pro-

tective and nonabusive. And without satisfactory explanation I would be constrained to make a finding of fact of neglect on the part of a parent or parents and thus afford the court the opportunity to inquiry [sic] into any mental, physical, or emotional inadequacies of the parents and/or to enlist any guidance or counseling the parents might need. This is the Court's responsibility to the child.[1]

Statutes which define neglect in terms of a child's environment do not present the same difficulty of proof as do those which address themselves to the parents' conduct. The fact that several injuries have occurred under inadequately explained circumstances can suffice to show that a child's "environment is injurious to his welfare."[2]

Juvenile court judges have a wide range of powers designed to give the highest practicable degree of flexibility in making dispositional decisions. A judge may warn parents or counsel them. He may order medical or psychiatric treatment for the child or the parents. He may place the child under protective supervision in his own home. He may remove the child from his parents should that extreme step be necessary. The judge also has ample power to act quickly in emergencies; but, unfortunately, a fast judicial response to emergencies may not, in fact, take place because a juvenile court judge may not be readily available.

Another important point is the leeway provided by this wide range of powers. Proof of neglect really involves answering two questions: (1) What really happened? (2) Are the "facts" to be characterized as "neglect"? What a judge is likely to characterize as "neglect" will, I believe, depend upon the action which he feels called upon to take.

The point to be grasped in Judge Felix's opinion is that he was not contemplating removal of the infant when he entered his judgment. Juvenile court judges surely are affected by a sense that the action taken by the court order must be related to the seriousness of parental unfitness as demonstrated by the evidence.[3] A severe spanking by a mother, harassed by the problems of everyday living, might sustain a neglect adjudication if the court were to make the adjudication to expedite further inquiry or to supply social services through the probation staff. It would hardly sustain the judgment if the court were to take the child away from home for any but the briefest period.

Protective supervision

The full use of juvenile court powers can keep a child in his home and still offer protection by providing official intervention into family life. The Children's Bureau has warned that protective supervision "should not be allowed to degenerate into mere watchfulness" but should be "a purposeful activity directed toward the improvement of the child's situation through the use of established casework techniques and the utilization of other community resources."[4]

However, we should not forget that many families will resent such official intervention. Court ordered protective supervision contains an important element of authority. Therefore, orders of protective supervision, should be periodically reviewed by the juvenile court with a view to termination if the intervention is no longer necessary. Indeed, the New York Family Court Act limits the duration of an order of supervision in a neglect case to a period of 1 year unless "the court finds at the conclusion of that period that exceptional circumstances require an extension thereof for an additional year."[5]

The problem of the juvenile court judges in abuse cases, of course, is to balance the interests of the parents against the likelihood of new harm to the child. No task is more difficult than predicting the recurrence of behavior which can endanger a child. The "balancing of interests" is made more difficult for a judge who is considering whether to take a child from his parents when under the evidence the degree of parental involvement in the child's injury is not perfectly clear.

Nevertheless, leaving in his home a child who bears the marks of unusual injuries which seem to have been intentionally inflicted is taking a chance with a child's life. Not all doubts should be resolved in favor of parents. Those who seek a court order to remove a child from a dangerous situation should not have to disprove every plausible explanation for the child's wounds. Temporary removal is not the same as a permanent change of custody. Parents who accept and profit by protective intervention can and do regain custody of their children when new evidence suggests that they are able to care for them properly. Parents have a right to their children, but their children have a right to live.

Protective services

In many States, the law has provided for "protective services" as a part of public programs of comprehensive child welfare services. In addition, some

States have granted charters to voluntary agencies to carry out protective services.

Protective services aim at effecting constructive change within the family in which there has been child neglect or abuse so that the child's environment may be improved. A key point is that the offer of services is made as a result of a complaint or referral from someone in the community and not usually at the request of one or both of the child's parents. Some of the parents most in need of assistance would never seek such help voluntarily.

Child protective services are offered without a court order although they may, in some instances, be identical with the services provided in protective supervision ordered by the court.

The Children's Bureau has proposed that a State or local welfare department be required to:

Investigate complaints of neglect, abuse, or abandonment of children and youth by parents, guardians, custodians, or persons serving in loco parentis; and on the basis of the findings of such investigation, offer social services to such parents, guardians, custodians, or persons serving in loco parentis in relation to the problem, or bring the situation to the attention of a law enforcement agency, an appropriate court, or another community agency.[6]

Thus, under proper child protective legislation, a welfare department would be *required* to "investigate" and to "offer social services" to families in cases of alleged child abuse. But the duty does not stop there. The offer of service may be refused. If so, the welfare department can "bring the situation to the attention" of others, including a juvenile court.

In some States, the laws require that protective services be established; in others, the services are merely authorized, leaving the final decision to local units of government. In any case, if the public welfare agency is to provide protective services to investigate complaints and serve abused and neglected children, the legislature must not only mandate or authorize these services but must also provide appropriations to make them a reality.

The "reaching out" with protective services, whether by a public welfare department or a voluntary agency, presents a problem which the good motives of the agency ought not to obscure. If help is offered when it is not wanted, the offer may contain an element of coercion. There is a danger of overreaching when the agency deals with the most vulnerable members of the community who may easily be cowed by apparent authority. The extent to which the offering of protective services should be reviewed by some judicial or administrative agency is beyond the scope of this paper. Here it is appropriate merely to note the problem. The privacy of a family ought not to be upset lightly.

Reporting laws

Whatever protection the criminal law, the juvenile court, or child protective services can offer to children, it can be offered only in respect to known instances of abuse or neglect. Therefore, statutes which encourage the reporting of suspected cases are an integral part of the law's attempt to protect children.

Bringing suspected cases to the attention of community authorities has been inhibited by many factors. Children, generally, cannot or do not speak out. Neighbors and friends hesitate to make accusations. An abusive father or mother, facile with explanations, often escapes discovery because of the common assumption, "certainly these respectable people couldn't do such a terrible thing to their children."

Over the years, many physicians have failed to alert the community's resources for child protection to suspected cases of abuse. For a number of special reasons they have kept their suspicions to themselves, treated the child for his injuries, and sent him home despite the possibility of repeated abuse. Some physicians have not reported such cases because of fear of civil or criminal liability. Others have been reluctant to play the role of "officious intermeddler," particularly when they might have to face angry parents. Some have regarded reporting as a breach of the special confidential relationship between physician and patient. Some have not reported because they did not know to whom to report and had no reason to believe that it would benefit the child.

In 1963, the Children's Bureau and The American Humane Association published model legislative language [7] and guidelines,[8] respectively, to assist States in drafting laws which would encourage physicians to report cases of suspected child abuse. In 1965, the Council of State Governments also published a statutory model for child abuse legislation.[9]

The theory behind these legislative suggestions is simple: Physicians possess the expert skill and judgment for recognizing a case of possible child abuse, a first necessity for bringing an abused child to the attention of the community's legal and social welfare resources. They regularly see cases of injured children and, in some instances, come to suspect that the injuries have not been incurred in the manner described by the caretakers. Therefore, physicians should report their suspicions so that the cases can be investigated and appropriate measures taken for the children's protection. The model laws would require physicians to report cases in which abuse is suspected, and free them from civil and criminal liability for doing so, and from any legal prohibition against testifying about the case in court.

Few legislative proposals in the history of the United States have been so widely adopted in so little time. During the past 3 years, 47 States passed statutes aimed at increasing the reporting of child abuse cases. At the beginning of 1966, only Hawaii, Mississippi, Virginia, and the District of Columbia were without such laws. This remarkable record has been achieved largely as a result of the publication of the proposals of the Children's Bureau and The American Humane Association, and of the wide publicity given the problem of child abuse in the medical and social work literature as well as in the mass media, including a drama in the "Ben Casey" TV series.

The proposals for reporting laws present a number of legislative issues, and as the 47 legislatures have tried to resolve them they have produced statutes with a great many differences.

All the State laws protect physicians against liability for reporting, although in Wisconsin legal immunity is provided only from criminal liability. In the six States where the statutes do not impose a duty to report, the extension of legal immunity is the only effect of the law aside from whatever encouragement to reporting may come from the passage of the legislation and the inclusion of the reporting scheme in the statute books. The statutes in these six States and a 1965 proposed statute drafted by the Office of the General Counsel of the American Medical Association [10] reflect a view held by some physicians that, for professional reasons, doctors should be allowed to retain some discretion in reporting. Other physicians, the American Academy of Pediatrics, and 41 State statutes support mandatory reporting.

A mandatory requirement for reporting can be of great assistance to a physician in explaining his decision to protesting parents. But there is another point in favor of a mandatory law. Whether cases of suspected abuse should be brought to the attention of the authorities responsible for child protection is not a medical question, but a question of social policy, properly answered by a legislature.

All 47 reporting statutes designate physicians of all kinds, and most of them also designate hospitals, as reporting agents. Some statutes and the American Medical Association's proposal reflect a judgment that the laws should also encourage reporting of suspected child abuse by members of other professions who see children regularly, such as nurses, dentists, teachers, and social workers. A few States provide that everyone who suspects a case of child abuse is covered by the statute.

The argument for focusing on reporting by physicians is very strong. Doctors face special confidentiality problems arising from the physician-patient relationship and are concerned about the threat of legal action. Actually, the chief aim of the legislation is to uncover cases which only medical skill can detect in the course of a medical examination and a review of the medical history. The obvious cases of maltreatment are likely to be identified by persons in the community who, at least in cases of serious injuries, bring them to the attention of some authority or agency which can take action. If the statute's reporting group is large, the impact of the reporting requirements may be diffused. Everybody's duty easily becomes nobody's duty.

Recipients of reports

The Children's Bureau proposal of 1963 recommended that reports of suspected child abuse be made "to an appropriate police authority." The police authority was designated originally because it "constitutes the only chain of services which is sure to exist in every community." [7] Moreover, police are available 24 hours a day. [7]

On the other hand, The American Humane Association has recommended that suspected cases be reported to the public or voluntary child welfare service which carries the child protective function in the community. [8]

Because, since 1963, public child protective services are becoming more widely available as part of comprehensive child welfare programs in the States, the Children's Bureau now recommends that in communities where a public welfare agency offers child protective service it be the agency designated to receive reports.

The 47 State statutes vary greatly with regard to the agency designated to receive reports. Some designate the police, another law enforcement agency, or the juvenile court. Some designate public or voluntary child welfare agencies, or both. In many States, more than one type of agency is designated.

The designation of the police or other law enforcement authority as the recipient of reports creates all sorts of problems. The investigative skills of the police, the sheriff, or the prosecutor are useful in answering the question, "Who did it?", but they are not likely to be of much use in answering: "Why was it done?", "What can be done to preserve the family?", or "How can this child be protected?" Law enforcement officers habitually look for a basis for prosecution, but are often blind to danger signs present in a home situation which would be apparent to a properly trained social worker. Investigation by a law enforcement agency is likely to engender defensive hostility in the parents and make successful intervention by a child welfare worker impossible. The child protective service of a child welfare agency possesses the greatest fund of desirable resources to focus on what happens to the children involved.

There is a growing trend, as evidenced by the statutes adopted or revised in 1965, toward the designation of the public welfare department either as one of the agencies to receive reports or as the agency to carry the chief responsibility for making the initial investigation following a report.

If reports are to be made exclusively to public welfare departments, however, some provision should be made to provide for round-the-clock emergency service. Illinois has initiated a unique system of statewide emergency service which can be reached by calling a well-publicized telephone number.

Statutes which provide a choice of agencies to receive reports in the same community bring uncertainty to administration and confusion to those who are obligated to report. Worst of all, none of the designated agencies may have a clear responsibility for action. Of course, a State may find it necessary to designate different agencies as exclusive recipients of reports for different parts of the State. Resources available in one community may be absent in another.

In two States, California and Illinois, under the provisions of State law, and in a few cities, for example, New York, under local administrative regulations, reports of instances of suspected child abuse are recorded in a central registry. Parents who abuse their children sometimes go from doctor to doctor and hospital to hospital in an attempt to es-

cape attention. A central registry helps to identify these "repeater" cases, and can help determine the significance of the present injury. Knowledge of a previous report of suspected abuse can help confirm suspicions that an injury is the product of abuse.

A central registry also serves an important statistical function, which can lay the basis for learning more about the nature and causes of child abuse. Some State and local welfare departments collect information for statistical and research purposes only, without making specific case information available to physicians and social workers.

Some questions about the effectiveness of reporting statutes probably never can be answered. For example, we cannot prove that reporting laws actually cause more cases to be identified than before. Records of casefinding were not previously kept. And, we do not know how many abused children, if any, are deprived of medical attention because their caretakers are afraid of being reported. Such cases are not recorded.

Nonetheless, the facts at hand provide a compelling argument that reporting laws are having an important impact. First, reports *are* being made under the statutes and in increasing numbers. Dr. David G. Gil of Brandeis University, director of a nationwide epidemiologic study of child abuse,[11] estimates that approximately 5,000 cases will be reported under these statutes alone in 1966. In the first year under the New York State reporting statute, reports involving 424 children were received. In the second half of the year, the rate of reporting increased.[12]

The reporting legislation has spurred the establishment of new public services aimed at child protection. In some States new legislation has been passed requiring or authorizing child protective services, and in others additional services have been provided under existing laws. In some States, after a reporting statute has been passed, legislators have made additional money available for child protective services.

Legislation alone does not bring reporting. In some places where the child abuse reporting laws have been most successful a burst of cooperative activity has taken place. Newspapers, medical societies, and welfare departments have alerted the citizenry and the medical professions about the reporting statute. Hospitals have established regular channels for reporting cases, and communities have created the machinery to help physicians comply with the law.

Reporting is, of course, not enough. After a report is made, something has to happen. A multidisciplinary network of protection needs to be developed in each community to implement the good intentions of the law. If child protective services are not available, reporters will no longer report. The promise of casefinding legislation, such as reporting laws, is that when a case is found, something is done about it. The legislatures which require reporting but do not provide the means for further protective action delude themselves and neglect children.

---

[1] *In the Matter of* S. 259 N.Y.S. 2d 164 (Fam. Ct. 1965).

[2] National Probation and Parole Association (now National Council on Crime and Delinquency): Standard juvenile court act, sec 8, 2(B). New York. 1959.

[3] Paulsen, Monrad: The delinquency, neglect, and dependency jurisdiction of the juvenile court. *In* Justice for the child. (M. K. Rosenheim, ed.) The Free Press of Glencoe, New York. 1962.

[4] U.S. Department of Health, Education, and Welfare, Social Security Administration, Children's Bureau: Standards for specialized courts dealing with children. CB Publication No. 346. 1954.

[5] New York Family Court Act, sec. 354.

[6] U.S. Department of Health, Education, and Welfare, Social Security Administration, Children's Bureau: Proposals for drafting principles and suggested language for legislation on public child welfare and youth services. 1957. (Multilithed.)

[7] U.S. Department of Health, Education, and Welfare, Welfare Administration, Children's Bureau: The abused child—principles and suggested language for legislation on reporting of the physically abused child. 1963.

[8] The American Humane Association, Children's Division: Guidelines for legislation to protect the battered child. Denver, Colo. 1963.

[9] Council of State Governments: Program of suggested State legislation. Chicago, Ill. 1965.

[10] American Medical Association: Physical abuse of children—suggested legislation. Chicago, Ill. 1965. (Mimeographed.)

[11] Gil, David G.: Epidemiologic study of child abuse—research in progress. Florence Heller Graduate School for Advanced Studies in Social Welfare, Brandeis University. 1965.

[12] Report of the New York State Department of Welfare, Albany. Nov. 30, 1965.

Child Abuse Laws — Are They Enough?

Larry B. Silver, MD, William Barton, MD, and Christina C. Dublin

The physicians in the Washington, DC, metropolitan area were questioned to assess their knowledge of the battered child syndrome, their awareness of the community procedures available, and their attitude toward reporting such cases under the protection of the new child abuse laws. Results suggest that methods of communication between medical and community organizations and the physician have not been completely effective in familiarizing the physician with the battered child syndrome or with the community procedures to be used for reporting. Several considerations appear to inhibit the physician from reporting suspected cases of child abuse.

In October 1961 a symposium on the "battered child syndrome" was held at the meeting of the American Academy of Pediatrics; the symposium brought into focus the increasing professional recognition of this problem.[1] In 1962 Kempe et al presented evidence of the prevalence of the battered child syndrome and, in so doing, alerted the physician to consider this diagnosis and to be aware of his duty and responsibility to the child.[2] Since that time numerous articles have been published on the incidence, clinical manifestations, and social and psychological characteristics of both the battered child and the battering parent, and about physician responsibilities.[3]

One of the major areas of effort involving the medical and social welfare professions has been in establishing child abuse laws. In 1963 the Children's Bureau of the Department of Health, Education and Welfare proposed model legislation on reporting the case of the physically abused child.[4] This model act has several basic features: (1) It recommends reporting by physicians or institutions of any case in which there is reasonable cause to suspect a battered child. (2) It suggests procedures for this reporting. (3) It provides immunity from liability for the physician. (4) It establishes that neither the physician-patient privilege nor the husband-wife privilege can be a ground for excluding evidence. (5) It states that anyone not reporting a suspected case of a battered child would be guilty of a misdemeanor.

Since 1962, forty-nine states and the Virgin Islands have passed statutes on child abuse, with legislation pending in Hawaii, Puerto Rico, and the District of Columbia. Each of these statutes is based, in general, on the model law.

From the beginning, the medical, legal, and social work professions have been concerned with the effectiveness of such a law. Reinhart and Elmer[5] felt that the law's concentration on the one child seen by the doctor failed to mention possible dangers to other children in the household. In addition, they expressed concern that the law might increase hazards for the injured child in that the publicity accorded a mandatory-reporting law could result in fewer injured children being brought to the doctor. Finally, they questioned the soundness of the suggested language of the law, which

From the Department of Psychiatry, Children's Hospital of the District of Columbia, Washington. Dr. Silver is a career fellow in child psychiatry.

Reprint requests to 2125 13th St NW, Washington, DC 20009 (Dr. Silver).

appeared to recommend the police as the appropriate agency to receive reports of alleged child abuse.

The General Counsel of the American Medical Association expressed concern over the new legislation in April 1964.[6] The major concerns noted were (1) that legislation should confer immunity from litigation and damage not only on physicians but also on lawyers, nurses, social workers, and others who seek to protect abused children by reporting; (2) that compelling the physician alone to report singles him out unwisely or causes the parent or guardian, for his own protection, to put off seeking medical care; and (3) that mandatory reporting in and of itself will not eradicate undesirable social conduct. The Committee on the Infant and Pre-School Child of the American Academy of Pediatrics recently stated that "mandatory reporting by physicians of suspected cases of child abuse is justified and that legislation for this purpose should be primarily of a protective rather than a punitive nature."[7]

Paulsen et al reviewed the legislative history of the child abuse reporting laws and expressed concern about the future[8]:

> Many supporters of child abuse reporting legislation viewed enactment as a means to strengthen the network of child protective services. The services are needed, but are by no means universally available. . . . Existing statutes will require additional appropriations for expanding child protective services [for] as child abuse reporting legislation [becomes] effective, it will add to the existing overburdened case load of the agencies.

They concluded, "To be a wise program for action, it should evolve on a solid basis of medical, psychiatric, and social research. Legislation should be formulated only after proposals are fully examined by a partnership of individuals, voluntary associations, and state government." Paulsen, in a study of the legal protections against child abuse, again expressed concern with the reporting laws[9]:

> Reporting is, of course, not enough. After a report is made, something has to happen. A multidisciplinary network of protection needs to be developed in each community to implement the good intentions of the law. . . . The legislatures which require reporting but do not provide the means for further protective action delude themselves and neglect children.

Since July 1965 the Child Abuse Research Group of the Department of Psychiatry of Children's Hospital of Washington, DC, has been concerned with the physician's role and the community structure for dealing with the problems of the battered child syndrome. As the Child Abuse Research Group worked with community agencies, hospitals, and practicing physicians, several questions were raised: (1) Are physicians aware of the established procedures within the community for management of suspected or proven cases of child abuse? (2) How effective has communication been between the physician and other members of the professional community? (3) What are the other considerations faced by the physician in reporting his suspicion of child abuse, even when he is protected by law?

Procedure

Questionnaires were sent to physicians in the greater metropolitan Washington, DC, area who would most likely come in contact with abused children. The physician population included pediatricians, general practitioners, and the hospital house staff servicing the emergency rooms of each hospital in the above area. The greater Metropolitan Washington, DC, area was defined as the District of Columbia, the neighboring Maryland counties (Montgomery and Prince Georges), the neighboring Virginia counties (Arlington and Fairfax), and the city of Alexandria.

Four hundred and fifty questionnaires were sent out, 150 to each of the above categories, ie, pediatricians, general practitioners, and hospital staff. The proportion of the total 450 questionnaires to each geographic area was determined by the percent of the physician population in each category living in that area. Each questionnaire consisted of ten questions: (1) What is your type of practice or hospital status? (2) When you see an injured child professionally do you consider the possibility of child abuse? (3) Can you think in retrospect of recent cases in which the possibility of child abuse could have been considered but was not? (4) In the course of an average month in your practice (emergency room) what would you estimate the number of suspected cases of child abuse to be? (5) When you suspect a case of battered child syndrome, to whom do you report the case? (6) If you report a suspected case of child abuse, do you know what type of follow-up is initiated by that agency or person? (7) Are there occasions when you make the diagnosis of battered child syndrome but do not report the case? (8) Assuming legal protection, would you report a case in which you suspected an abused child but did not have full evidence to confirm such a diagnosis? (9) Assuming legal protection, what are the reasons you might not report a case in which evidence exists for a diagnosis of battered child syndrome? (10) Where did you obtain your knowledge about the battered child syndrome?

The 450 questionnaires sent out represented approximately 80% of the pediatricians, 50% of the general practitioners, and 80% of the hospital emergency room house staff in the greater metropolitan Washington, DC, area. The questionnaires returned for this study represented a 51% return for the pediatricians (76), a 42% return for the general practitioners (63), and a 40% return for the hospital staff (40). Therefore, the data used in this study represent approximately 41% of the pediatricians, 21% of the general practitioners, and 32% of the hospital staff population in this metropolitan area.

Results

The results on each question are summarized in Tables 1 to 9.

A strikingly high percentage of the physicians suggested a lack of awareness of the battered child syndrome or a lack of knowledge about community procedures. One in five physicians reported rarely or never considering child abuse when seeing an injured child. One in six physicians reported mistakenly not having considered child abuse. Over one half of the physicians did not know the correct procedure to follow in their community. One in three physicians did not know what follow-up procedures were initiated by an agency after reporting a case of suspected child abuse. The observation that only the hospital emergency room staff reported seeing more than two cases of child abuse per month suggests that parents may bring their children for care only when the injury is serious enough to require emergency medical attention and under conditions which they think are less likely to involve them in disclosures regarding family relationships.

Concerning the effectiveness of the child abuse reporting laws, almost one of every four physicians stated that he would not report a case of suspected battered child syndrome, even given legal protection. The major concern seemed to be that the evidence would not stand up in a court proceeding. As might be expected (since the major literature on the battered child syndrome has appeared since 1962), most of the hospital staff learned of this syndrome in medical school and in medical journals, while most of the pediatricians became aware of the problem through specialty training or medical journals, and most of the general practitioners through medical journals.

Comment

These data suggest that physicians are not sufficiently aware of the battered child syndrome or of community procedures for the management of a case of child abuse. The lines of communication to the individual physician from community agencies and professional groups have not been fully effective. Medical publications, medical school education, and hospital training seem to be the best

Table 1.—When you see an injured child professionally, do you consider possibility of child abuse?

	Always or Usually		Often or Occasionally		Rarely		Never	
	%	No.	%	No.	%	No.	%	No.
Total physicians	44	88	35	70	18	36	3	6
Pediatricians	44	34	34	26	21	16	1	1
General practice	41	26	29	18	25	16	5	3
Hospital staff	47	28	43	26	7	4	3	2

Table 2.—Can you think of recent cases when child abuse could have been considered but was not?

	Yes		No	
	%	No.	%	No.
Total physicians	16.5	33	83.5	167
Pediatricians	10	8	90	69
General practice	14	9	86	54
Hospital staff	26	16	74	44

Table 3.—In an average month in your practice, what is the estimated number of suspected child abuse cases?

	0-2		3-5		6-10		More Than 10	
	%	No.	%	No.	%	No.	%	No.
Total physicians	90	180	7.5	15	2	4	0.5	1
Pediatricians	100	77	...	0	...	0	...	0
General practice	100	63	...	0	...	0	...	0
Hospital staff	66	40	25	15	7	4	2	1

Table 4.—When you suspect a case of battered child syndrome, to whom do you report it?

	Correct Answer*		Incorrect Answer†		No One		I Don't Know		Other‡	
	%	No.	%	No.	%	No.	%	No.	%	No.
Total physicians	48	96	3.5	7	9	18	24	48	15.5	31
Pediatricians	48	37	5	4	7	5	23	18	17	13
General practice	43	27	3	2	13	8	35	22	6	4
Hospital staff	53	32	2	1	8	5	13	8	23	14

*Police department, hospital medical director.
†Head nurse, community medical society, community medical director.
‡Practicing physicians noted social service, psychiatrist, pressure to family, or refer to hospital, or avoided answer. Hospital staff noted social worker or chief resident, or avoided answer.

Table 5.—If you report a suspected case of child abuse do you know what type of follow-up is initiated?

	Yes		No	
	%	No.	%	No.
Total physicians	34	68	66	132
Pediatricians	42	32	58	45
General practice	21	13	79	50
Hospital staff	38	23	62	37

Table 6.—Are there occasions when you make the diagnosis of battered child syndrome, but do not report the case?

	Yes		No	
	%	No.	%	No.
Total physicians	11	22	89	178
Pediatricians	8	6	92	71
General practice	13	8	87	55
Hospital staff	13	8	87	52

Table 7.—Would you report a case when you suspect an abused child but do not have full evidence to confirm diagnosis?*

	Yes		No	
	%	No.	%	No.
Total physicians	77	154	23	46
Pediatricians	74	57	26	20
General practice	76	48	24	15
Hospital staff	82	49	18	11

*Assuming legal protection.

Table 8.—What are reasons for not reporting a case when evidence exists for diagnosis of battered child syndrome?*

	Legal Time Lost		Implications To Family		Diagnostic Evidence Insufficient		Other†		Did Not Answer	
	%	No.	%	No.	%	No.	%	No.	%	No.
Total physicians	9.5	29	15.5	31	54	108	4.5	9	25.5	51
Pediatricians	6	5	14	11	60	46	6	5	20	15
General practice	6	4	21	13	46	28	...	0	38	24
Hospital staff	17	10	12	7	57	34	7	4	20	12

*Assuming legal protection. Many physicians gave multiple answers.
†The physicians stated that if they suspected such a case they would report it.

Table 9.—Where did you obtain your knowledge about the battered child syndrome?*

	Medical School		Special Training		Medical Journal		Lay Press		Other†		Not Familiar	
	%	No.	%	No.	%	No.	%	No.	%	No.	%	No.
Total physicians	21.5	43	29.5	59	65.5	131	17.5	35	6.5	13	5	10
Pediatricians	4	3	52	40	65	53	8	6	10	8	1	1
General practice	9	6	3	2	73	46	16	18	3	2	13	8
Hospital staff	57	34	28	17	62	32	18	11	5	3	2	1

*Many physicians gave multiple answers.
†Lectures, personal experience.

means of reaching the physician; however, still other means are needed.

In addition to the difficulty of reaching the physician, other considerations appear to inhibit the physician from reporting his suspicion of child abuse, even when he is protected by law. The data from the questionnaires, work with community agencies, and contact with physicians suggest several possible reasons for this problem: (1) Some physicians may find it difficult to accept the reality of willful child abuse. (2) The meaning and scope of many basic terms and concepts associated with the understanding and description of varying degrees of neglect and abuse are not clear. (3) The responsibility and limitations of the physician, child welfare agency, child protective service, police, juvenile court, and criminal court are not fully defined.

Some physicians are resistant to the possibility that there are, in fact, battering parents. Kempe et al state[2]:

Physicians have great difficulty both in believing that parents could have attacked their children and in undertaking the essential questioning of parents on this subject. Many physicians find it hard to believe that such an attack could have occurred and they attempt to obliterate such suspicions from their minds, even in the face of obvious circumstantial evidence.

Child abuse, once accepted by the physician as a clinical phenomenon, must be studied within a range of symptomatology encompassing various types and degrees of physical and emotional neglect. Without full clarification of both terms and concepts, physicians will continue to find difficulty in referring to and cooperating with community agencies. Cheney, in discussing the legal problems of providing protective services, questioned the definition of "neglect"[10]:

"Neglect" . . . is a concept which permits no degree of certainty, either in legal definitions or social application. . . . Most neglect statutes. . . . define the conditions on which the State may act [using] standards [that] do no more than import vague subjective tests into a legal criterion.

He also questions the spectrum of clinical or social situations which could fit within certain basic definitions, and he wonders where professional groups should draw the line. For example, at what degree of family deterioration is intervention by a social agency to take place? Cheney raises the question of the possible continuum of situations in which the term "neglect" could be used. Is emotional and social neglect the same as physical neglect? He feels that before emotional and social neglect can be dealt with as is physical neglect, psychiatrists need better to delineate standards of psychological welfare. As he notes, "The need for action in behalf of emotionally disturbed children is difficult to translate into legal standards because the medical guidelines themselves are uncertain."[10] In the same discussion, Cheney notes that there are almost no written juvenile court opinions dealing with neglect, and few appellate decisions. Thus, a child protective service worker, in determining whether to refer a case to court, must rely on his personal or hearsay knowledge of what the judge has done in the past.

The Committee on Infant and Pre-School Child of the American Academy of Pediatrics feels that the practicing physician might be handicapped when encountering a case of suspected maltreatment in his office practice because of the traditional physician-patient relationship, and because of the lack of time for obtaining an accurate history.[7] Also, it is suggested by this committee that the physician may lack laboratory facilities, x-ray, etc, to make a suitable evaluation. This committee recommends that the physician should hospitalize the child for such an evaluation. Hospitalization would provide the necessary time and equipment. Such a diagnostic evaluation would be more complete, would support the private physician in his role with family, and would minimize the involvement of the private physician in legal suits or time lost in legal actions.

The lines of communication to the individual physician from community agencies and professional groups and the resistance of some physicians to reporting suspected cases of child abuse need to be explored and analyzed by professional organizations before the practicing physician can either know of or feel comfortable in his role as the reporting physician. The role of the child welfare, protective service, police, and court, and their interrelationships, should be reviewed in terms of the therapeutic needs of the family and the protection of the child.

The willingness of hospitals to accept the challenge presented by the Committee on Infant and Pre-School Child of the American Academy of Pediatrics in suggesting to physicians that they depend on the hospital for medical evaluation, diagnosis, and disposition in cases of child abuse should be fully explored.

Local medical societies, the Law Department, or other committees or councils of the American Medical Association, interested medical specialty groups, and the American Hospital Association must concern themselves with these and other phases of the child abuse dilemma. This work must be done in cooperation with their counterparts in the legal and social welfare professions at the local, state, and national levels. Information resulting from these contacts must then be disseminated to individual physicians and other workers, through educational and professional media.

Conclusions

Methods of communication from medical professional organizations and from government and community agencies have not been completely effective in familiarizing the physicians in a metropolitan area with the battered child syndrome or with the community procedures to be used for reporting. Child abuse laws will not be enough until these lines of communication are improved. There are several areas of resistance which inhibit some physicians from reporting suspected cases of child abuse. A need exists to further educate physicians, to clarify many basic terms and concepts, and to define the responsibility and limitations of the individuals and agencies involved in cases of child abuse (eg, physician, child welfare agency, child protective service, police, juvenile court, and criminal court).

As the physician learns more about the scope of the child abuse problem and about the community facilities available to him, he will be more able to overcome some of his concerns and to work as a team member within his community.

The medical profession must spearhead the efforts of those individuals and groups concerned with the child abuse problem, with the ultimate goal of an integrated program for prevention, protection, and assistance for the abused child and the family.

This study was supported in part by the Philip M. Stern Family Fund and the Mary B. Meyer Memorial Fund.

References

1. Bain, K.: The Physically Abused Child, *Pediatrics* **31**:895-898 (June) 1963.

2. Kempe, C.H., et al: The Battered-Child Syndrome, *JAMA* **181**:17-24 (July 7) 1962.

3. *Bibliography on the Battered Child,* Clearinghouse for Research in Child Life, Children's Bureau, Dept of Health, Education and Welfare, Jan 1966.

4. *The Abused Child—Principles and Suggested Language for Legislation on Reporting of the Physically Abused Child.* Children's Bureau, Dept of Health, Education and Welfare, 1963.

5. Reinhart, J.B., and Elmer, E.: The Abused Child: Mandatory Reporting Legislation, *JAMA* **188**:358-362 (April 27) 1964.

6. Battered Child Legislation, Office of the General Counsel, AMA, *JAMA* **188**:386 (April 27) 1964.

7. Maltreatment of Children: The Physically Abused Child, Committee on Infant and Pre-School Child, American Academy of Pediatrics, *Pediatrics* **37**:377-382 (Feb) 1966.

8. Paulsen, M.G., et al: Child Abuse Reporting Laws—Some Legislative History, *George Washington Law Rev* **34**:482-506 (March) 1966.

9. Paulsen, M.G.: Legal Protections Against Child Abuse, *Children* **13**:42-48 (March-April) 1966.

10. Cheney, K.B.: Safeguarding Legal Rights in Providing Protective Services, *Children* **13**:86-92 (May-June) 1966.

In this article Vincent De Francis, Director of the Children's Division of the American Humane Association, deals with the need for legislation requiring that evidence of physical abuse of children be reported, particularly by doctors and medical personnel, to appropriate public authorities. The central objective, he underlines, should be to protect children rather than to punish parents. With this end in view he suggests a number of approaches, legal and otherwise. And he points to a wide range of laws, most of them mandatory, enacted in forty-seven states in the last three years for reporting of child abuse.

Laws for Mandatory Reporting of Child Abuse Cases

by Vincent De Francis

FEW RECENT social causes have aroused public sensibility or created as much concern as has the current awareness that child abuse is a shocking reality and a growing problem. It is a phenomenon common to every community. It knows no bounds in relation to the economic or educational levels of parents. Cases of abuse are reported from the seemingly well regulated home and from the seriously disorganized or broken home, from the country club district and from the slum area.

Although the wave of public concern is of comparatively recent origin, the problem itself is very old. It dates back to ancient times when fathers had powers of life and death over children; to the era when children were sold into slavery or were maimed and mutilated to make them more effective for street begging. Those were harsh and cruel times, characterized by rigorous, primitive standards; might was right, and children were chattels with few rights in the eyes of the law.

Public indignation at this gross disregard for the rights of children and for the tradi-tional protective role of parents is frequently turned toward punitive action against parents who transgress our cherished ideals about family responsibility for children. In the process of pursuing sanctions against offending parents, the need for constructive planning and services on behalf of the abused child is often relegated to a secondary consideration or is completely overlooked.

THE SIZE OF THE PROBLEM

While there are no accurate national statistics on the incidence of child abuse cases, several studies serve as an index of the size of the problem.

Of particular significance is a study by the Children's Division of the American Humane Association. In 1962 it studied cases of child abuse reported in United States newspapers. The study amassed information on 662 incidents, culled from newspapers in forty-eight states. The cases represented the grossest types of child abuse—situations which were reported to law enforcement authorities and which were deemed "newsworthy" by the local press. The severity of abuse involved may be judged from the fact that in 178 of the cases, almost one-fourth of the total, the child died from the injuries.

The 662 cases studied in 1962 represent only that portion of child abuse incidence which was identified and reported. For each such case making the headlines there may well be a hundred or more, unseen, unreported and unidentified.

Educated estimates place the probable incidence of serious child abuse in the nation at more than 10,000 cases a year. There are no doubt many additional thousands of cases in which the mistreatment is of less dangerous proportions. A recent editorial in the American Medical Association Journal said that child abuse "may turn out to be a more frequent cause of death than such well recognized diseases as leukemia, cystic fibrosis and muscular distrophy, and may well rank with automobile accidents."

How to find and identify the vast number of child abuse cases hidden from public view? This question posed the problem which now has resulted in the move for mandatory reporting legislation.

WHY A REPORTING LAW?

The need to discover and identify child victims of abuse is the compelling reason for devising a case-finding tool such as the reporting law. Medical personnel came to be selected as the target group of the law's mandate as a result of ferment within medical circles, where research and study was producing irrefutable evidence that child abuse can be determined by medical diagnosis.

Numerous articles in current medical journals implore practitioners to exercise great care when examining children brought to them for treatment of injuries. All too frequently, they are told, doctors accept glib stories about such injuries resulting from accidental cause. The use of X-rays and a study of all symptoms may reveal findings inconsistent with the history given, and may provide the doctor with reasonable cause to suspect inflicted, rather than ac-cidental, injury. Failure to recognize the "Battered Child Syndrome" could subject the child to additional or repeated injury and even death.

The logic and force of medical concern as expressed in the literature has focused attention on the doctor as the probable first responsible contact with child victims of abuse. Doctors are the first "outsiders" with opportunity to see and examine the child, and the first competent persons capable of assuming repsonsibility for positive action on behalf of the child. Thus they are seen as the best resource for early identification and reporting of cases.

But would doctors be willing to voice their suspicions by reporting these cases when the diagnosis of inflicted injuries was not clear cut—particularly in the face of continued denial by the parents? Would such reporting expose doctors to the possibility of a legal action for money damages? Would doctors feel that such reporting would run counter to ethical considerations in regard to privileged communication between doctor and patient?

To overcome these blocks to free reporting, legislation has been proposed by various authorities which provides immunity from legal action to persons making a report, and a waiver of the doctor-patient privilege. Waiver of the husband-wife privilege also is to be recommended, to free a spouse to testify about abuse committed by the other.

Procedural matters in regard to the manner and method of reporting are dealt with in the legislative proposals. An immediate oral report by telephone, to be followed by a written report, is suggested. Also included are details covering content—i.e., names, addresses, age of the child, etc.

PHILOSOPHY, PURPOSE OF THE LAW

The most important consideration in the whole concept of mandatory reporting is a definition of the purpose to be served by the report. Obviously, the core objective is early identification of children who have been physically abused, so that they can be (1) treated for their present injuries and (2) protected from further abuse.

Achieving the first prong of this objective—treating children's injuries—presents no serious problem except when parents, for religious or other scruples, may refuse permission for needed medical care. Depending on the specifics of each case, this can be dealt with by invoking the authority of the juvenile court to order necessary medical care over parental objections.

For the second prong of the objective different approaches may be and are being used. Here we are looking at how the community treats the situation so as to protect the child from further injury. We need to examine what process the community employs to prevent additional abuse.

Several circumstances impinge on the ultimate pattern employed. Most basic, however, is the emotional climate in the community toward violators of the moral code and the rule of law and order. Of equal impact is community awareness and understanding in terms of social planning in the best interests of children.

THE EMOTIONAL CLIMATE

As noted earlier, the general reaction of people to the problem of child abuse is shock and anger when confronted with the brutal facts. A natural consequence is a desire to exact retribution—to punish unnatural parents for their acts of cruelty.

Where this philosophy pervails, reporting legislation would be viewed as a tool for identifying parents who mistreat children so that society may deal with them for the crime of child abuse.

The space limitations of this article will not permit more than a superficial exploration of the merits of this approach. On the positive side, we can say that justice, in the strictly legal sense, would be served. The negatives, however, are many.

Prosecution requires proof through evidence which establishes culpability of the parent beyond a reasonable doubt. Because these acts usually take place in the privacy of the home, without outside witnesses, lack of evidence makes it impossible to identify which parent was the offender, or to sustain the legal burden of proof. An unsuccessful prosecution may subject the child victim to increased hazards, exposed as he now may be to a parent embittered by his experience with police and court. And the parent may view the prosecution's failure as a license to continue to abuse.

Two other factors mitigate against this use of mandatory reporting. If seeking medical attention for the injured child may expose a parent to the possibility of criminal prosecution, fear of possible consequences may prevent taking a child for medical help until the situation becomes acute—or, perhaps, until too late to help the child. Of equal weight is the concern of doctors who may resist reporting cases if by so doing they become involved as witnesses in a criminal proceeding against the parents. Because doctors identify with the "helping" ethic, they would find repugnant anything which places them in a punitive role. The net result could be a stalemate—and a defeat of the law's objective to encourage reporting and early case-finding.

This is not to say that parents should never be prosecuted for child abuse. Certainly the community has a duty to act against parents who commit heinous crimes against children. Where a felony has been committed, this duty cannot be evaded. But the decision of whether or not to prosecute in a given case should rest with the county prosecutor. And no decision to prosecute parents can afford to overlook adequate planning for the abused child and other children in the family.

SOCIAL PLANNING FOR CHILDREN

The other approach is rooted in a philosophy which sees the purpose of case-finding to be the discovery of children who, because of abuse, need the care and protection of the community. The community carries out its responsibility by making available the social services in order to (1) prevent further abuse of the child and (2) meet the child's needs through planning to assure maximum protection.

This approach is best served if the reporting, at the outset, is directed to the child protective program in the community. Such services are usually found in the public child welfare agency.

Child protective programs are especially qualified to "reach out" to families where children are neglected or abused. Their functional responsibility requires that they (1) explore and determine the facts of neglect or abuse, (2) assess and evaluate the damage to children, (3) initiate appropriate social work services to remedy the situation, and (4) invoke the authority of the juvenile court in those situations where removal from parental custody must be sought in the best interests of children.

The "helping-through-social-services" philosophy is stretched to include the parents. This is based on recognition that destructive parental behavior is symptomatic of deeper emotional problems. Rarely is child abuse the product of wanton, willful or deliberate acts of cruelty. It results from emotional immaturity and from lack of capacity for coping with the pressures and tensions of modern living. The parents involved are frequently people with personality defects or character disorders. They may be neurotic, emotionally disturbed or mentally ill. The outer symptoms of their disorganized states are manifested in deviant behavior and bursts of violence or anger directed at other people, including their children.

Many of these parents have themselves been victims of parental neglect or abuse, and their behavior as parents is a reflection of what they were exposed to as children. Most of them are not capable of providing adequate care for their children without outside help.

What such parents need is help—help and treatment. They need services to guide and counsel them toward accepting their responsibilities as parents—to rebuild their damaged personalities, to give them strength and stability to live up to their parental roles.

But while many parents will respond to skilled services, some parents cannot be helped, or cannot be helped soon enough to avoid the risk of exposing their children to more abuse. In such cases the protective service will take action through the juvenile court to remove the child from a dangerous situation. The best interests of the child—his very safety—may dictate his removal from the home as an immediate and necessary action. Decisions of this type require mature, experienced judgment, plus skill and training in handling children's problems.

LEGISLATIVE ACTION

The pressure of public concern and recognition of need for social action resulted in prompt attention by state legislative bodies in 1963. Eleven of eighteen legislatures in which such bills were introduced that year enacted mandatory laws requiring the reporting of child abuse. These were the first such laws anywhere. Some of the bills introduced were hastily conceived, and reflected public indignation against abusing parents. Most of the eleven which passed were more thoughtfully prepared, and showed awareness of the imperative need for protective services on behalf of abused children. About half of them, in varying degrees, followed suggested language prepared by national organizations active in promoting the law.

The law-making tempo continued in the legislative off-year of 1964 when ten more legislatures passed reporting laws. The momentum reached full pitch in 1965, in which similar laws were enacted in twenty-six more states. Thus, in three legislative years a total of forty-seven legislatures have passed laws seeking reports of injuries inflicted on children. Several states were on their second go-round in 1965, in which their sessions passed amendments to reporting laws enacted in 1963 or 1964.

The forty-seven state laws are characterized by many differences in form and substance. Some of the differences are minor, and may be attributed to the differing administrative or organizational set-ups in each state. Others are more generic and reflect variance in the philosophy of how to treat the problem of child abuse. This is particularly true in relation to the approaches discussed earlier.

Study of the forty-seven laws reveals many areas of conformity to the suggested legislation developed by a Council of State Governments committee * and similar models. However, a review of differences will serve to highlight the range of viewpoints and philosophies.

Jurisdiction—Age

An element regarding which much variation is found is the age limit used in defining an abused child. The range is from a low of 12 years to the high of 21 when a child is no longer a minor. See Table A.

TABLE A

Under 12	Colorado, Georgia, Missouri, Oregon
Under 14	Maryland
Under 16	Alabama, Alaska, Arizona, Arkansas, Florida, Illinois, Indiana, Kansas, Maine, Massachusetts, Minnesota, New Hampshire, New Mexico, New York, North Carolina, South Carolina, Tennessee, Vermont
Under 17	Louisiana, Michigan, Oklahoma
Under 18	Connecticut, Delaware, Idaho, Iowa, Kentucky, Montana, Nevada, New Jersey, North Dakota, Ohio, Pennsylvania, Rhode Island, South Dakota, Texas, Washington, West Virginia
Under 19	Wyoming
Minor Child	California, Nebraska, Utah, Wisconsin

Report—To Whom

Most confused and confusing are the great differences in defining who or what agency receives the report of child abuse. This is the most sensitive area in the whole concept of reporting legislation. Designating the agency which can most effectively act on behalf of the abused child is crucial. Unless the child is protected, immediately and constructively, in terms of his future well-being, the reporting law may accomplish nothing. Differences in this connection are shown in Table B.

TABLE B

State	Report Directed To
Alabama, Alaska, Idaho, Massachusetts, Nevada, New Hampshire, New	State Dept. of Welfare or County Dept. of Welfare

*See *Suggested State Legislation, 1965*, developed by the Committee of State Officials on Suggested State Legislation, the Council of State Governments, pp. 66-68.

TABLE B—Continued

State	Report Directed To
York, Rhode Island, Wyoming	
Colorado, Georgia, Illinois, North Carolina, Utah	Dept. of Welfare or Police & Sheriff
Indiana, Maine, Michigan	Dept. of Public Welfare or County Prosecutor
Pennsylvania	Dept. of Public Welfare or Juvenile Court
North Dakota	Department of Public Welfare, Juvenile Court or Prosecutor
Iowa	Dept. of Public Welfare, Police or Prosecutor
Oklahoma	Dept. of Public Welfare, Juvenile Court, Police or Prosecutor
Arizona, Arkansas, Kentucky, Louisiana, Maryland, Minnesota, Missouri, Ohio, South Carolina, Washington	Police or Sheriff
Vermont, Wisconsin, California	Police or Prosecutor
Montana, Nebraska, New Jersey, New Mexico, West Virginia	Prosecutor
Texas	Police, Juvenile Court or Prosecutor
Florida, Kansas, Tennessee, Delaware, South Dakota	Juvenile Court or Family Court
Oregon	Medical Investigator
Connecticut	Health Dept., Welfare Dept., and Police

Compulsory or Permissive—Immunity

The purpose of the law as proposed by interested national organizations, is to mandate reporting. Permissive laws may promote reporting by providing immunity for those who do report, but are obviously not as far-reaching as the mandatory measures. Legislation of the permissive type has been adopted in Alaska, Missouri, New Mexico, North Carolina, Texas and Washington.

Wisconsin's act does not provide immunity to those who make reports. California lacked this element in its 1963 law, but a 1965 amendment added it.

Waiver of Privileged Communications

States which did not incorporate waiver of the doctor-patient or the husband-wife privilege are listed in Table C.

TABLE C

No doctor-patient waiver	California, Connecticut, Georgia, Illinois, Kansas, Massachusetts, Michigan, Minnesota, Rhode Island, South Carolina, Tennessee, West Virginia, Wyoming.
No husband-wife waiver	Alabama, California, Connecticut, Florida, Georgia, Illinois, Kansas, Massachusetts, Michigan, Minnesota, Montana, New Jersey, New Mexico, New York, Oklahoma, Pennsylvania, Rhode Island, South Carolina, Tennessee, South Dakota, West Virginia, Wisconsin, Wyoming.

NOT THE END OF THE PROBLEM

Mandatory reporting legislation does not end the problem of child abuse. It is only a tool for discovering and identifying the child who is abused.

The legislation only makes a beginning. States and communities must be prepared to implement the case-finding law by developing the full complement of services necessary to treat the problem. They must provide the funds for adequate staffing of child protective programs and the specialized treatment resources to aid protective agencies in rehabilitating these families or, when indicated, in planning care for abused children away from their homes.

Role of the Police in the Protection of Children From Neglect and Abuse

By Lynn D. Swanson

*Consultant on Specialized Police Services for Children and Youth, Technical Aid Branch
Division of Juvenile Delinquency Service, U. S. Children's Bureau*

DEPENDENCY AND NEGLECT cases in the United States totaled 124,000 in 1958. These cases increased by 9 percent between 1957 and 1958.[1] Preliminary data for 1959 indicate a further increase of about 3 percent to a total of 128,000 in that year. Thus, the upward trend which began in 1951 and occurred in each subsequent year, except 1956, continues. Other than those reaching the court, additional cases were dealt with by certain community agencies without referral to court.

Throughout the country, services for neglected and abused children may be provided by a variety of community agencies, such as child guidance and mental health clinics, family service and child welfare agencies, and recreational and other character-building agencies.

While it is generally recognized that police departments have an important function in protecting children who are neglected in most communities, no agreement has been reached by either police departments or community agencies as to the appropriate role of the police. Nor has there been effective coordination of police activities with activities of other agencies.

Because the role of the police in this area of community services has not been clearly defined, many questions arise. Should police officers receive and respond to complaints about neglected children? Are investigations of these complaints an appropriate function of the police? What constitutes an "evaluation" by the police? What should be the role of the police in taking children into custody and in using shelter care facilities? How can the police and community agencies work together in planning services for neglected and abused children?

The aim of this paper is to discuss certain aspects of neglect raised by these questions and to help clarify the role of the police in the community network of agencies working together to protect children from neglect and abuse. The areas to be discussed include: the investigation of neglect cases, referrals to community agencies, taking children into custody, use of shelter care, and community planning for the protection of children from neglect and abuse.

Traditional Role of the Police

Police officers are responsible for the protection of life and property and for the preservation of peace in the community. Specifically, they investigate, apprehend and bring to the attention of appropriate prosecuting officials persons who have been involved in criminal offenses, both felonies and misdemeanors. In addition, the police have regulatory activities, such as directing vehicular and pedestrian traffic and inspecting a variety of licensed establishments.

The Police Role in Cases of Neglect

Generally, the role of the police in cases of neglect can be broken down into receiving and investigating, verifying, evaluating, and disposing of complaints.

Receiving and Investigating Complaints.—Situations involving neglect of children usually are brought to the attention of the police by someone other than the parents. Other instances of neglect are observed by the police responding to other complaints, such as domestic disturbances. Many of these complaints concern children caught in the middle of family crises such as destitution, loss of the home, violent fights of parents, and parents who threaten suicide. These crises often lead to children being left alone, locked in closets, undernourished, or severely beaten. The following examples are typical of the many complaints received each year by the police throughout the country:

Responded to a complaint concerning three children, ages 2 to 6, left alone in a parked car for several hours. Observation indicated that the children were dirty and unkempt, cold and hungry, poorly clothed and in need of medical care.

Responded to a domestic disturbance where drinking parents had been fighting. Children were frightened and appeared to be abused by parents. The home was in disorder.

Responded to a complaint about several children, ages 3 to 7, left alone in a small apartment for several hours. Complaint indicated that this situation was not new but was being reported to an official agency for the first time.

A variety of sources point out the authority and responsibility of the police for receiving and responding to complaints of the type illustrated.

These authorities[2] see the police department as an appropriate agency investigating complaints of this type, filing petitions for court hearings, and referring cases to community welfare agencies. They recognize that police procedures in cases of neglect are in many respects similar to those used in cases of delinquency and that the investigation of offenses is primarily a police function. Another authority states that the police are permanently in the field of child protection since no other community service is organized to perform all of the functions of the police in relation to neglect and abuse.[3]

A certain amount of overlapping is evident in regard to the police departments and community agencies receiving and responding to complaints of neglect. A question can be raised whether the police department or any other community agency can handle, by itself, all complaints of neglect which arise in a community. Neglect is not confined to an 8-hour day. Just because the police department is the only agency with responsibilities in this area that is open 24 hours a day and 7 days a week, it should not be expected to deal with all complaints of neglect. However, the police department is probably in the best position to respond to emergency complaints of neglect where children are in immediate danger since it provides continuous service and has the means to move into such a situation without delay. On the other hand, complaints which appear to be chronic or nonemergency in nature should be referred directly to the community agency providing service in this area.

To insure an effective program, police departments and community agencies need to work together to coordinate their efforts in responding to complaints about neglect and alternative methods might be c ceiving and responding to such c these are a central referral un tions by the police and commu provisions for joint consultation.

Verifying Complaints.—The initial question which should concern the police in responding to reported complaints of abuse or neglect of a child is: Does neglect or abuse exist? This fact should be established by a proficient police investigation, based upon knowledge of the law and of the offenses governed by law, rules of evidence, and previous police experience in handling such complaints. Methods to gather evidence include statements of witnesses and complainant, interviews with parents and children, and general observation.

"A variety of sources point out the authority and responsibility of the police for receiving and responding to complaints of the type illustrated. These authorities see the police department as an appropriate agency investigating complaints of this type, filing petitions for court hearings, and referring cases to community welfare agencies. They recognize that police procedures in cases of neglect are in many respects similar to those used in cases of delinquency and that the investigation of offenses is primarily a police function. Another authority states that the police are permanently in the field of child protection since no other community service is organized to perform all of the functions of the police in relation to neglect and abuse."

Obvious cases of abuse or neglect can be verified immediately by observation. In cases less obvious, more facts and information may be needed before the complaint can be verified. Unsubstantiated cases of abuse or neglect should be closed after the police officer completes his investigation.

Evaluating Complaints.—After observing and investigating home conditions and discussing the case with the family and witnesses, an evaluation of the situation is made by the police officer. This evaluation includes those aspects of the case regarded as legally and socially significant; the seriousness of the situation, the need for immediate protection of the child, observations concerning the physical condition of the child, attitudes of parents, statements of witnesses, and general conditions of the home. This evaluation is not a social history—since it differs in purpose, scope, and degree—but is simply a process for arriving at police disposition.

emergency or chronic cases of abuse or neglect present a more difficult problem since many of the factors causing neglect are less obvious and generally require a more skilled diagnosis. Police officers should refer these cases to other community agencies after the initial investigation. Ordinarily, such cases might more appropriately be referred to a community agency in the first instance.

Disposing of the Case.—Generally, a police officer has discretion in disposing of complaints that have to do with neglect of children. One reason for this is that he is concerned not only with violations of law but also with the welfare of the persons involved. Dispositions generally fall into the following four categories:

Case Closed, No Further Action Needed.—A number of cases can be closed by warning or reprimand. Generally, the release from further police involvement, with or without a reprimand, is regarded as a final police disposition. Based upon the information contained in the evaluation, certain cases can be disposed of at the home or at the station. An officer may indicate to the parents or other persons involved the possible repercussions in the event that the act is repeated. In addition, "on the spot" suggestions or appropriate educational material may be given to the family.

Before disposing of certain cases, the officer generally should check records of the police department and, in some cases, may also contact other community agencies to determine whether the family has been known previously. In any event, adequate records should be maintained regarding the complaint, facts of the investigation, and the police disposition.

Referral of Case to Police Unit Specializing in Children's Cases.—Making a disposition in some neglect situations may be quite difficult. Many complex factors may be involved. In addition, the patrol force, being limited by scope of assignment, tour of duty and confinement to a patrol area, may be unable to make a disposition in certain cases. Many of these cases must be investigated more thoroughly to obtain additional facts and social information before a sound police disposition can be made. When an officer is uncertain as to the best disposition of a case, he should be able to request assistance from, or refer the case directly to, a juvenile unit in the police department having specialized functions and competence to deal with cases of families and children. Police departments in rural and semirural areas oftentimes do not have the services of special police juvenile units. Therefore, when confronted with difficult neglect situations, these officers should seek advice from whatever resources are available such as welfare and probation departments, private social agencies or visiting teachers.

Such special juvenile police units should be trained to refer these families to appropriate community resources. In police departments which do not have these specialized units, one officer often is assigned this responsibility, which may be in addition to his regular duties.

Referral to Community Agencies.—When an officer believes that court action is not necessary, but that certain factors indicate the need for some kind of help, he should refer the case to the appropriate community agency. Referrals to such agencies for service or care should be made only with the consent of the child's parents. Primarily, these cases would be minor, chronic or nonemergency in nature. In departments having juvenile police specialists, one of these officers should have the responsibility for handling referrals to community agencies. Agreements on type of cases to be referred and methods of referrals should be developed between the police department and the social agencies in the community.

Referral to Juvenile or Family Court.—The police should always refer cases of neglect and abuse to the court when a child is removed from his home and placed in a shelter care facility. Most of these children either have been abandoned, are without care or supervision or are in situations of immediate danger to their health or welfare. Even where it is not necessary to remove the child from his home, certain cases may need to be referred to the court.

Generally, the police are required by statute to refer to court children taken into custody and placed in shelter care. Exceptions would be lost children or children whose parents have left their homes for a short time. In any event, when the police believe official action is necessary, the child's case should be referred to court. From that point on, the court should assume responsibility.

Taking Children Into Custody

Taking children into custody is primarily a

police function. By law, the police have the responsibility and authority to take immediate custody of children in danger of violence or serious injury. This authority may also be vested in other administrative agencies, such as a society for prevention of cruelty to children. Usually, such an agency is granted this authority by law.[4]

In any event, persons having the responsibility for taking children into custody or for arresting parents involved in neglect situations should be informed concerning the laws covering such action, including the law of arrest; instructed in the use of force and as to the limits of force; trained in self-protection in order to minimize the danger to themselves and the public in certain situations, such as when confronted with intoxicated and mentally deranged persons; and trained to decide whether a criminal charge can be taken against an adult. Generally, the police have this knowledge and training, as well as the responsibility to take this action.

"All communities should have some type of shelter care facility to take care of children in emergency situations. The lack of such a facility presents a serious problem in many communities, often resulting in children having to be held in detention homes or jails. Every effort should be made by the police to find suitable temporary care through an appropriate community agency."

When questions arise as to the need to take a child into custody, the police, if possible, should consult with social agencies about the desirability of such action. Distinction should be made between the desirability of taking children into custody and statutory grounds for such action. The police cannot take children into custody merely upon the request of an individual or a social agency. They must determine whether sufficient grounds exist for such action. Since the police have the responsibility and authority, the final decision to take children into custody must rest with them. Where another community agency has such powers conferred upon it by law, that agency may, of course, also take such action.

Not all children taken into custody by the police must come under the jurisdiction of the court. Exceptions are lost children and children left alone because of emergency family situations, such as hospitalization of one or both parents. Such children may be held temporarily pending arrangements by the parents for permanent care or return home.

Statutes of some states provide certain safeguards governing the process by which children are placed in shelter care. For example, a number of state juvenile court statutes are similar to the *Standard Family and Juvenile Court Acts* which provide that the officer or other person who brings a child to a detention or shelter facility shall at once give notice to the court and that no child shall be held in detention or shelter care longer than 24 hours, excluding Sundays and holidays, unless a petition has been filed.[5]

All communities should have some type of shelter care facility to take care of children in emergency situations. The lack of such a facility presents a serious problem in many communities, often resulting in children having to be held in detention homes or jails. Every effort should be made by the police to find suitable temporary care through an appropriate community agency.

"When an officer believes that court action is not necessary, but that certain factors indicate the need for some kind of help, he should refer the case to the appropriate community agency. Referrals to such agencies for service or care should be made only with the consent of the child's parents. Primarily, these cases would be minor, chronic or nonemergency in nature. In departments having juvenile police specialists, one of these officers should have the responsibility for handling referrals to community agencies. Agreements on type of cases to be referred and methods of referrals should be developed between the police department and the social agencies in the community."

When proper shelter care facilities are not available, the police often attempt to find relatives or friends of the family to care for the children temporarily. Unless the relative's or friend's home is approved for temporary placement by an agency, police officers should be cautious about such placements. In some instances, that action has led to children being exposed to additional risks of neglect or personal injury. An alternative is to hold the child temporarily in a facility, such as a sheriff's home.

Handling of Adults Involved in Abuse and Neglect Situations

Police officers should be permitted to exercise some discretion with respect to referring parents for prosecution in cases of neglect. Often, cases which at first appear to involve willful neglect may not be so judged after all the facts become available and are evaluated. These cases might be referred to a community agency, such as a family or child welfare agency. In any event, police action in cases of neglect of children by parents should be based, insofar as possible, on the fact that "the continuing relationship between child and parent will need to be taken into consideration in deciding whether or not the adult is to be charged."[6] In many communities, the juvenile court staff is available to advise as to the desirability of such action.

Community Planning of Services for Neglected Children

Every community needs an adequate program for the protection of children from neglect and abuse. The police, the court and other community agencies involved must all take part in the necessary planning.

Some progress in this area has been reported. For example, the police and social agencies in one community reached agreements regarding the type of cases to be referred by the police and accepted for treatment by the social agencies. Another community has a police officer assigned to a social agency with the responsibility for investigating certain complaints of neglect. Still another community is using a joint police-social worker investigation of neglect complaints. This service is available both day and night.

Further study and research is needed to evaluate the effectiveness of such programs. Nevertheless, these experiments do indicate a spirit of cooperation among agencies. Such cooperation does not happen overnight. Working agreements among the community agencies and departments come about only after many conferences and much effort. These agreements usually lead to understanding of the philosophies and goals of

> "When questions arise as to the need to take a child into custody, the police, if possible, should consult with social agencies about the desirability of such action. Distinction should be made between the desirability of taking children into custody and statutory grounds for such action. The police cannot take children into custody merely upon the request of an individual or a social agency. They must determine whether sufficient grounds exist for such action. Since the police have the responsibility and authority, the final decision to take children into custody must rest with them. Where another community agency has such powers conferred upon it by law, that agency may, of course, also take such action."

all the agencies involved, frank discussion of issues hampering effective coordination of services, and flexibility in administrative policy and

direction in developing experimental pilot projects.

Although some progress is being made in coordinating community programs for neglected children, still in many communities throughout the United States the only service for the protection of children from neglect and abuse is provided by the law-enforcement agency. The degree or manner in which this protection is exercised varies from community to community.

> "Although some progress is being made in coordinating community programs for neglected children, still in many communities throughout the United States the only service for the protection of children from neglect and abuse is provided by the law-enforcement agency. The degree of manner in which this protection is exercised varies from community to community."

Much more work needs to be done to standardize law-enforcement services for neglected children. And even before that, a common philosophy in regard to cases of neglect needs to be adopted by all the police, from the recruit to the experienced officer. In addition, basic police training should provide all police officers with more knowledge and skills to work with children and families. Police officers having specialized duties in this area should have intensive training.

But more is needed to assure protection of children from abuse and neglect than well-trained and qualified law-enforcement officers. Important as this is, an effective program is not possible without teamwork with the court and other community agencies—teamwork brought about by mutual recognition of and respect for the contribution each agency makes to protect abused and neglected children.

[1] *Juvenile Court Statistics, 1958.* Statistical Series No. 57. Washington, D.C. Children's Bureau, U. S. Department of Health, Education, and Welfare, 1960, p. 5.

[2] *Standards for Specialized Courts Dealing with Children.* Children's Bureau Publication No. 346. Washington, D.C.: Government Printing Office. 1954. p. 11; *Child Welfare Services.* Children's Bureau Publication No. 359. Washington, D.C.: Government Printing Office. 1957. p. 11; John P. Kenny and Dan G. Pursuit, *Police Work with Juveniles,* 2nd ed. Springfield, Illinois: Charles C. Thomas Publisher. 1959. p. 260; *Municipal Police Administration.* 4th ed. Chicago: International City Managers Association. 1954. p. 1.

[3] "Neglect, Social Deviance, and Community Action," *NPPA Journal,* Vol. 6, No. 1, January 1960, p. 22.

[4] *Standards for Specialized Courts Dealing with Children,* p. 45.

[5] *Standard Family and Juvenile Court Acts.* Article IV, Section 16. New York: National Probation and Parole Association. April and October 1957. p. 129 and p. 357.

[6] *Police Services for Juveniles,* Children's Bureau Publication No. 344. Washington, D. C.: U. S. Government Printing Office, 1954. p. 36.

Procedural Problems Inhibiting Effective County and Community-Wide Resolution of Battered Child Problems

By O. J. Tocchio

ABOUT THE AUTHOR: *Prior to entering the field of criminology as a professor, Doctor Tocchio spent thirteen years in law enforcement in Quincy, Massachusetts. Through both field experience and advanced education, he has dealt with every facet of police work including: patrol, criminal investigation, personal identification, criminalistics, traffic, vice, juvenile procedures, communications and records, training and administration, and retail and industrial security.*

The author has taught at The American University, Washington State University, and at his present position at Fresno State College. At The American University, he was instrumental in the development of the police program, and was its first Instructor.

During the past fifteen years, Doctor Tocchio has been a consultant, researcher, author and lecturer on numerous police problems. He has been awarded recognition in Pi Sigma Alpha, National Political Science Honorary; Chi Psi Omega, Honorary Academic Fraternity for Graduate students; Alpha Phi Sigma, Honorary Police Science Fraternity, Who's Who Among Students in Colleges and Universities; Who's Who In American Education, and Who's Who In The West. Amongst his professional affiliations are: The International Association of Chiefs of Police, The California Police Officer's Association, and the Knights of Columbus.

In examining the legal and functional procedures presently being utilized in Fresno County, California, for the effective control and resolution of the "battered child syndrome," it became immediately apparent that those legal limitations and procedural barriers to more effective county and community-wide resolution of this problem in California do not differ markedly from those noted among the writings of other authorities concerned with this tragic problem, both in the United States and throughout the world. Although several of the problems outlined in this writer's doctoral dissertation[1] have already been somewhat resolved through the tireless efforts of a conscientious Fresno County Battered Child Committee, and through the efforts of members of state and local organizations throughout California who have labored for the passage of badly needed child abuse legislation, additional problems inhibiting a more effective resolution of this problem continue to exist. Because it is certain that problems, identical to those discovered through Fresno County's attempt at an interdisciplinary approach to the battered child syndrome, exist not only in the United States but also in other parts of the world, it seems appropriate that data regarding the problems discovered in Fresno County be delineated here for the express purpose of aiding others involved with this problem to meet their objectives of its control and probable resolution.

PROBLEMS CONFRONTING THE PROBATION DEPARTMENT AND THE JUVENILE COURT

Although there are numerous legal limitations and procedural barriers inhibiting the Juvenile Court and the Probation Department in Fresno County from effectively controlling and eradicating child abuse problems in this county, it became apparent during the early stages of the study that one of the most significant problems confronting the staff of the County Probation Department was the lack of continuity of policy and procedures among Juvenile Court judges in the Juvenile Court system for handling this particular type of case. Therefore, in order to effectively delineate this and other problems confronting probation officers, it became necessary to discuss these two units of government together, so that one might be shown how these problems affected both the court and the probation officer, and that it was often difficult to maintain *esprit de corps* among them. Thus, the first problem needing examination and resolution is the changing philosophy of the Juvenile Court,

---

[1] Tocchio, Octavio J.: *Legislation and Law Enforcement in California For the Protection of the Physically Battered Child.* dissertation unpublished, American University, Washington, D. C., 1967.

Address: Doctor O. J. Tocchio, Department of Criminology, Fresno State College, Fresno, California 93726.

with its yearly turnover of judges. Nowhere, perhaps, has the underlying philosophy of this court been stated in more beautiful language than in the court opinion repeatedly quoted in a California appeal decision from *The People v Superior Court*, 104 Cal. App., 276, 282 which states:

> From its very nature, and because of necessary qualifications for doing the work for which it is intended, the Juvenile Court is not designated as a trial court in the ordinary sense. Not only is its purpose more reformative than punitive, but its method of operation is very different from that of a criminal court. Technicalities and formalities are largely done away with and its simple procedure is designed to gain the confidence of those coming within its operations, and to enable the judge thereof to best guide and control its wards, with more consideration for their future development than for their shortcomings. The circumstances attendant upon contested jury trials are not only out of place there, but might have an injurious effect not only upon the methods, but upon the atmosphere and confidence that have been built up around the work of the Juvenile Court, and which are so largely responsible for its success.

Thus, for nearly seventy years, the Juvenile Courts continued to solidify their acceptance of the judicial pattern of *parens patriae* in sharp contrast with adult proceedings, even though judges in certain areas were selected from the bench on a semi-permanent basis, while others rotated among members of the judiciary, none wanting to accept the responsibility on a full-time basis. In addition, some courts were provided with referees to assist these judges, and in larger operations, probation services were made a part of the court's function. Then, in 1961, a new pattern, beginning in the East and South, began to take shape on the west coast, long a leader in juvenile work and a stronghold of the Juvenile Courts and Probation Departments. California, like other western states, adopted what is in reality an adult criminal process for juveniles (incorporating all of the safeguards of the criminal court) in place of the *parens patriae* (which held the judge to be a wise and kindly parent acting in the child's best interests). In addition, this unique operation includes a full-blown adversary proceeding, without a criminal conviction possible, with counsel provided for the juvenile, but no provision for a prosecutor. Herein lies part of the problem or conflict which confronts agencies wishing to take Juvenile Court action to protect abused and battered children.

With this yearly turnover of judges and these policies in the Juvenile Court, probation officers subject to these policies are further placed in the position of having to revise their procedures to bring them into alignment with this yearly turnover. This, of course, defeats the principle or process of policy making, that is, policy should be more or less continuous, being changed gradually rather than suddenly. How an agency such as the Department of Probation can function adequately with the uncertainty of yearly turnover in policy, is difficult to comprehend. Nevertheless, it must be done and with a degree of effectiveness. It is expected by those looking to probation for the services needed. A program implemented under one judge may very quickly be curtailed by another, but when one is asked about the value of a permanent Juvenile Court judge, the respondent almost shudders at the thought. Perhaps the court may not be as well off as one would think under the yearly turnover rule, but it may very well be the lesser of two evils. But, the problem of a lack of standard operating procedures for neglected, abused, and battered children remains. Research is definitely needed to rectify this dilemma, and should be conducted before changes in the present system for selection and tenure of Juvenile Court judges is altered.

This lack of continuity of Juvenile Court philosophy due to the yearly turnover in judicial assignments, brings up the second problem confronting the probation officer and centers around the means by which continuity of philosophy and procedures can be maintained, especially in the handling of child battery or maltreatment problems. In an attempt to maintain some concept of continuity of procedure by which these problems can be effectively controlled, probation officers find themselves more inclined to bring their problems to the attention of the Juvenile Court referee rather than to the new Juvenile Court judge, since the referee represents the only continuity of philosophy found within the court system. This presents another dilemma in the system, since a number of Juvenile Court referees do not have a legal background, even though many of them have an accumulation of years of experience in the handling of juvenile matters. Although this experience is recognized, there are certain probation officers and deputy probation officers who wonder whether or not Juvenile Court referees should be held responsible for child abuse cases, especially those of the type and severity seen in Fresno and other counties and cities throughout the nation.

During the first year of the Fresno County Battered Child Committee deliberations, 1963, it became apparent that a third problem which confronted juvenile probation officers, as well as the police, was the problem of obtaining petitions in the Juvenile Court under the *Cali-*

fornia Welfare and Institutions Code, Section 600(b).[2] Petitions are difficult to obtain even in situations where officers have felt that sufficient evidence existed that the child in question was living in a home "unfit for him because of neglect, cruelty and depravity" on the part of one or both of his parents. Most of the members of the Committee could not understand why this difficulty existed. Nevertheless, it did exist, and the only answer given was that the Juvenile Court judge simply could not be convinced that the case definitely required the filing of a petition under this section of the Code. On other occasions, the same applied to W.I.C., Section 600(a).[3] Presently, however, philosophy appears to have changed due to the activities of the Battered Child Committee (whose membership contains officials from the six key agencies responsible for child protection in the county), and the more adequate presentation of cases by the agencies so involved. This was evidenced by the fact that there was a more even distribution of petitions to the Juvenile Court in the following year under both sections of this code. One thing is certain, and that is that counties and cities experiencing similar problems must re-examine existing child legislation, and update this legislation with the protection of the battered child in mind.

Another problem confronting both the probation officer and the Juvenile Court, as well as the Criminal Courts in the county is the problem of psychiatric examination and therapy for aggressive parents in child abuse cases. In the Juvenile Court, examination and therapy for the parent is strongly encouraged, but inadequate funds and facilities make this practically impossible. Some demonstration of the effectiveness of such therapy might convince the County Administrative Officer and other county officials that this would be a valid expenditure of county funds. Nevertheless, even with the recent enactment of the Short-Doyle Act in California, and the allocation of federal funds to the counties for local programs in mental hygiene, no program has as yet been established to include treatment for battering parents or guardians. At the present time, very little is known as to whether or not these programs will eventually include battered child problems in Fresno and other counties, since the entire Act has not as yet been implemented. Definite legislation requiring psychiatric examination and therapy for aggressive parents in child abuse cases, with accompanying funds for staff and facilities, is badly needed for the handling of and resolution of child abuse problems.

---

[2]Welfare and Institutions Code, Section 600 (b).

[3]Welfare and Institutions Code, Section 600 (a).

Another problem confronting the probation officer, child welfare caseworker, and the Juvenile Court judge is evidence that a battering parent or guardian has been satisfactorily rehabilitated, and is now capable of resuming the caliber of custody and control which will assure these practitioners that a previously traumatized child will not suffer repeated trauma. This is important because of the high mortality rate in battered child cases, and because children who have been prematurely returned to such parents have suffered repeated trauma and death. Practitioners need to assure themselves that abused children will return to a safe and healthy home environment.

During the yearly review of the case, the probation officer and the court must look for a definite change in the family life of the parent or guardian batterer that will give them assurance of improved treatment of the child to be returned to his custody. Resolving this problem will not be easy, since it has been shown that much research is still needed in this particular aspect of child abuse. At the present time, it has been extremely difficult to place the kind of evidence before the court that can prove that battering parents or guardians have been adequately rehabilitated or can ever be rehabilitated.

PROBLEMS CONFRONTING POLICE AGENCIES

Among the police problems which presently exist are: First, the need for adequate training of patrolmen, deputies and constables in the ramifications of the battered child syndrome, since these officers often make the first contact with abused and maltreated children. Second, the need to develop specific juvenile unit policies within police agencies so that the personnel of these units can take the leadership in the establishment of crime prevention programs within the community complex. This can result in the development of a combined community effort of preventing both initial and repeated incidents of child abuse. Third, the need to encourage both public and private social work agencies to assist law enforcement personnel in controlling and resolving child battery and maltreatment, especially when and where child protective services do not presently exist. Fourth, the need to keep abreast of existing inadequacies in legislation relative to this problem. Fifth, the need to develop inter-agency procedures and extra-departmental planning for countywide protection of abused and maltreated children.

PROBLEMS CONFRONTING THE FRESNO GENERAL HOSPITAL

The establishment of a Central Index File System at Fresno General Hospital greatly aided the hospital staff in resolving some of the problems which existed at this hospital prior to the establishment of the system. Other problems, however, still remain. Among these are: First, the loss of valuable summary data for its central index due to the substitution of a Battered Child Card File in the Probation Department for the extensive summary case file at the County Hospital. Second, the uncertainty as to whether the Battered Child Committee has completed its objectives and should be disbanded, or whether it should now go into another and much needed phase of research, namely, the rehabilitation of battering parents and guardians. Although the battered child syndrome is a parent-child dysfunction, most of the research has centered upon the abused child, with little or no research being conducted on the parents in these cases. Third, conflicts in authority often arise between medical prognoses and *Welfare and Institutions Code* procedures, especially relative to the length of time a physician may hold a child in a hospital for medical care. Fourth, county hospitals need to know what to do about battered children who remain in the hospital when medical attention is no longer needed, and the parent, guardian, welfare social caseworker, or other responsible party fails to retrieve the child. Fifth, a need exists to keep county, city, and private medical practitioners apprised of the most recent changes in the battered child syndrome and its ramifications, thereby encouraging greater interest in reporting incidents of child abuse.

PROBLEMS CONFRONTING THE WELFARE DEPARTMENT

Among the chief problems confronting the social caseworkers at the Department of Public Welfare are the difficulty in locating adequate foster homes for battered, abused, and maltreated children, and the difficulty of encouraging suitable parents to assist in these programs; lack of adequate staff to handle the tremendous caseloads presently in need of social casework; the need for orientation and training of social workers who will handle most of the child battery cases; and the great need for legislation which will make it mandatory for each state to establish county or statewide Child Protective Services Agencies to handle child battery and related problems affecting infants and minors, thereby absorbing some of the caseload presently burdening social welfare workers in the county.

When it is noted that intensive helping efforts over a period of time fail to change the behavior patterns of battering parents or guardians, especially those who show little concern over the problems facing their children, it may become necessary to reassess parental ability and willingness to give proper care to the child, and it may then be necessary to use the authority of the Juvenile Court. Such use of the court, however, should not be regarded as a threat or a punitive measure, but as another supportive technique to help parents face the reality consequences of their behavior.[4]

Where a lack of progress is determined after a period of time, this may be indicative of deeper seated problems in the child or parent, or in their interaction. Here, the caseworker and court may need to determine first, whether psychiatric treatment is needed by either; second, whether institutional care is needed; and third, whether temporary placement of the child outside of the home is indicated. Where there is resistance to the child's removal, the court must take action to protect the child.[5]

Where satisfactory protection for the battered and maltreated child cannot be assured through foster home placement, social casework assistance, satisfactory reha-

TABLE I

PRESENT APPROACH TO PUNITIVE AND PROTECTIVE ACTION IN CHILD BATTERY CASES

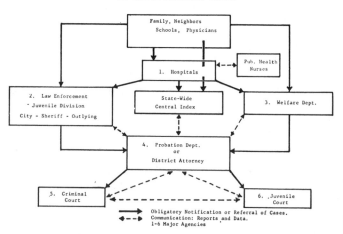

bilitation through psychiatric examination and therapy, or any other means which will assure effective and lasting protection for these children, every effort must be made to seek the best means available for the permanent separation of parent and child, and placement of the child for adoption. This needs to be accomplished even if it means that specific legislation must be enacted in order to enhance the life of the abused child. Otherwise, the ultimate results may be the homicide of the

---

[4]Wald, Max: *Protective Services and Emotional Neglect.* Children's Division, The American Humane Association, Denver, 1961, p. 13.

[5]*Ibid.*, pp. 13-14.

child, as has already been noted in cases throughout the nation as well as in California.

Experience in both Metropolitan Los Angeles and Fresno County, as well as an examination of nationally conducted studies, has shown that the prosecution of aggressive parent or guardian batterers, in most cases, is neither the best solution for correcting existing parental behavior in battered child cases, nor a satisfactory means of protecting the vicim of parentally inflicted trauma. Although other communities in California and throughout the nation may employ any of a variety of methods for protecting its children from severe child abuse, Fresno and Los Angeles have altered prior methods of handling this problem in favor of taking punitive and protective actions in both criminal and juvenile courts simultaneously. To insure more adequate protection of their charges, these communities have developed a system of inter-agency dialogue through which more effective resolution of child battery cases may be engendered. The diagram in Table I[6] shows how this system of interdisciplinary dialogue is currently maintained.

Although it appears that both communities agree that greater protection for battered and maltreated children can be assured by referral of child abuse cases to a Child Protective Services' agency or a Humane Association, such an agency does not presently exist in California, even though legislation has recently been enacted to establish Protective Services within the State's Counties.

TABLE II
PREFFERED APPROACH TO PROTECTIVE ACTION IN CHILD BATTERY CASES

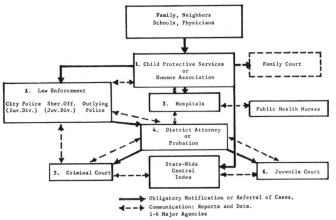

Table II[7] snows how cases ought to be referred through this agency to other agencies, and to the courts when necessary. Because of the apparent legal and procedural barriers which exist in both the punitive and protective approaches presently in use in Fresno County, neither system is as highly effective in the resolution of the

problem as one would like to see them. Nevertheless, of the two court systems, the Juvenile Court appears to have been more effective than the criminal court system in resolving child abuse in this county within the past several years. To strengthen either or both systems, however, thereby making both of them more effective as a means of controlling and eventually resolving the battered child syndrome in this and other counties in California, or throughout the nation, either revision of existing legislation, a more effective enforcement of existing legislation, or both, become paramount in importance.

Perhaps another solution to this unfortunate problem and its present dilemmas can be found in the following quotation by a past chairman of the Fresno County Battered Child Committee, a well-informed former Sergeant of the Juvenile Division of the Sheriff's Office. In the words of Christopher Flammang, Instructor, Fresno City College Police Program:

> At present, I do not believe that the Juvenile Court with its probation supervision or the prosecution of the offender is necessarily adequate as a resolution of the battered child syndrome. Nor do I believe that protective legislation should come under this Penal Code. In answer to the dilemma facing practitioners in this State attempting to resolve the problem of child abuse, I envision new legislation with an informal judicial hearing wherein both the adult offender and the traumatized child would be handled within the setting of a new court.[8]

CONCLUSIONS

An examination of procedures in Fresno County for handling cases of battered and maltreated children revealed that among the problems confronting practitioners and community leaders in this county were the following:

(1) The effect of annual replacement of Juvenile Court judges on the operating procedures of the Probation Department, and on the effective disposition of child abuse cases.

(2) The wisdom of allowing untrained and unqualified Juvenile Court Referees to adjudicate child abuse cases, even when this may be the only means by which continuity of policy may be maintained between the Probation Department and the Juvenile Court.

(3) The feasibility of providing psychiatric examinations and therapy for psychologically and physically battered children.

(4) The kinds of data needed by Juvenile Court judges, probation officers, and child welfare workers prior to the yearly review to determine whether or not

[6]See Table 1.

[7]See Table II.

[8]Statement taken from questionnaire on Battered Child, with respondent's permission.

the batterer has been satisfactorily rehabilitated and is capable of resuming the care and custody of his child.

(5) The means by which other hospitals throughout California and the nation can be encouraged to examine and perhaps adopt the procedures for handling battered child cases as presently utilized by Fresno General Hospital.

(6) The resolution of conflicts between necessary in-hospital medical care and legal technicalities in state laws, especially when such conflicts may hinder satisfactory completion of medical attention in child battery cases.

(7) The desirability of encouraging California and other counties and metropolitan areas throughout the nation confronted with child abuse problems to both examine and give serious thought to adopting an approach similar to Fresno County's system for handling child battery and maltreatment cases.

(8) The desirability of encouraging and supporting both initial and continued research relative to child abuse, battery and maltreatment by professional committee action throughout the nation, as had been done in Fresno County, California, by the Battered Child Committee.

(9) The desirability of encouraging both public welfare and probation to increase the quantity and quality of their personnel, so that both agencies will be in a better position to handle and supervise present and future child battery cases.

(10) The means by which public and private physicians and other practitioners can be encouraged to become more aware of child battery problems in their communities, thereby being in a better position to make more referrals to the statewide central index.

(11) The means by which Fresno and other counties and cities throughout the nation can obtain a sufficient number of foster home and other placement centers for abused children, and the means by which public support regarding this problem might be engendered.

(12) The desirability of encouraging legislation which will both establish and implement Child Protective Services as needed in every state throughout the nation.

(13) The desirability of Fresno County, and other counties confronted with the problems of child abuse throughout the nation, undertaking a training program in the battered child syndrome for all county and city practitioners.

(14) The means by which private and public social welfare agencies might be encouraged more adequately to assist law enforcement agencies in the control, suppression, and eradication of child abuse problems.

(15) The conditions under which Fresno and other counties throughout the nation would utilize the grand jury, if necessary, to examine and make recommendations for the control and resolution of child battery and maltreatment.

(16) The clarification and resolution of those legal technicalities in the *California Welfare and Institutions Code,* Section 600, and comparable laws relating to children throughout the nation, which hinder satisfactory petitioning of the Juvenile Court in child abuse cases.

(17) The means by which procedures for the psychiatric examination and therapy of battering parents or guardians deemed rehabilitatible by the courts might be established and administered.

(18) The desirability of encouraging the development of juvenile unit policy geared toward crime prevention in the community complex, especially as this policy affects the prevention of child battery and maltreatment.

(19) The means by which county and city police administrators can be encouraged to upgrade investigative procedures for the collection and preservation of physical and scientific evidence in order to strengthen cases in which documentary evidence is either weak or difficult to obtain.

(20) The desirability of encouraging administrators to develop and maintain extra-departmental planning regarding child abuse problems, thereby increasing the effectiveness of a community-wide approach to this problem.

(21) The need to give serious thought to the recommendations of former Sergeant Christopher Flammang of the Fresno County Sheriff's Office, that what may be needed to resolve this problem is new legislation with an informal judicial hearing, wherein both the adult offender and the traumatized child would be handled within the setting of a new court.[9]

★★★

---

[9]*Ibid.*

SUMMARY

From the preceding articles, we have had glimpses into the complex role of the criminologist in relationship to child abuse. A number of observations can be made.

Child abuse is a continuing and increasing problem in the United States today.

It was not until the early 1960s that effective legislation for the protection of the children themselves and citizens who became involved with these children was enacted.

Detection and reports of child abuse must be made before children can benefit from the protection that was established by these laws.

Every state in the Union believes that its primary obligation is to the child even though each state has its own distinctive procedure used in handling child abuse cases.

Although some of the child abuse protection programs have certain weaknesses, most are strong in the use of interagency cooperation and a central registry file.

Child abuse is an existing and growing problem. It is one that feeds upon its predecessors: a child that is beaten or neglected very often develops into an adult who in turn neglects his child. The cycle appears to be vicious and unending. To break this cycle, the entire public, and especially the criminologist, must become more aware of the problem and must also be willing to become involved in order to protect these children.

STUDY QUESTIONS

1. Why is it necessary for educators, law enforcement agents, and medical personnel to understand the world of the abused child?

2. Should professional people be willing to become involved in child abuse cases? What obstacles deter them?

3. What is the proper procedure to follow if an educator or medical worker feels that he is working with an abused child?

4. Do educators, law enforcement agents, and medical personnel recognize the difference between abused and seriously injured children?

5. How can teachers and medical workers be made aware of the behavior signs of the abused child?

6. What particular contribution do law enforcement agents make in helping the battered child?

REFERENCES

A. Readings Included in This Text

DeFrancis, Vincent. "Laws for Mandatory Reporting of Child Abuse Cases." *State Government,* 39 (1966):8-13.

Felder, Samuel. "A Lawyer's View of Child Abuse." *Public Welfare,* 29 (1971):181-188.

Harper, Fowler V. "The Physician, The Battered Child, And The Law." *Pediatrics,* 31 (1963):899-902.

Paulsen, Mongrad G. "Legal Protection Against Child Abuse." *Children,* 13 (1966):42-48.

Silver, Larry B.; Barton, William; and Dublin, Christina C. "Child Abuse Laws—Are They Enough?" *American Medical Association Journal,* 199 (1967):65-68.

Swanson, Lynn D. "Role of the Police in the Protection of Children From Neglect and Abuse." *Federal Probation,* 25 (1961):43-48.

Tocchio, O. J. "Procedural Problems Inhibiting Effective County and Community-Wide Resolution of Battered Child Problems." *Police,* 14 (1970):16-21.

B. Suggested Additional Readings

Bechtold, M. L. "Silent Partner to a Parent's Brutality." *School and Community,* 52 (1965):33.

Foster, H. "Battered Child Legal and Professional Immunity." *American Bar Association Journal,* 52 (1966):1071-1073.

"Helping Physicians Protect Children; Illinois Law to Exempt Physicians from Libel Suits by Parents." *Christian Century,* 82 (1965):516.

Paulsen, Monrad G. *et al.* "Child Abuse Reporting Laws—Some Legislative History." *George Washington Law Review,* 34 (1966):482-506.

Paulsen, Monrad G. "Child Abuse Reporting Laws, the Shape of the Legislation." *Columbia Law Review,* 67 (1967):1-49.

Shepherd, Robert. "The Abused Child and the Law." *Washington and Lee Law Review,* 22 (1965):180-195.

IV

The Sociologist and Social Worker Take a Look

INTRODUCTION

The stereotyped child beater characteristically has been portrayed as coming from the low socioeconomic family group. These people are pictured as poor, uneducated, often slovenly parents who constantly batter their children. After World War II, research indicated that this stereotype was indeed an incorrect one. Studies now have established that a large number of child abusers also come from the middle and upper strata of our society as illustrated in the central part of this chapter.

Rather than having economic background in common, these parents have similar emotional and social problems usually stemming from inadequacies in their upbringing. In such cases the children soak up the suppressed feelings of their disturbed parents and in return are not able to give their own children the security, love, and safety that they themselves never had.

Originally, protection of children was primarily a law enforcement function. The objective was to protect children from parents by removing them from a hazardous situation; the agencies would also arrest, prosecute, and punish the parents. Today old methods and techniques are often criticized because of their emphasis on punitive action rather than on rehabilitation.

Public and voluntary child welfare agencies in a number of places have demonstrated that many parents can be helped to grow and improve in the care, protection, and guidance of their own children. When this happens, the child's own home is preserved and his family strengthened. In many cases some children may also be saved from delinquent behavior or from becoming neglectful parents themselves as will be seen in the readings of this chapter.

Social service for neglected or abused children and their parents is a basic child welfare service that should be available in every community throughout the country.

PAUL V. NYDEN *is Deputy Commissioner, Westchester County Department of Public Welfare, White Plains, New York. Mr. Nyden gave this paper at the Association's 1965 Northeast Regional Conference.*

The Use of Authority

In a society that has achieved the level of affluence and sophistication that ours has and in a period of history where we have made so much material and social progress, it seems incredible that it is necessary to address ourselves to this topic. Most people find it hard to believe that there are parents who severely neglect and abuse their children. When cases of severe child abuse are brought to light, the public becomes angered, demands punishment of such parents; thus many laws have been enacted with a punitive motivation. Parental abuse of children represents a complex area of human behavior, and it is our task to examine one aspect of the problem.

Before developing the central theme of this paper, I would like to review some historical facts relevant to our subject which, hopefully, will help set this presentation in proper perspective.

THE CHILD-PROTECTIVE PROGRAM

Having worked 17 years with a private child protective agency, I am most cognizant of the place of the private agency in the child protective movement and the role that it can still play. On the other hand, we must recognize that the provision of adequate child-protective services is such a vast task confronting our society that it cannot be done solely as a private or voluntary agency effort. It is a task that requires the agency organization, services, and funds available only in the public welfare setting. It is a task that quite properly should be supported by tax funds. We will not discuss the whole range of child-protective services today, but it must be clear that protecting children from abuse is part of child-protective services and that any program, whether private or public, must include services to the abused child among its protective services to children and families.

Although in the past many public welfare departments have overlooked the provision of child-protective services in their programs and even today the provision of adequate child-protective services is spotty, no one will quarrel with the concept that child-protective services should be part of every public child welfare service.

Child abuse is nothing new in human society, and its alleviation was not anything that was discovered yesterday. But it is only relatively recently that social workers as a group—public welfare workers, and others engaged in child welfare—have recognized the existence of the problem and are taking steps to meet it.

BEGINNINGS OF THE CHILD-PROTECTIVE MOVEMENT

In order to understand the setting for protective services, it is appropriate to refer to the beginnings of the child-protective movement. In 1874, in New York City, there occurred a flagrant instance of the brutal abuse of a little child who, in the absence of laws for the protection of children, was rescued and protected under the law providing protection for animals. As a result of the great publicity given this case, many similar cases were brought to the attention of the Society for the Protection of Animals, and it became apparent that there was need for a similar society to protect children. This need was met in 1875 by the formation of the New York Society for the Prevention of Cruelty to Children, the first such society in the world. On May 28, 1875, the first anti-cruelty case was initiated by the society and was prosecuted in the New York City Court of Special Sessions. A man by the name of Newell was tried, convicted of beating his son with a heavy whip, and sentenced to prison.

At the time of the establishment of the New York SPCC in 1875, there were no laws on the statute books in New York State, or elsewhere for that matter, specifically offering protection to children. It was a time when children were exploited in the theater, by circuses, and by traveling road shows; in industry children were often forced to work long hours. Moreover, there were no specific laws offering children protection from sexual and physical abuse. In the first few years of the New York SPCC, the leaders of that society influenced legislation to the extent of placing on the statute books most of the laws for the protection of children which are still in force in New York State today.

Originally, responsibility for the protection of children from neglect, abuse, and exploitation was assumed by agencies whose function was primarily law enforcement. The focus of their activity was to protect children from their parents by removing them from hazardous situations and to arrest, prosecute, and punish parents. By today's frame of reference and according to standards for good social work practice, there are many grounds on which to criticize the methods and techniques used by the founders of the child-protective movement: their use of police methods, their close identification with police and law enforcement agencies, their emphasis on punishment rather than rehabilitation, and their aloofness from other social agencies.

PIONEERING EFFORTS

Despite the negative aspects of this early his-

tory, recognition must be given to these leaders of the early years of the child protective movement; they did provide a valuable service which was a pioneering effort at a time when no one was really concerned with the problem. They were fighters for human rights in a day when children, women, immigrants, minority groups of one kind or another, and labor were exploited. They felt their mission was to work on behalf of exploited and abused children. They were *progressive* in that they saw a problem and did not pass it by but tried to change and improve conditions. They were *aggressive* in that they moved into the streets and the homes to find children who were abused, exploited, and cruelly treated. They were *social actionists* in that they moved into state legislatures to get laws on the statute books, and they moved into courts to see that laws were enforced and children protected. Their achievements seem almost incredible when one reviews the number of laws that were enacted for the protection of children through their efforts. I am sure that those of you who have been associated with any group trying to influence the passage of legislation realize what a tremendous task it is; these men in New York State were instrumental in setting up a whole new structure of law for the protection of children—all before the profession of social work was born.

As noted before, the great tragedy of the movement of these early days was that these leaders did not keep pace with other developments in the field of social welfare; it was a tragedy that they set themselves apart from other groups whose methods were different but whose goals were similar. As a result, child protection fell out of the mainstream of the movement of social welfare. Let me add, however, that not all societies were in this category because progressive leaders in New York State and elsewhere, particularly along the eastern seaboard, kept the spark of child protection alive.

Today, a significant segment of social welfare is concerned with protective services to children. New services are being launched and old programs are being revitalized or merged with newer services. The movement, which was largely privately supported at first, or quasi-public in some areas, now has become primarily tax supported. A serious concern that I must voice in passing is that there is an insufficient number of trained and qualified persons also to move into this field, and this area of service may not develop as rapidly and as soundly as we would hope.

In 1961 Dr. Harry Kempe, Chairman of the Department of Pediatrics of the University of Colorado Medical Center helped focus attention on the abused child when he coined the now much-used term, "the battered child syndrome." Dr. Kempe's survey revealed some shocking statistics. Seventy-one hospitals reported that they had treated a total of 302 serious cases of child abuse in one year; 33 of these children died, and 85 suffered permanent brain damage.

PUBLIC AWARENESS

Since that time, more research on the subject has been started and the public is becoming more aware of the problem. It is encouraging to note that the press, radio, and TV are reflecting the concern that professional people—physicians, social workers, lawyers—have about this problem of child abuse. I was intrigued that in its July 2, 1965, issue the *Wall Street Journal* had a long article describing current developments and activities on the subject of child abuse.

The incidence of abuse cases is not restricted to any economic group. However, the less affluent and more deprived parent has a harder time covering up his behavior and often is more exposed to detection.

There should be no dispute that the problem of physical abuse to children exists. In a nationwide survey of Child Abuse conducted by the Children's Division of the American Humane Association in 1963 we learn the following:

The forms or types of abuse inflicted on these children is a negative testimony to the ingenuity and inventiveness of man. By far the greater number of injuries resulted from beatings with various kinds of implements and instruments. The hairbrush was a common implement used to beat children. However, the same purpose was accomplished with deadlier impact by the use of bare fists, straps, electric cords, TV aerials, ropes, rubber hose, fan belts, sticks, wooden spoons, pool cues, bottles, broom handles, baseball bats, chair legs and, in one case, a sculling oar. Less imaginative, but equally effective, was plain kicking with street shoes or with heavy work shoes.

Children had their extremities—hands, arms and feet—burned in open flames as from gas burners or cigarette lighters. Others bore burn wounds inflicted on their bodies with lighted cigarettes, electric irons or hot pokers. Still others were scalded by hot liquids thrown over them or from being dipped into containers of hot liquids.

Some children were strangled or suffocated by pillows held over their mouths or plastic bags thrown over their heads. A number were drowned in bathtubs and one child was buried alive.

To complete the list—children were stabbed, bitten, shot, subjected to electric shock, were thrown violently to the floor or against a wall, were stamped on and one child had pepper forced down his throat.[1]

Statistics that are released from various child protective agencies in many areas of the country substantiate the fact that the problem seems to be growing. It is hoped that, as more publicity is given to the problem, abusing parents can be reached and children helped.

In considering the relation of authority to child abuse cases, we first think of the legal mandate that gives the agency its reason for existence and, second, the law, insofar as it can be applied to the situation of a parent or other adult who has abused a child.

The Social Welfare Law in New York State gives public welfare commissioners broad powers protecting a child from neglect, abandonment, destitution, cruelty, or abuse. The 1962 amendments to the Federal Social Security Act, which have provided for the strengthening of services to public assistance clients through the defined services program, also have provided for strengthening child welfare services. Encouragement in the form of Federal reimbursement is given to public welfare agencies which establish protective services to children. These developments mark a further step in assuring that child-protective services will become a reality in every community. It is, of course, incumbent on the several states and local communities to take advantage of these resources, to develop new services if they do not exist, or to strengthen existing services that might require it.

Child-protective services actually are based on the concept of the state as *parens patriae*—which in today's context of law means the state's concern as the guardian of social interests and the concept that the state has both the right and the duty to see that the physical, mental, and moral welfare of its children is safeguarded. In this country the inherent rights of the control and custody of children are firmly fixed in the home,

---

[1]Vincent DeFrancis, *Child Abuse—Preview of a Nationwide Survey* (Denver, Colorado: Children's Division, American Humane Association, 1963), pp. 5, 6.

and in the natural parents. In the absence of abnormal circumstances within the domestic circle, the state has only a limited right to intervene in matters pertaining to the child's upbringing.

However, it is also clear that the state has a sovereign power, by means of its legislative acts and the authority vested in its governmental divisions and in certain private or quasi-public agencies to protect the child whose parents, because of their mistakes and failures, neglect to do so. The objective of the state in such a situation is to protect the best interests of the child.

Particularly within the past century and a half, the concept of the state's authority as being superior to that of neglectful parents has developed. During this time there has come to be more and more general recognition and practical application of the principle that it is the right and duty of the public authorities to intervene in cases of parental cruelty or gross neglect that might seriously injure the health and morals of children and to remove children by force if necessary and place them in an environment more conducive to their safety and proper development. In recent years, many definitions of child-protective services have developed. I do not intend to reiterate them here, but merely to refer to three fundamental components necessary in any service to protect children.

COMPONENTS OF CHILD PROTECTION

Inherent in any definition of child protection is the concept that protective services are a representation of a community's concern for its children. The authority of the agency stems from the will of the people to safeguard the rights of children; this authority is based in law and granted by charter in the case of the private agency or written into the law itself for the public agency. The authority to protect children from abuse derives from the same source.

A second distinguishing feature in providing services to the abused child is that the services of the agency are involuntary. This means, of course, that the agency and its staff must be equipped legally and psychologically to move in to provide help to a child whether a parent requests such help or not. The agency must be competent to assess complaints, act on them, and move to remedy the situation. This may be done by the casework process or the use of the court or both.

A third component in child protection is the responsibility that the agency has to pursue a complaint and provide service until the matter has been resolved. The agency cannot desert a child who may be mistreated but must stay with the case until the child is safe. These components give the agency its legal base and form the basis of authority in dealing with child-abuse cases.

For many years social workers were suspicious of the use of authority as a tool in casework, for reliance on authority was construed by some as a weakness. People were to be motivated to change by casework methods. An outgoing approach by the caseworker and the use of authority was considered not only a weakness of practice but also an invasion of an individual's right. This reticence to use authority, and the accompanying suspicion of the agency using it, diverted many social workers from entering the child protective field. There was the cocoon approach with the reliance on the theoretical basis of casework that led far too many workers to feel that they would not do a good job in an authoritative setting. To use a word that appears far too often in our literature, they were not "comfortable" in working with authority.

The use of authority demands the highest professional skill and competence. The factor-by-factor analysis of home situations by caseworkers which has contributed indispensable data to the knowledge of the "anatomy" of home life is part of the authoritative agency's approach.

No less an authority than Dr. Gordon Hamilton wrote many years ago,

> The psychologically well equipped worker is not afraid to use authority on a positive basis after it has been diagnosed as appropriate for the individual and the function of the agency. Much protective work is simply casework with deeply disturbed or neurotic parents. Caseworkers have had to learn about authority, just as they have had to learn about the principles of "rights" and "needs."[2]

Fortunately, for the profession of social work in general, and for the field of child protection in particular, aggressive casework, out-reaching services, and assertive approaches have become acceptable methods in our time to approach social and casework problems. Even some family agencies espouse these techniques. The use of authority

---

[2] Gordon Hamilton, *The Theory and Practice of Social Casework* (New York: Columbia University Press, 1940), p. 289.

by the child-protective agency must therefore include the philosophical approach of the validity of the use of authority by the agency and its staff.

WORKING FOR CHILDREN

Originally, child-protective agencies were almost exclusively child-centered in their approach. The "rescue" type of service, with its emphasis on the enforcement of the law and the punishment of the parent saw its only responsibility to be that of helping the child. Protective services today still consider the child as their main focus, but the worker sees the child in its familial and social environment. The child-protective worker may do more intensive work with the parents than with the child, for the worker knows the child's needs cannot be fully met until the family's needs are met. In short, the child-protective worker in using his authority works *with parents for children*.

A social worker can approach the treatment of child abuse cases from the classical concept of the social casework process of: (1) social investigation, (2) social diagnosis, and (3) social treatment.

First of all, a worker must investigate the facts to determine the nature and extent of the problem. In abuse cases involving infants or very young children, we must of necessity rely on external observation, medical diagnosis and draw our conclusions from such physical evidence at hand, for such children are too young to explain what happened to them. Often physicians in their private practice or hospital doctors examining children with injuries may suspect that such injuries were externally inflicted by an adult, namely a parent or guardian. On occasion in my experience in child protective work, we did receive referrals from private physicians and hospitals where doctors were suspicious of the cause of injuries and where a particular physician felt strongly motivated to ask the intervention of the law or the services of a child-protective agency. However, there is never a guarantee that such will be the case, for many physicians have not been trained in this skill of diagnosing the battered child, and thus this possibility often escapes detection. Furthermore, there is a reluctance to report cases of abused children because of fear on the part of the physician that he might be sued by angered parents.

MANDATORY REPORTING LAWS

To correct this problem many states, including New York, have passed what are termed "mandatory reporting laws." These laws include the definition of the abused child which generally means a child who has injuries inflicted by other than accidental means by some adult—which might be the parent, guardian, or even some other adult.

These laws require a physician or surgeon who treats a child with such injuries to report them; hospital directors, nurses and others may also be the reporting persons.

Different states have different practices as to whom cases should be reported; but among the group are the police or law enforcement agency, a child welfare or protective agency or a department of welfare. The hope is that the receiving agency for these reports should be a child welfare service. In those jurisdictions where the police are to be notified, there should also be the requirement to notify the child welfare services.

One distinguishing feature of this kind of law is the provision granting immunity from civil or criminal action to medical personnel reporting cases of inflicted injuries on children. This is essential to insure protection of those who in good faith and in the pursuit of good medical practice refer for help and protection those children whom they treat and who apparently have been abused.

In the practice of child protection in the case of an older child, referrals to the agency are often made by school personnel, e.g., school nurses, doctors, and school social workers who may have observed external evidence of beatings and assaults. With children of any age beyond infancy, who can articulate what happened, one might assume that there would be an "assist" to the worker exploring the facts. However, more often than not, a severely abused child is so traumatized that he cannot, nor does he dare, reveal what happened to him. In some situations where children themselves may report abuse, the social worker must be aware of the possibility of fantasying by the child.

THE PROCESS OF DIAGNOSIS

Continuing the process of diagnosis, the worker will want to determine whether the abuse was a

PREVENTING MALTREATMENT OF CHILDREN

willful act on the part of the adult inflicting the abuse. In many abusing parents we find characteristics of aggression and hostility; most of these parents are dependent and insecure individuals. Some show rigidity and lack of warmth and a rejective attitude toward their children. Such parents tax the skill of the caseworker and are often his most difficult, harassing, and time-consuming clients. Thus child protective services require staff of high professional competence.

The case material of a protective agency reveals certain striking patterns. In case after case one sees a repetition of the same basic disturbances, varying somewhat in symptom pictures, but having similar roots. A large number of neglectful (or abusing) parents came from neglectful homes themselves. Their parents failed them, and often the present home atmosphere is but a carbon copy of the home in which they themselves grew up. Upon further examination it is frequently observed that their ego structures are severely damaged.

In the nationwide survey of child abuse conducted by the Children's Division of the American Humane Association in 1963, certain facts emerged. Among them was the fact that abuse is generally not willful, that a significant number of abusing parents are emotionally immature; many incidents arise from an emotional explosion often triggered by some irrelevant cause. Some parents suffer from acute depression, and a significant number have a history of mental illness and institutionalization. Some parents committed mercy killings on children who were suffering severe handicaps or whose mothers feared they would become victims of handicaps.[3]

Treatment Alternatives

The experienced child-protective worker with his understanding of human motivation must choose from many alternatives what is best for the child. In some situations it might be determined that intensive casework with the parents is required. In those situations where parents deny the assault and where there is definite evidence of abuse, steps must be initiated immediately to invoke the authority of the court so that the child may be removed from the dangerous environment.

The use of the court may be part of treatment, but the present-day child-protective worker does not see his role as using the court to punish parents. It is, of course, far more helpful in most cases to bring proceedings on behalf of the child in a juvenile court than to prosecute a parent in a criminal action. Since guilt must be proven beyond a reasonable doubt in criminal proceedings, the lack of evidence may make it impossible to obtain a conviction. There are constitutional safeguards to protect witnesses from incriminating themselves in a court of law. Parents cannot be forced to testify against their own interests—even in a civil proceeding when the facts which are being elicited from them tend to indicate that they have committed a crime.

When such a prosecution fails, the child may remain in the care of parents who may then feel even more justified than before in their abusive treatment, and the publicity which surrounds such trials may make it more difficult to work with the parents.

Often it is not left to the discretion of the agency to decide whether retributive action against parents should be taken. This is the prerogative of the public prosecutor, and it is imperative that the agency cooperate with such authorities in carrying out the mandate of their office.

In the case of severely abused or seriously neglected children it is imperative to remove such children from the dangerous environment; but even here a proper diagnosis must be made, for all of us in public welfare know the disadvantages of foster home and institutional care and that all problems—even from poor homes—are not solved by placement in a new environment. We are aware too that children from such environments are difficult to place and manage in a foster home setting. However, we cannot afford to become immobilized from taking action by being wedded to the idea that the best place for a child is in his own home. This is not true with hostile homes and with rejecting parents. In these serious situations where the life of the child may be at stake, his rights become more important than his parents' rights. Then the authority of the agency must be invoked to remove a child from his own home promptly.

The use of authority may be part of the treatment process decided upon in working with parents. In such process, authority often becomes the

---

[3]Vincent DeFrancis, *op. cit.*, pp. 9-12.

supportive tool in casework with parents. It is agreed that many of those parents have weak ego structures and often suffer from severe emotional disturbance, and who, in a sense, are "people who can't help themselves." The role of the child-protective worker is much like the role of a parent; the need of these dependent individuals often is to relate to parental authority.

In an article some time ago on the subject of "Worker-Client Authority Relationships," Dr. Eliot Studt stated among other things that:

> One of the significant characteristics of this client group is its vulnerability to the exercise of authority. Individuals would not be clients if they were not at least temporarily handicapped in taking responsibility for some aspect of their personal lives. In such situations they are particularly dependent on the authority person who can link them to the social and psychological resources which are necessary to repair damage and to reinstate their ability to manage for themselves. They are impelled to seek help because of internal or external difficulties which matter to them.

Dr. Studt asserted that:

> the profession must therefore, be concerned with the possibility of motivating involuntary clients to make constructive use of the authority relationship; and with the skills by which this is accomplished.[4]

These principles are certainly applicable to the abusing parent. Can you find a more involuntary client than a parent who has beaten his child? Working with such parents demands the highest degree of professional competence.

In a similar vein, a report on observations and treatment of children and parents by the staff of the Children's Hospital of Philadelphia includes the following significant observation and comment:

> In our dealings with parents of seriously neglected or abused children brought to our hospital we have used a non-critical, non-punitive approach, not only for purposes of sound data collection on which to base practical plans for protecting children, but also in order to protect parents from further acting out their frustrations on their children.

Very significantly the report continues,

> This has been based on our recognition that parents who neglect and batter their children are actually speaking their parental incapacities in action language and are asking to be stopped in behaving as they do. Why else do they bring their children to hospitals and so run the high risk of punishment? We think that parents run this risk because the risk of total, internal, personality disintegration is even more terrifying—a risk they run in continuing the care of their children.[5]

CONCLUSION

We have defined the problem of child abuse as more prevalent than most people know. We have asserted that the child-protective agency must find its basis in law and that authority properly applied is a casework tool of inestimable value. By the use of authority the child-protective worker may give supportive help to emotionally deprived, fear-ridden, acting-out, deficient parents.

While punishment of parents is not a primary goal, the protection and safeguarding of children is our chief objective, and the authority of the law may have to be invoked to remove children from their homes to assure their security.

As in other areas of social work practice, the child-protective worker does not pursue his role alone. This is a cooperative service dependent on the medical profession—including the psychiatrist; the legal profession—including the courts, the law enforcement community—including the police and the prosecuting attorney, other community resources such as schools, hospitals and other social agencies, and the community at large whose support of the agency must be real and vital.

---

[4]Elliot Studt, "Worker-Client Authority Relationships," *Social Work*, Vol. IV (January, 1959), pp. 23, 24.

[5]Marian G. Morris *et al.*, "Toward Prevention of Child Abuse," *Children*, Vol. XI (March-April, 1964), p. 56.

A demonstration project to protect
children by restoring . . .

COHESION, DIGNITY, AND HOPE FOR MULTIPROBLEM FAMILIES

MIRIAM O. PAGE

Training Consultant, Vermont Department of Social Welfare, Montpelier

A DEMONSTRATION project to help multi-problem families achieve a better quality of home life for their children has been operating in the Vermont Department of Social Welfare since August 1959. Jointly financed by the department and the Turrell Fund of New Jersey, the project is the result of a long-time conviction of the department and the Vermont Conference of Social Welfare that adequate service to families could reduce the number of children committed to the department for foster care. The project involves the services of two full-time social caseworkers, Enna M. Bates and Barbara N. Ward, a part-time supervisor—the writer of this article—and a secretary. Originally set up in one area of the State for one year, it has since been extended to August 1961. If support can be achieved from the General Assembly, it will be continued as a regular department service in three areas of the State, and eventually throughout Vermont.

The project serves families whose children have problems severe enough to give the department, under its protective function, the right to go into homes unasked; but they are families who have enough strengths for the worker to be able to tell them honestly: "In spite of these problems we think you can and should stay together as a family." We have been careful not to call on any family until we have been sure that a serious problem exists which is affecting the children. We have, however, been liberal in our definition of "strengths," since we believe that most families can and should stay together if help is available to them.

The area in which we are operating includes nine small towns with populations ranging between 485 and 2,271, and a small city with a population of 8,500. As of October 1, 1960, we were working with 34 families having 145 children. Six of these families live in the most deprived section of the city. In this neighborhood, which includes 45 families with about 150 children, we have also been working on a neighborhood improvement project.

Individual Casework Service

In the beginning, the caseworkers visited each superintendent of schools and overseer of the poor in the area to describe the project to them and to ask if they knew of families that might be helped by it.

Of the 37 families accepted for individual casework service, 20 were referred by the public assistance and child welfare divisions of the State department of social welfare. The schools referred seven; the overseers of the poor, five. Two families themselves asked for help. The project initiated service to two families, on the basis of probation reports available to the department, and to one family living with a project family.

The manner in which these families were referred differed considerably from the way complaints had usually been made to our department—when everyone had "come to the end of their rope" and wanted the child removed immediately from the home. Those referring children to the project obviously felt that they were helping to keep families together. That they referred families about whom they might have complained at a later date is indicated not only by the problems in these families but by the fact that the child welfare division has had only one complaint of child neglect from the entire area during this period.

All the families had difficulties in relationships within the family and between the family and the community. In 25 of the 37 families there was severe economic deprivation; in 18 at least one of the parents had a serious health problem; in 14 the parents had marital problems; and in 7, one or both of the parents drank heavily. In 10 families the father was not in the home, and in 5, the mother was working. Seventeen of the families included children with school problems; 14 included children who exhibited behavior problems in the home and in the community; 8 included children with serious health needs.

In October 1960, a review of the families receiving counseling indicated that 21 of them (including the six engaged in the neighborhood project) had shown some improvement, real enough for the worker, the referring source, and the family to recognize. However, we had closed no cases except those in which the family had moved out of the area. In many instances, the situations bringing about the referral had cleared up rapidly, but the family and worker had become aware of many contributing problems on which they still needed to work. At present six cases are about ready to be closed. In these, the parents have learned something new about solving problems; have had time to test and gain confidence in their ability; and have learned to use resources within their communities.

Methods

We have profited much from material from the Family Centered Project in St. Paul, especially the casework.[1] One difference has been that we have met much less initial resistance to the service than was reported by the St. Paul project. In spite of the fact that the workers have been very direct in pointing out the problems affecting children, a few families have enthusiastically welcomed the worker at the first interview and almost all have done so after a few visits. These families have had far fewer contacts with social agencies than had the urban families in the St. Paul project and are rather intrigued with the idea that someone is interested enough to seek them out. Also, in many instances the referring source has prepared the family for the project's worker by presenting the service as likely to help. Each referring source has been willing to let the project worker use his name as she introduces herself to the family.

Fathers have shown more resistance than mothers, but we have insisted that, since they are heads of their households, the family casework service must include them. This has meant that the caseworkers have made visits in the evening as well as during weekends since some of the fathers are lumbermen who go into the woods on Monday morning and return Saturday night. In the few instances in which we could not succeed in involving the father, our help has been much less productive. The participation of disabled fathers has seemed especially important in reestablishing family morale.

Ordinarily our workers see the father and mother together, unless there is some indication of a need for individual interviews. For most of the parents, talking things over with the worker in these joint interviews is perhaps the first time they have talked things over together. The experience usually helps them to begin working out problems together even without the worker's presence.

The caseworker makes every effort to help the families relate appropriately to available community resources. These include a few social agencies, churches, schools, doctors, dentists, and recreational organizations. Few of the parents whose children were in trouble at school had ever been there to talk with the teachers or had ever attended PTA meetings. Few of the families attended church. Most of them were afraid of medical or dental care. One mother who has made amazing strides in other respects is still wondering whether she "dares" to go to a hearing clinic.

Many of these families had long felt ostracized by the community. Consequently they had sometimes acted defiantly. While there was a considerable amount of negative feeling about these families in the community, there was also concern for them and a willingness to help as soon as it was found that someone could offer suggestions and give encouragement to persons wanting to help.

Each time something has been needed by a family, the worker has not only contacted the agency able to help but has also managed to involve the family in achieving something for themselves.

A family with 14 children found it impossible to pay for the nine school lunches required each day. The overburdened mother was worn out from her efforts to feed 16 people three times a day. After the worker talked with the school principal, the school authorities agreed to give the lunches free. However, the worker also asked the parents whether there was something they could contribute from their garden. They said they had extra cabbages. She suggested that perhaps the next year the parents could ask the school officials what vegetables they needed and plant a section of the garden for this purpose. The worker then told the principal that the family would be offering the cabbages. These parents had never talked to anyone at the school about the school difficulties of one of their sons, but after the cabbage arrangement was worked out they and the school authorities made plans to keep in touch with each other in the boy's behalf.

Project visits are scheduled at hours most convenient for the family, whenever possible. Weekly visits are usual at the beginning, but gradually the visits are spaced at longer and longer intervals so that parents can grow confident in managing on their own. At the start of the project, the families were offered a choice of either office or home visits. Only one parent wanted to come to the office, and we have come to believe that home visits are more appropriate for this kind of service.

Neighborhood Clubs

Because of the parents' need for some recreational outlets besides the corner bar, and because we thought the agricultural extension service could impart knowledge and skills which the mothers could use, the project supervisor talked with the service's home demonstration agent about starting mothers' groups in the most deprived area of the city where four of the project families lived. While this area is composed of small, poorly built houses, with few facilities and much overcrowding, the population remains rather stable. The people seem to regard themselves as a separate community united against the "outside," although far from united in internal affairs. Public welfare expenses are high; police are frequently called to settle family and neighborhood rows; the men work only in the summertime; and a jug of wine is one of the few happy things to look forward to. One of the project workers knew nearly everyone in the community, having been there many times in the past as a child welfare worker following through on complaints of child neglect.

The home demonstration agent expressed considerable interest in working with these families, but she realized that everything would not go smoothly. We were all pleasantly suprised at the enthusiasm expressed by the five women whom the agent visited one by one to invite into the proposed club. They were to meet at the home of the R's, a project family, the only recipient of the project's casework service among the five. Because it seemed important for the families to make their own decisions about whether to join the club, the worker did not mention

her part in the plan. Mrs. R told about the club and seemed pleased that the first meeting would be at her house.

On the evening of the meeting, the worker met Mr. R going home from work, gave him a ride, and at his suggestion stopped in for a moment. She found the usually dirty and unkept house sparkingly clean, and Mrs. R nervous about whether she had enough chairs and other things. The worker spent a little time trying to encourage her, leaving about 2 hours before the meeting was to be held.

The next morning the home demonstration agent told the worker that the house was dark when she arrived 5 minutes before the scheduled time for the meeting. One of the R children said her mother had been taken to the hospital, but was vague about the details. The agent waited in the car until long past the meeting time, but no one came. She then visited two of the women who had been invited: one said she had not felt well that day; and another, that she had a sick child. Both said they would like being in a club. An inquiry to the hospital revealed that Mrs. R had not been there.

As we of the project staff talked this experience over together, we became aware of the enormity of our request of Mrs. R. Not only had she never entertained, she had never been entertained. She had had so few successes in her life that she would not have been able to face it if her neighbors had not liked her home. Mrs. R later told the worker that she had turned off the lights a few minutes before the home demonstration agent's arrival. She said she had never been so scared in her life.

We decided Mrs. R had done well to go as far as she had. We felt responsible for adding still another failure to her already long list. As we talked, we searched for any positive thing of common significance to these five women and finally came up with the project worker who was so well known in the community. We realized we had been wrong in not identifying her with the plan from the start.

A few weeks later, in October 1959, at the project worker's request, Mrs. R's stepmother invited the same five women to her house for coffee. When the worker arrived, no one but the hostess was there. All five women (including Mrs. R) came as soon as the hostess put her head out of the window and shouted that the worker had arrived. After finding out that the women really wanted a club, the worker asked what objectives they had in mind. They mentioned three:

1. They wanted to clean up their streets and make them attractive with flowers. They thought their husbands would

make window boxes, and they could exchange plant slips and start new plants indoors this winter. They did not like the way the rest of the city referred to their section.

2. They wanted to get permission from the owner of the vacant lot to clean out the junk there and make play space for their children. The children were playing in the streets and two of them had recently been hit by cars.

3. They wanted to get their names in the paper for something "good"—not just "bad" things.

The women formed the West Side Women's Club in January 1960. Although there have never been more than 10 mothers at any meeting and a few families have actively opposed the club, 35 of the 45 families in the neighborhood have been active in attaining its objectives. Some teenage girls asked to be admitted, but their mothers wanted the club as their own.

The girls were therefore helped by the worker and by the county 4-H club leader to form two 4-H clubs. Their parents first volunteered to serve as leaders, then became scared because they had never heard of 4-H before, nor had they ever led anything. The two caseworkers, therefore, assumed active leadership of the club, but the parents came to the meetings and helped. Although the 4-H county leader also helped in an advisory capacity, she could not assume direct leadership of these clubs, and we were unable to find leaders from outside the neighborhood.

At the second meeting of the women's club, husbands also asked to join, but they were not included until the spring when their talents were needed in the cleanup campaign and in other projects. The club then became the West Side Community Club. The project worker assumed responsibility for guiding the group since the home demonstration agent and the assistant county agricultural agent, who helped on special projects, could not arrange to take on the task of regular leadership. The boys began a 4-H group but leadership again was a problem. Last fall, however, the county agent agreed to be the regular leader of the boys' group.

Achievements

A year after the first meeting of the six women who began the club, their original objectives had been met along with a lot of others that would have seemed overwhelming at the start. In addition, they have had a lot of fun. Here is the record:

• *Beautifying the community.* Seven truckloads of junk were carried away by the city dumptruck which was paid for out of the club treasury. Five hundred donated tulips were planted. Window boxes appeared on many houses. Flowers were planted in front lawns and vegetable gardens in back-yards. Nearly every backyard now has some play equipment and many houses have been improved.

• *Making a playground.* The club earned money for clearing the vacant lot and for buying playground equipment. This was done by holding a food sale, selling chances on a quilt, holding a pot-luck supper, and selling articles made by the members. The men made benches and stools, fixed the sand-boxes, and repaired broken equipment.

Mothers volunteered for playground duty, but within a week it became apparent that they were not yet able to handle the responsibility, and the project workers had to take over. However, they continued to bring refreshments each day and to assist the workers. By the time we realized the mothers' inadequacy, the project workers were so involved in seeing that the playground did not fail that they had no time to search for supervisory help outside the neighborhood.

• *Achieving good publicity.* The caseworker talked with the newspaper editors who gave fine coverage to the activities. The first election of officers was reported on the society page of one paper. Another paper carried a story about some people in the project neighborhood who did wood carvings in a series on hobbies. As time went on, newspaper coverage of the neighborhood activities was the same as that accorded any organization in the area although pictures were used more extensively for the club stories. The assistant agent of the county farm bureau helped the families with their gardens and presented the neighborhood's efforts in this respect on several of his regular TV shows on gardening.

All this publicity has greatly helped these people to achieve a sense of pride and to feel as though they were part of the larger community.

As the neighborhood project gathered momentum, one worker was assigned full responsibility for it. The other worker carried a higher proportion of families receiving individual casework service and during the summer took responsibility for leading a 4-H club and for some playground leadership.

Neighborhood Changes

Since the beginning of these activities, the city has reported a drop in relief costs in the neighborhood and the police have been called on less frequently to settle neighborhood rows. They report that several persons who used to be brought home with regularity from the local taverns have not been seen there lately. New foods have been introduced into family menus, as a result of the cooking practice the women had in getting ready for the food sale, of their exchange of recipes, and of their increased garden produce. Homes are cleaner. There have been no complaints of child neglect, and school authorities have commented favorably on the change in appearance and attitude of many of the children. One mother, without any suggestion by the worker, canvassed the community to get parents to take their children to the well-baby clinic, which they had previously ignored.

Today whenever someone becomes sick, neighbors

rally around and try to help. Several families have returned to their churches after a long period of no attendance.

At a 4–H club picnic held in May, a minor altercation between two children suddenly spread into a neighborhood row which brought to the surface all the pent-up feelings and enmities which had temporarily been put aside. Since the president of the neighborhood club was the main figure in this, the club's very existence seemed threatened. The worker recorded:

I dreaded to go back to the neighborhood the following day but felt that I must reassure those who are still hopeful. They expressed regret that such a thing had happened during the children's picnic, but instead of my encouraging them, they were encouraging me. They said that the community plans could still go ahead and that they would work on it under a new leader. Four people had small gifts for me in an effort to be consoling. . . . Mr. A and Mr. V argued and each declared they'd never try to work on anything together. The day following, they had apologized and started building tables and benches which they displayed proudly. . . .

The city truck was due in the neighborhood on the day following the row, and, while there were mumblings, everyone came out of his house to put his junk on the truck. The last club meeting for the season had been scheduled for that night and some dentists had been invited to speak. (Children and parents had been surprisingly enthusiastic over the dental care provided through the project!) The president said she did not want to go through with the meeting, but supposed she had to since the dentists had been asked to come. The project worker encouraged her; the meeting was held and went well.

The neighborhood did not become a cohesive community again during the summer, but all the children did come to the playground, all the mothers helped, and the 4–H clubs got through to a fine "Achievement Night." attended by most of the parents. In October 1960, club elections for another year were held. Few seemed happy at the outcome but all had so much to do in planning neighborhood Christmas parties for the children, that they got to work. One mother said to the worker, "You've been helping the 4–H girls to learn to work together. We need to learn the same thing."

The workers report that no rehearsal for 4–H Achievement Night ever took place without somebody getting mad and quitting. An excerpt from the record states:

At a meeting of the older 4–H group, one of the younger girls {we will here call Louise} wanted to participate. We told her that she could not take part, as it was rather crowded. Louise stood in front of the house with a couple of boys shouting and throwing stones, and one of the plastic ducks on Mrs. J's lawn was broken. The girls were all for chasing Louise home. I said I would go over to her house and ask her mother to keep her home during the rest of the meeting. I said I should have done this in the beginning. We had a lesson in avoiding trouble rather than looking for it. Louise was very angry for the moment. We didn't accuse her of breaking the duck, but merely asked the mother whether Louise could play by herself so that we could rehearse. Her mother cooperated; Louise was kept in the house.

The group decided that money from the treasury should be used to pay for the duck. However, on the following day, Mrs. J told us not to bother as she had been able to repair it.

The club had been told from the beginning, as had all the project's families, that the worker could give no assurance of being with them after August 1960. Its members had already had some success in petitioning the city government for a street light, so that they had decided just before the row to write to the Commissioner of Social Welfare asking for continuation of the project. While feelings were still high, the group forwarded 60 letters to the Commissioner in 1 envelope, addressed by the club member with the most flourishing handwriting. All were worded differently, but most of them carried this message: "Please leave the worker here for one more year until we have finished what we have begun." The Commissioner replied very soon saying that the Turrell Fund had agreed to support the project another year, that these letters would help him get similar services for other neighborhoods.

Analyzing what the worker has done in this community, we find most important her helping the people to work for what they wanted. She called on people in the neighborhood explaining the club's plans. She helped the president write her speeches, the secretary her reports, and the treasurer her checks. She knew persons who could help the club with its programs—a woman who could teach the women how to do home permanents, another who knew how to crochet afghans, a store in which wood carvings could be exhibited, a dentist who would talk to them, and the proprietor of a place in which a food sale could be held. She introduced the assistant county agent, the 4–H club leader, and the home demonstration agent to the neighborhood. She worked with city officials to achieve a more enlightened method of work relief, and kept them informed of progress in the neighborhood, so that they were glad to attend a pot-luck supper on St. Patrick's Day.

When a suggestion for planting tulips was made, some club members predicted that the children would run over them if they ever came through the ground.

The worker asked, "Whose children are these?" The tulips were planted and many grew to flowers. When some families complained about the distribution of Christmas baskets, the worker asked why they themselves could not provide Christmas for their children. When the club members wanted a neighborhood Christmas tree, she agreed to find a place where the men could cut the tree; furnished two strings of lights *after* the club members had managed to get others; and suggested that each family bring some light bulbs. When difficulties have occurred, she has bluntly reminded the club members that they started the clubs, that they have done in them what they wanted to do; and that they cannot blame her when things go wrong.

This worker is besieged by people who want to tell her something, want to ask her, want her to see. This usually concerns something about their own family troubles or triumphs. She discusses these problems as they are brought to her attention, but does not attempt to carry on a continuous casework relationship with each family. She has used casework skills to help individuals move into, stay in, and contribute to the group. She has made it possible for them to use many community resources and specialized facilities which they knew nothing about and could not use without continued individual understanding and support.

Complementary Services

The four families in this neighborhood who have been participating in the counseling part of the project since the beginning, were all eventually drawn into the neighborhood activities. In addition, we are working individually with two families who asked for counseling help after they became involved in the neighborhood improvement program. The following example illustrates the interaction of individual casework service with the group activities:

The K's were on the point of divorce when they were referred to the project. Mr. K had several serious disabilities for which he refused treatment. He also refused to do what work he could because he feared loss of the family's ADC grant. He abused and bullied the whole household and accused his wife of extramarital sexual relationships. Mrs. K had ceased to consult him about family matters; instead she sought advice and support from other relatives. The ADC grant, though at the maximum, was inadequate to meet the family's needs.

A year after the family began to receive counseling help,

Mr. and Mrs. K told the worker that the biggest change that they saw in themselves was that they now discussed family problems together and were able to function as a family unit. During the year Mr. K had taken some treatment for his disabilities; he now did odd jobs whenever he could and was talking about the possibilities of getting steady work.

The worker had begun her work with this family by talking with Mrs. K about how Mr. K might feel about his disabilities and his inability to support his family. She had then encouraged Mr. K to talk out his fears about losing the family's steady income if he got well; and had accompanied him to the clinic. She had also seen Mr. and Mrs. K together for discussion of family matters. She had made arrangements for one of their children, who was sick, to continue schoolwork at home.

Mrs. K became one of the earliest and most active members of the women's club. She obviously had fun at the meetings, participated in community improvement efforts, and sang at the pot-luck supper where city dignitaries were guests. These activities gave her a sense of accomplishment which made her better able to bear Mr. K until he could change. She began the club's garden project—in a few weeks it become "theirs"—and Mr. K was as active and proud as she. Both now talk about neighborhood needs and developments. The children have been active in the 4–H club.

Conclusion

In our work with both individual families and with groups, we use basic casework principles: we try to find out from the families themselves what they are most immediately concerned about and to help them do something about it. We feel sure that their ultimate goals and ours are the same, though our priorities are often different.

All neighborhoods do not have the same specific objectives as the neighborhood we have discussed here, but most of them, like most families, want the things which these objectives point to: self-respect growing out of accomplishment; improved opportunities for their children; a better relationship with and recognition by the community at large. No matter which of these three objectives comes first, the others will follow if the families can be helped to achieve whatever they want most. Every community has resources needed by those of its families who seem unable to cope with the problems of everyday living. But few such families will use the resources to best advantage, or even at all, unless a caseworker is at hand to reach out to them and give them the courage to go ahead.

[1] Overton, Alice; Tinker, Katherine H., et al.: Casework notebook Greater St. Paul Community Chest and Councils, Minn. 1957.

Maurice J. Boisvert

The battered-child syndrome

Casework planning would be more efficacious if a typology could be established which could predict, according to classification, any future injuries

Maurice J. Boisvert is executive director,
Youth Opportunities Upheld, intensive probation,
Worcester, Massachusetts.

This article is based on a study which was undertaken to support or disprove a similar study by James Delsordo which analyzes families in which there has been physical abuse of children by parents.[1] The ultimate goal of the research was a typology for classification and treatment, with the hope of providing the rudiments of a guide for planning intervention strategy.

A valid typology requires the systematic identification of where the basic problem lies; what causes and maintains the problem behavior despite pressures toward social conformity; and what can be done to eliminate or ameliorate the problem and its consequences.[2] Thus, a typology should point out the typical and recurring features of cases in the specific problem area under consideration —in this case, child abuse. The fact should be noted that any specific behavior problem also has related aspects to behavior in general.

In social work, human behavior is typically seen as being determined by the following factors:

1. The individual's personality system (e.g. his basic pattern of id/ego/superego functioning).

2. His significant interpersonal relationships— especially the nuclear family of which he is a current member, but also extended kinship and important friendships and work, and any other activity-oriented relationships.

3. His values, which reflect cultural and subcultural influences.

4. The number, complexity, and congruence of—and his relative mastery over—the social roles he performs.

5. His physical make-up and condition—i.e. physical assets, liabilities, disabilities, chronic or acute illness, and so on.

6. The amount of stress or support provided by the external environment, in physical-social-cultural-political-economic resource terms (e.g. depression, discrimination, opportunity, rapid social change, barren terrain, and natural catastrophes).[3]

Any typology which makes reference to a specific problem such as child abuse must also keep a perspective of the analytic framework described above.

This study was concerned with the abuser, and the criterion for locating the abuser is the abused. Under the requirements of recently enacted state legislation (1964) designed to assure a greater measure of protec-

---

[1] James D. Delsordo, Protective Casework for Abused Children, *Children*, 10:213–18 (November–December 1963).

[2] Samuel Finestone, Issues Involved in Developing Diagnostic Classifications for Casework, *Casework Papers 1960* (New York: Family Service Association of America, 1960), pp. 152–53.

[3] Serapio R. Zalba, The Abused Child: II. A Typology for Classification and Treatment, *Social Work*, 12:70–79 (January 1967).

tion for the significant and apparently increasing number of children suffering such traumas, cases of injury or abuse to children are subject to reporting to the Division of Child Guardianship (DCG) of the Massachusetts Department of Public Welfare by the examining physician. The abused or battered child is defined by the law as a child under sixteen years of age, examined or treated by a physician who has reasonable cause to believe that the child is suffering from serious physical injury or abuse inflicted by a parent or other person responsible for the care of the child.

Among the many types of injuries frequently covered by the law are broken bones (especially arms, legs, and ribs), single and compound fractures, such head injuries as concussions or skull fractures, internal injuries such as ruptured livers, spleens, or lungs, bruises and multiple welts of various kinds, swelling, split lips, blackened eyes, lost teeth, and burns. Not included in this legislative act are the less serious forms of neglect such as malnutrition, failure to thrive, or substandard general physical care.

The main concern of social workers covering these cases of inflicted injury is the protection of the abused in the future. Once casework intervention has taken place, it is important to determine what would be the immediate danger of further harm coming to the child in his present environment and what would be the best treatment strategy according to the pathology and degree of danger. Casework planning would be much more efficacious if a typology could be established which could predict, according to classification, any future injuries. It was hoped that this study would be able to establish some major criteria for such predictions.

Method

Chapter 119 of the General Laws of the Commonwealth of Massachusetts, section 39A, specifically states:

Every physician and intern or medical officer registered as provided in section 9A of chapter 112 who professionally examines or treats a child under the age of 16 years and has reasonable cause to believe that such child is suffering from serious physical injury or abuse inflicted by a parent or other person responsible for the care of such child, shall report such injury or abuse to the Department of Public Welfare in accordance with the rules and regulations of the Department.

It also stipulates that "any information given in good faith by such physician, intern or medical officer shall not constitute slander or libel," thus safeguarding the doctor and his practice.

The term *battered child* as employed here is defined by the above law. The inflicted-injury cases used in this research were those reported to the Worcester district office of the DCG during 1965 and 1966—a total of twenty such cases.[4] These cases were carefully studied, and the workers on the respective cases were consulted.

Each case was carefully studied for the following points:

1. typical characteristics and pathology of the abuser
2. age of the abused
3. nature of the inflicted injury
4. any legal action
5. the casework plan
6. recidivism of abuse

The first point studied established what had caused the abuse: a psychotic episode, an impulsive act, a sadistic act. The typical characteristics of each case were carefully noted. The pathology of the case was then determined by clinical evaluation already written into the record by a psychiatrist, psychologist, or social worker. If no clinical evaluation had been made, the case was placed in a classification on the basis of information in the record or information given by the worker concerning the typical recurring features of the abuser's personality. Each case was thus classified according to the pathology

[4]Grateful acknowledgement is made by the writer to Gerald Nugent, director of the Worcester district office of the Division of Child Guardianship, for permission to conduct the study on which this article is based.

or the typical characteristics of the abuser.

Under each classification, the characteristics of the abused were determined by variables 2 and 3 (the age of the child and the nature of the injury). Casework strategy for each classification was then determined by variables 4 and 5 (any legal action taken and the casework planning). The treatment plan was differentiated in terms of one or more of the following: (1) authority-based control and environmental manipulation (police intervention, court action, institutional commitment of parent, or removal of child); (2) reality-based planning and use of community resources for child care; (3) relationship-based casework (as described by Beatrice S. Reiner and Irving Kaufman)[5] or traditional psychoanalytically oriented psychotherapy; (4) group therapy where social performance and relationship dynamics are confronted and awareness and skills in interpersonal relationships are developed; (5) conjoint family therapy; and (6) ego-supportive surveillance. Variable 6 (recidivism of abuse) was employed as an indicator of danger of further harm to the child.

Each case was divided into a typology of either *uncontrollable* or *controllable abuse* and then delimited into classes according to the pathology of the abusing parent or parent-substitute as given by the above data.

Results

Typology: uncontrollable battering

Classification 1: the psychotic personality. Abuse is always unpredictable and uncontrollable. The child who is attacked plays some idiosyncratic role in the fantasies of the psychotic attacker. In only one of the cases studied, the natural mother was the abuser. Her abusing was part of a bizarre ritual. She insisted that "some man" had broken into the house and had attacked her child. She was later diagnosed at the Worcester State Hospital as schizophrenic, paranoid type. The abused child was one of six children. He was two years old and suffered lacera-

---

[5] Beatrice S. Reiner and Irving Kaufman, *Character Disorders in Parents of Delinquents* (New York: Family Service Association of America, 1959).

tions of the face and multiple contusions. This child, along with the other siblings, was in serious danger. When the psychotic abuser will not voluntarily accept psychiatric help, the police should be notified immediately. In this case, relatives notified the police and had this mother committed to the Worcester State Hospital for treatment. The children were then placed with relatives until such time as their mother was considered capable of caring for them. If and when a reunion occurs, continued casework support will be imperative.

If the abuser and abused cannot be separated voluntarily or through the commitment of the abuser, a care-and-protection petition should be filed through the courts on behalf of the abused child. Separation is therefore the primary strategy for the caseworker. Effective placement of the child, where he will receive proper care and protection, along with referrals for psychiatric treatment of the abuser in a closed setting are secondary concerns.

Classification 2: the inadequate personality. The abuser is irresponsible, immature, and very impulsive. He or she has a low tolerance for frustration. The parents, if not divorced or separated, relate to one another on a superficial level, usually biologically. Characteristic of this type is a messy home, a list of evictions, alcoholism, and inability to maintain any definite pattern of work. The marriages of these people seldom last for any length of time.

The focus of the problem here is the conflicting needs of the very dependent child and the very impulsive, inadequate parent. An aggressive, hostile reaction to conflict is usually characteristic of the abuser. He is often anxious and tense, but very seldom admits his guilt. If the abuser is still married, his mate will usually support any story he employs to account for the injury. These families are usually noted for neglect as well as inflicted injury.

This class accounted for 30 percent of the battered-child cases reported. In all six cases the abused child was under twelve months old, which is the most dependent age. The nature of the injury was usually multiple bruises or mild fractures.

Caseworkers in their planning should always realize that this type of home is very dangerous for infants. These abusers are usually relatively cooperative and wish to allay any feelings of guilt, although they will seldom admit this guilt verbally. Therefore voluntary, temporary placement of the child is usually the best intervention strategy. Effective placement of the child away from the abuser is vital, whether completely voluntary or not. The caseworker may then be able to build upon the few strengths of the inadequate personality of the abuser. Counseling from state welfare agencies and family service agencies, along with close supervision from the caseworker, may result in a much more mature adult.

Here again, if the abuser is not willing to cooperate and is not amenable to casework, a care-and-protection petition should be filed on behalf of the child. If there are older children in the home, they may also be suffering from neglect and abuse which might go undetected. These children, too, should be considered in the planning for this family. If the older children do remain in the home, supervision by the worker should be maintained, even though the battered child has been placed.

In summary, the caseworker should be aggressive in employing legal sanctions, including court wardship and police intervention when necessary. He should also provide homemakers' services, counseling services, group therapy, or foster home placement when needed.

There does not seem to be any recurrence, once casework intervention has taken place, except when another child is born to the abuser. It therefore seems in order that the name of the abuser be given to the hospitals in the area; then if another child is born the hospitals can notify the worker who can supervise more closely the potential problem.

Classification 3: the passive-aggressive personality. Abuse represents hostility and anger at having to meet the expectations of others. Usually only one child is abused. This child is seen as a source of competition or as the representation of the abuser's failure to meet role expectations (husband, father). The child is usually either a stepchild or illegiti-

mate. The main personality feature of the abuser is dependency. The abuser finds it difficult to fulfill social roles; the demands of these functions overwhelm him just as his marriage does. There are usually many underlying marital conflicts.

The abuser never admits his guilt and is very unresponsive and unemotional in speaking about the abuse. He is defensive about his feelings and is usually depressed and unhappy. The child toward whom the hostility is directed is definitely in serious danger. This class accounted for 10 percent of the cases studied.

The children who are abused tend to be about two or three years old, an age when they are beginning to seek independence through locomotion. They usually suffer internal wounds or multiple bruises.

The abusers are very uncooperative, and aggressive casework is necessary for the protection of the child; the abusers do not seem amenable to casework, and the prognosis is poor. Relationship-based therapy, however, has been found to be somewhat effective with these abusing parents.

Legal sanctions, court action, and police intervention are often necessary. In the cases studied, the children were placed in a foster home through the guardianship of the courts; the caseworkers had found it necessary to call upon the support of the court.

A recurrence of physical abuse is usually evident if immediate separation of abused and abuser is not effected. Long-term foster care or adoption seems to be the best plan for the child. The protection strategy for the remaining siblings, if they have not been abused, is contingent upon the treatment of the abusive parent and the amount of supervision which the protective agency can give. Here again, homemakers' services, psychological therapy, and casework are vital to the protection of the remaining children.

Classification 4: the sadistic personality. The abusive parent has a history of sadistic behavior, usually including frequent beating and killing of animals. This basically aggressive-destructive pattern has been well developed over a long period of time. There is no strong emotional involvement with the act of abuse, no sign of anxiety or guilt. In some cases, the abuser is also masochistic. There are almost always marital conflicts underlying the family constitution. The abusive parent is often a heavy drinker.

The abused children tend to be older than four years of age. Their injuries are usually skull fractures and concussions or fractures of other limbs. This class accounted for 20 percent of the cases studied.

Casework should always be aggressive, since the abusive parent is usually hostile and defensive to the worker. Legal action (court and police intervention) is almost always necessary. Here it was necessary in 75 percent of the cases. The child is in very serious danger. Treatment strategy should always be in terms of immediate separation of abused and abuser. The prognosis is poor.

If the abuser and abused are not separated, abuse tends to recur even where casework support has been initiated. Here it occurred in 75 percent of the cases. If the abuser is not removed from the home, either voluntarily or through the courts, then long-term foster care or adoption is the best plan for the child. The rest of the family should then be kept in close contact with the caseworker in order to protect the rest of the children, since abuse is usually not isolated to one child. It may be wise to file a care-and-protection petition on behalf of all the siblings.

Homemakers' services and counseling are usually rejected by this type. The only effective means of coping with these sadistic personalities is to forcibly control them by commitment to prison or to a closed psychiatric setting, through the courts.

Typology: controllable abuse

Classification 1: the displacement of aggression. Abuse is the result of displaced aggression. The locus of the problem is marital conflicts. The abuser is usually the mother (80 percent of the cases of this type studied) who is hostile and angry at her mate, the aggressor. Because she cannot return the aggression to the original source, she displaces it onto the defenseless child. The abusive parent manifests much anxiety and guilt concerning the abusive act which she herself cannot understand. The abusive act is impulsive and is usually immediately regretted. The abuser is generally adequate, but cannot cope with her marital difficulties. She cannot control her behavior at moments of greatest stress. This class accounted for 25 percent of the cases studied.

The abused child tends to be over two years old and is usually a bed-wetter and withdrawn. The injuries tend to be multiple bruises or fractures.

Abusers are usually cooperative with the caseworker. They are desirous of relief from the anxiety and guilt which is burdening them. The most suitable planning will include group therapy for the parents or conjoint family therapy which would include the children. If one family member dominates, individual therapy may be preferable, but since treatment should be directed at exposing the marital conflict that is the basis for the abuse, the group approach would seem to be the best plan to help the family relate more harmoniously.

The child may be placed voluntarily in a foster home for a short period of time, while the parents work on their marital problems. Placement, however, is not always necessary.

Court action and police intervention is seldom necessary. The child is not in grave danger, and recurrence after casework has been initiated is infrequent.

Classification 2: the cold-compulsive disciplinarian. Abuse is in reaction to the child's need for closeness and loving affection. The main personality trait of the abuser is usually compulsiveness: He is usually compulsively clean and neat, and cold, rigid, and unfriendly in his interpersonal relations. Abusive parents are often upstanding citizens who defend their right to discipline their children. They generally appear cooperative in order to end the protective supervision and intervention. Often the abuse is an isolated incident. This class accounted for 10 percent of all cases studied.

The abused children tend to be over seven years of age. The nature of the injury is normally lacerations or bruises.

Casework strategy should be in terms of continued home supervision with group therapy for the parents. Therapy should be oriented toward the expression of feelings and emotions, with the explication of fears, and toward warmth and intimacy; in this controlled environment (the group setting), the parents should be able to learn to give and receive emotionally oriented communication. The child is not in grave danger, and legal intervention is usually unnecessary.

The future

It is hoped that this study will contribute to a greater knowledge of the battered-child syndrome. The caseworkers covering the families in which child-battering has taken place are concerned with the future welfare of the abused child. It seems clear, in the light of this study and the findings of Delsordo and others, that they are justified in sounding an alarm. A recent study reported to the American Academy of Pediatrics by Dr. Grace Gregg and Elizabeth Elmer of the University of Pittsburgh reveals that of those children who suffer multiple skeletal trauma inflicted by abusive parents early in life, only about 10 percent fully recover; the remaining 90 percent are still marked by physical, mental, and emotional scars as they approach adolescence. Few of the children studied gave promise of becoming self-sufficient adults, according to the investigators.[6] Their analysis is substantiated by the fact that 70 percent of the cases reported on here showed that the abused child had received head injuries of one kind or another.

An added complication is the fact that social workers continue to find that many professional people—physicians and attorneys, in particular—are still reluctant to participate actively in solving this problem. Many of the case histories studied for this research point up this fact. In one specific instance, the abused child was hospitalized for very serious injuries (skull fractures, compound fractures of other limbs) four times before the examining doctor would actively aid the caseworker by signing a complaint and then testifying

in court. This lack of communication between the physician and caseworkers has caused further abuse to some children. In the example mentioned, the child was crippled for life.

In order to elicit future cooperation from all physicians, social workers must play a role in educating doctors who have had little experience with this problem. It is hoped that studies such as this will bring the problem into focus. Under the new law, physicians' fears of being sued for libel should be dispelled, yet many are reluctant to appear before the courts to testify on behalf of the child because of possible legal, social, and economic repercussions. These fears must be allayed by the social worker, who is familiar with laws.

Lawyers retained for a fee by the abusing parent also play a vital role in the child's welfare. Many attorneys have been able to employ fine legal maneuvers to protect the "rights" of their clients, with the result that the defenseless child is not adequately protected. In many cases studied, a petition for the care and protection of the child was filed, but the child was returned to his hostile home because of the legal maneuvers of the parents' lawyers. Often this resulted in further harm to the child. Usually, however, once a child has been beaten on more than two occasions, the courts and the attorneys will be cooperative. It would be useful if the caseworker also had the benefit of legal representation, but as it stands now the state does not provide this service. Perhaps a part-time attorney in each district office of the DCG would save some of these battered children from future abuse.

The writer must conclude with Delsordo's wise comment on his own earlier study:

While this study sheds some light on child abuse, it clearly indicates that much more needs to be known about the distorted views of abusive parents and the mechanisms which trigger their damaging behavior. To undertake a study of the entire problem of abused children is obviously bigger than any one profession. Satisfactory results may be obtained only through joint professional endeavor.[7]

---

[6]Grace S. Gregg and Elizabeth Elmer, Battered Child's Trauma Found to Be Lasting, *RN*, 30:28 (April 1967).

[7]Delsordo, Protective Casework.

Agency Structure
and the Commitment
to Service

ANDREW BILLINGSLEY, Ph.D.
NAOMI STRESHINSKY
VONNIE GURGIN

Dr. Billingsley and his associates have summarized in this paper material from a study of Child Protective Services currently in progress with the support of the Children's Bureau, Welfare Administration, DHEW. The findings of the study thus far indicate to these researchers that child protective services should be a part of a child welfare function and associated with other child welfare services within the structure of public welfare. This does not rule out the delegation of this responsibility within public assistance divisions of public welfare agencies. In fact, there are many public welfare agencies in which it is being done effectively within the public assistance framework. The point is that children are protected and safeguarded from harm. Dr. Billingsley is Assistant Professor, School of Social Welfare, University of California, Berkeley. Miss Streshinsky is Research Associate and Miss Gurgin is Research Assistant.

The provision of social welfare services to families who need them is one of the responsibilities of county public welfare departments throughout the United States. The 1962 Amendments to the Social Security Act make it mandatory for welfare departments to provide social services in addition to financial assistance to families who are needy and eligible for these services.

One of the particular types of social services that welfare departments can and do provide is child-protective services on behalf of children who are subjected to parental mistreatment. In a typical protective services case, children are actually or potentially in danger of psychological and/or physical harm and may need immediate assistance. Their parents are unwilling to see the problem or ask for help and may be overtly hostile to agency services. These special circumstances call for a considerable degree of professionalism, flexibility, innovation, and the full use of agency and community resources.[1] Our interest here is in the analysis of conditions under which such services are offered.

It has become apparent to us in field visits to a number of welfare departments that specialized services to families involved in neglect and abuse may be provided in the context of several different structural arrangements within the welfare department.[2] These services may be provided in the child welfare division, that sector of the welfare department specializing in such services as adoptions, foster care, licensing, parent-child counseling, and protective services. Such services may be provided in the family assistance division, encompassing those programs focused primarily

[1]For further discussion, see *Standards for Child Protective Services* (New York: Child Welfare League of America, 1960); Andrew Billingsley, "Bureaucratic and Professional Orientation Patterns in Social Casework," *Social Service Review*, Vol. XXXVIII (1964), pp. 400-407.

[2]Observations in this paper are based principally on field visits we made to nine county welfare departments located in five states on the West Coast, the Midwest, and the East Coast. All these departments have in common a fairly well-developed program of child-protective services.

on the provision of financial assistance to needy families and individuals, such as Aid to Families with Dependent Children, Aid to the Blind, Aid to the Disabled, and Old Age Assistance. Even where welfare departments are not specifically organized into two distinct divisions, there are often some operational equivalents of a child welfare division and a public assistance division. Protective services may be carried out in either or both of these divisions.

Even when lodged specifically within one of these major divisions of the welfare department, child-protective services may be further organized into specialized units within the division or into generalized units carrying not only protective cases but other types of cases known to that division.

The most common pattern is for protective services to be organized in specialized units within the child welfare division. However, each of the above patterns is represented among the different county welfare departments in the state of California alone. In many agencies throughout the United States, even when there is a specialized protective services unit, cases of neglect and abuse are frequently found in the caseloads of the regular AFDC units in the public assistance division.

The primary focus of our analysis has been on the specialized child-protective units in the child welfare division and generalized AFDC units in the public assistance division, as alternate structures for the possible location of child protective services.

What difference does it make as to the type of structure in which these services are located? This is the central question for this analysis. Our view is that it may make a great deal of difference because each of these types of organizational structure has its own attributes and "subculture" which have important implications for efforts to provide protective services.

As we discuss these alternate settings for protective services, we will examine their differing features along five dimensions—the clientele, the size of operation, bureaucratic procedures, professional considerations and ancillary services.

CLIENTELE

The first major difference between these two organizational settings concerns eligibility for service. Families served in the public assistance divisions are only those who qualify for financial assistance under particular eligibility requirements relating to income, residence, property, and so forth. When a family no longer meets these requirements, the case is closed.

The primary eligibility requirement for service in protective services units is suspected or confirmed evidence that parents are mistreating their children.

In the child welfare division, where protective services units are housed, financial eligibility is not a relevant factor, although clients receiving financial assistance may be served in the child welfare division concerning other problems. A range of services are offered in child welfare divisions: for example, parent-child counseling, adoptions, foster home placement.

There are several consequences of the agency's decision as to who gets service where. In general, clients of the child welfare division are of a higher socioeconomic status than public assistance clients, and this status differential is reflected in the treatment accorded them by the community, and in the latitude and discretion shown them by the social work staff in that division. In contrast, the AFDC program, in particular of all public assistance programs, is under heavy public criticism concerning the manner of the expenditures of public funds; and the AFDC clients are publicly vulnerable because of a high incidence of separation, divorce, and illegitimacy. These clients often come from disadvantaged minority groups and low-income families with long histories of economic dependency, with resulting negative community attitudes toward them.

In contrast, in the child welfare division, the main purpose is safeguarding children; and this brings immediate public sympathy. Much of the work is with foster parents and adoptive parents who not only have the public's acceptance but are in a position to give or withhold service from the agency. The agency and the workers are, in a large sense, dependent on them; and this has strategic importance for the worker's job. In a study of the public assistance division and the child welfare division of a public welfare department, Richard Scott confirmed a previously developed hypothesis that the more dependent the worker is on his client, the less bureaucratic the worker will be.[3] The social position of the public

[3]See W. Richard Scott, "A Case Study of Professional Workers in a Bureaucratic Setting (unpublished Ph.D. dissertation, University of Chicago, 1961), pp. 228-29, for references to studies relating dependence on clients to degree of bureaucratization. Among these are Elihu Katz and S. N. Eisenstadt, "Some Sociological Observations on the Response of Israeli Organizations to New Immigrants," *Administrative*

assistance client lessens his respectability and power. Consequently, the public assistance worker is more restricted by rules and less likely to be flexible in the use of rules in a discretionary way. We would add that these workers are also more susceptible to public criticism and community pressure.

SIZE OF OPERATION

The second element which distinguishes the subculture of the public assistance division from the child welfare division is magnitude. This is reflected in two respects. First, the operations of the public assistance division were much larger than those of the child welfare divisions in all the communities we visited. This sheer size of operation requires a more rigidly bureaucratic structure. One of the effects of this difference is that the workers in the smaller units are nearer to the source of the rules, and the result of these differences can be seen in the following examples.

In a large AFDC division, a worker was uncertain about allowing a particular kind of special need in the family's budget. He consulted his manual with no success, and then went to his own supervisor for consultation. There had been a recent directive relating to this, and the supervisor was not sure how this might be interpreted. He in turn went to the district supervisor. Again, there was uncertainty, and the district supervisor phoned the AFDC specialist in the department's central office. The specialist in turn took the case to the assistant director, who interpreted the rule but cautioned that this was to be applied only to this case. He stated that he would ask for a formal interpretation of the rule from the state welfare agency in the near future.[4]

Consider a contrasting example which we witnessed during our study. In a small protective services unit, a worker came to the supervisor asking about the eligibility for service of an eighteen-year-old mother who was adequately caring for her own child, but who was herself being mistreated by her own mother in whose home she lived. Could she provide protective services to the eighteen-year-old girl? The supervisor considered the present caseload size, the general flow of recent intake and decided on the spot that their intake could be extended to include this girl. The worker knew immediately that she could proceed with service to her client.

The smaller size also makes it possible for the protective services worker to feel himself part of a more closely knit, perhaps more autonomous unit than the AFDC worker who is one of fifty or more similar workers in the agency.

Second, the caseloads of the regular AFDC staff are also uniformly larger. In our study, we found these to range from 75 to 150, and rarely less than 75 except in isolated instances where a caseload of 60 had been instituted to meet Federal requirements for 75 percent matching funds. As a rule, child welfare workers had 20 to 25 cases. From the standpoint of time alone, the child welfare workers have less pressure from the agency in serving clients than the regular AFDC workers.

One of the concomitants of actual numbers is that the nature of case assignments and transfers is different in the two divisions. In child welfare units, assignments are more likely to be made on the basis of the nature of the case and the skill and experience of the worker. A supervisor of a protective services unit told us that she assigns cases to her workers on the basis of their workload, their ability to handle different kinds of cases, and their facility with different aspects of treatment. In our study, this seemed characteristic of assignments in specialized units. In regular AFDC caseloads, assignment and transfer are usually made on a geographic basis.

In our study, we found an interesting paradox in agency policy which relates to this. In one county, the agency encourages all of their regular AFDC workers to offer services to families beyond the financial one; and in reviewing their records, the reader is impressed by the workers' considerations of many social and psychological factors in discussions with clients. One is also impressed by the frequent change in workers, as transfers of caseloads are made for administrative reasons. The result is that an individual client may have a series of workers, each one discussing many important social and emotional problems, but with a glaring lack of continuity, because of frequent change of workers. The aim of total service to the client is superseded by other adminis-

---

Science Quarterly, Vol. V (June, 1960), pp. 117-19; Samuel A. Stouffer *et al., The American Soldier: Combat and Its Aftermath* (Princeton, N. J.: Princeton University Press, 1949), p. 100; Charles H. Page, "Bureaucracy's Other Face," *Social Forces,* Vol. XXV (October, 1946), pp. 89-94; Seymour M. Lipset, Martin A. Trow, and James S. Coleman, *Union Democracy* (Glencoe, Ill.: Free Press, 1956), p. 139.

[4]Scott found that the rules tend to discourage any additional work to set aside policies in a particular case. His term for such discouragement is the "preservation of apathy" (Scott, *op. cit.,* p. 211).

trative aims of the agency, and we have an example of the "pathologies of bureaucracy,"[5] even in view of the agency's attempts to have it otherwise.

BUREAUCRATIC PROCEDURES

The next factor to be considered is the relatively greater reliance on agency manuals in the public assistance division. This factor is intimately related to the others discussed.

A characteristic of contemporary public welfare is the proliferation of rules which surround the provision of financial assistance. Jests are common about oversized manuals and the constant flow of new regulations, as if from automated machines. Two-inch-thick manuals are a reality and so is the steady flow of modifying rules. One supervisor reported to us that she found it necessary to shield her workers from the flow of new directives. She felt they would be overwhelmed and unable to function if they had to assimilate all of them. She discussed a new rule only as a particular worker's situation called for it. A district director of another agency commented that she and all of the supervisors had spent several hours just trying to understand the meaning of a new regulation before feeling able to impart the information to the line workers.

As a consequence of the extensive rules and the provision of financial help, the AFDC divisions are required to complete a bewildering array of forms. These may include eligibility applications, budget computations, budget revisions, change-of-address forms, change in family structure forms, different versions of case movement scales, denials of aid, termination of aid, ad infinitum. One worker said, "All of us dislike completing these forms. They actually get in the way of our serving clients rather than being of any help."

A comment from an administrative review of one welfare department touches on this.

The case abstract, although completed in duplicate with one copy going to the caseworker for filing in the case record and the other for the substantiation of claiming, actually is of no value to the caseworker because the latter uses a county devised form which requires all that which is required by [the new state form].

Pressure on the workers to complete forms

which, like the one just described, may be just a duplication, comes from differing sources. The pressure may derive from concern for the client, when his subsistence depends on the worker's completion of paper work. The pressure more often comes from the administration whose accounting procedures depends on the worker's paper activity.

Scott's findings in the public assistance divisions are relevant here.

Seventy-two percent of workers believed that their caseloads were too large to allow them to perform adequate casework with their clients, and 85 percent felt that they were required to spend too much time filling out the various forms required by agency procedures. In short, workers in County Agency believed that the kind of services they could perform for clients—their professional function—was rather severely constrained by the administrative and legal framework within which they were required to operate.[6]

The problem of magnitude, then, as represented both by the size of the agency operation and the size of workers' caseloads seems to intensify the reliance of the public assistance division on rule oriented behavior in sharp contrast to the child welfare division, where smaller units and caseloads, and primarily nonfinancial services require far less of a *bureaucratic* framework.

PROFESSIONAL CONSIDERATIONS

We also observed that the level of professionalism in the public assistance divisions, while varying widely from one community to another, was consistently lower than in the child welfare division in the same community. We found that typically agencies required only a B.A. degree for workers in regular AFDC divisions, though it is not uncommon for supervisors in public assistance divisions to have graduate social work training. In the child welfare division, however, at least one year of graduate work appears uniformly required and frequently all workers in the protective service units have M.S.W. degrees.

The divisions are affected in several ways because of the different degrees of professionalism. Those divisions in which there are more trained workers enjoy both the tangible and intangible evidences of higher status. Administrators of public welfare departments show their higher valua-

[5]Harold L. Wilensky and Charles N. Lebeaux state that necessary and useful aspects of bureaucracy can become exaggerated into "pathologies" of bureaucracy (*Industrial Society and Social Welfare* [New York: Russell Sage Foundation, 1959], p. 246).

[6]W. Richard Scott, "Reactions to Supervision in a Heteronomous Professional Organization," *Administrative Science Quarterly*, Vol. X (1965), pp. 69-70.

tion of the workers in the child welfare divisions by paying them higher salaries. The entire agency —administration and both trained and untrained casework staff—believe there is more prestige attached to graduate training. The director of the child welfare division in one community told us that the high status for their protective services units seems to be, in part, related to their salary, training, and position, and, in part, related to the fact that they concentrate on providing casework services and do not get involved in public assistance and other tangible services except by referral. Often within the already highly valued child welfare divisions, the protective services unit is considered an elite group. We were told, "Workers like to transfer into these units from public assistance units but very seldom wish to transfer out."

A director of casework services described the difficulties in keeping trained staff in the public assistance divisions, even in the intensive services units. "The workers," she said, "do not like to administer the public assistance part of their job because of all the rules and regulations and paper work. They want to spend most or all of their time in providing casework services." She added, "I am afraid we will have trouble keeping them." A public assistance worker in another agency told us that an in-service training program had been established for the public assistance division, but that most workers did not attend the seminars. She felt this was because there was little incentive provided by the agency for such attendance in terms of salary increments or status changes for the workers.

ANCILLARY SERVICES

One of the more important ancillary services is that of other professional consultation, particularly psychiatric consultation. Consultation is more readily available in child welfare than in assistance units. The prestige which the social work community attaches to psychiatry, medicine, and law is associated with the child welfare units much more than with the regular AFDC units.

In addition, the use of such facilities as foster care, day care, and homemaker services is a usual part of the child welfare division. The regular AFDC units must refer to others in a different division for these services.

An agency administrator told us that over a million dollars was spent in the previous year in providing extra services to clients of protective services and child welfare units. "This amount," he said, "does not include the salaries of the workers who provide direct services to clients, but it does include extra services such as psychiatric services, medical services and other supports that the client might need. In addition, there are available to these workers the services of two psychologists and a part-time psychiatric consultant, as well as a medical consultant."

CONCLUSION

In this paper we have suggested that the public assistance division of the welfare departments we visited may be distinguished from the child welfare divisions as a location for child protective services in three major respects. The public assistance division is much more highly rule-oriented, exhibits a much lower level of professionalism, and commands a much narrower range of ancillary services than the child welfare division. In general, public assistance divisions are more restrictive of the social worker's role. Even in those communities where the public assistance divisions are under public attack, the staffs of the child welfare divisions have more professional autonomy and discretion and are less vulnerable to these repressive elements than the personnel of the public assistance divisions.

The relevance of these observations to the provision of child protective services may be stated simply. The standards of the Child Welfare League of America, our own experience, plus the general observations of all our informants during the course of our field visits all suggest that the provision of child-protective services, because of the nature of the client problems involved, require a social work role characterized by flexibility, autonomy, and innovation and heavy reliance on collaborative relations among a variety of agencies. These conditions seem more likely to be met within a structural framework strongly committed to service.

These observations provide support for our general view that child protective services should be conceptualized as a child welfare function and structurally associated with other child welfare services rather than grafted on to the public assistance function.

SERVICES TO NEGLECTED CHILDREN

ANNIE LEE SANDUSKY
Consultant on Social Services to Children Living in Their Own Homes, Children's Bureau

WE ONLY HAVE TO READ the newspapers to know that serious neglect and abuse of children by parents is all too frequent. Today hundreds of children pass through our juvenile courts and into foster care because of neglect or abuse. Many delinquent children are also neglected children. Social services for neglected or abused children and their parents are therefore a basic child welfare service that should be available in every local community throughout the country.

Social work experience has shown that many neglecting parents want help in learning to be better parents and can benefit from it. Public and voluntary child welfare agencies in a number of places have demonstrated that many parents can be helped to grow and improve in the care, protection, and guidance of their children. When this happens the child's own home is preserved and his family is strengthened; parents and children are spared the trauma of separation; the community has been spared the high cost of supporting children in foster care; and some children may be saved from future delinquent behavior or from some day becoming neglecting parents themselves.

Children suffering from neglect or abuse are brought to the attention of the agency through someone other than the parent whose acts or behavior jeopardize the child's well-being. These children arrive at the agency because of the community's concern for them. The conscience of the community has been outraged and its expectancy in regard to parental care violated.

Neglect or abuse of a child may be a symptom of many types of problems among parents. These include deep-seated emotional difficulties, immaturity, drunkenness, marital problems—to name but a few. The agency is not free to refuse to help families with such problems on the basis that "our workers are not equipped to deal with them." It must see what can be done.

Child welfare workers are learning from experience with such parents that, as Helen Perlman has said, "the whole of living may be benignly affected by the resolution of one problem and the restoration of balance." [1] Often when parents are helped to achieve success in one small area, major problems become less overwhelming.

The K family, consisting of Mr. and Mrs. K and five children ranging in age from 11 years to a few months, were referred to the child welfare agency because of gross neglect of their children. Living conditions were deplorable. The children were usually dirty and unkempt, and school attendance was poor. Work with the parents revealed marital difficulty to be one of the major problems underlying the neglect. Mr. K was about to leave Mrs. K for another woman.

While Mr. and Mrs. K were discussing their marital difficulties with the worker at their home, 8-year-old Jean came into the room quietly crying. When the worker asked what was troubling her, Jean came to the worker, put her head on her shoulder and sobbed. She finally said, "I want to live with grandma." The worker asked Jean if she was worried about things at home and the child replied that she was. When asked where she would rather live, Jean said: "With Mommy and Daddy, but they don't seem to want me." The worker said a problem like that must be very hard for a little girl to think about. Jean tearfully and vigorously nodded. The worker then asked if Jean was afraid she had come to take her away. Again the child nodded, sobbing uncontrollably. The worker assured Jean that she was there to help Mommy and Daddy make things better for her and not to take her away.

Mr. and Mrs. K sat silently watching. The worker turned to them and asked whether the incident had meant anything to them. Mr. K replied, "It meant a lot. We have been so concerned with our own affairs we haven't thought what this was doing to the children." Mr. K made the decision that he was going to stay with Mrs. K. When she asked him for how long he replied, "Forever." [2]

The problems of these immature parents were not solved with this decision. Improvement in their care of the children came slowly, with some reversal to former habits of uncleanliness and carelessness. But they did stay together and family relationships did improve.

The circumstances that prevent parents from being able to ask for help also make it difficult for some of them to face the fact that they have been neglecting or abusing their children. Yet, until the parents are able to face this fact, their energies are not freed for them to do something about the problem. A great amount of understanding, respect, acceptance, and skill is required to help parents who are caught in a struggle of denial and projecting blame on others. Many child welfare workers are acquiring competence in this.

The C family was referred to the child welfare agency by a hospital which treated the 6-year-old boy, Wade, for a broken arm suffered in a beating by his mother. Mr. C began the first interview with the worker by saying: "I want to say directly at the beginning that I approve of all my wife has done." He said the neighbors were prying into his business and they were "neurotic about the whole affair." Mrs. C agreed with him.

Mr. C then tried to deflect the conversation from the beating of the child by talking about the neighbors' interference in the past. The worker listened attentively but brought the subject back to the beating by saying that he could see they had had some trouble with their neighbors but the report of serious abuse of the children was the main concern now. Both parents said they whipped their children because they believed in firm discipline and they challenged the worker's right to question this. Mr. C again attempted to avoid the subject of Wade's beating by describing at length how strict his parents had been with him. Mrs. C said the children had "evil in them" which had to be controlled.

The worker said he could understand how Mr. and Mrs. C felt about his being there. He granted that the parents had the right to discipline their children, but pointed out that when a child is injured "the community wants to find out what the problems are and try to help the family. That's why I am here."

Mr. C maintained that there was not any problem. He began talking about one of the other children's difficulties in school, and with Mrs. C went into a long tirade about "young teachers" not being firm enough with youngsters.

Again the worker brought the conversation back to the Cs' own disciplinary practices by saying that children had to be dealt with firmly, but the injury of a child was a serious matter. He added: "I can understand that one may be so upset he has trouble controlling himself." Mrs. C hesitatingly said, "I was so upset and too angry" and broke into tears. The worker replied that if together they could try to understand why Mrs. C gets so upset, perhaps the behavior would not continue. Mr. C, who had been silent for a while, said he realized it was serious and that he did not approve of Mrs. C beating the children but did not know what to do. He had told her that this was bad for the youngsters but she continued. Mrs. C remarked that looking back on Wade's beating was a terrible experience. She did not realize she had injured him until his arm became swollen. She supposed it was her anger and her temper that did it. She would like to talk to someone and she does need help. [3]

In addition to reaching out to parents and initiating help, the agency must stay with the problem until more adequate care of the child is reasonably assured. At times this must be done in the face of the parents' objections.

Neighbors complained that a young mother was seriously neglecting her 4-month-old daughter, the first and only child. When the child welfare worker visited the home, she found the baby looking very pale and listless and apparently not in good physical condition. She persuaded the mother to take the baby to a clinic, where the child was found to be seriously malnourished and to have a severe diaper rash. On her next visit to the home, the worker found that the mother had apparently done nothing to carry out the doctor's instructions. As the worker talked to the mother about her lack of care and the seriousness of the baby's condition, the mother ordered her out of the house. The worker agreed to go but explained that she would have to continue her responsibility for seeing that the baby had more adequate care even to the point of filing a petition at court, if necessary.

The worker called in a public health nurse who helped the mother follow the doctor's instructions. The mother told the nurse how sorry she was about the way she had treated the child welfare worker and asked the nurse to tell her to return. The worker went back promptly and from then on was able to help the young mother and her husband grow in their ability to care for their child and to get pleasure from it. The child blossomed in her parents' care. [4]

Mutual Decisions

Workers providing casework services to children in situations of neglect and abuse are always faced with the crucial decision—can the child be helped in his own home or is foster care required? To answer this question, the worker must have knowledge, skill in its use, sensitivity, and creativity in the diagnostic process. In addition he must understand parents and the meaning parenthood has for the individual.

The transition from being merely marriage partners to being capable parents is a developmental process that most parents achieve without too much difficulty. But this is not true for all parents. Sometimes because of circumstances in their past or present, their capacity for parenthood is blocked and cannot develop. With removal of pressures, fears, anxieties, or other impediments their capacity for parenthood may grow. In some instances however, because of their own previous deprivations, parents may lack the capacity to develop *at this time* the emotional maturity required for successful parenthood. The question is how to determine this.

I am constantly amazed and gratified at the growing skill of child welfare workers in evaluating the capacities of parents who have been neglecting their children. In many instances parents who at first seem hopeless in their parental relationships have developed with the child welfare worker's help into adequate parents, though often slowly and haltingly.

In others, the child welfare worker has helped parents face the fact that the best way to carry out their parental role is to release their child for adoption so that the child can have security and loving care in a family of his own. These decisions, of course, are not the worker's alone. They are decisions arrived at by worker and parents together.

Because social services provided in cases of child neglect and abuse have the primary purpose of protecting the child, child welfare workers sometimes give parents the impression that they are there to protect the child against the parents. It is natural and easy to identify with a helpless child who has been mistreated by adults and to feel that one must protect him against his dreadful parents. But such an attitude puts a barrier between worker and parents. Since help to the child must come through the parents by way of increased capacity to give him better care, the worker must begin at the point of the parents' interest in their child whatever that may be. For instance, the Cs' interest in their children's "good behavior" was the point at which the worker began by supporting them in their conviction that children should be disciplined. The worker did not, however, condone their method. Such an approach helps to relieve the parents' fear of blame and condemnation by the worker.

Frequently, as with Mr. and Mrs. K, parents' own needs and problems are the stumbling blocks to their being more adequate parents. Before parents can even begin to think about the needs of their children, the worker must relate to the parents in terms of their own needs. Thus, a connection between the worker and the parents is made and movement can begin.

Any social agency providing casework services in relation to child neglect must make provision for temporary care of children in emergencies. Sometimes neglected or abused children are in immediate danger when called to the attention of child welfare agencies, and need more adequate care at once. Some child welfare agencies have carefully selected families to be available on a 24-hour basis to receive children into their homes for emergency foster care. Other child welfare agencies have established group-care or shelter-care facilities, which are under their administration.

A few agencies are experimenting in the use of homemaker services in emergencies. For example, when young children have been left unattended by parents, the agency instead of suddenly moving them to a strange environment sends a homemaker into the home to care for the children until the parents can be located. Homemakers are also being used in cases of neglect to help parents learn to give better care to the home and children, and, in some instances, to be a source of emotional support to immature parents.

Place of Other Agencies

Providing social services to neglected children brings a child welfare agency into relationships with law enforcement officials and juvenile courts. Frequently instances of neglect, abuse, or exploitation are reported to law enforcement officials and sometimes investigated by them before the case is referred to a social agency. On the other hand, when a child welfare worker finds that an immediate danger requires removal of children from their homes without the knowledge or consent of their parents, she calls on the police, a sheriff, or other law enforcement officer to carry out this function. Thus child welfare workers and the police learn to understand, respect, and accept each other's functions. As understanding grows, the police are apt to refer to the agency more children and their parents in need of child welfare services for a variety of reasons.

The majority of all children coming to child welfare agencies for foster care have been committed by the courts. However, in many instances, the agency has had no part in determining the need for foster care. When there is good cooperative effort between the child welfare agency and the court the rights of the child and his parents are safeguarded and careful attention is given to the need of the child for foster care before he is committed to the agency for placement.

Sometimes a child's welfare makes it necessary for him to be cared for away from his own home. Only the court can interfere with the parent's right to the possession of his child. When a child is removed from a situation of immediate danger and placed in shelter care, an order from the court is required to detain him.

Since child welfare services for neglected children and their parents involve referrals to and from other agencies, they require the agency also to have a close working relationship with the public assistance agency, the schools, health agencies, mental health clinics, housing authorities, religious organizations, and other agencies. All of these relationships to be effective must be based on clear interpretation of agency function, goals, and methods of work, and well-thought-out plans for coordination of services.

As child welfare agencies provide more services to neglected children they insure for many of these children security in their own homes with their own parents. Nevertheless, foster care will continue to be needed for some children. But the purpose of placing a child in foster care will be clear, and the goal to be achieved through it will be thoughtfully planned as part of the decision to place him. Moreover, only those children who need foster placement to promote their well being will be placed in foster care.

Blocks to Service

Today, however, many communities do not provide services to help families overcome problems leading to child neglect. Why have the majority of local public child welfare agencies not assumed responsibility for providing help to parents with such problems *before* the situation becomes so bad that court action is necessary? Part of the reason may have to do with tradition.

Historically child welfare agencies were begun out of a concern for children who had no families. Their emphasis was, therefore—and still is largely—on placing children in foster care or for adoption. Neither their staffs nor the community regarded them as responsible for strengthening the family life of children in order to keep children and their parents together.

However, today we know that we cannot regard children as if they were isolated entities who live in an emotional vacuum. We realize more clearly that a child, because of his immaturity and dependency, must always be viewed in relationship to adults, preferably his own parents—that social services for a child are services given to him in relation to his parents and the rest of his family, whether he lives in his own home or in a foster home or institution. The goal for each child is a secure family life.

Originally the protection of children from neglect, abuse, and exploitation was the province of "protective" or "humane" societies that in the beginning were not considered social agencies. Many of the early humane societies were set up to protect animals from cruelty and abuse and later took on the function of protecting children. In their early days these societies considered themselves law enforcing bodies rather than social agencies. They were empowered by law to remove children from their homes in situations of immediate danger without the knowledge or consent of parents and to arrest parents for neglecting or abusing their children. Over the years some of these societies have changed from law enforcement to social work agencies, employing competent social work staff and using social work methods to help neglected children and their parents. Some have given up their law enforcement functions while others have retained them.

These voluntary agencies, however, do not cover the country. Moreover, they are finding it increasingly difficult to meet all the need in the areas they were incorporated to serve. Some of them have had to limit the number of cases of child neglect they will accept.

At the present time many communities are recognizing that social services for neglected children and their parents should be a part of the public child welfare field. In community after community where studies have been made to determine the extent of child neglect and the need for services, the recommendation has been made that the public welfare agency provide such services.

In Cleveland for example, the welfare department has recently established a program of services in cases of child neglect as a result of a recommendation made by a citizens' committee. This committee had been appointed by the local welfare council to find a way to get services to neglected and abused children when it became apparent that no agency in the area was accepting complete responsibility for such children. Its recommendations were based on studies of the literature in the field, the State laws in regard to neglected children, and the practices of the local social casework agencies in relation to child neglect.[5]

One of the blocks to the development of social services for neglected children is the lack of legislation defining the public welfare agency's responsibility in this regard. Some States have no legislation empowering the public welfare agency to provide such services. In other States the enabling legislation is couched only in a general requirement that the State cooperate with the Federal Government in "extending and strengthening public welfare services for homeless, dependent and neglected children, and children in danger of becoming delinquent." Other States have laws giving overlapping responsibilities to public welfare agencies and juvenile courts. In these States the public welfare agencies tend to rely upon the court, which often receives the initial complaint, to act in all instances of neglect.

In some States the legislation is permissive—the welfare agency *may* provide service in neglect situations. But permissive legislation does not assure the availability of service. Mandatory legislation specifically defining the public welfare agency's responsibility for children who are neglected or abused is the best way to make sure that all such children will receive social services.

Some factors in the development of social casework itself have hampered the expansion of programs of social services for children who are neglected and abused. As the profession of social work began to incorporate psychoanalytic concepts into its knowledge and practice, the notion that a person's ability to ask for help was an indication of his ability to benefit from help began to hold sway. As a result, if an individual needed help he had to ask for it. For many years most social agencies would not reach out to offer help to people who did not request it even though their need was evident.

The very nature of neglect problems prevents the people involved from asking for help. Being a *good parent* is one of the highest attainments and basic expectancies in our culture. To admit failure in one of the most fundamental aspects of human relationships—that of parent and child—is a terrible onslaught on the ego. Most neglecting parents cannot come to a social agency and say: "Help me—I am neglecting my child."

As our knowledge of human behavior and experience with people continues to grow we in social work are beginning to see that to ask for help is not in itself conclusive evidence that the applicant is ready to take help, and conversely, that the fact that a person has not asked for help does not mean that he does not want help or is unable to use it.

Confusion in Terms

Another factor inhibiting the development of services to neglected children and their parents is the confusion about what these services are and what they can accomplish. Part of the confusion grows out of the fact that terms have been carried over from earlier days when law enforcement was the sole function of protective societies. In social work literature and elsewhere, the terms "authoritative agency" or an agency "with more authority" are often used in referring to an agency providing services to neglected children. This frightens administrators as well as child welfare workers. Some agency administrators have thought they must have some special kind of authority to reach out to people who have not requested help even though legislation has given them responsibility in neglect situations. The truth is, an agency providing casework services to neglected children has no more authority than a social agency providing casework services in relation to other social problems. The agency does have a responsibility to respond to information about child neglect by reaching out to the family unasked in order to ascertain the validity of the facts of the complaint, evaluate the total situation, and determine a plan of action.

The agency initiates the contact, offers the parents help, but it cannot force them to take help. However, motivating parents to *want* help is part of the casework process. Child welfare workers cannot go into the home if the parents do not want them nor stay in if they are asked to leave. Their authority, as in all casework, lies in their knowledge and professional skill. When plans need to be made for taking children away from their parents, the court is the constituted authority to interfere in the relation between parents and child.

Other words carried over from the era of law enforcement confuse and confound us, such as complaint, complainant, investigation, and the like. These are not social work terms; they are legal terms.

The term "protective services" is confusing in tending to set these services apart from other casework services for children. Adoption and foster placement describe types of care. But what does "protective services" describe? All services for children are in a sense protective. To use such a broad term in so narrow a sense compounds confusion. Staff of the Children's Bureau have discontinued the use of the term "protective services." Instead we refer to services for children who are neglected, abused, or exploited.

There are some identifiable specifics in providing social services in relation to child neglect. These are: work with the referring person or agency; reaching out to parents who have not asked for help; determining whether or not neglect exists; knowing what is admissible evidence when seeking to file a petition at court; accepting responsibility to stay with the situation until the child's welfare is reasonably assured. The helping process, however, is the application of basic casework techniques to the problem of neglect and abuse.

Toward Progress

Though the growth of social services for neglected children has been slow, nevertheless progress is being made. State and local public welfare agencies are increasingly developing these services. In some agencies providing such services knowledge, understanding, and skill in evaluation and treatment are steadily improving.

Unfortunately, however, not all public welfare agencies giving services in child neglect are providing a top quality of services. The inadequacies usually stem from lack of administrative understanding and conviction about what good service is. Too often all the blame is put on the lack of trained personnel.

There is much that a public child welfare agency can do to develop a good service in spite of a shortage of trained, experienced child welfare workers. It can select nonprofessional staff members to work in child welfare who have interest, personality qualifications, and a college education, and provide them with educational leave for professional training. It can develop inservice training and provide competent supervisors to guide the workers and help them give services to parents and children. It can reduce caseloads to a size that will allow workers to give families the continuous help and support they need.

The fact that effective services are being provided to neglected children and their parents by some public child welfare agencies shows what can be achieved.

The best measure of what we can accomplish for all children lies in what we do for the abused and neglected child. Persons concerned with child welfare must move much more aggressively and at a much faster pace to see that social services are available for neglected children and for their parents. This requires community action as well as an increase and refinement of professional knowledge and skill on the part of child welfare workers. All of this must be achieved quickly because children cannot wait.

[1] Perlman, Helen Harris: Social casework. University of Chicago Press, Chicago, 1957.

[2] New Hampshire State Department of Public Welfare. Case record (disguised for publication).

[3] Juvenile Protective Association, Chicago, Ill. Case record (disguised for publication).

[4] Children's Aid and Society for the Prevention of Cruelty to Children. Buffalo, N.Y. Case record (disguised for publication).

[5] Ward, David M.: Citizens' responsibility in the development of protective services to children. Paper presented at the 1959 forum of the National Conference on Social Welfare.

HOMEMAKER SERVICE IN NEGLECT AND ABUSE

II. A Tool for Case Evaluation

ELIZABETH A. STRINGER

Associate Director, Foster Care Services
Children's Aid Society, New York

THE GENERAL PUBLIC, and even professional persons, find it difficult to believe that a parent will willfully and intentionally harm his child. Yet, not long ago, the New York papers carried headlines about a 7-year-old crippled child who was beaten to death by her mother and the mother's "boy friend" solely because "we enjoy beating her." Such incidents are not unusual, and have in recent years become the subject of nationwide concern.

As Elizabeth Elmer has said, there are ". . . unbelievably primitive transactions that take place beyond our gaze, safe from our curious questions." [1] These acts range from battering a child in impulsive rage to deliberate intent to murder. In such situations, the use of homemaker service to assist a social caseworker in the evaluation of family strengths and weaknesses, and to provide facts based on direct observation, can be invaluable in helping a responsible agency to take appropriate action for the protection of the child.

The value of the homemaker's role in clarification of the vague and uneasy impressions of hospitals and social agencies that there is need for intervention has been shown in many cases. Sometimes the homemaker has been the only source through which the actual facts have become known, enabling an agency to take court action.

Obviously, homemaker service is a resource which could be used increasingly by all communities to obtain a clearer picture of family relationships and incidents taking place in the home. Necessary action to protect children who are in danger has all too long been hampered by "the maze of contradictory statements and lack of real facts which so often surround cases of seriously neglected or battered children." [2]

This is illustrated in the case of Paul, age 9 months, who will never walk, and who has had four hospital admissions for injuries in his few short months of life. Yet he has been sent home again and again to become the repeated object of his father's rage and violence. Even when his father acknowledged the acts that resulted in Paul's becoming a hopeless cripple, the legal, medical, and social professions were reluctant to heed this family's unspoken appeal for Paul's protection.

Both Paul's parents are deaf-mutes. His father's history is full of evidence of frustration and rage over his inability to communicate and compete on a level with others. The parents met as adolescents on a social outing and were married after pregnancy with their first child occurred.

Although the father had occasional explosions of temper, he seems to have managed to sustain himself and his family without untoward incident until the conception of the second child, Paul. He then became so depressed that he lost control of his actions. This continued after Paul's birth, and worsened when Paul's mother proved to be totally unable to manage the two babies, less than a year apart in age. The father gave up his job and accepted public aid in order to remain at home to help his wife.

Outwardly, Paul's father seemed to be elated with the new baby, rocking him, kissing him, and holding him very tight. However, only 1 month after his birth, Paul was admitted to the hospital with a fractured skull. The parents reported he had been screaming and crying, and that his father, who was holding him at the time, accidently dropped him on his head. Even before this, Paul had been treated for fractures, though not hospitalized.

Paul was treated and sent home only to be readmitted to the hospital at the age of 4 months, so badly beaten and bruised that he developed a spastic condition of both legs which will prevent him from ever walking. His father, who brought Paul to the hospital, admitted that the injuries occurred when he punched the baby in the abdomen.

At that point, the hospital reported the matter to the authorities. The father was arrested and admitted to a hospital prison ward, where he remained for a month. He was then released on bail and returned home. His trial was postponed and later dismissed.

The point was made in a recent issue of CHILDREN that parents who neglect and batter their children are actually expressing their parental incapacities in action, and are asking to be stopped in their brutal behavior. Why else do they bring their injured children to hospitals, thus running a high risk of punishment? [2]

This was certainly true in the case of Paul's father, who asked for readmission to the hospital for himself because of depression and self-hate, which he admitted he displaced on the baby. However, he was diagnosed "not actively psychotic" and was released.

When Paul was sufficiently recovered to leave the hospital, he was once again discharged and taken home. This decision was made on the basis of his father's diagnosis, and because both parents had agreed to seek psychiatric help, along with social service and homemaker service.

Enter a Homemaker

By this time, several community agencies were interested in the family—the hospital, a psychiatric clinic, the family court, and the public welfare department. On a purchase-of-service agreement with the public agency, the Children's Aid Society, a voluntary agency, placed a homemaker with the family; she remained for 6 weeks.

The homemaker's observations proved invaluable in enabling the various interested agencies to obtain a clear picture of the family relationships, and to conclude that, without question, the child was in constant danger as long as he remained with his father.

The homemaker graphically described the father's handling of the baby: overfeeding him; hugging and kissing him so roughly that the baby often cried; shaking him violently when he did cry; giving him the bottle so forcefully that blisters were raised on his mouth.

The mother communicated with the homemaker by note and told her that the father stayed up late to watch television and that she was afraid to go to bed before he did because he might harm his son. On the other hand, the mother was unable to bring herself to make a formal complaint against the father.

Paul's parents did not follow through on the psychiatric referral. Therefore, on the basis of the homemaker's observations, a consultation between the children's agency providing homemaker service and the referring agency resulted in a decision to appeal to the court for the baby's permanent removal.

Later that same day, Paul was readmitted to the hospital suffering from a brain concussion. He had been dropped on his head by his father when he started crying during a feeding.

The case was referred to the family court and is still in process of investigation. Paul is in the custody of the court, pending decision.

Other Cases

The unique value of homemaker service in case evaluation, and even in casefinding, is illustrated in other family situations posing danger to children.

Such an example is the Grey family, with five children, age 5 and under. This family was referred to a protective agency by the pediatric clinic of a hospital because of the physical condition of the youngest child.

The homemaker—on 8-hour-a-day, 5-day-a-week assignment—learned that Mr. Grey, in his early thirties, had formerly been a compulsive drinker given to abusing his wife and family when drunk. He had joined Alcoholics Anonymous, and turned to this organization for his outside contacts, going from its meetings directly to his night job. He came home about 9 a.m., and slept most of the day, leaving Mrs. Grey to care for the children day and night on her own.

Her method of retaliation was to lock the children in the bedroom, so that they could not wander away. Often the homemaker would arrive in the morning to find the mother still in bed, and the locked-in children's physical needs completely unattended.

After 4 months, psychiatric consultation was scheduled. The psychiatrist felt that both parents were probably psychotic. The father was regarded as posing more danger to the children than the mother. His need to feel omnipotent was seen as the cause of his rages, during which he beat his wife and children.

The protective agency strongly urged court action to remove the children from the home.

Often the factor which precipitates a referral for homemaker service is one which is incidental to the total problem mosaic of the family, and extended observation and evaluation are needed. This is illustrated by the "Rivera case," which, after a year of homemaker service, still requires additional observations and tests before a suitable therapeutic plan can be made.

The Rivera parents are in their early twenties, their four children ranging in age from 4 years to a few months. Homemaker service was first provided to enable Mrs. Rivera to keep medical appointments at the center for her two younger children. She was unable to manage taking all four children to the clinic by herself.

The homemaker's observations made it immediately apparent that the family's problems were much greater and more complicated than they were originally thought to be. The mother alternated screaming at the children with bribing them to be good. She readily acknowledged that she had no control over them, and stated that both she and her husband wanted to place them in foster care so that they might work to pay off their debts. On the basis of these and other early impressions, full-time home-

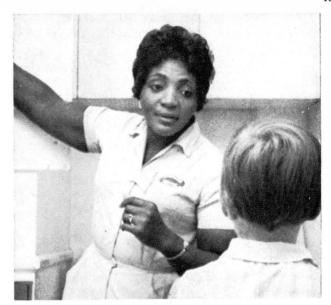

"A . . . homemaker can . . . help many neglecting parents by . . . direct teaching by demonstration and example . . . ."

maker service was offered the family to help relieve immediate pressures and make possible further evaluation.

Soon after full-time homemaker service began, it became that the situation was seriously complicated by the behavior of the 3-year-old child, described by his mother as having been "nothing but trouble" from birth. He was hyperactive, given to severe temper tantrums without apparent cause, enuretic, day and night, and was eating dirt, wood, and plaster. The parents agreed to a psychiatric evaluation of this child, which resulted in a tentative diagnosis of childhood psychosis with homicidal and suicidal tendencies. Hospitalization of the child, though urgently needed, was delayed owing to lack of inpatient psychiatric facilities for a child of 3.

Meanwhile, the home situation had worsened. The mother began to clean the house compulsively, sweeping the floors several times a day, washing the kitchen floor before lunch and again after lunch, and changing the children's clothing two or three times a day. Her moods alternated between silence and excessive talking.

She almost totally ignored the children, except to scream at them, push them, or hit them if they got in the way of her cleaning. If the homemaker had not been present, the mother would have let the children harm themselves, or each other, by her neglect. Two of the other children began to imitate the 3-year-old's tantrums and plaster eating.

On one occasion the mother became so enraged at a tantrum of the oldest child, a girl, that she took off her shoe and beat the child until the homemaker intervened. Later that day the mother said that she might have beaten the child to death, had it not been for the homemaker. She made numerous references to children's deaths.

The psychiatrist's opinion is that this mother is either psychotic or reacting with abnormal behavior to the strain of the 3-year-old's behavior. A true assessment cannot be made until this child is removed. Short- or long-term placement of all of the children may be indicated.

A Grave Responsibility

We have been a long time in acting on the child welfare principle that children have an inherent right to the kind of care and nurturing that will enable them to grow up into healthy adults who will be able to give adequate care to their own children. The first step in such a procedure, and one which is immediately demanded by the uncovering of an alarming number of children in need of protection, is to find ways of obtaining the facts and acting quickly to protect those children whose lives are in danger. Helen Boardman has warned:

... Experiences with the repetitive nature of injuries indicate that an adult who has once injured a child is likely to repeat. Police warnings, court action, and probationary status have not been adequate deterrents. *The child must be considered to be in grave danger unless his environment can be proved to be safe.* The adult, too, needs protection from the consequences of his own explosive behavior.[3]

Yet, from the legal point of view:

The right of the parents to the care and custody of their children creates a strong presumption in favor of the parents in any proceedings to remove the child. Judicial decisions indicate that the conduct of the parents must amount to *forfeiture* or *abandonment* of their right to custody. . . .

In the face of these rights, it is obvious that any petition requesting removal of a child from his family must be based on solid and substantial reasons, established by plain and certain proofs of the neglect. The rights of parents are protected by tradition and precedent, and vague or ambiguous allegations will not be sufficient to show that the parent has forfeited these rights.[4]

Obviously, there is a need for clarification, early identification of the problem, and active steps toward a solution.

Immediate authoritative action is needed in some instances to protect the life of the child in danger. In other instances, parents can be helped by a professional caseworker and a homemaker working in combination to achieve more healthy family relationships and to adopt better methods of child care, as the preceding article by Louise Foresman makes clear. A homemaker can also help many neglecting parents by the direct teaching by demonstration and example which is so clearly in the homemaker's province. The placement of a homemaker, along with the services of the caseworker, can be invaluable in obtaining a well-rounded picture of the family dynamics and of the parents' actual or potential readiness to use help.

As has already been pointed out in CHILDREN,[2] many types of services are needed in combination to protect children from neglect and abuse. Homemaker service should be in the forefront of these. Morris and Gould have found that "services constructively engaging parents into society and putting them in contact with those who exercise nurturing parental roles are most effective in protecting children and in promoting social public health." [5]

Most important is the necessity of establishing the facts early in the child's life, not only to preserve his life but to use whatever forms of intervention can and should be used to alter the course when physical and personality damage is being inflicted.

Services must be provided long before the child enters school, for, by that time, it is often too late and the damage is often irreversible.

If we are to prevent the development of the kinds of personalities which can murder a President or, without reasonable provocation, murder his murderer, *we must reach these personalities before the mold is set.*

[1] Elmer, Elizabeth: Abused young children seen in hospitals. *Social Work*, October 1960.

[2] Morris, Marian G.; Gould, Robert W.; Matthews, Patricia J.: Toward prevention of child abuse. *Children*, March–April 1964.

[3] Boardman, Helen E.: A project to rescue children from inflicted injuries. *Social Work*, January 1962.

[4] Downs, William T.: The meaning and handling of child neglect—a legal view. *Child Welfare*, March 1963.

[5] Morris, Marian G.; Gould, Robert W.: Role reversal: A concept in dealing with the neglected battered-child syndrome. *In* The neglected battered-child syndrome; role reversal in parents. Child Welfare League of America, New York. 1963.

Providing Preventive and Protective Services to Children in a Public Welfare Agency

MYRA J. MITCHINER, ACSW

In North Carolina, we have long considered public welfare's responsibility to be to the total family. Consequently, in our state we have an integrated public welfare program administered locally by county departments under the supervision of the State Board of Public Welfare. I should like to quote briefly from an article written in 1962 by Dr. Ellen Winston (then Commissioner, North Carolina State Board of Public Welfare) and by Miss Myrtle Wolff (then Director, Division of Child Welfare in North Carolina).

"Throughout its history the public welfare program in North Carolina has reflected close cooperation between public assistance and child welfare services at both the state and the county levels.

"In line with the agency's philosophy of maintaining an integrated service program, the staff has included persons from a variety of disciplines selected to carry out the varying aspects of a diversified, broadly based service program. There has been no dichotomy between public assistance staff and child welfare staff. Rather, the agency has set policies on qualifications and compensation that are uniform for all staff members doing similar work and carrying comparable degrees of responsibility; the qualification requirements for general caseworkers and child welfare caseworkers are exactly the same with respect to education and experience, and so also are the salary ranges. The term *general caseworker* is used in preference to the term *public assistance worker* because most workers carry other service cases in addition to their public assistance cases." [1]

---

[1] Ellen Winston and Myrtle P. Wolff, "Integration of Services in a Public Welfare Program," *Social Casework*, XLIII (1962), 403–404.

The agency has held to the necessity for staffing the public welfare program with properly qualified professional personnel. In North Carolina, only a college graduate can be employed in a preprofessional position in a county department of public welfare. No one can qualify for a casework classification, or for a supervisory or administrative position, unless he has had at least one year of graduate education. Many positions require a master's degree in social work.

It should be emphasized that all services offered to children through the public welfare program are available equally to the child who is receiving financial assistance and to the child who is not. In some instances, depending on the particular problems evident in the family situation, an AFDC case may be carried by a child welfare worker. In many instances, the general caseworker responsible for the public assistance caseload carries cases in which there are special problems relating to children. Another administrative policy of the agency provides for only one worker to carry a case. The general caseworker assigned an AFDC case is expected to (1) make available to the family those resources appropriate to meeting the family's needs and (2) handle all of the casework services required.

It has been said many times that AFDC is our first line of defense in assuring that the total needs of children are met. Caseworkers carrying AFDC caseloads have a real opportunity to help parents provide the best possible homelife for their children within the limitations of the program. It is significant that the 1962 Amendments to the Social Security Act set forth a plan requirement, which became effective July 1, 1963, in relation to public welfare's responsibility

---

MRS. MITCHINER *is Director, Division of Public Assistance, North Carolina State* Board of Public Welfare, Raleigh. *This paper was presented at the CWLA Eastern Regional Conference, Philadelphia, May 1964.*

for each dependent child receiving AFDC. In meeting the requirement of a plan for each child, the agency is responsible for maintaining current knowledge of the conditions under which each family lives; the adequacy of, and problems in, child care and rearing; and the specific needs of each child. Through considering each child individually in working with the family, children who require special planning are usually identified. Under this plan requirement, agencies *must* provide services to children *whose care and supervision are inadequate* and to children with special problems. The Federal public assistance policy goes on to state:

"Where there are serious threats to the welfare of children and they are in need of special protection, the agency is responsible for developing and carrying out an adequate plan for care and protection of the children within the home or in substitute arrangements. It is preferable that substitute arrangements be made voluntarily by the parents, but when this is not possible, court action becomes necessary in order to protect the children. . . . The emphasis is upon individualizing the children and knowing any particular needs or problems which should have agency attention." [2]

A Plan for Each Child

In addition to spelling out the responsibility of public welfare for developing a plan for each dependent child, the 1962 Amendments also require coordination between public assistance and child welfare. The following statement emphasizes this:

"Public assistance and child welfare programs are basic resources for meeting the responsibilities which State public welfare agencies carry to provide social services to families and children. Both programs have common objectives to strengthen family life and safeguard the welfare of children; to provide services which support, strengthen or restore the capacities of parents to carry responsibly the parental roles; and to encourage and promote the sound development of the State's program of family and child welfare service. The State agency carries responsibility for planning to develop and utilize to best advantage the program resources of both public assistance and child welfare." [3]

Thus, we see the need for sound adminis-

trative planning in the area of services to children, basic overall agency policy reflecting a concerned agency philosophy, and open lines of communication between the two divisions. Policies should be developed cooperatively and could include broad areas, such as the care of children born out of wedlock; the employment of mothers; the nature of home conditions, parental behavior, money-management or other problems considered to be detrimental to the welfare of children; and criteria to be used in assessing whether such problems result or are likely to result in inadequate care, protection, or neglect of children.

There should be a clear understanding of the types of services needed in various situations for the guidance of both general workers and child welfare workers. This will assure the best and most complete service to families and children and, at the same time, will prevent duplication of services and confusion in responsibility.

Specifically let us look at what is required of the general caseworker carrying an AFDC caseload. She must have a knowledge and understanding of agency function and overall policy, agency and community resources, public assistance policy, methods used in establishing eligibility for public assistance payment, dynamics of human behavior and family relationship, and child growth and development. She must also have the ability to diagnose social problems, evaluate the possibility of treatment, and arrive at a plan of attack on those problems that appear most amenable to solution; the ability to reevaluate, as the plan of treatment proceeds, the effects of service and the need for change in focus; and the ability to acknowledge that some situations cannot be changed and that plans must be made for the children away from their parents.

In comparison, let us consider the responsibilities of the child welfare worker in giving services to children in their own homes. Upon the examination of the above listing, we find that the child welfare worker carries the same responsibilities as the general caseworker—with the exception of those items relating to public assistance. Consequently, it is our belief that the general caseworker responsible for the public assistance service should continue to serve the family even though a neglect situation develops. (We are assuming, of course, that adequate professional supervision is available.)

---

[2] "Social Services in Public Assistance," in *Handbook of Public Assistance Administration* (Washington, D. C.: Bureau of Family Services, Welfare Administration, U. S. Department of Health, Education, and Welfare, 1962), Part IV, Section 4260.

[3] *Ibid.*, Section 4270.

In meeting the requirement for developing a plan for each child in the AFDC caseload, the general caseworker completes a social study of each family. In doing this, she becomes well acquainted with each member of the family, considers the strengths within the family and each family member, and evaluates the family's ability to cope with its problems.

Thus, within this framework, special attention can be given to each child separately. The worker gets to know the child in relation to his adjustment in school; his recreational interests and activities; relationships within the family group, with other children in the neighborhood, and with those at school; any unusual behavior or delinquency; special medical problems; etc. Because of these many factors, the needs and problems of children in families receiving public assistance require a wide range of social services, focused not only on the protection of children whose well-being is in jeopardy, but also on the prevention of problematic situations. It is this area in which the general caseworker responsible for the public assistance function can make her most valuable contribution—the early identification of potential neglect situations.

Coordination of Services

Providing the wide range of social services requires full and coordinated use of the resources of the total agency, both public assistance and child welfare. Even though both services are concerned with the child's total needs, this dual responsibility for the provision of services becomes especially apparent in such problem situations as: serious behavior problems of children; unmarried parenthood and births out of wedlock; neglect, abuse, or exploitation of children; children with mental or physical health problems; children in conflict with the law; and children in need of guardians. The large majority of these problems can very easily appear on public assistance caseloads.

When these types of situations do arise in AFDC cases, the general caseworker carries the primary responsibility for seeing to it that the services needed are made available. If the situation is hazardous for the child, the general worker should be responsible for seeing that services are provided to correct the condition or that appropriate protection is found for the child. The direct services of the general worker are focused primarily on helping the parent or surrogate parent to maintain, or regain, and to use effectively his parental relationship.

The resources of the public assistance program itself are used to meet the family's economic need and to sustain and strengthen the family in dealing with individual and family problems. It goes without saying that the service basic in public assistance to families with children is decent payment. As has been said so many times in so many different ways: no amount of service can fill a child's empty stomach or assure him of adequate clothing for school, needed medical care, and other necessities of life. Likewise, when parents are assured the security of a decent payment with which to meet the needs of their children, they are more likely to turn a listening ear to the worker and to be more accepting of other services from the agency and community.

The general caseworker has much to learn from the child welfare worker in the area of protective service. As we mentioned earlier, there should be open lines of communication between the two divisions. If, in the process of serving an AFDC family, the general worker notes signs of potential neglect or finds that neglect does, in fact, exist, the child welfare division should be called in for consultation. In this way the general worker receives help in understanding the dynamics of the situation, possible methods of treatment, and recommendations regarding the direction toward which services should be focused. This type of collaboration will assure that the family receives the best possible service the agency has to offer.

It may develop that the case should be referred to the child welfare division. This should be done if it appears that the child must be separated from his natural family and placed in foster care. Another type of situation that should properly be referred to child welfare involves an unmarried mother who is considering the release of her child for adoption. In addition, some case situations in which court action has removed the custody of the child from his parents should be referred to child welfare. But, if the child is to be placed with specified relatives and is to continue to receive AFDC, consideration should be given to continuing the case on the AFDC caseload.

With the plan now available for prescribed or defined services in AFDC under Federal regulations, general workers carrying a limited AFDC caseload (of not more than 60 cases) are in a position to offer specialized services to children in their caseloads. Because of the magnitude of the AFDC program and the overall responsibility of the program itself to plan in behalf of dependent children, caseloads must be sufficiently small to allow the worker time to become well acquainted with the family.

Some families carry family responsibilities capably. So long as they know how to reach the worker and feel sure of the worker's attention when problems arise, these families manage well. Other families need regular visits. The one-parent family with several young children, the unmarried mother, and the parent with limited intellectual ability generally need frequent and regular contacts with the worker, who supports and encourages them and makes practical suggestions about home management and child care. Workers must have time to visit each family as frequently as is necessary to meet that family's need for agency service.

As we have indicated earlier, there must be effective coordination between public assistance and child welfare in order for children to receive the protection they need. Careful definition of the two programs serving children and a wise use of all community resources are basic means by which to achieve the goal of adequate preventive and protective service in behalf of children.

RECEIVED AUGUST 6, 1964

A Sociocultural Perspective On Physical Child Abuse DAVID G. GIL

A broad study—on a nationwide scale—of physical child abuse, conducted by Brandeis University, stressed the sociological and cultural aspects of this phenomenon. The findings suggest a series of measures as a basis for prevention through education, legislation, elimination of poverty, and social services.

Throughout history children have frequently been subjected to various forms of abuse in many human societies.[1] This phenomenon, which seems to be one consequence of the inequality in physical strength and social status between children and adults, has always aroused the concern of human individuals and groups. In recent decades public and professional interest in child abuse has increased markedly in the United States and in many other countries.

In this country the heightened interest goes back to the years right after World War II, when pediatric roentgenologists, psychiatrists and social workers identified violent physical attacks by parents and other caretakers as the probable cause of a frequently observed, puzzling association between multiple fractures of the long bones in very young children and subdural hematomas.[2] This discovery caused shock and dismay among professionals who had studied the phenomenon, and gradually, also among the public at large, once the

David G. Gil, D.S.W., is Professor of Social Policy, Florence Heller Graduate School for Advanced Studies in Social Welfare, Brandeis University, Waltham, Massachusetts. This article is based on his book Violence Against Children (Cambridge, Mass.: Harvard University Press, 1970). The study reported here was supported by the U.S. Children's Bureau, under grant PR-288-1.

news media began reporting it in gruesome detail.

In the 1950s and 1960s several books and numerous articles were written on the subject by professional authors and journalists,[3] papers were presented at conferences of physicians, social workers and lawyers, and radio and television networks outdid each other in presenting programs on child abuse. This intensive publicity and the correspondingly intensive interest of professional groups and public authorites led during the 1960s to the swift enactment throughout the country of legislation requiring physicians, and at times other professionals, to notify welfare and law-enforcement authorities of incidents of suspected physical abuse of children.[4]

This growing concern also stimulated efforts to investigate the scope and nature of the phenomenon. However, studies usually involved relatively small and unrepresentative samples of cases known to hospitals, clinics and social welfare agencies.[5] The orientation and methodology of these studies was clinical, and the general conclusion suggested by their findings was that physical abuse of children resulted from psychological disorders of the abusing caretakers, or, at times, of the abused children themselves, from pathological family relationships, and from stressful environmental conditions. Students of child abuse also suggested that the phenomenon was widespread throughout all groups of the population, that it involved primarily very young children, and that it was an important cause of mortality and morbidity among children.

The implementation throughout the United States of laws on reporting child abuse opened up possibilities of conducting epidemiologic studies involving relatively large and more representative cohorts of abused children. At the initiative of the U.S. Children's Bureau and with its support, Brandeis University carried out a nationwide survey of all incidents reported through legal channels during 1967 and 1968, a total of almost 13,000 cases. The method, find-ings and conclusions of this survey have been reported in detail elsewhere.[6] The following observations represent highlights from this survey.

The Brandeis study attempted to transcend the clinical understanding of individual incidents of child abuse, and to unravel the underlying sociocultural dynamics of this manifestation of interpersonal violence. It was expected that such understanding would yield suggestions for primary preventive measures aimed at the configuration of forces that seem to cause this destructive phenomenon.

Systematic study of child abuse had been hampered in the past by lack of an unambiguous conceptual definition. Investigators tended to derive definitions from observable consequences of abusive attacks such as injuries inflicted upon children, rather than from the motivation and the behavior of perpetrators of abuse. Consequences of abusive attacks, however, are likely to be due to chance factors as much as to the behavior of perpetrators, and constitute thus an inappropriate basis for developing a conceptually sound definition. In view of this, physical abuse of children was defined in the Brandeis studies as "the use of physical force by a caretaker toward a child, in order to hurt, injure, or destroy the child." This conceptualization is broad, but unambiguous and free of relativism and arbitrariness. It includes every act of physical aggression directed against a child, irrespective of consequences.

The Sanctioning of Force

The foregoing conceptual definition leads to the realization that physical abuse of children is actually endemic in American society, since the cultural definition of child rearing in the United States does not exclude the use of physical force toward children by parents and other caretakers. Rather, the use of some physical force in child rearing is encouraged in subtle, and at times not so subtle, ways by communications disseminated by the press, radio and television, and by popular and professional publications. Moreover, children are subjected to physical abuse in many schools and child care facilities and even in juvenile courts.[7] Against this background of public sanction of the use of violence toward children, it should surprise no one that extreme incidents occur from time to time in the interaction between individual caretakers and children in their care.

It should be noted that adult persons in American society have legal protection against physical attack by other persons. Children are not assured such protection. This seems to be a denial of "equal protection under the law," an apparent violation of the 14th Amendment to the U.S. Constitution.

The culturally sanctioned use of force in child rearing thus constitutes the basic level of all physical abuse of children. Different social classes and ethnic and nationality groups tend to differ in their child-rearing practices, and also in the extent to which they approve of physical force as a socialization method. These variations among social classes and ethnic groups constitute a second dimension of the phenomenon. The third dimension is determined by environmental chance factors that may transform "acceptable" disciplinary measures into unacceptable outcomes. The fourth dimension is a broad range of environmental stress factors that may weaken a person's psychological mechanisms of self-control and thus contribute to the uninhibited discharge of aggressive and destructive impulses toward physically powerless children. The final dimension is a broad range of deviance in physical, social, intellectual and emotional functioning of caretakers, and at times of children in their care, as well as of entire family units to which they belong. Physical abuse of children appears thus to be a multidimensional phenomenon rather than a uniform one with a single set of causal factors.

Before presenting recommendations based on the foregoing conceptual framework, several comments seem indicated concerning major substantive findings of the nationwide surveys. In spite of its strong emotional impact and the tragic aspects of every incident, the phenomenon of child abuse needs to be put into a balanced perspective. Its true incidence rate has not been uncovered by the nationwide surveys, but the scope of physical abuse of children resulting in serious injury does not seem to constitute a major social problem, at least in comparison with several more widespread and more serious social problems that undermine the developmental opportunities of many millions of children in American society, such as poverty, racial discrimination, malnutrition, and inadequate provision for medical care and education.

Cohorts of officially reported incidents of child abuse are likely to represent the severe-injury segment of the physical child abuse spectrum, since severity of injury is an important decision criterion in reporting. If the 6000 to 7000 incidents that are reported annually through official channels are as a group an approximate representation of the severe segment of the nationwide abuse spectrum, the physical consequences of child abuse do not seem to be serious in the aggregate, for more than half these children suffered only minor injuries, and the classical "battered-child syndrome" was found to be relatively infrequent. Even if allowance is made for underreporting, especially of fatalities, physical abuse cannot be considered a "major killer and maimer" of children in the United States.

Precipitating Factors

Turning to an epidemiologic perspective, it should be noted that physical abuse of children, and especially more serious incidents, was found to be over-concentrated among the poor and among nonwhite minorities. Although it may be valid to argue that overrepresentation of the poor and nonwhites in cohorts of reported child abuse may be in part a function of reporting bias, it must not be overlooked that life in poverty and in the ghettos generates additional stressful experiences likely to become precipitating factors of child abuse. Moreover, the poor and members of ethnic minorities have fewer alternatives and escapes than the nonpoor in dealing with aggressive impulses toward their children. Finally, there is an additional factor, the tendency toward more direct, less inhibited expression and discharge of aggressive impulses, a tendency learned apparently through lower class and ghetto socialization, which differs in this respect from middle-class mores and socialization.

Of considerable interest in terms of forces contributing to child abuse are relatively high rates of deviance in areas of bio-psycho-social functioning of children and adults involved in abuse incidents. Deviance in functioning of individuals was matched by high rates of deviance in family structure, reflected in a high proportion of female-headed households and of households from which the biological fathers of abused children were absent. It is also worth noting that, as a group, families of physically abused children tend to have many more children than other American families with children under age 18.

The age distribution of abused children and their parents was found to be less skewed toward younger age groups than had been thought on the basis of earlier, mainly hospital-based, studies. This difference seems due to the fact that younger children tend to be more severely injured when abused and are, therefore, overrepresented among hospitalized abused children. More boys than girls are subjected to physical abuse, yet girls outnumber boys among adolescent abused children.

Although more mothers than fathers are reported as perpetrators of abuse, the involvement rate in incidents of child abuse is higher for fathers and stepfathers than for mothers. This important relationship is unraveled when account is taken of the fact that nearly 30 percent of reported abuse incidents occur in female-headed households. Altogether, nearly 87 percent of perpetrators are parents or parent substitutes.

Many children in the study had been abused on previous occasions. Also, siblings of many abused children were abused on the same or previous occasions. Many perpetrators were involved in incidents of abuse on previous occasions and many had been victims of abuse during their childhood. The high rate of recidivism reflected in these findings indicates that the use of physical force tends to be patterned into child-rearing practices and is usually not an isolated incident.

Recommendations

Applying a public health model of preventive intervention to physical abuse of children, and proceeding on the foregoing conceptualization of its etiology, the following measures can be suggested:

(1) Since culturally determined permissive attitudes toward the use of physical force in child rearing seem to constitute the common core of all physical abuse of children in American society, systematic educational efforts aimed at gradually changing this aspect of child-rearing philosophy and developing clear-cut cultural prohibitions and legal sanctions against the use of physical force in rearing children are likely to produce over time the strongest possible reduction of the incidence of physical abuse of children.

As a first step, the U.S. Congress and state legislatures could outlaw corporal punishment in schools, juvenile courts, correctional institutions and other child care facilities. This would assure children the same protection against physical attack outside their homes as the law provides for adult members of society. Moreover, such legislation would be likely to affect child-rearing attitudes and practices in American homes, for it would symbolize society's growing rejection of violence toward children.

Giving up the use of physical force

against children may not be easy for adults who were subjected to physical force and violence in their own childhood and who have integrated the existing value system of American society. Children can sometimes be irritating and provocative in their behavior and may strain the tolerance of such adults to the limit. Yet, in spite of these realities, which must be acknowledged and faced openly, society needs to work toward the gradual reduction, and eventual elimination, of physical violence toward its young generation if it is serious about preventing the physical abuse of children.

Rejecting corporal punishment does not imply favoring unlimited permissiveness in rearing children. To grow up successfully, children require a sense of security inherent in nonarbitrary structures and limits. Understanding adults can establish such structures and limits through love, patience, firmness, consistency and rational authority. Corporal punishment seems devoid of constructive educational value, since it cannot provide that sense of security and nonarbitrary authority. Rarely, if ever, is corporal punishment administered for the benefit of the attacked child; usually it serves the needs of the attacking adult, seeking relief from anger and stress.

(2) The multiple links between poverty and physical abuse of children suggest that one important route toward reducing child abuse is the elimination of poverty from America's affluent society. No doubt this is only a part answer to the complex issue of preventing violence toward children, but perhaps it is an important part of the total answer, and certainly a part without which other preventive efforts may be utterly futile. This nation possesses the resources for eliminating poverty, assuming willingness to redistribute national wealth more equitably.

(3) Deviance and pathology in areas of physical, social, intellectual and emotional functioning of individuals and of family units were found to be another set of forces that may contribute to the incidence and prevalence of physical abuse of children. These conditions tend to be strongly associated with poverty and, therefore, the elimination of poverty is likely to reduce, though by no means to eliminate, their incidence and prevalence. The following measures should be available in every community as components of a comprehensive program for reducing physical abuse of children, and for helping individuals and families once abuse has occurred:

(a) Comprehensive family planning programs, including the repeal of all legislation limiting medical abortions. The availability of family planning resources and medical abortions is likely to reduce the number of unwanted and rejected children, known to be frequent victims of severe physical abuse and infanticide. Families with many children and female-headed households are overrepresented among families involved in physical abuse of children.

(b) Family life education and counseling programs for adolescents and adults in preparation for marriage and afterward. Such programs should be developed on the assumption that there is much to learn about married life and parenthood that one does not know merely on the basis of sexual and chronological maturity.

(c) A comprehensive, high-quality, neighborhood-based, national health service, financed through general tax revenue, and geared not only to the treatment of acute and chronic illness, but to the promotion of maximum feasible physical and mental health for everyone.

(d) A range of high-quality, neighborhood-based social services geared to the reduction of environmental stresses on family life and especially on mothers who carry major responsibility for the child-rearing function. Any measure reducing these stresses would also indirectly reduce the rate of child abuse. Homemaker and housekeeping services, mothers' helpers and baby-sitting services, and family and group day care facilities for preschool and school-age children are examples of such services.

(e) A system of social services geared to assisting families and children who cannot live together because of severe relationship or reality problems. Physically abused children frequently are in this category, and in such situations the welfare of the child and of the family may require temporary or permanent separation. The first requirement in such situations is comprehensive diagnostic facilities capable of arriving at sound decisions that take into consideration the circumstances, needs and rights of all concerned. Next, a community requires access to a variety of facilities for the care of children away from their homes.

The measures proposed here are aimed at different levels and aspects of physical abuse of children. The first set would attack the culturally determined core of the phenomenon; the second would eliminate a major condition to which child abuse is linked; the third approaches the causes of child abuse indirectly. It would be futile to argue the relative merits of these approaches. All three are important, and a beginning should be made in utilizing them all. The basic question seems to be not which measure to select for combating child abuse, but whether American society is indeed committed to the well-being of all its children.

It is important to keep in mind that physical abuse committed by individual caretakers constitutes a relatively small problem within the array of problems affecting the nation's children. Abuse committed by society as a whole against large segments of the next generation through poverty, discrimination, malnutrition, poor housing and neighborhoods, inadequate care for health, education and general well-being are far more dangerous problems that merit the highest priority in the development of constructive social policies. ◆

References

1. J.H.S. Bossard and E.S. Boll: *The Sociology of Child Development* (New York: Harper and Brothers, 1966); S.X. Radbill: "A History of Child Abuse and Infanticide," in R. E. Helfer and C.H. Kempe, eds.; *The Battered Child* (Chicago: University of Chicago, 1968).

2. J. Caffey, "Multiple Fractures in the Long Bones of Infants Suffering From Chronic Hematoma," *American Journal of Roentgenology*, LVI (1946), 163.

3. *Bibliography on the Battered Child*, U.S. Children's Bureau (Washington, D.C.: Government Printing Office, 1969).

4. *The Abused Child: Principles and Suggested Language on Reporting the Physically Abused Child*, U.S. Children's Bureau (Washington, D.C.: Government Printing Office, 1962); *The Child Abuse Reporting Laws—A Tabular View*, U.S. Children's Bureau (Washington, D.C.: Government Printing Office, 1966).

5. Elizabeth Elmer, "Abused Young Children Seen in Hospitals," *Social Work*, V, No. 4 (1960), 98; Helen E. Boardman, "A Project to Rescue Children From Inflicted Injuries, *Social Work*, VII, No. 1 (1962), 43; C.H. Kempe, F.N. Silverman, B.F. Steele, W. Droegemueller, H.K. Silver, "The Battered-Child Syndrome," *JAMA*, CXXCI (1962), 17; I. Kaufman, "Psychiatric Implications of Physical Abuse of Children," in V. DeFrancis, ed.: *Protecting the Battered Child* (Denver: American Humane Association, 1962), 17-22; H.D. Bryant *et. al.*, "Physical Abuse of Children: An Agency Study," *Child Welfare*, XLII No. 3 (1963), 125-130; M.G. Morris and R.W. Gould, "Role Reversal: A Concept in Dealing With the Neglected/Battered Child Syndrome," in *The Neglected/Battered Child Syndrome* (New York: Child Welfare League of America, 1963), 29-49, V. DeFrancis, *Child Abuse Preview of a Nationwide Survey* (Denver: American Humane Association, 1963); L.R. Young, *Wednesday's Children* (New York: McGraw-Hill, 1964), 1-195; R. Galdstone, "Observations on Children Who Have Been Physically Abused and Their Parents," *American Journal of Psychiatry*, CXXII, 440; I.D. Milowe and R.S. Lounie, "The Child's Role in the Battered-Child Syndrome, "*Abstracts of the Society for Pediatric Research* (1964), 1079.

6. David G. Gil, *Violence Against Children* (Cambridge, Mass.: Harvard University Press, 1970).

7. Jonathan Kozol, *Death at an Early Age* (Boston: Houghton Mifflin Co., 1967); Howard James, *Children in Trouble* (New York: David McKay, 1970).

Child Neglect Among the Poor: A Study of Parental Adequacy In Families of Three Ethnic Groups

Research on parental neglect has generally been based on comparison between neglectful families and the general population. This study, restricting its field to low-income families, examines factors that differentiate the adequate parent from the neglectful parent, with the families subdivided ethnically.

JEANNE M. GIOVANNONI

ANDREW BILLINGSLEY

In a recent review of research on child neglect, Kadushin listed three principal factors apparently associated with it: (1) low socioeconomic status, (2) a one-parent family structure, and (3) a large number of children.[1] The research from which these findings emerged was based upon a comparison of selected populations of neglectful families with those in the general population. Since such studies do not hold socioeconomic status constant, they are not useful in elucidating ways in which poor families who do not neglect their children differ from those who do. The present research effort was directed toward that question. The study compared a group of poor families recognized by the community as neglectful with poor families recognized as adequate or not seriously neglectful.

Methodology

The study population was obtained from two sources—the caseloads of public health nurses in the San Fran-

cisco Department of Health and the caseloads of the Protective Services Units at the Department of Social Services. The latter included no cases of physical abuse, and constituted our sample of neglectful families. The public health nurses rated the families whose names they submitted for study on a scale dealing with six areas of childrearing.[2] For each case they noted whether the parent had a problem in each of the six areas. Parents rated as not having any problems constituted our sample of adequate families. Those rated as having problems in all areas comprised our third group, designated as potentially neglectful.[3] The study population was further subdivided according to eth-

2. This and other measures mentioned in the paper are available from Dr. Giovannoni upon request.

3. Dr. Hylan Lewis delineated three types that correspond with the types conceptualized in this study: the "adequate," the "preclinical," and the "clinical neglect" families. See Lewis, "Childrearing Practices Among Low-Income Families in the District of Columbia," paper presented at the National Conference of Social Welfare, Minneapolis, 1961.

1. Alfred Kadushin, *Child Welfare Services* (New York: Macmillan, 1967), 222-228.

Jeanne M. Giovannoni, Ph.D., is Acting Associate Professor, School of Social Welfare, University of California, Los Angeles. When this paper was written she was Research Associate, School of Social Welfare, University of California, Berkeley. Andrew Billingsley, Ph.D., is Associate Professor, School of Social Welfare, University of California, Berkeley. A more extensive version of this paper was

presented at the CWLA South Pacific Regional Conference at San Francisco in 1969, and is available on request to Dr. Giovannoni. The research was supported by grant PR-1100 (C3) from the Children's Bureau, U.S. Department of Health, Education, and Welfare. Members of the San Francisco Department of Social Services and the Department of Health cooperated with the authors.

nicity, with representation of black, Caucasian, and Spanish-speaking families.[4]

This procedure yielded a nine-cell study design, with a final sample breakdown by ethnicity and parental adequacy grouping as follows: black, 24 adequate, 20 potential neglect, and 22 neglectful; Caucasian, 21 adequate, 15 potential neglect, and 18 neglectful; and Spanish-speaking, 28 adequate, 20 potential neglect, and 18 neglectful.

The study procedure consisted of a single, structured interview designed to tap information about the families in the following areas: social and family background of parents, current situational factors, mothers' social functioning in informal and formal social systems, and their child-rearing practices. All respondents were interviewed in their homes and were paid $5 an interview. The interviewers were second-year social work students, matched for ethnicity with the respondents.

Results

All of the data were analyzed with ethnicity held constant; within each of the three ethnic groups, the association between each variable and that of the maternal adequacy grouping was investigated, and chi-square tests of statistical significance were applied. When the data for each of the ethnic groups showed a similar pattern, ethnicity was dropped as a control variable, and the data were combined into a single cross-tabulation.

Family and Social Background

Three characteristics of the families in which the mothers had grown up were examined: family structure, family stability, and patterns of parental role dominance. Not one of these background characteristics was associated with the present status of maternal adequacy among these mothers.

Two other factors in the data are of note. First, there was a high incidence of both family instability and one-parent homes among all of these mothers, which may be attributable to the fact that this was a low-income population. Since neither variable was associated with maternal adequacy, it is suggested that the practice of studying only neglectful families, and then comparing them to the general population, may lead to spurious associations because of the confounding of low-income status, neglectful status, and family patterns.

Secondly, it should be noted that past family stability and past family structure were not related. Stability was defined as the number of major changes in family composition; structure referred to the predominant family composition, i.e., one or two parents. The data here would not support any notions that the one-parent home is invariably an unstable home.

Other social background variables investigated in relation to present maternal adequacy included the respondents' places of birth and early socialization, their parents' education, and their own education.[5] None of these bore any remarkable relationship to maternal adequacy, save for place of national origin among the Spanish-speaking mothers. Among them, U.S.-born mothers predominat-

---

4. In requesting names of persons for interviews these restrictions were made: (1) only those of the three ethnic groups described; (2) only families with less than $5000 a year income; (3) only families where the mother had either been married at some time in her life or had lived independently of her own family at some time; (4) only families who have at least one preschool child in the family; and (5) for families submitted by nurses, only those not known to either protective services or juvenile court.

5. Place of birth and socialization was dichotomized differently for each ethnic group: for black mothers it was Northern-born vs. Southern-born; for white mothers, born in or out of state; and for Spanish-speaking mothers, born in United States, vs. Mexico or Central America.

ed in the neglectful group, while Central American and Mexican-born mothers were most common in the more adequate groups. Such a finding would certainly not support a prevalent opinion that acculturation problems contribute to child neglect.

Current Social Situational Factors

Age and childbearing patterns. For all ethnic groups, the number of children a woman had borne was associated with maternal adequacy, with the adequate mothers having had fewer children than either the potentially neglectful or the neglectful ($x^2 = 6.42$, 3df, $p < .05$). Childbearing patterns were associated with maternal adequacy, but differed among the three ethnic groups. Among the black families, the neglectful mothers were significantly older than the more adequate ones, but were still as likely to have had a child in the last year. Among Spanish-speaking mothers, older age was also associated with neglectful status, but these neglectful mothers were unlikely to be still bearing children. ($x^2 = 15.90$, 4df, $p < .01$). The Caucasian neglectful mothers were not significantly older than the adequate mothers; however, they were much less likely to have had a child recently ($x^2 = 8.11$, 4df, $p < .10$). This indicates they probably started their families earlier, but were not increasing them.

The data corroborate earlier findings regarding the relationship of unusually large families and the presence of neglect. They further suggest that although all neglectful mothers share this added burden of many children, these black and Spanish-speaking mothers had an added burden of being older, and the black mothers had the still further hazard of having more children.

Current family structure and stability. Both family structure and stability were related to maternal adequacy for all three ethnic groups.[6] The overwhelming majority of the neglectful families had only one parent, while a two-parent pattern predominated among the adequate families ($x^2 = 16.47$, 3df, $p < .001$). Similarly, when stability of the family in the last year was examined, a considerably higher rate of marital disruption was found among neglectful parents in all ethnic groups than among the adequate families.

Income. It should again be pointed out that the entire study population was, by design, a low-income group. Since finding differences within a group already homogeneous with respect to a given characteristic is always difficult, we attach particular importance to the association found between financial condition and maternal adequacy.

Two basic poverty levels were used in analyzing the relationships between poverty and maternal adequacy: (1) those with less than $2000 a year income for two persons, and (2) those with $2000 to $4000 for two persons. With all ethnic groups combined, 63 percent of the adequate mothers were in the extreme poverty group, 84 percent of the potentially neglectful, and 88 percent of the neglectful families ($x^2 = 65.68$, 2df, $p < .001$). Thus, even within a group of families all of whom can be considered "poor," there was higher incidence of extreme poverty among neglectful parents.

For all ethnic groups the source of family income had been relatively stable: only 30 percent had experienced change in the source of income during the year. Stability of income was not related to maternal adequacy for any group. This finding indicates that the extreme poverty of the neglectful

6. Twenty of the 186 mothers had never been married. They were combined with those not currently living with a spouse. There was no indication that unmarried motherhood predominated in any one maternal type.

families was of long standing and preceded the marital breakdown, which most often had occurred during the last year. Thus it cannot readily be assumed that the lowered incomes of the neglectful mothers were attributable to their husbands having left them; rather, the reverse situation might well have been so.

Material resources. Going beyond information about simple dollar resources, a number of questions were asked to assess the material resources of the families, including adequacy of housing, sleeping arrangements for children, and possession of a telephone, wrist watch, and automobile. The results were: (1) In all instances the Caucasian families most often had these resources, the Spanish-speaking families next often, and the black families least often. (2) In all instances the adequate mothers more often had such resources than did the neglectful mothers. In all ethnic groups, inadequate housing and inadequate sleeping arrangements for children were significantly associated with neglect status. Among black mothers, possession of a wrist watch and telephone also significantly differentiated the adequate mothers from the neglectful.

These data on the lack of material resources among neglectful families extended the information on income. In sometimes seemingly small ways the inability to purchase "conveniences" may, day in and day out, from hour to hour, contribute to a condition of child neglect.

Social Functioning

The interest in the mothers' social functioning was based on an assumption of the interdependence of performance in the parental role and performance in other roles. In an industrial, urbanized society no parent can adequately rear a child alone. All parents are dependent upon an array of services and supports, supplied by a variety of community systems and subsystems, in giving adequate care and protection to their children.

Informal social systems. In general, this aspect of the study indicated that relationships within the kinship system were more important correlates of maternal adequacy than were those either with friends or with neighbors. There were no significant differences among the three maternal types in either the qualitative or quantitative aspects of the relationships to friends.

The area of interaction with neighbors was the only one where the potentially neglectful mothers distinguished themselves from both the adequate and the neglectful. They reported much greater involvement with their neighbors. In the previously reported data on life strains, these mothers were found to be less fortunate than the adequate mothers, but not in such severe circumstances as the neglectful mothers. Their extensive neighborliness may be for them a means of dealing with these stresses, but one in which the neglectful mother is too overburdened to indulge herself.

The responses of the mothers to questions concerning their relationships to extended kin indicated that relatives were an important factor in their lives. Although few of the women lived with relatives, the great majority had relatives living in the immediate area. Simply having relatives nearby was not associated with maternal adequacy; however, the frequency and nature of contacts with relatives were. A definite picture of estrangement from kin emerged among the neglectful mothers. The typical pattern for the adequate mothers was to have seen all of their relatives sometime during the year. The less adequate mothers had seen few relatives, and often none at all. Beyond this lower limit of interaction with relatives—yearly contact—a number of questions relating to both the frequency of contact and the number of relatives seen were combined into a single measure of kinship interaction.[7] Examination of this measure revealed that among black and white women daily contact with a number of relatives was characteristic of the adequate mothers, but not of the neglectful mothers ($x^2 = 29.27$, 3df, $p < .001$). This relationship between kinship interaction and maternal adequacy did not hold for the Latin American mothers, about whom the findings were inconclusive.[8] A measure of psychological attachment to family revealed that the white adequate mothers had a much higher degree of positive attachment to family than did the neglectful mothers ($x^2 = 6.44$, 2df, $p < .05$). The results were less dramatic for the black mothers, all of whom showed a higher level of attachment than the other ethnic groups.

Another set of questions dealt with the types of activity shared with relatives. The most common activities described were recreational, e.g., visiting and watching television. Among the black mothers, however, mutual-aid activity, such as babysitting and housecleaning, was an important category, and one in which the adequate mothers engaged much more frequently than did the neglectful ones. This factor, coupled with the data on psychological attachment, suggests some differences between the black and white mothers in the relevance of kin in their lives. Although relatives are definitely an asset to maternal adequacy for both, among black adequate

mothers an active, supportive, instrumentally oriented contact was as integral as more affectively oriented ones; among white mothers the latter appeared to be crucial.

In general, all of these measures indicated that relationships with extended kin were highly salient features of the lives of the women in this study, and when absent or impaired, a matter that impinged upon maternal adequacy.

Formal social systems. Most of the supports and services that parents need to rear their children are provided through the community's various bureaucratic structures. Therefore, we asked questions of the mothers concerning their level of information about, and their behavior in, such community structures. Specifically, we asked about the church, the political system, and various service systems, including public utilities, recreational facilities, medical care, housing, education, and welfare.[9]

Only in one area was the mothers' functioning found to be significantly related to maternal adequacy, and that was in church attendance. Although the church is a formal community structure, church activities often bring members into closer informal contacts. This was so with many of the women, particularly the black mothers, who reported attending church functions other than worship service. In general, the adequate mothers were much more often engaged with the church than were the less adequate ($x^2 = 7.32$, 2df, $p < .05$). The church probably was a source of support to these women, and possibly an untapped resource of assistance for neglectful parents.

The most striking aspect of results on other community systems was re-

---

7. This was a four-point scale which ranged from weekly contact with at least three relatives down to no weekly contact with any relative.

8. This is thought to be attributable to two factors—the cultural heterogeneity within the group due to differences in national origin, and the possible inappropriateness of the questions asked to tap significant matters in Spanish-speaking kinship relations.

9. See Joan Gordon, *The Poor of Harlem: Social Functioning in the Under Class,* a report to the Welfare Administration, Office of the Mayor, Interdepartmental Neighborhood Service Center, New York, 1965.

lated not to maternal adequacy, but to ethnicity. In all areas of questioning, the Spanish-speaking mothers were severely lacking in information. There was no community system about which more than 30 percent of the Spanish-speaking mothers had even minimum information.

Both black and white mothers were generally much better informed. However, there were also marked differences between them. The white mothers were much better informed than the black mothers about the political system, the services and recreational systems, and the medical care system. On the other hand, the black mothers were somewhat better informed about housing, welfare, and the school system.

These findings regarding knowledge of community systems may have practical implications for extending services to neglectful mothers. Considering the many strains on the neglectful mothers, and their relative lack of supports in the informal systems, one might anticipate that they would have a heavier reliance upon community services to meet their children's needs. Our data indicated that the Spanish-speaking and black mothers, especially, were not equipped to cope with these systems and to obtain necessary services.

Childrearing

The final area of functioning that was studied concerned the childrearing practices of these mothers. These were selected partly on the basis of some of our own work,[10] and partly on the work of Leontine Young,[11] as being areas that distinguished neglect-

ful and nonneglectful parental behavior. The practices were: medical care; routine and organization, assessed through questions about the timing and patterning of household activities; supervision and protection, through questions concerning the age at which mothers permitted their children to engage in an inventory of activities; general emotional nurturance; and finally, methods of discipline.

Only two of these measures significantly differentiated neglectful mothers, across ethnic lines. These two measures can be seen as interrelated. The first was a simple question. "At what age do you like children best?" The neglectful mothers much more frequently than the other mothers stated a preference for older children, as opposed to babies ($x^2 = 14.86$, 2df, $p < .01$). The related measure was devised from a series of questions asked about the mother's youngest child, such as "How often do you tell stories to your child?" "sing to him?" "play music?" etc. Here, the neglectful mothers had significantly lower scores on this measure of general emotional nurturance than did the others ($x^2 = 7.46$, 2df, $p < .05$). These findings augment those of Young,[12] who used a single word to characterize the relationship of neglectful parents to their children—"indifference." However, these data on preference for the less dependent, older child and the impoverishment of emotional nurturance, when coupled with the other data on the numerous strains and lack of supports of these mothers, suggest the situation may not be so much one of indifference, as one of despair.

Summary and Conclusions

Previous research in the area of child neglect has highlighted the higher incidence of the problem among lower socioeconomic groups.

---

10. Andrew Billingsley, *et al., A Study of Child Neglect and Abuse* (Berkeley, Calif.: University of California School of Social Welfare, 1965).

11. Leontine Young, *Wednesday's Children: A Study of Child Neglect·and Abuse* (New York: McGraw-Hill, 1964).

12. Young, *ibid.*, 31.

This study was an attempt to elucidate additional factors that might distinguish neglectful parents from more adequate ones, within a group of mothers all of whom were of low-income status. One hundred and eighty-six low-income, black, Caucasian, and Spanish-speaking mothers were interviewed about their past and current life situations. Two groups of mothers had been prejudged as "adequate" or "potentially neglectful" through ratings made by public health nurses who knew them. The third group consisted of "neglectful" mothers known to Protective Services. Data analysis sought to find factors that would distinguish these three maternal types within each of the three ethnic groups represented. The results:

(1) Social and familial background factors did not significantly differentiate neglectful mothers. Although the measures of past family life were gross indicators, such as family breakdown and family structure, it seems doubtful that more subtle indicators of qualitative family relationships would yield more positive results. These data do not support the proposition that the early family life of neglectful parents was significantly different from that of adequate parents.

(2) The current life situation of the neglectful mothers was considerably more stressful than that of the more adequate ones. The neglectful mothers were much more likely to have more children, to be without a husband, to have experienced recent marital disruption, to be poorer, and to be without necessary material resources for caring for their children. Other studies have documented the higher incidence of poverty, large families, and marital disruption among neglectful parents relative to the general population. This study indicates that there is a higher incidence of these stresses among neglectful parents, even when they are compared with other low-income families.

(3) Indicators of the role performance of these women, apart from the parental role, pointed to an impoverishment of relationships with extended kin among neglectful parents, while adequate mothers enjoyed frequent and rewarding contacts with relatives. Although the many strains on the neglectful mother and her lack of familial support would indicate a heavier reliance upon formal community systems for assistance in rearing children, the neglectful parents appeared to be no better informed about such systems nor more skillful in using them than the less needful adequate parents.

(4) Measures of childrearing practices, attitudes, and homemaking behavior indicated that the major area in which neglectful mothers deviated from adequate ones was in acceptance of and in meeting the dependency needs of very young children.

(5) Ethnic variations noted throughout, and particularly in the area of kinship relations, functioning in formal social systems, and in childrearing practices, underscored the continuing importance of evaluating and understanding families within the ethnic context.

In sum, the low-income neglectful parent is under greater environmental and situational stress and has fewer resources and supports in coping with these stresses than does the adequate mother. It is the current situational strains that predominate among neglectful parents, not those of their past life. The picture that emerges is not one unique to neglect. The difficulties these families face are similar to those described among "multiproblem," "culturally deprived," "disadvantaged" families (and other euphemisms for poverty). Even if these mothers do not neglect their children, they are a group of women facing severe hardships and in need of services to alleviate these hardships. This is not to suggest that poverty is an invariant concomitant of neglect. Rather, the implication is that poverty exposes parents to the increased likelihood of additional stresses that may have deleterious effects upon their capacities to care adequately for their children. There are implications here for the protective services practitioner, the planners of services, and the child welfare field in general.

For the practitioner, it seems clear that the results of this study call for an increased emphasis on manipulation of the environment of poor, neglectful mothers. That this mode of practice is already more characteristic of protective services workers than caseworkers in other types of agencies has already been documented. However, protective service workers are also known to experience more frustration than some others.[13] Alleviating the strains on mothers such as those in this study and reconstituting or substituting for the lost familial supports is no easy task. The protective service worker is not a magician. Without an adequate array of community resources and backup services such as day care and homemakers, the protective service worker can face stalemate with such families. And this may be so whether he adopts an environmental approach or a more psychotherapeutic one.

Planning, obtaining, and integrating the services and resources needed by the women in this study goes beyond the individual protective services worker and beyond the agency itself. These are community problems, requiring communitywide action, and extracommunity action. It is unlikely that protective services, no matter how broadly or well conceived, are going to eliminate poverty. Nonetheless, when a community defines a problem such as child neglect, which seems so inextricably bound to poverty, any program sought by that community to alleviate neglect must also encompass aspects directed toward the alleviation at least of some of the ravages of poverty. As Kahn has noted, "The community as a whole is responsible for the adequate rearing of its children.[14]

If this is so, any community concerned about families such as those described in this study must reevaluate its participation in the rearing of its children. Reference here is not simply to the neglectful families, but to all poverty-stricken families, the potentially neglectful and the adequate as well. On the one hand, commendation is due the many adequate, though extremely poor, mothers. On the negative side, it is not inconceivable that as the stresses of poverty continue to bear upon them, the adequate mothers of today's study may be the neglectful ones of tomorrow's. A sound program of prevention would seem to have as an imperative the availability of supportive childrearing services to all of these women, even those not currently considered problematic.

Perhaps what the child welfare field needs most is not a more exacting definition of "child neglect," but a reconceptualization of the entire problem. This means relinquishment of any notion of "child neglect" as a static, discrete, diagnostic entity. Among low-income people "neglect" would seem to be a social problem that is as much a manifestation of social and community conditions as it is of any individual parent's pathology. ◆

---

13. Andrew Billingsley, "The Role of the Social Worker in a Child Protective Agency," Child Welfare, XLIII No. 9 (1964), 472-479.

14. Alfred J. Kahn, *Planning Community Services for Children in Trouble* (New York: Columbia University Press, 1963), 325.

SUMMARY

At long last the community and social workers are trying to bring about some meaningful solutions to the problems of the battered children and their parents. Methods of group therapy are being employed, parent rehabilitation is being sought, and mothers are organizing groups to help one another.

All in all, we are finally emerging from the "dark ages" of this acute social problem. The problem of the battered child is no longer being overlooked. Society is finally waking up and taking action on behalf of the innocent. Society is now trying to deal with the problem at its roots—in the inadequacies of the disturbed parent.

Social workers are currently trying to improve services for families in which children are receiving substandard care. This area can also be labeled protective services.

The social worker, responding to the reality of the battered child, must be prepared to move from the level of shock to the level of action. The action is that of providing the child with experiences that will enable him to acknowledge and eventually accept—and love—real people instead of retaining the distorted images that have passed as parental models in his life. In the case of severely abused or seriously neglected children, it is imperative to remove such children from their dangerous environment.

Agencies are also concerned about abusing parents, who do not typically come asking for help with their problems. The circumstances that prevent parents from being able to ask for help also make it difficult for some of them to face the fact that they have been neglecting or abusing their children. Yet, until the parents are able to face this fact, their energy is not freed for them to do something about the problem.

In working on child abuse cases, three considerations must be kept in mind by the agency in making treatment decisions and in determining treatment goals for these families. These are the degree and extent of the pathology in the family, the apparent need of immediate protection for the child based on the extent of the abuse perpetuated, and the prognosis for success in helping the parent to effect change in the areas that stimulated the abuse.

STUDY QUESTIONS

1. How and when did child protective services originate in this country?

2. What is the relationship between the social worker and law enforcement agencies in cases concerning child abuse?

3. What are some personal obstacles the social worker must first overcome in order to perform an effective service to parents and children?

4. What are the characteristics of abusing parents?

5. Under what circumstances should an abused child be allowed to remain in the home?

6. Under what circumstances would an agency take a child from his parents before notifying them?

REFERENCES

A. Readings Included in This Text

Billingsley, Andrew, Streshinsky, Noami; and Gurgin, Vonnie. "Agency Structure and the Commitment to Service." *Public Welfare,* 24 (1966):246-251.

Boisvert, Maurice J. "Battered-Child Syndrome." *Social Casework,* 53 (1972):475-480.

Gil, David G. "Sociocultural Perspective on Physical Child Abuse." *Child Welfare,* 50 (1971):389-395.

Giovannoni, Jeanne M., and Billingsley, Andrew. "Child Neglect Among the Poor: A Study of Parental Adequacy in Families of Three Ethnic Groups." *Child Welfare,* 49 (1970):196-204.

Mitchiner, Myra J. "Providing Preventive and Protective Services to Children in a Public Welfare Agency." *Child Welfare,* 45 (1966):224-227.

Nyden, Paul V. "The Use of Authority." *Public Welfare,* 24 (1966):239-245, 252.

Page, Miriam O. "Cohesion, Dignity, and Hope for Multiproblem Families." *Children,* 8 (1961):63-68.

Sandusky, Annie Lee. "Services to Neglected Children." *Children,* 7 (1960):23-28.

Stringer, Elizabeth A. "Homemaker Service in Neglect and Abuse: A Tool for Case Evaluation." *Children,* 12 (1965): 26-29.

B. Suggested Additional Readings

Bechtold, Mary Lee. "Silent Partner to a Parent's Brutality." *School and Community,* 52 (1965):33.

Boardman, Helen E. "A Project to Rescue Children from Inflicted Injuries." *Social Work,* 7 (1962):43-51.

Blue, M. T. "The Battered Child Syndrome from a Social Work View Point." *Canadian Journal of Public Health,* 56 (1965):197-198.

Boehm, Bernice. "An Assessment of Family Adequacy in Protective Cases." *Child Welfare,* 41 (1962):11-16.

Bryant, Harold D.; Billingsley, Andrew; Kerry, George A.; Leefman, Walter V.; Merrill, Edgar J.; Senecal, Gordon R.; and Walsh, Barbara G. "Physical Abuse of Children—An Agency Study." *Child Welfare,* 42 (1963):125-130.

Butler, Raymon V. "Lend the Client an Ear." *Public Welfare,* 23 (1965):105-107.

"Children in Peril." *Nation,* 214 (1972):293-294.

Cooper, Vera E. "What Happens in Child Protection." *Canadian Welfare,* 38 (1962):66-69.

D'Ambrosio, R. "No Language But a Cry." *Good Housekeeping,* 171 (1970):64-67.

Davies, Joan. "When the Agency Must Intervene." *Public Welfare,* 23 (1965):102-105.

Davies, Joann E., and Jorgensen, James D. "Battered Not Defeated: The Story of an Abused Child and Positive Casework." *Child Welfare,* 49 (1970):101-104.

Hammell, C. L. "Preserving Family Life for Children." *Child Welfare,* 48 (1969):591-594.

Helfer, Roy E. "A Plan for Protection: The Child Abuse Center." *Child Welfare,* 49 (1970):486-494.

"Help for Child Beaters." *Newsweek,* 80 (1972):66, 69.

Herre, Ernest A. "A Community Mobilizes to Protect Its Children." *Public Welfare,* 23 (1965):93-97.

Jacobziner, Harold. "Rescuing the Battered Child." *American Journal of Nursing,* 64 (1964):92-97.

Kelly, Joseph B. "What Protective Services Can Do." *Child Welfare,* 38 (1959):21-25.

Oettinger, Katherine B. "Protecting Children from Abuse." *Parents,* 39 (1964):12.

Schmidt, Delores M. "The Challenge of Helping the 'Untreatable'." *Public Welfare,* 23 (1965):98-102.

Schaffer, Helen B. "Child Abuse: Search for Remedies." *Editorial Research Reports,* 1 (1965):343-357.

Silver, Larry B.; Dublin, Christina C.; and Lourie, Reginald S. "Agency Action and Interaction in Cases of Child Abuse." *Social Casework,* 52 (1971):164-171.

Tenhave, Ralph. "A Preventative Approach to Problems of Child Abuse and Neglect," 64 (1965):645-649.

Toland, Marjorie. "Abuse of Children—Whose Responsibility?" *Connecticut Medicine,* 28 (1964):438-442.

Zalba, S. R. "Battered Children." *Science Digest,* 70 (1971): 8-13.

Zauner, Phyllis. "Mothers Anonymous: the Last Resort." *McCalls,* 99 (1972):57.

V
The Medical Worker Takes a Look

INTRODUCTION

Child abuse has existed, often with social sanction, in all ages and locations. Different forms of mutilation have been justified for many centuries, and many abuses have been practiced under the guise of religious rites, child disciplining, and cosmetics. Urbanization and the machine age inaugurated sweatshop child labor abuse. Agriculture, especially among migrant workers, produced child labor abuses still tolerated and lawlessly "not noticed," or extolled as the admirable means of developing the work ethic.

Periodic waves of sympathy have reached their peak and declined. The recent stimulation of concern has been due to pediatric radiology. Through studies of X-rays, the startling fact was brought out that many injuries were willfully inflicted.

In 1961, the Academy of Pediatrics proposed the term the "Battered Child Syndrome" and since then a variety of services and programs have been combined to make child abuse treatment and concern a total community cooperative program.

The type and degree of physical attack on children varies from one extreme to another. There is the direct murder of children and deliberate mutilation, injury, or torture. At the other extreme is the near-abusive parent who needs help because he fears his ability to continue his restraint. He is the one who feels at the end of his rope, but has no one to whom he can turn for help, whose understanding he can trust. He feels a deep fear and guilt but can not face the response to his need which he feels (often justifiably) will be punitive and condemning.

When parental assault is under consideration, radiologic examination is necessary not only for confirmation, but also as a guide in treatment. Many times the severely beaten child comes in with internal injuries, in convulsions, or in a coma. If assault is seriously suspected, the child must be hospitalized not only for his protection, but also for additional observation.

The role of the medical profession is not only one of diagnosis and treatment, it is also one of prevention. The preventive aspect of the battered child syndrome is early detection. However, once the injury occurs, the physician's primary concern is the immediate care of the patient. After the patient is under the care of the physician, he must direct his energy to the family and fulfill his moral and legal responsibilities.

The children who are abused are scarred physically, emotionally, and mentally, and many will not reach their optimum potential. The abused child of today is the potential psychopath, the potential drug abuser, the potential hard core criminal, and the potential child abuser of tomorrow.

Pediatrics

| VOLUME 31 | JUNE 1963 | NUMBER 6 |

COMMENTARY

THE PHYSICALLY ABUSED CHILD

THE SYMPOSIUM, "The Battered Child Syndrome," held at the American Academy of Pediatrics meeting in Chicago in October, 1961, brought into focus the increasing professional recognition of a new significance to an old problem. The phrase "the battered child" was, of course, arresting and accounted in part for the large audience. The interest shown, however, was not simply a response to the sensational but rather an expression of the need to clarify a vague and ill-defined area that had long troubled many physicians. The presentation recalled to the memories of many of the participants cases never fully solved to their satisfaction, and defined an entity into which many of these would fit.

Typical skeletal lesions consisting of multiple fractures of the long bones accompanying subdural hematoma were described by Caffey[1] in 1946. In 1953 Silverman[2] in reporting additional cases ascribed such lesions to trauma, unrecognized or unadmitted. Woolley[3] in 1955 seems to have been the first to point to inflicted injury as the etiologic factor in many of these cases.

Within the last 5 years, and more especially within the last 2, the subject of the physically abused child has appeared in the medical literature and in the lay press with increasing frequency.

From one or two papers per year on the abused child complex, the volume increased to about 15 papers in 1961-62.[4] Simultaneously articles have appeared in popular magazines—a reversal of the attitude expressed by one editor several years ago that "this isn't the sort of thing the American family wants to read about at breakfast."

Whether the true incidence of child abuse is actually rising is not clear, though the increasing number of cases reported in newspapers would seem to indicate this. No valid incidence figures are available, nor are they likely to become so. The entity has only recently been described for physicians and is still unknown to many of them. Hospitals have no diagnostic symbol through which they can retrieve records of cases on which a diagnosis of physical abuse may have been made or suspected. Some indication of the magnitude of the problem can be obtained from surveys such as that of Kempe and his associates,[5] who reported 302 cases in one year from 71 hospitals and 447 cases from 77 district attorneys, and from reports of series of cases from individual institutions, such as the article in this issue by McHenry, Girdany, and Elmer. Such reports can indicate only a small fraction of the cases. Undoubtedly the great majority, including those which do not result in broken bones or gross disability, never come to the attention of physicians.

In a study[6] of 180 children in 115 families

PHYSICALLY ABUSED CHILD

referred to the Massachusetts Society for the Prevention of Cruelty to Children in 1960 for child abuse, a significant fact for the medical profession emerges. Only 9% of the cases were referred by hospitals or physicians, though they had been involved in over 30% of them. Case histories from many hospitals substantiate the fact of repeated medical contacts without action to prevent recurrences. This failure on the part of physicians probably has several causes. The first is missed diagnosis. The syndrome of multiple skeletal injuries occurring over a period of time has only recently been the subject of scientific papers. Since few doctors are yet aware of this fairly definite complex, it is understandable that isolated or first injuries are missed. Even when strong evidence of this confronts the physician, he may find the idea that parents could abuse their children so abhorrent that he denies the facts. Often young physicians, interns, or residents especially, finding such behavior too bizarre for belief, try to explain the physical signs as manifestations of some rare disease.

A further reason for the physicians' failure to act in behalf of the child is the absence in some, fortunately only a few, of a social conscience. Just as there are abusing parents, there are neglectful doctors. Some take the attitude expressed by a resident, "I am here to treat the child. I am doing everything I can for him medically and that is all you can expect of me." Others hide behind exaggerated fears of court procedures or adverse publicity, or even of suit for false accusation.

Probably many physicians have failed to act because they did not know what to do. Though they may have suspicions, they usually have no proof. A good medical social worker is, of course, their best ally. She has interviewing skills through which she can get valuable information from the family and she knows the community resources which can be used to protect the child. But often resources are meager or agencies are slow, the family removes the child and disappears, and the physician is left with the uneasy feeling of having gone too far or not far enough.

The experience of the group at the Children's Hospital of Los Angeles[7] in using the requirement in California law for reporting by doctors and hospitals of inflicted injuries provides evidence that this method of starting action can be effective. Aroused over the fate of children who after discharge from the hospital died or were severely injured as the result of additional attacks, they explored what legal machinery was available to them. When their diagnostic skills were reinforced by the recognition of definitive radiologic findings, the doctors and social workers found in their existing law, which requires such reporting, a way of developing a working relationship with law enforcement officials and the juvenile court that resulted in protective procedures for the children. This experience led a group of consultants meeting with the Children's Bureau in January, 1962, to recommend the development of a Model State Law. Subsequently the Children's Bureau called together a group of experts, largely from the legal profession, to lay down the principles on which legislative language could be drafted. Elsewhere in this issue is a discussion of the proposal for such legislation and its interpretation by Professor Fowler Harper of Yale (see pp. 897-902).

Obviously arguments can be raised for and against requiring physicians to report cases of suspected physical abuse of children. The rationale of reporting is that a case of suspected child abuse constitutes a medical and social emergency. The pattern in these cases is for abuse to be repetitive, and prompt preventive action must be taken. Reporting, though based on the premise that a crime has been committed, and though it may result in action against the parents, is primarily for the purpose of protecting the child.

For the physician, reporting is to some degree a protection also. Just as in reporting of gunshot wounds, when reporting of evidence of inflicted injuries to a child is required, this relieves the physician of the burden of choice. This requirement also may relieve him of feelings of guilt toward the parents.

No one believes that requiring doctors or hospitals to report cases of suspected physical abuse will end, or even lessen, such abuse. Such a law, and the process of enacting it and implementing it, would focus on the problem, alert the medical profession to its existence and its seriousness, and perhaps set in motion community action to provide better protective social services for children. Even though abused children are identified, either by voluntary or required reporting, unless adequate provision is made for their subsequent care and for the rehabilitation of their parents, nothing will have been accomplished.

Gross physical abuse is only one segment of a much wider problem of parental neglect. The unloved child, the emotionally traumatized child, the socially and emotionally deprived child, become part of our pool of neurotic, disturbed, retarded, or delinquent adults. Out of this morass of social breakdown, current interest is being focused on one specific malady which can be identified and for which the physician has a primary responsibility for diagnosis. Any physician seeing children should develop a high level of suspicion for possible inflicted injury. Any case in any social class where the injuries are not fully explained by the history should be tagged and explored. At present, the only solution in many cases is to remove the child from the home by court order. Many of the parents are themselves so psychologically damaged that they are beyond the reach of our present therapeutic measures. We need studies of the kinds of parents who abuse their children and of criteria that will identify those parents that can be helped. Some beginnings along these lines are recorded by the Children's Bureau's Clearinghouse for Research in Child Life.[4]

For many years some communities have provided help for these families and their children through the public child welfare program or through private agencies such as the Society for the Prevention of Cruelty to Children. Getting the child identified before it is physically or emotionally ruined has been difficult. Obviously the role of the physician is of crucial importance.

KATHERINE BAIN, M.D.
Deputy Chief, Children's Bureau
Department of Health, Education,
    and Welfare
Washington 25, D.C.

REFERENCES

1. Caffey, J.: Multiple fractures in the long bones of infants suffering from chronic subdural hematoma. Amer. J. Roentgenol., **56**:163, 1946.
2. Silverman, F. N.: The roentgen manifestations of unrecognized skeletal trauma in infants. Amer. J. Roentgenol., **69**:413, 1953.
3. Woolley, P. V., Jr., and Evans, W. A., Jr.: Significance of skeletal lesions in infants resembling those of traumatic origin. J.A.M.A., **158**:539, 1955.
4. Bibliography on The Battered Child, Clearinghouse for Research in Child Life, Children's Bureau, Department of Health, Education, and Welfare, March, 1963 (Revised).
5. Kempe, C. H., *et al.*: The battered-child syndrome. J.A.M.A., **181**:17, 1962.
6. Merrill, E. J.: Physical abuse of children—an agency study; *in* Protecting the Battered Child, Children's Division, The American Humane Association, Denver, Colorado, 1962.
7. Boardman, H. E.: A project to rescue children from inflicted injuries. Social Work, **7**:43, 1962.

An Insidious and Disturbing Medical Entity

VINCENT J. FONTANA, M.D. *is Director, Department of Pediatrics of Saint Vincent's Hospital Medical Center of New York City and Director of Medicine of New York Foundling Hospital. This paper was presented at APWA's 1965 Northeast Regional Conference in New York City.*

In the last decade the major pediatric problem involving child neglect and physical abuse has become more apparent. During 1962, 4,000 cases of child neglect came to the attention of the Children's Court in New York City. In the first nine months of 1962, a newspaper clipping service, to which the American Humane Society subscribed, submitted newspaper accounts from 47 states related to apparent child abuse. There were 378 cases involving 446 children and 109 fatalities. Since not every case is in the newspapers, these figures constitute but a fraction of the true incidence. The Chief Medical Examiner's Office in New York City has also reported that there appears to be an increase in the number of deaths of children resulting from injuries inflicted by their parents.

The National Vital Statistics Division of the United States indicated cancer to be the major cause of pediatric deaths, a rate of 8.1 percent per 100,000 population in 1959. Accidental deaths shown for the same year ranked 175 percent higher than did the deaths due to cancer in children between the ages of 1 and 14 years. The question arises as to how many of these so-called accidental deaths were not actually "accidental" but were due to unsuspected maltreatment.

NATURE OF ABUSE

The story of the abused child is not new; but prior to these reports this pediatric problem of the maltreated child had, for the most part, been unsuspected and has gone unrecognized by society, and legal agencies of our country, and the medical profession.

The neglect and abuse of children involves situations ranging from the deprivation of food, clothing, shelter, and parental love to incidents wherein children are physically abused and mistreated by an adult, resulting in obvious physical damage of the child and, unfortunately, often leading to death.

The problem of infanticide and the salvaging of abandoned children was one of the motives that prompted the establishment of the New York Foundling Hospital about 100 years ago by the Sisters of Charity of Saint Vincent DePaul. It had as its principal objective the reduction of the appalling rate of infanticide in New York City. Most of these deaths were attributable to abandonment and exposure. The first year of operation, 61 percent of the infants admitted were dying. While it may be an exaggeration to say that the streets of New York were covered with dead and dying children, it certainly would not be an exaggeration to say that it was commonplace. Indeed, as late as 1892, 200 foundlings and 100 dead infants were found on the streets of New York City.

Accurate statistics concerning the incidence of this pediatric entity are unobtainable, since only a small portion of the neglected and abused children are taken to the physician or hospital for medical attention.

Kempe and his associates have described this repeated physical abuse of children and call it "the battered-child syndrome." Other reports in the medical literature have referred to this disease of maltreatment as "unrecognized trauma."[1] Unfortunately, both of these terms do not fully describe the picture of this often life-threatening condition. A maltreated child often shows no signs of being "battered," as this is the last phase of the spectrum, but shows multiple minor physical evidences of emotional and, at times, nutritional deprivation, neglect, and abuse. In these cases it is the most acute diagnostic acumen of the physician that can prevent the more severe injuries of inflicted trauma that are a significant cause of childhood death. The willful neglect and injury of these children by parents or others may range from cases in which the child is malnourished and physically neglected to those in which he is the victim of premeditated trauma leading to permanent crippling and death.

Symptoms of Maltreatment

Clinical criteria are necessary in making the diagnosis and in recognizing the maltreated child. The child who is maltreated is often brought to the hospital or private physician with a history of "failure to thrive," malnutrition, poor skin hygiene, irritability, a repressed personality, and other signs of obvious neglect. The more severely abused children are seen in the emergency rooms of hospitals with external evidences of body trauma, such as bruises, abrasions, cuts, lacerations, burns, soft-tissue swelling, and hematomas.

[1] C. H. Kempe et al., "Battered Child Syndrome," Journal of the American Medical Association, Vol. CLXXXI (July 7, 1962), pp. 17-24.

Inability to move certain extremities because of the dislocations and fractures associated with neurological signs of intracranial damage or brain damage is an additional signal that should arouse the suspicion of the physician. Children manifesting the maltreatment syndrome give evidence of one or more of these complaints, with the most severe of the maltreatment cases arriving at the hospital or physician's office in coma or convulsions or even dead.

Therefore, the signs and symptoms indicating maltreatment of children range from the simple undernourished child who is reported as failing to thrive to the more severe signs of the battered child who is seen with evidence of gross trauma, multiple fractures, and other inflicted body injuries. Soft-tissue lacerations, abrasions, burns, and hemorrhages involving any part of the body should cast a suspicion on the cause of the present complaints. Even more enlightening is the presence of healed or scab-covered "old" lesions, abrasions, or contusions of the skin.

The Maltreatment Syndrome of Children

It is not difficult, therefore, to see that a more precise term, an all-encompassing term, would be the "maltreatment syndrome of children" rather than the "battered-child syndrome." The battered child is the last phase of this all-important spectrum. The physician, the social worker, and the legal organizations of our society must be clearly aware of the symptoms and signs of the maltreatment syndrome. Only this awareness and recognition of the maltreated child can prevent the last phase of the battered child, many times avoiding permanent physical and mental crippling as well as death.

Because of parental fear of legal entanglements, many of these children are not taken to the physician or the hospital for medical care until the child is in acute distress or until the parents become alarmed of impending death. For this reason, X-ray evidences of fractures may be present in various stages of reparative changes. On the other hand, if no fractures or dislocations are apparent on examination, bone injury may remain obscure during the first few days after inflicted trauma. In these cases, evidences of bone repair may appear within weeks after the specific bone trauma. It is, therefore, important to remember that, although X-ray findings are not available on seeing the child, if the child is observed for several days these bone lesions become apparent.

X-ray examination more commonly reveals definite and unusual bone changes that assist the physician in making the diagnosis. Fragmentation of various parts of the bone caused by twisting or pulling of the afflicted extremity is apparent. There may be some squaring of the long bones secondary to new bone formation on the metaphysis fragments. Hemorrhages along the sides of the bone are noted frequently, since the covering of the bone in infants is not securely attached to the underlying bone. This is followed by calcification of the hemorrhage which becomes apparent from four to seven days after the fracture. This layer of calcification around the shaft of the bone should always arouse suspicion of inflicted trauma and should elicit further investigations into the cause of the fracture. Therefore, the findings from X-ray examinations revealing repairing bone changes, excessive new bone formation, or previously healed fractures with reaction along the shafts of the bone should be considered diagnostic when correlated with other manifestations of child abuse and neglect.

Obtaining Information

Maltreatment of children by parental abuse and neglect may occur at any age with an increased incidence with children under 3 years of age. In view of this, an infant or child cannot tell a story of how the trauma was inflicted; and many young children are reluctant or afraid to tell the entire story. The history that is related by the parents is very often at variance with the clinical picture and the physical findings noted on examination of the child. Seeking out information involves a precise detection of previous hospital admissions and the physician's interest in uncovering a possible cause of the physical findings. The physician will often discover that the mother has taken the child to various hospitals and doctors in an attempt to negate any suspicions of parental abuse. There is usually complete denial of any knowledge of inflicted trauma to the child and often the attitude of complete innocence is transmitted to the examining physician. Difficulty in obtaining any kind of history is often encountered, and the diagnosis depends on physical examination, X-ray findings, and a high index of suspicion on the part of the physician.

Studies evaluating parental feelings and motivations leading to child abuse and death are now in progress, but at the present time are wanting. Preliminary observations in this field have indicated that the child-abusing parent presents features of rigidity, compulsiveness, immaturity, antisocial behavior, and a lack of warmth toward the maltreated child.

Social service investigations also revealed that usually one child in the family is selected and made the target for abuse and neglect, while all the other siblings usually show evidence of overprotection. Often these abused and neglected children are made symbols of the parents' expression of hostility to society based on their disapproved sexual and social patterns of existence.

Society must face up to the fact that the incidence of the maltreated child syndrome is startling and appears to be on the increase. This is a problem of increasing importance calling for the full cooperation among the medical, social, and legal organizations of our country.

Reasons for Not Reporting Cases

Various reports from child protection agencies reveal that less than one-third of the child-abuse cases seen by a physician are reported to the law enforcement or social agencies available to the community. This defect lies in the fact that the physician is unaware that parents can and often do willfully inflict serious damage to their children or even kill them. There is a definite lack in medical education concerning the maltreatment syndrome in children. The physician is often reluctant to report cases of child abuse in his practice or hospital duty, since it may involve entanglement in legal matters and hours away from his medical chores. The moral responsibility of the examining physician is to the maltreated child. He must be cognizant of the fact that over 50 percent of these children are liable to secondary injuries or death if appropriate steps are not taken to remove the child from this life-threatening environment.

The physician should refer cases involving suspected maltreatment of children to a hospital for thorough diagnostic study and social investigation if he is unsure or reluctant to report the child that comes to his attention in private practice or in the admitting room of a hospital facility. The physician or medical authorities should report, under present law in the state of New York, any child who is physically abused or neglected to the Department of Social Welfare, Bureau of Child Welfare. The physician must be available for court appearance; otherwise the maltreatment of children by the parents will continue. The courts rely on, and are influenced a great deal by, the testimony of the physician. My personal appearance at court hearings of child abuse resulted in temporary placement of these children. The court has been most cooperative in realizing the physician's limited time and arranges an appearance that is acceptable and convenient.

The cases seen at Saint Vincent's Hospital and Medical Center and the New York Foundling Hospital give evidence that childhood deaths can be avoided if physicians are alert to the problem. We have seen patients who were pronounced dead on arrival; we have seen others who have had irreparable damage and suffered irreversible signs of mental retardation due to inflicted injuries; and again we have seen cases that have been diagnosed as the maltreatment syndrome. These children, after thorough investigation, were referred to the appropriate agencies with resulting court action and placement of the child in a foster home. These children, we feel, have been saved from future abuse and possible death.

Agencies' Obligations

Society must acknowledge that the problem of child abuse and neglect does exist. There must be recognition of this syndrome as an index of social delinquency so that further community cooperation through various organizations, protective agencies, and courts can be integrated in an attitude of cooperation, leading to better child protection. These societies should be given the utmost in financial support necessary to establish child protection agencies with authoritative and administrative structures.

Social service workers play an all-important role in the integration of the medical, legal, and social aspects of this disease. They are responsible for planning and presenting the social and medical findings of the cases to the court authorities. Social service personnel assist in identifying any

existing destructive drives within the family unit and in protecting the child from further traumatic experiences. Attempts should be made to enable the parents to accept and receive psychiatric help which will strengthen family understanding and protect the parents from future consequences of abnormal social behavior.

Use of Laws and Welfare Services

Instructive use of laws should safeguard the rights of the abused child, the parents, and the physician. Such a law is presently active in New York State. However, in the past year it has been found that physicians are apparently still reluctant to report suspected cases of child beating to the welfare authorities. In the past year, approximately 245 cases have been reported to the Bureau of Child Welfare. There were 294 cases reported to the registrate; of these, 4 cases were reported by private doctors, 120 by city hospitals, 90 by voluntary hospitals, and 6 by medical examiners. The other referrals have come from school physicians, skilled child health centers, the department of welfare, and the police department.

It would seem that the lack of physician cooperation may be due to a deficiency in recognition of the maltreatment syndrome, unfamiliarity with the existing law pertaining to child-abuse cases, or a fear of becoming involved in the court action that many of these cases demand. It is not difficult to see why a private physician is reluctant to report one of his private patients to a public authority. At the same time, if he suspects maltreatment, neglect, or abuse in one of his private patients and he is himself reluctant to report this child, it would certainly be feasible to have the child admitted to a hospital for further diagnosis and confirmation of his suspicions. The hospital, in turn, after consultation with the physician, a social worker, and a psychiatrist, will make the appropriate report to the Bureau of Child Welfare. I believe that this will encourage more physicians to report cases that they suspect of being maltreated.

Immediate assistance must be made available to the abused child by the appropriate community and child welfare service. The utilization of law enforcement agents should be considered if the child is a victim of gross, severe, abusive parental actions. This often requires prompt removal of the child from the threatening and hazardous home environment.

ROLE OF THE COURTS

The juvenile courts are available to review petitions for prosecution. The courts are established to prevent the parents from maltreating the children further through the acceptance of evidence which casts guilt on a parent beyond any reasonable doubt. The courts must become cognizant of this real and important aspect of parental delinquency. The courts need also to re-evaluate the benefits of the normally accepted dogma that "the child belongs with mother." This concept must be re-evaluated in view of presently existing evidence that such a decision might be detrimental to the well-being of the child as well as to that of the mother.

It must also be stressed that the law and the courts should protect the parent or the individual inflicting injury in situations which will result in further neglect and injury of the child, often leading to death. This can be accomplished by the temporary placement of the child by the courts and the treatment of the parents by whatever therapy or counseling is indicated.

In conclusion, the maltreatment of children is a pediatric disease as well as a parental disease which often leads to permanent mental or physical crippling of the child and even death. It is a preventable disease which can be diagnosed, recognized, and treated. The responsibilities of the community, the physician, and the legal agencies of our society must be upheld. I would make a plea that there be proper integration and cooperation between these various agencies for the greater good of child protection. Attention must be focused on this insidious and disturbing medical entity to prevent unnecessary deaths of children.

Current Practice CHILD CARE IN GENERAL PRACTICE

Trauma in Childhood

ROBERT ROAF,* M.CH., F.R.C.S.

Trauma in the neonatal and intranatal period will not be considered in this article. It should, however, be noted that the results of neonatal trauma are not always immediately apparent, and indeed some conditions—for example, spasticity and Erb's palsy—are often recognized only at a later date when they manifest themselves as chronic orthopaedic conditions. Once the newborn child has survived the trauma of birth one would expect him to be relatively immune to trauma until he reaches the toddling stage, but two aspects of modern life have altered this state of affairs—the development of the internal combustion engine and the increasing recognition over the last few years of the " battered baby " syndrome.

Mechanical Injuries

The babe in arms, whether as a passenger or as a " pedestrian," is liable to be quite badly injured in accidents involving motor-cars. Such trauma does not follow any definite pattern, but like other severe direct injuries may lead to very serious consequences in the young babe.

The recognition of fractures and dislocations in young babies by radiography may be difficult, and if the mother and child are brought into hospital either as a result of being knocked down by another car, or because the car in which they were passengers was involved in an accident, it is essential to examine the baby very carefully, particularly looking for evidence of gross swelling or haematoma formation, as this may well indicate serious underlying damage. It is important to realize that injuries and haematoma formation in small children may closely mimic bacterial infection. Locally there is a hot, red, painful fluctuant swelling ; the baby is pyrexial and fretful, appetite is impaired, and there is a leucocytosis. In addition, a haematoma acts as an ideal culture medium and may become secondarily infected. Any hot, red swelling in a child should be aspirated under aseptic conditions. I have seen a swelling in a haemophiliac boy closely resemble an abscess, so it is wise to be sure before using a knife. The injection of chymotrypsin into the haematoma after aspiration may aid in resolution.

In these days of increasing mechanization on the roads, in the home, and on the farm serious mechanical injuries are increasingly common. These do not follow any set pattern and each case must be treated on its merits. However, compared with adults, the powers of restoration in children are amazing. This means that these lesions must be treated with the utmost conservatism—for instance, a guillotine amputation of the index finger in an adult would need trimming of bone and formal skin closure, but the same injury in a child could be safely treated with a sterile dressing, when the raw area will become epithelized, thus preserving the maximum possible length.

* Professor of Orthopaedic Surgery, University of Liverpool.

Battered Baby Syndrome

The battered baby syndrome has become more commonly recognized in the last few years (Griffiths and Moynihan, 1963). The child is usually teething and is often brought to hospital by the parents with one or more grossly swollen limbs, or perhaps a grossly swollen face, with evidence of haematoma formation. The parents deny that it could have been injured, and it is common to suspect some serious condition—for instance, a blood dyscrasia, infection, or even tumour formation. In the early stages radiographs are not always informative, but those taken a few days later will often show subperiosteal formation of new bone at the ends of the long bones (Fig. 1) and the syndrome is characterized by fracture separation of non-ossified cartilaginous epiphyses. Usually, but not invariably, these children suffer from a certain amount of malnutrition. By now a number of these patients have been described and it is recognized that the syndrome is nearly always due to injury inflicted by the baby's own parents or by baby-watchers. The condition was first clearly described and made widely known by Caffey (1957), but it must be differentiated from the other syndrome described by Caffey and Silverman (1945)—namely, "infantile cortical hyperostosis," in which there is swelling of the jaws and often of the scapulae and long bones, and in which subperiosteal new bone formation is also increased. Alternatively, the child may present with cerebral symptoms—vomiting and "inexplicable" coma—due to an intracranial haematoma. If undiagnosed, a cranial injury from parental assault can prove fatal, and in the absence of a history of injury diagnosis may be very hard.

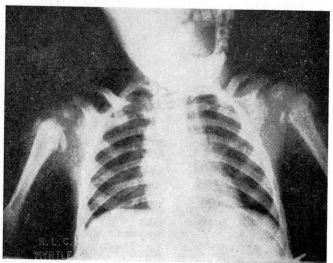

Fig. 1.—Bone changes at upper end of humerus in battered baby syndrome.

Unless one is aware of this syndrome it may be difficult to recognize it, and even when it is suspected it is not always easy to prove that trauma is the only cause ; indeed, it is almost mandatory that the child should be admitted to hospital and fully investigated, and other causes excluded. When the condition has been diagnosed it is extremely hard to know what is the right course of action to take in the interests of the child, for it is not unusual, when the child's condition has improved and he has been sent home, for the parents to assault him again.

The treatment of the physical injuries does not usually present any serious problem, but preventing the recurrence of the assaults is a far more complex procedure. It is essential to have full consultation between the parents' own general practitioner, the medical officer of health, and the various welfare services. Probably in the long run the parents' own doctor is in the best position to advise about the best course of action to take in the ultimate interests of the child.

Common Fractures

Greenstick Fracture.—At a slightly older age, when the child is a toddler, he is likely to fall, and at this age the most frequent injury is a greenstick fracture of both bones of the forearm, or a spiral fracture of the tibia or femur. Treatment is usually extremely simple, and, even if the fracture is not fully reduced, the powers of growth and remodelling in the small child are very considerable. Within a year or two even 30° of angulation or 1 in. of shortening will be corrected by nature alone (Figs. 2a and b).

Elbow Fractures

Pulled Elbow.—Another common syndrome at this age is a "pulled elbow." The history is usually that the child has been lifted by one hand, after which the elbow becomes painful and the child is unable to rotate his forearm. Radiographs do not show any abnormality. It is usually believed that this syndrome is due to the head of the radius being pulled down into the orbicular ligament and becoming impacted in this position. A push on the head of the radius associated with a pronation-supination movement will usually cure the condition.

Fracture of Capitellum.—When the child is slightly older the most common elbow injury is a fracture of the capitellum after a fall on the outstretched hand (Figs. 3a and b). The elbow becomes swollen and a radiograph reveals considerable outward displacement and rotation of the capitellar epiphysis. It is extremely important to recognize this injury as, if the capitellum is left unreduced, non-union, failure of growth, and gross deformity will result (Fig. 3). It is usually impossible to reduce the capitellum satisfactorily by conservative means, and open operation and fixation are required—either with a Kirschner wire or a screw, which require removal later, or a catgut suture—to hold the capitellum in perfect alignment. This will ultimately restore the normality of the elbow.

Supracondylar Fracture of Elbow.—Another important injury of the elbow in children is a supracondylar fracture of the elbow. As with so many injuries its real importance lies not in the fracture itself but in the complications which go with it (Fig. 4). The most important of these is Volkmann's ischaemic contracture. As a result of a fall on the outstretched hand the elbow becomes swollen and the classical signs of impaired circulation appear. Of these the first and most important is pain in the hand aggravated by passive extension of the fingers ; the child is also unable to extend the fingers voluntarily. At a later stage there will be absence of the radial pulse, impaired peripheral capillary circulation, and either pallor or cyanosis of the hand with swelling of the fingers. Later still blistering and complete paralysis of the forearm muscles appear. However, the condition should be suspected long before these signs are apparent.

The treatment of a threatened Volkmann's ischaemic contracture is a matter of some controversy. It is of course important that all splints and bandages should be removed and the child's general blood-pressure maintained. With the help of these measures the collateral circulation will very often be adequate to maintain a good blood supply to the muscles of the forearm and hand even though the brachial artery has been occluded by direct pressure or spasm. However, if, after having elevated the arm, released all constricting bandages, and placed the elbow in a semi-extended position, there is still evidence of impaired circulation it will usually be wise to perform an operation. Two main types of operation have been described. The first method, associated with the name of Professor George Perkins, is to approach the bone fragments posteriorly and replace them by direct open reduction so that the lower fragment, instead of lying posterior to the upper fragment, lies in line with it, or even in front. The other operative approach is to expose the brachial artery anteriorly and if it contains a

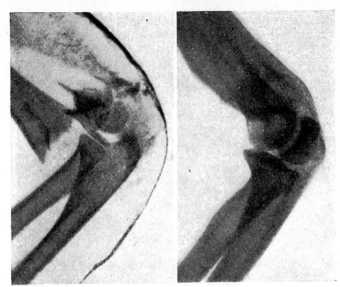

FIG. 2a   FIG. 2b

FIG. 2.—Remodelling of supracondylar fracture: (a) radiograph after reduction; (b) two years later.

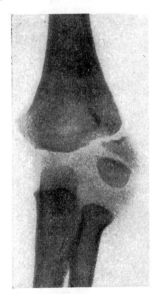  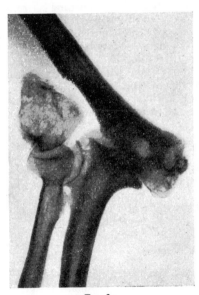

FIG. 3a   FIG. 3b   FIG. 3c

FIG. 3.—Fracture of capitellum:

(a) before reduction;   (b) after reduction;   (c) untreated fractured capitellum.

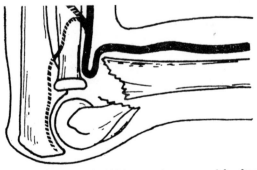

FIG. 4.—Nipping of brachial artery in supracondylar fracture of elbow.

thrombus or blood clot then this should be removed. If the arterial wall is hopelessly damaged it is probably best to resect the affected portion and ligate the artery above and below it.

Owing to the small size of the artery in children it is only rarely possible to do an excision and direct suture of a damaged segment of the artery or to perform a replacement graft.

It will be clear that even after heroic measures such as these function may not be completely restored. Obviously far more important than the ability to undertake major and complicated surgery is that of recognizing the threat of Volkmann's ischaemia and taking immediate steps to prevent its occurrence. If these measures are taken early enough it is rare for the child to develop serious contracture at a later date. This is undoubtedly the most serious complication of closed fractures of the limbs in children.

Monteggia Fracture.—Another serious fracture occurring around the elbow in children is the so-called Monteggia fracture—that is, dislocation of the head of the radius associated with a fracture of the ulna. In this condition there is usually tearing of the interosseous and orbicular ligaments and widespread separation of the radius and ulna. Though it may be possible to reduce these injuries by conservative means, it is usually wise to operate. The head of the radius is reduced and fixed in place by a reconstruction of the orbicular ligament. Internal splints are then applied to the ulna by means of either a plate or an intramedullary nail.

Naturally in any fracture or injury around the elbow there may be damage to one of the surrounding nerves. Of these the median nerve is the most important, though the radial nerve is the most commonly damaged. Again it is of the utmost importance to recognize such a complication at the earliest possible date and point out to the parents that it is caused by the injury and not by the treatment.

Most other fractures in children have a strong tendency to unite, and even if there is some mal-union growth usually restores normality ; the nearer the fracture is to the growing end of the bone the more quickly this natural correction occurs. The opposite occurs if there has been damage to the epiphysis ; under these circumstances progressive deformity and shortening will result. The epiphysis may be damaged in early childhood —usually from infection or at a later stage from injury—for example, a fall on the outstretched hand may damage the lower radial epiphysis and produce a Madelung's deformity, or damage to the trochlear epiphysis often produces progressive cubitus varus or " gun-stock elbow."

Ankle Injury

At an older age—around 12 or 13—an inversion injury to the ankle may damage the lower tibial epiphysis ; as a result there is progressive varus deformity of the ankle due to failure of growth of the medial part of the lower tibial epiphysis, and continued growth of the fibula.

General Considerations

The characteristics of a child's reaction to injury are his amazing powers of repair and restoration, both of function and appearance, even when a fracture has been imperfectly reduced. It requires considerable judgment and experience to know when a given position is " acceptable " or when strenuous efforts should be made to improve the position, and the surgeon must always bear in mind that most injuries in childhood have a favourable outcome provided that they are not over-treated. This applies particularly to elbow injuries, where excessive manipulation may delay recovery and cause serious complications such as Volkmann's ischaemia. In fractures of the shafts of long bones in children open operation and internal fixation are rarely necessary.

A possible source of diagnostic confusion in children is that the child may have been suffering from some constitutional disturbance before the injury—for instance, classical rickets is not uncommon among the immigrant population in big urban areas. It may also be necessary to exclude renal rickets and other conditions such as fragilitas ossium, especially in cases of multiple fractures. In this connexion a greenstick fracture of both bones of the forearm in children of 5 or 6 presents a special problem. For some ill-understood reason re-fracture is not uncommon and the parents frequently suspect either that the child has some underlying bone disease or that the fracture has not been treated properly. It is therefore wise to warn them of this possibility when treating a fracture of the forearm.

Nerve, Tendon, and Blood-vessel Injuries

With the exceptions mentioned above closed injuries of children's limbs do not usually produce serious consequences. On the other hand, cuts—especially round the wrist—may lead to severe loss of blood or division of tendons and nerves. Provided these are promptly repaired the prognosis with regard to ultimate function is usually excellent in children, but immediate diagnosis is all-important.

Sensory testing is exceedingly difficult and often unreliable in children—even a complete division of the median nerve in a child may not be easily detected by sensory testing alone, as the area of autonomous distribution is relatively small. If there is any possibility of a nerve or tendon being damaged and if there is an open wound at one of the important anatomical sites—for example, the wrist or round the elbow—it is better to explore the wound and examine the tendon and nerves rather than fail to diagnose. Primary repair of severed tendons is usually desirable, but, unless the wound is exceptionally clean, nerves should usually be sutured six weeks later when the skin has healed.

Burns

Burns in children are exceptionally serious, not only from the point of view of producing deformity but also as a danger to life, and in this respect the skin loss due to avulsion of skin or crushing is very similar to that due to burns. The management of extensive burns or other forms of skin loss is of course a complicated problem requiring the services of a plastic surgeon, but it is all-important in the early stage that the area should be protected from infection by applying a large sterile dressing and that the child should be treated for shock—if necessary by intravenous therapy—as soon as possible.

REFERENCES

Caffey, J. (1957). *Brit. J. Radiol.*, **30**, 225.
—— and Silverman, W. A. (1945). *Amer. J. Roentgenol.*, **54**, 1.
Griffiths, D. Ll., and Moynihan F. J. (1963). *Brit. med. J.*, **2**, 1558.

Trauma in Childhood—*Roaf*

WHICH PARENTS ABUSE CHILDREN?

"One or two children are being killed at the hands of their own parents in this country every day."—Vincent J. Fontana, M.D., *The New York Times, August 16, 1971*

By VINCENT J. FONTANA, M.D.

Mrs. K. writes: "I was a battering parent appalled to discover that after the birth of my first child I had spells of unprovoked viciousness toward the child. With the craftiness of a sick mind I hid all evidence of scars or bruises, or lied to explain them away. But something rational still operated enough to insist that my behavior was highly abnormal, and that I needed help. The horrible thing was that I did not know where to go for help, and even when I finally forced myself to the offices of various social agencies, I was so afraid of having the child taken away and my behavior thus exposed to friends and relatives that I could hardly speak of the problem. Even when I could, I found that social workers could not really help me.

"At this time, we were living in one of the states that did have a law on reporting the mistreatment of children. But to my confusion, the sick portion of my personality that willfully burned, beat, and terrorized the child covered its own tracks so well, that when I sat in someone's office, rational and calm, and explained what I had done, I was not taken seriously. I thoroughly wished that there was someone to stop me and help me.

During a six-month period in New York City this year, 2,200 cases of child abuse were reported

"Finally I moved up through bureaus and agencies to a psychiatrist. Here I obtained help, but I might add that many people could not afford this. It remains my contention that parents who maliciously mistreat their own children can be helped . . . but only by the most expert and advanced forms of treatment. The whole personality has to be remade to stop this one dangerous manifestation of mental illness, because that's what it is. I knew other parents with the same problem. I was somewhat primed to spot them . . . and none of them showed enough change to indicate they were undergoing treatment. From my own experience, it took three years from the time the behavior began until I was finally getting competent help, and at that, I was actively seeking help.

"As for the statistics on such parents, some of them certainly fit. I spent my early years in welfare homes, acquired a stepfather at the age of five and he beat me regularly until I left home at 17. I married, woefully immature and pregnant, at 18 to a boy as young and inexperienced as myself. And undoubtedly the pressures of helping my husband work his way through five years of college, with two children before he graduated, added to the frustrations that erupted in violence against an innocent child. Incidentally, for a note on the other parent involved, since it is usually only one who abuses a child, my husband was unable to give me all the emotional support I needed, but he also felt helpless. He protected the child when he was there, but of course, I only waited until he wasn't home. He did not want to take any action himself as to reporting me, because that would involve breaking up his own family. He could not believe for a long time that my behavior could be so unbalanced, a hard thing to accept about someone you love and need."

This letter was written by a parent who sought out competent help and finally did solve her problem. However, thousands of other parents with similar child-beating tendencies are continuing their as-

sault on children in this ostensibly civilized world.

The medical profession has, in the past decade, been alerted to what is now called the maltreatment syndrome in children. The spectrum of childhood neglect and abuse ranges from the infant suffering from "failure to thrive" and malnutrition to the battered child, the result of severe physical abuse. It is estimated that perhaps one to two children are being killed each day at the hands of their caretakers in the United States.

In New York City from January 1, 1971 to June 28, 1971, 2,200 cases of child abuse and neglect were reported to the Central Registry; the total percentage increase of child abuse cases reported in New York City from 1966 to 1970 was 549 percent. The number of battered children being reported in the medical literature and recorded by child protective agencies throughout the country appears to be increasing. A recent *JAMA* editorial expressed the view that as-

Dr. Fontana is Director of Pediatrics, St. Vincent's Hospital and Medical Center of New York; Medical Director, New York Foundling Hospital; Professor of Pediatrics, New York University Medical Center; Chairman of the Mayor's Task Force on Child Abuse and Neglect.

CHILD ABUSE

saults on children could turn out to be a more frequent cause of death than such diseases as leukemia, cystic fibrosis, and muscular dystrophy, and might even rank with automobile fatalities.

In a recent text on human violence, Wertham[8] stated that "the battered child syndrome or maltreatment syndrome is a recent phenomenon. It is increasing and seems to occur as a mass phenomenon in the United States. The parents belong to a generation which has grown up with crime, horror books, and the violence of other media. They live in a time when war and foreign policy are almost interchangeable terms and nonviolence is regarded as a radical invention. In a considerable portion of the cases,

alcohol plays a very important causal or contributing role in both mothers and fathers. Without the lubrication with alcohol some of the cases would not have happened.

"This syndrome in all its aspects is the most important symptom of our time. It is a link in the documentation of the thesis that the spirit of violence is rampant in our society. It is a matter not only of the occurrence of these heartless cruelties against defenseless children, but of the inadequacy of the steps taken so far to prevent them. Physicians, legislators, and the childcare agencies have taken up the question belatedly. Even now no proper solution has been found. This is one of the forms of violence which society calls 'incredible' and is unequipped to deal with."

The physician's index of suspicion is heightened when the parents relate a history that is at variance with the physical findings noted by the physician, or are reluctant to given information concerning the child's physical condition. Further investigation may reveal that the parents have made multiple visits to various hospitals with the child in order to lessen the suspicion of abuse. There is often a history of family discord, financial stress, alcoholism, psychoneurotic tendencies, sexual problems, and drug addiction. Physical examination may reveal signs of physical neglect, poor skin hygiene, malnutrition, an irritable and repressed personality, bruises, abrasions, burns, soft tissue swellings, hematomas, and/or old skin lesions. Evidence of dislocation or fracture of the extremities may also be obvious on examination.

The child who has been battered may arrive in the emergency room with physical evidence of abuse such as subdural hematoma, intra-abdominal injuries, coma, and convulsions. X-ray examination of the skull and long bones may reveal subperiosteal hemorrhages, fractures, dislocations, epiphyseal separations, periosteal calcification, and squaring of the metaphysis resulting from the laying down of new bone. If X-rays are taken immediately after the traumautic incident, periosteal reaction may not be present; when there is suspicion of child abuse, the child should be hospitalized and the X-rays repeated in a week's time. The physician should not make a definitive diagnosis of battering unless he has carefully ruled out the presence of scurvy, rickets, infantile cortical hyperostosis, infantile syphilis, osteogenesis imperfecta, and last but not least, the possibility of accidental trauma.

The abusing parents usually manifest at least some of the following traits: impulsive personality, a low frustration level, immaturity, lack of affect, psychosis, alcoholism, drug addiction, and a history of abuse in their own childhood. A large number of these parents were battered by their own parents, and the battered child of today often becomes the battering parent of the future, thereby creating a vicious cycle

What traits are manifested by abusing parents?

of violence breeding violence. The inner tensions and conflicts of these parents have an inevitable breaking point which may lead to the battering syndrome. One early aspect of treatment, therefore, should consist of exposing the realities of the parents' personalities and assessing the psychosocial pathology that is responsible for their reactions toward their own children.

In some of these parents, the abuse they inflict on their children may be a means of asking for help. Drs. Steele and Pollock have indicated that the child abusers had severe identity problems in their parental roles. The moments preceding aggressive acts are often only partially remembered, and during this cloudy period it may be that the abusive parent regresses to an earlier stage in his development, transfers identity with his own frustrating parent, and punishes the child as if he were punishing himself. The physician must direct those parents who are receptive to help to the appropriate community services, which must be immediately available if the abusing parents are to be given any meaningful assistance.

The most immediate aspect of this problem is the physician's responsibility to a child who is in a life-threatening situation. He must have an acute awareness of the maltreatment syndrome, be suspect on behalf of any child who shows signs of questionable care, neglect, or abuse, and know the diagnostic criteria necessary to confirm suspicions. He must report suspected cases to the child protective agencies or the law enforcement bureaus in his area. Only by fulfilling his medical, moral, and legal responsibilities in protecting the maltreated child from further abuse can the medical profession truly fulfill their obligation to the child and assist in stemming the tide of child battering.

The following summary of characteristics of the maltreatment syndrome may be helpful to the physician:

- Child is usually under three years of age.
- General health of the child indicates neglect.
- Characteristic distribution of fractures.
- Disproportionate amount of soft tissue injury.
- Evidence that injuries occurred at different times and are at different stages of resolution.
- Cause of recent trauma is in question.
- Suspicious family history.
- History of previous similar episodes.
- No new lesions occur during child's hospital stay.

If the physician is reluctant or unsure in diagnosing or reporting a case of child abuse or neglect, for whatever reason, he should send the child to a hospital facility for a complete medical survey.

A hospital team or Child Abuse Committee in the hospital can be very helpful in assessing any suspected cases of child abuse and neglect; a team judgment regarding diagnosis and management of the child is helpful in the immediate acute situation and in presenting the case to the courts. After removing the child from a life-threatening family environment, the team should continue their involvement in the case by considering the plight of the parents, in order to offer intensive therapy and thereby decrease the likelihood of repeated attacks on the child. The committee or team should be composed of a pediatrician, a psychiatrist, a social worker, and a nurse.

Part of the physician's resistance to personal involvement may be overcome by clear directives concerning his responsibilities in reporting these cases and his role in protecting the child from future inflicted abuse. Today there are child abuse reporting laws in all 50 states. Their aim is protection of the parents when presented with invalid evidence; protection of the child by making it mandatory for physicians to report cases of maltreatment; and protection of the physician by legislation preventing possible damage suits by the parties involved in any legal action. Therefore, under these laws, every physician who has under his charge or care any child suspected of having any wounds due to willfully inflicted injury or giving evidence of unjustifiable mental suffering must report the case to the appropriate child protective agency or law enforcement bureau in his community.

Physicians are the first line of defense in the fight to decrease the incidence of child maltreatment. But laws in themselves will do little to help alleviate the plight of the abused and neglected child. Reporting of abuse and neglect cases is not enough, it is the action taken after the reporting that is important.

These children who suffer from abuse and neglect, whose early lives are scarred by trauma, starvation, and maternal deprivation, have little chance of growing up normally. If they survive, they may be mentally retarded or physically disabled; they may develop psychotic illness. As a result, many of these battered children become the hard-core criminals or the battering parents of the future. The child must be protected by prompt removal from a life-threatening environment, and assisted by all possible means to obtain the opportunity of growing up without isolation, without trauma, and without neglect. The physical, moral, spiritual, and emotional status of America's future generation depends on the action of society towards this problem of maltreatment today.

This problem of child abuse is real, it's sizable, and it is pressing! We must recognize the problem and all its implications if it is ever to be adequately met and resolved by individual involvement that will result in remedial action and permanent legal reforms. ☐

1. Fontana, Vincent J. The maltreatment syndrome in children. N. E. J. Med., 269:1389, 1963.
2. Kempe, C. H., et al. Battered child syndrome. J.A.M.A., 181:17, 1962.
3. Fontana, V. J. The neglect and abuse of children. N. Y. J. Med., 64:215,1964.
4. Fontana, V. J. Further reflections on maltreatment of children. N. Y. State J. Med., 68:2214, 1968.
5. Kempe, C. H. and Helfer, R. The Battered Child. Chicago University Press, 1968.
6. Fontana, V. J. The Maltreated Child, 2nd edition. Charles C. Thomas, Springfield, Illinois 1971.
7. Fontana, V. J. The maltreatment syndrome in children. Hospital Medicine, March 1971, p. 7.
8. Wertham, F. A Sign For Cain: An Exploration of Human Violence. Macmillan, New York, 1966, pp. 48-49.

ROSS timesaver

VOL. 14-NO. 3
MAY-JUNE 1972

feelings

Guest editors of this issue are: Ray E. Helfer, Associate Professor, Department of Human Development, Michigan State University, East Lansing, and John S. Wheeler, in pediatric practice in Allentown, Pennsylvania. Dr. Helfer was Chief of Pediatric Residency at St. Christopher's Hospital for Children, Philadelphia, in 1958 and 1959, when Dr. Wheeler was in pediatric residency at that hospital.

Dr. Helfer is a recognized authority on child abuse in the United States. Dr. Wheeler is one of the key forces behind establishment of a unique Child Abuse Program in Allentown.

Child Abuse and the Private Pediatrician

Significant contributions to clinical medicine are frequently preceded by chance happenings, which might be dismissed as insignificant, were it not for acute observation of perceptive and inquiring attendants.

During the early 1960's, Dr. Brandt Steele, a psychiatrist, and Dr. C. Henry Kempe, a pediatrician, both at University of Colorado Medical Center, were intrigued by a statement made by a young mother: "I've waited all this time to have my baby; and when she was born, she never did anything for me." With further questioning the mother added, "Then when she cried, it meant she didn't love me . . . so I hit her."

The baby, only 3 months old, was seriously injured. The mother was in desperate need of help.

This emotionally charged incident of some 10 years past marked commencement of an intensive study of child abuse. From this embryo, nationwide interest in "Battered Child Syndrome" developed.[1,2]

Sometime later, a seriously injured, 2-month old was brought to the office of one of the authors, a pediatrician in private practice. This incident stimulated development of a coordinated, community approach to problems of child abuse in Allentown, Pennsylvania. Feelings generated in the pediatrician by that event are expressed in a letter written shortly after the incident.

"A week ago, a 2-month-old baby was admitted to my private service in Allentown General Hospital.

"I saw this child a month ago when the father brought him in, because 'he had a sore arm.' X rays revealed a fracture of the humerus. The history provided by the father stated that the child 'must have rolled over in bed or fallen onto the floor.' I didn't think much of this at the time; but in retrospect, it is quite obviously a feeble explanation. My feeling was to deny that this could be a case of child abuse, since I knew both parents to be 'good.' Somehow, I believed the father. I didn't *want* to admit that this could be a battered child case.

"When the baby was brought back last week with a swollen, painful left leg, and X rays revealed a fracture of the femur, again with no reasonable explanation, I went into something of a mood of depression. My earlier denial of child abuse gave way to the very obvious and objective facts before me.

"I subsequently went through the inescapable phases of antagonism toward and dislike for the parents, pity for the child, anger at the policeman who had somehow gotten into the act, failure of the social system to act after my report was made, the manner in which the newspaper handled the situation, and the final realization that those whom I disliked most, the parents, were in greatest need of help.

"Although I dealt with child abuse when we were residents on the ward services together, I have never before had a case in my own practice. Things surely look different from this vantage point. Pediatricians are not trained to handle feelings of dislike for child-abusive parents.

"When this incident occurred, I found myself giving more and more attention to the child, by overtly avoiding making rounds on the ward when I thought the parents might be there.

"In the beginning, I made little or no attempt to involve the parents, except to give them rather cursory reports on how the child's fractures were healing.

"The first time I saw the child, I denied that cause of injury could possibly be nonaccidental. I wanted to believe the parents' history—and did. This denial tended to reinforce a very selfish and underlying need, since I realized that to make the diagnosis of suspected child abuse would require a time and emotional commitment which I was not prepared to make. I don't think I thought of all these things at the time, but it is clear to me now what happened. I never faced up to the fact before that some parents might not be telling me the truth.

"I really became concerned when I finally recognized my tremendous desire to seek revenge by turning the case over to the police, thus washing my hands of the whole mess. I finally mastered these feelings, and I sat down with the parents and talked with them at length. I told the parents that I felt this was a case of battered child syndrome, and that all the other pediatricians in the hospital felt the same way—since this case had been presented at conference. The parents were furious and said that they would obtain legal counsel and go to court. I responded that we were glad they had decided to obtain counsel. I added that we also had decided to go to court, and added that in doing so, *we* were fighting to save the child's life. I told the parents that I was going to leave the room for 10 minutes so they could 'talk it over.'

"When I returned, the father confessed. He broke down during our conversation, and he stated that he actually was grateful that we had gotten in on the case. He said he realized that they needed outside help in the situation.

"Now I found myself reacting in a peculiar way. I discovered that I did not dislike the parents as much as I thought, and I even began to understand how this event might have happened. Ironical as it seemed, I now wanted to protect the parents from the very system which I had thought earlier might punish them.

"My anger began to be directed more toward the social system and away from the parents. I guess I had to be mad at somebody.

"A psychiatrist was brought in on the case. It was discovered shortly after that the father himself had been a battered child.

"We also arranged for psychiatric help for the mother. We explained to both parents that it would be necessary to place their child in a foster home temporarily, but that they eventually would get their child back.

"I often have wondered where the blame lies in battered child cases which are handled ineffectually. I have seen doctors bear the brunt of criticism by agencies concerned with child welfare, and I have seen doctors blame these agencies. I realize now that the physician is in a unique position, and he very often deserves the blame when a child-abuse case is not handled well. For one thing, social service agencies are hamstrung if the physician does not give his support and help.

"You and I know that child abuse is a nasty business. When parents are confronted with possibility that their child is a victim of child abuse, some of the more hostile human feelings are likely to be evoked. No one, including a physician, wants to become involved in a deluge of accusations, denials, threats and indignation. I feel that this factor alone makes many physicians shy away from reporting suspected child-abuse cases. Although there is little possibility of involvement in a lawsuit, I feel that loss of time through necessity to appear in court to testify deters physicians from reporting suspected child abuse. Nevertheless, child abuse can be a matter of life and death, or a matter of permanent crippling for the child. The physician has a moral obligation to help."

Two to three percent of all reported child-abuse cases result in death, and 25 to 30 percent result in permanent injury. Not knowing where to turn for help explains in part why of 2,800 reported cases of suspected child abuse and neglect in New York City in 1970, only eight were reported by physicians in private practice.

The Abusive Pattern

The following, from the introduction to the book, *Helping the Battered Child and His Family*, summarizes the pattern seen in abusive families: [3]

"In order for a child to be physically injured by his parents or guardian, several pieces of a complex puzzle must come together in a very special way. To date, we can identify at least three major criteria.

"First, a parent (or parents) must have the *potential to abuse*. This potential is acquired over the years and is made up of at least four factors:

"1. The way the parents themselves were reared; i.e., did they receive the mothering imprint?

"2. Have they become very isolated individuals who cannot trust or use others?

"3. Does either have a spouse that is so passive he or she cannot give?

"4. Do they have very unrealistic expectations from their child (or children)?

"Second, there must be a *child*, one who is seen differently by his parents; one who fails to respond in the expected manner; or possibly one who really is different (retarded, too smart, hyperactive, or has a birth defect). Often the perfectly normal child is "seen" as bad, willful, stubborn, demanding, spoiled or slow.

"Finally, there must be some form of crisis, or a series of *crises*, that sets the abusive act in motion. A washing machine's breaking down, a job lost, a husband's being drafted, absence of heat, insufficient food or a mother-in-law's visit might be the precipitating factor. The simplistic lay view that child abuse is caused by parents who 'don't know their strength' while disciplining their child has been shown to be false."

The Allentown Program

Learning to handle emotions and concerns commonly experienced by physicians confronted by overt child abuse requires significant time and motivation. One of the first steps of those starting a program for rehabilitation of child-abuse families in Allentown, Pennsylvania was to enlist assistance of a capable psychatrist with an active interest in group therapy. Second, a child-welfare agency was identified which, prior to this time, had experienced significant difficulty trying to coordinate services that families of abused and neglected children require. This agency was willing to make a small quantity of funds available, which enabled one of the community pediatricians to delegate sufficient time to coordinate and develop an ongoing program.

A variety of services and programs has been combined to make the Allentown child-abuse and -neglect effort a total community, cooperative program. Weekly clinics for abusive parents and their children are held in the Allentown Hospital, a group therapy program is available, an emergency-room alert file and a photographic file have been developed, and an educational program for teachers, nurses, and court

workers has proven to be most effective. Liaison with the District Attorney's office, the Attorney for Child Welfare, police, courts and news media have all been combined to improve coordinated community services.

Services provided to referred families are selected to be appropriate to the outcome of counseling. In cases where abuse *has* occurred, available consultants and specialists provide a multidisciplinary approach to the problem.

Cases referred by local physicians and community service agencies have varied considerably, but all initially showed symptoms implying child abuse. Not all children concerned have been found to be abused.

Case Study—Child Abuse

A 2-year-old girl was hospitalized for extensive subgaleal hematoma—without history of trauma. The child purportedly was under care of a baby-sitter at time of injury. However, the child had undergone three sets of skull X rays in the past year for trauma at other local hospitals. On two of these three occasions the child was under care of her divorced mother.

Attending physicians talked with the mother very frankly about all possibilities which might explain the cause of injuries, one such being child abuse. She immedately became defensive, blamed the baby-sitter and, when confronted with the fact that two episodes of head injury had occurred previously under *her* care, became belligerent and stormed angrily from the hospital before further questioning could be conducted. She went directly to her lawyer to seek advice.

The next day the mother had calmed somewhat and was willing to discuss her feelings toward the child, as well as her own rearing, with the community Pediatric Child Abuse Consultant. She finally accepted the fact that a child-abuse form notifying the Child Welfare Department of suspected cause of injury had to be submitted.

The mother still brings the child to see the physicians periodically. Now, 2 years later, due to help and reassurance given by interested physicians, this parent is sufficiently comfortable that she has not found it necessary to further abuse the child. There has been no further evidence of trauma.

Case Study—False Alarm

Another 2-year-old girl, with multiple generalized bruises, was seen in the physicians' child-abuse clinic after being referred by the hospital. She was covered with ecchymotic areas on the face, chest, abdomen and legs. Child abuse was suspected, and hospitalization was advised to enable further study. Suspicions of attending physicians were discussed with the parents who, although not angry, were indeed puzzled. The father looked to the mother and said, "Maybe it's the babysitter."

Nothing further was discussed with these parents until diagnostic studies were done, which revealed a platelet count of 12,000 and clear-cut evidence of idiopathic thrombocytopenic purpura. The child recovered and was discharged with no further ecchymotic areas noted.

This proved *not* to be a case of child abuse. The parents, accordingly, were reassured by attending physicians that initial diagnosis had been erroneous, and that what had at first aroused suspicion of child abuse was in reality thrombocytopenic purpura.

Components of a Community SCAN Program

The most important aspect of any such Suspected Child Abuse and Neglect (SCAN) program is early identification and acquisition of one or two highly motivated persons willing to carry through the difficult first stages of development. The next step is to identify community organizations and agencies capable of providing services to abused children and their families. At least one person in each agency with a particular interest in child abuse and neglect usually can be located. Since primary responsibilities of such persons are to the agencies by which they are employed, it usually is advantageous to select persons from "outside the system" to coordinate organization and, sometimes, implementation of the program.

Organizers can anticipate opposition and lack of cooperation. As in any other new program, uncommitted bystanders want a demonstration of effectiveness before they will offer support or even acceptance. Judicious use of newspaper, radio and television media can help develop widespread interest and support.

A recommended structure for a community SCAN program, one having distinct and separate components pulled together by a Coordinator, is shown below.

FIGURE I
Structure of Community
SCAN Program

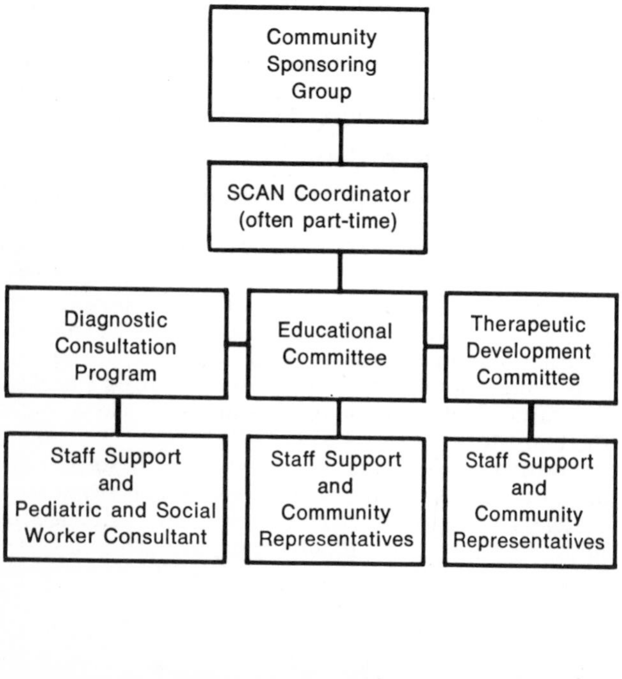

Each of the three segments has a specific task to perform:

The Diagnositc Consultation Program: The main function is assisting the individual physician, nurse, teacher or agency requesting consultation. Assistance is given in gathering and compiling data, keeping records and serving as a referring locus. This segment of the program should be available 24 hours per day. As in Allentown, the pediatrician and social worker probably will be part-time.

Educational Committee: This segment makes resource material and general information about child abuse available to any agency in the community desiring such assistance, promulgates the image and purpose of the program and assists in organizing lectures, classes and special educational sessions on child abuse and neglect.

Therapeutic Development Committee: This segment defines various therapeutic programs and available options, determines personnel required, and helps identify local individuals and agencies capable of helping. It must remain one step ahead of the Diagnostic Consultation Program to provide resources for use in making recommendations for disposition of families evaluated.

It is important to keep the three segments of the SCAN program separate, since each has its specific role, and there is a tendency to duplicate effort when segments lose autonomy.

Increased understanding of psychodynamics of abusive parents has permitted development of multiple treatment options. The Therapeutic Development Committee, therefore, has a number of programs from which to choose. These include the self-help group of Parents Anonymous, group therapy, specialized homemakers, preschool therapeutic day-care centers, community/hospital consortiums, parent-aides and foster grandparent programs, and special roles for public-health nurses and homemakers. Most of these are described in detail in references 2 and 3.

Role and Responsibility of the Private Pediatrician

The practitioner who sees large numbers of children has four distinct responsibilities to patients and community in dealing with problems of child abuse and neglect:

1. *Early identification* of families that have the potential to abuse small children;

2. *Admitting the child* to the hospital when child abuse and neglect is suspected. Hospitalization allows both physician and parents to "calm down" so that necessary information can be obtained objectively. Hospitalization for diagnostic and evaluation purposes is much less costly than are consequences where diagnosis is not made;

3. *Making every attempt to confront parents with the problem* in such a way that it ultimately will be seen as a helpful gesture, rather than one that increases their distrust, antagonism, and feeling of isolation; [2,3]

4. *Making arrangements for early referral* to a community-coordinated, child-abuse and -neglect consultation and therapeutic program.

If a community SCAN program is not in existence, the physician has an added responsibility (as was the case in Allentown). The local medical society, hospital staff and community agencies must be made to see each incidence of child abuse as a high priority project. Problems that arise in trying to help an abusive family are much too diverse—and chance of failure much too great—to risk handling the case in a solo manner by an individual practitioner or even by a single community agency. If child abuse is to be handled effectively in the community, a cooperative program must be initiated. The pediatrician is often the *only* person able or willing to get a community SCAN program started.

References:

1. Helfer, R. E., and Kempe, C. H., *The Battered Child*, 1st ed., University of Chicago Press, 1968.
2. Kempe, C. H., Silverman, F. N., Steele, B. J., Draegemueller, W., and Silver, H. K.: "The Battered Child Syndrome," JAMA 181:17, 1962.
3. Kempe, C. H., and Helfer, R. E., *Helping the Battered Child and His Family*, Phila., Lippincott, 1972.

SUMMARY

From the articles in this section, we might conclude that, according to police statistics, indigent blacks and whites are the usual aggressors. However, it was pointed out that detailed studies indicate all socioeconomic levels are involved and that private physicians are less likely to report willful abuse to the authorities than their counterparts in emergency wards of hospitals. Again, the most striking finding in these reports is that the parents of battered children were abused or neglected by their parents.

Fifteen percent of the children five years old who are brought into hospital emergency rooms are battered. This indicates that the battered child syndrome is one of the most serious epidemic diseases in America. As previously pointed out, more children under five die from injuries inflicted by a parent or guardian than from tuberculosis, whooping cough, polio, measles, diabetes, rheumatic fever, and appendicitis combined. Some staticians say more die from abuse than in automobile accidents.

It has been estimated that at least 60,000 children are willfully beaten, starved, burned, and smothered each year in the United States. These children who suffer from abuse and neglect, whose early lives are scarred by trauma, starvation, and maternal deprivation have little chance to develop normally. If they do survive, they may be physically or mentally disabled, emotionally deprived, and, in their turn, child abusers. So the vicious and pitiful spiral will be perpetuated unless prevention and/or effective treatment intervenes at the earliest stages.

STUDY QUESTIONS

1. Should it be considered a misdemeanor if a physician does not report willful trauma to protective agencies?

2. What type of in-service education should maternity wards provide to all mothers to support the infant-mother-family relationship?

3. What is the role of the physician and nurse in a multi-disciplinary approach to assisting the battered child?

4. What can hospitals do to help discover and protect children who are being mistreated?

5. Since the physician is the primary source of medical care and, in many cases, the first to discover child abuse, should he spearhead the counseling with parents? Why do many fail to act in any way?

6. Why do parents subject their offspring to the kinds of assaults mentioned in these readings?

REFERENCES

A. Readings Included in This Text

Bain, Katherine. "The Physically Abused Child." *Pediatrics,* 31 (1963):895-897.

Fontana, Vincent J. "An Insidious and Disturbing Medical Entity." *Public Welfare,* 24 (1966):235-239.

Fontana, Vincent J. "Which Parents Abuse Children?" *Medical Insight,* 16 (1971):18-21.

Helfer, Ray E., and Wheeler, John S. "Child Abuse and the Private Pediatrician," *Feelings,* 14 (1972):1-4.

Roaf, Robert. "Trauma in Early Childhood." *British Medical Journal,* 1 (1965):1541-1543.

B. Suggested Additional Readings

Adelson, Lester. "Slaughter of the Innocents." *New England Journal of Medicine,* 264 (1964):1345-1349.

Alverson, Charles E. "Protecting Children: Medical, Legal Drive Aims to Spot, Reduce Cases of Child Abuse." *Wall Street Journal,* 166 (1965):1.

"Child Abuse: An Anonymous Answer?" *Medical World News,* 12 (1971):6.

Cochrone, W. "The Battered Child Syndrome." *Canadian Journal of Public Health,* 65 (1965):193-5.

Greengard, Joseph. "The Battered-Child Syndrome." *American Journal of Nursing,* 64:98-100.

Harper, Fowler V. "The Physician, The Battered Child, and The Law." *Pediatrics,* 31 (1963):899-902.

Milowe, Irvin D., and Lourie, Reginald S. "The Child's Role in the Battered Child Syndrome." *Journal of Pediatrics 65,* No. 6, 1079-1081, December 1964.

Rhymes, Julina P. "Working with Mothers and Babies Who Fail to Thrive." *American Journal of Nursing,* 66 (1966): 1972-1976.

Russell, Patricia. "Subdural Hematomas in Infancy." *Medical Science,* 15 (1964):82-91.

Shade, Dolores A. "Limits to Service in Child Abuse." *American Journal of Nursing,* 69 (1969):1710-1712.

Storey, B. "The Battered Child." *Medical Journal of Australia,* 2 (1964):789-791.

Wooley, Paul. "The Pediatrician and the Young Child Subjected to Repeated Abuse." *Journal of Pediatrics,* 62 (1963): 628-691.

VI
The Educator Takes a Look

INTRODUCTION

The battered child syndrome is a problem that the parents, the community, and the schools have obscured, or pretended did not exist, until the last few years.

It will be seen from the material in this chapter that the classroom teacher can become one of the most important links in the prevention and protective chain, since his daily contacts put him in the strategic position to observe early indications of abuse.

The teacher's own behavior is also either stimulating or therapeutically deterrent to abusive tendencies in children, which will influence their adult behavior. Most abusive incidents occur in the course of disciplining children. Therefore, a teacher who uses physical force against a child teaches that child and all children in the classroom that physical force is an appropriate means of human interaction.

Schools and other services in our society must be based on a constructive and therapeutic—rather than a punitive—philosophy if they are to serve the ultimate objective of reducing the general level of violence in the country and to raise the level of human well-being throughout the entire society.

The writers of the articles that follow not only discuss the general problems of the battered child and what the schools can do, but also provide clues for the identification of battered children.

The headline Battered Child Syndrome Reaches Epidemic Level *recently appeared in newspapers around the country. Increasingly newspaper readers note articles about children who have been abused or even killed by their own parents. These are the battered children to which this article refers.*

During the last few years educators have had their attention called to numerous classifications of children whose special problems require special attention. We now try to provide special help for the mentally retarded, emotionally disturbed, physically handicapped, and so forth. However, it has only been since we have developed means of identifying these children and have been willing to admit that these problems exist that it has been possible to try to provide assistance.

It is not so many years ago that the mentally retarded child was considered a stigma on the family and society and hid in an attic, secretly placed in an asylum, or confined to his own home, lest someone find out about him. Today the battered child is similarly considered. Parents want to hide the fact that they are mistreating one or more of their children;

and society at large does not want to admit such things are occurring. Thus, the battered child, usually one young in years, has no protection and is left to the mistreatment of one or both parents.

According to the figures provided by the U.S. Children's Bureau in Washington, D.C., between 50,000 and 75,000 children were grossly mistreated in 1964. Other sources estimate that ninety percent of these children were under ten years of age and half of the total under four years of age. Parents, singly or together, were responsible for three out of every four cases. One out of every four of these battered cases ended in the death of the child. It is likely that brutal physical punishment by parents causes more deaths among children than such recognized diseases as leukemia and muscular dystrophy.

The amount of systematic research on the problems of child abuse and neglect is conspicuously scant. Some material is available about individual mistreated children and particularly abusive families. Records reveal that youngsters have been punched, kicked, bitten, scratched, and flung against hard objects. They have been hit by everything from sticks and strap buckles to furniture and garden tools. They have been deliberately burned, locked up, chained, and put outdoors in zero weather.

Little is known about the long-term effects of abuse on the child or on the nature of the factors which determine the outcome of rehabilitative efforts with the family. Even less is known

The battered child

JEROME E. LEAVITT is Professor of Education, State College, Portland, Oregon

plus the taboo of our society regarding even the mention of abuse and gross neglect of children, put the discussion of this topic out-of-bounds. The situation of the battered child of today is as bad as that of the mentally retarded child of a century ago, who was hidden from the family and community lest the sensitivities of these persons be offended. Physically he is no better off than the child slave of yesterday who was bartered, sold, or disfigured for profit. Few objective standards for child protection have been established.

The battered child is not an isolated case or something that happens some other place. Battered children live or die in every city and in every state of the United States. And they, unlike some other types of problems, exist in every strata of our society.

With many thousands of battered children coming to school each year, educators need to understand the problems faced by these children and their parents. First, educators need to learn all they can from professionals in medicine, law, and the behavioral sciences. Second, they need to develop means by which to identify and work with these children and their parents.

Physicians as a group have been as idealistic as the rest of us and did not believe that conditions could be as they are. It was not until the routine use of the X-ray on patients being admitted to hospitals that the problem showed up. Now that physicians have the evidence, they are very much concerned with the problem. Actually there are two problems — the battered child suffering under abuse; and parents who are probably (to say the least) immature, impulsive, self-centered, hypersensitive, and quick to react with poorly controlled aggression. According to Mr. Vincent De Francis, Director of the Children's Division of the American Humane Society, the problem of the battered child is

about both the short- and long-term effects on the learning of the abused child and his ability to function in society. However, it is believed that brutal punishment may be a major cause of brain and nervous system damage.

Child abuse is not new. Until recently the lack of research fostered the belief that "civilization" did away with such things. This belief, really the problem of the battering adult.

As a teacher you can expect that some of the three out of every four battered children who live will appear in your classroom. How will you identify them and what will you be able to do to help them?

By the time a child reaches first grade most of the battering damage has been done, although the alert teacher will recognize, on occasion, unusual physical damage done to a child. At such times the first step is to refer the child to the school doctor or nurse who can then follow up to determine the cause and the extent of the damage. If deemed advisable, they in turn can make a referral to the appropriate legal authority. In many cases the damage, such as lashes on the back, will not show. Under these conditions the only clue may be the unusual behavior of the child. Sometimes the child's health and other records will provide information.

Another possible means of identification is the parents. Such parents tend to be meek, dependent, reject their children, and are more concerned with their own feelings and pleasure. They show an inability to love their children or to feel protective towards them. Of course teachers have to be exceedingly careful, for all parents that fit the previous description do not batter their children.

Extremely nervous and upset children or those with brain damage may also be victims of battering. In most cases teachers will never know. With children in these groups one can only proceed as they would with any other child suffering with the same problem regardless of the cause.

In the classroom the actual identification of the battered child, difficult at best, is not actually the important thing. What is most important is being sensitive to the needs of the crippled, meek, fearful, lonesome, or aggressive child, regardless of the cause, and then working with him to make him feel that here in school he belongs, that he is wanted, and that somebody cares.

One of the most important ways a teacher can help is through the role as a citizen—doing everything possible to see that appropriate laws are passed for the protection of children. So far only a few states have child protection laws. The Children's Bureau of the United States Department of Health, Education, and Welfare, Washington 25, D.C. can provide suggestions on how to assist and also supply sample child protection laws for consideration of legislatures. As a professional educator you can get your state education association interested in this problem and have them go on record in support of adequate child protection laws.

As I entered a taxi recently, the driver remarked that his last passenger had said that if we scaled the history of the world as a yardstick, 26 of the 36 inches would represent our scientific advance in the last twenty years; and 1½ inches our total social advance in the history of the world. This got me to thinking that it's about time that we started giving as much consideration to people as we do to "things."

Persons interested in reading more about this problem and in knowing what they can do about it are referred to the book *Wednesday's Children* by Leontine R. Young (McGraw-Hill); and the magazine articles "Parents Who Abuse Children" by Vincent De Francis in the November, 1963, issue of *The PTA Magazine,* and "The Shocking Price of Parental Anger" in the March, 1964, issue of *Good Housekeeping.* The two best general sources of publications and information are the Children's Bureau, United States Department of Health, Education, and Welfare, Washington, D.C. and the Children's Division of the American Humane Association, Denver, Colorado.

EDITORIAL NOTE: At the present time the author of this article is interested in securing aid in developing two projects to familiarize teachers with the battered child. One is a paperback reprint of all pertinent articles so far published in this area. The other a conference of researchers and practitioners from all the disciplines concerned, to work with a group of educators in developing a program for reporting and dissemination of the latest material in the field. He will welcome your suggestions.

The battered child

IT IS HARD FOR MANY OF US TO BELIEVE that any parent would wilfully inflict physical injury upon his baby or young child. Yet across the Nation cases of "battered children" are reported daily. These are usually young children, sometimes infants. They may be burned, choked, beaten, thrown against the wall or down the stairs. In some cases they are dead on arrival at the hospital. The severity of their injury seems to be in direct relation to the anger or emotional imbalance of the parent who inflicts the injury.

This is a serious national problem. Child abuse is not new in our society, but its occurrence seems to be on the increase. It also is receiving more prominent attention in hospitals and in social agencies.

It is a matter of grave concern to doctors who see these children and to social agencies who suspect injury and try to work with the parents to prevent further mistreatment. But it must be a matter of equal concern to all who are concerned about the welfare of children.

The "battered child syndrome," as this condition is called, was brought into sharper focus in 1961 when Dr. C. Henry Kempe, of the University of Colorado School of Medicine, and others undertook a nationwide survey of hospitals to find out how often this syndrome occurred. In a single year in seventy-one hospitals, 302 cases of child abuse were reported. Thirty-three of the children died, and eighty-five suffered permanent brain injury.

The Children's Bureau has long been interested in finding ways to stop this shameful abuse of children. After the Kempe findings were reported, we called two conferences of authorities in the medical, legal and social work fields to discuss effective ways to deal with this problem.

The Abused Child

By KATHERINE B. OETTINGER

It has many ramifications. Our first concern, naturally, is for the protection of the child. If his parents are going to injure him repeatedly, ways must be found to keep him away from harm even if this means removing him from his own home. In every case, effort must be made to work with the parents to prevent further harm to the child.

The initial problem, of course, is to identify the abused child so that steps can be taken to safeguard his health and —in too many cases—his life.

Reporting Cases of Child Abuse

The Children's Bureau, with the help of experts, has issued guiding principles and some suggested language to require reporting of the physically abused child by doctors.

The purpose of these guides is to identify children in danger so that they can be protected. It is not to punish parents, although criminal action may result from an investigation of the action.

Some doctors may be fearful of reporting cases where they suspect child abuse because criminal or civil suit may be brought upon them by the parent or caretaker. The suggested legislative guides grant them immunity from such liability.

The suggested legislative language is directed principally to the protection of the very young child who cannot speak for himself. Reporting abuse incidences of older children also would be required under the suggested guides.

Improved radiological techniques, now readily available, will help the doctor to

Katherine B. Oettinger, chief, Children's Bureau, Welfare Administration, United States Department of Health, Education, and Welfare, states that society has a responsibility to protect and preserve the rights of children when parents are wilfully abusing them.

determine whether he is dealing with an "accidental" injury or whether the child shows previous injuries in various stages of healing.

Copies of the Children's Bureau's guides for legislative action to protect the abused child have been widely distributed throughout the country. About a third of the States now have taken legislative action so that, in one form or another, there are laws on their books making it mandatory for doctors to report cases of child abuse to the appropriate authority.

This is an important step, but it is only the first step in the concerted efforts of both public and voluntary officials to meet this problem. The American Humane Association, for one, is working hard to bring this problem to the attention of the public, as is the Children's Bureau.

Social agencies, the courts, the police and the community all have their role to play in dealing with the "battered child syndrome." Once the child is identified, perhaps the heaviest burden will fall upon the public or voluntary social agency which deals with the case. This agency must take whatever steps are necessary to be sure that the child is not again exposed to the danger of abuse at the same time that it works with his parents.

Study of Parents Who Abuse Children

What do we know about these parents?

They do not seem to be confined to any economic level in our society or to any one group of professions or jobs.

The study of parents who abuse their children show that these parents were themselves subjected to much the same types of abuse or misuse when they were children. Most of them experienced more severe physical abuse as children than other groups in our population. Some of these parents see a world that is demanding, inconsiderate and punishing.

The Children's Bureau, with the help of psychiatrists, pediatricians and welfare groups, is supporting an in-depth study at the University of Colorado to find out some of the answers to this most important question.

What Do We Know About the Abused Child?

What we generally know about the abused child himself adds to this body of developing knowledge. He may be the product of an unwanted pregnancy. He may be in a home where there is a stepfather or stepmother and where one child in a family may be subject to severe abuse while others are cared for lovingly.

With this background of information, it is urgent that everyone concerned seek an end to these abuses, either by working with the parents or by taking other steps to be sure that children are not wilfully maimed or crippled by their parents. We must be concerned in those situations where parents are either not willing or are unable to fulfill their responsibilities of parenthood and actually are harming their children.

A duly authorized agency must have the official responsibility to take action necessary for the child's protection. This may in many instances be a social agency. The social agency has access to the court to petition for holding the child in custody or placing him temporarily to avoid further injury. In some instances, children returned to their homes instead of being kept in protective custody have been hurt again, sometimes fatally.

Educators should not only be informed about the "battered child syndrome" but should alert community leaders to the importance of mobilizing efforts of agencies in curbing this problem.

For centuries the child has been considered the "property" of his parents until he fends for himself. Society has a responsibility to protect and preserve the rights of the child who is too young to defend himself. This responsibility should be carried out through whatever means are necessary and appropriate.

We cannot afford the wastage of life and emotional damage produced by failure to give children protection.

What Can the Schools Do About Child Abuse?

DEAN E. ROCHESTER, *director of educational research, Southern Illinois University, Edwardsville; with* **MARY ANN ELLIS** *and* **SAM C. SCIORTINO,** *counselors, Parkway Public School District, Chesterfield, St. Louis County, Missouri.*

There was an old woman
Who lived in a shoe.
She had so many children
She didn't know what to do.
She gave them some broth
Without any bread
And whipped them all soundly
And put them to bed.

Does the school have a moral obligation
with regard to known
or suspected cases of child abuse? If so,
what action should be taken and by whom?
Today's Education presents the
following article in the hope that the
information it contains will prompt reader
response from across the nation
as to the proper role of the school
in dealing with the battered child syndrome.
Reports of actions taken and of results
achieved will also be welcome. The editors
hope that enough material will come in to
provide a follow-up article in a later issue.

● **This nursery rhyme** reflects the methods of handling children that were prevalent in the eighteenth and nineteenth centuries. The theory was that all children, because they resulted from carnal sin, were possessed of the devil, which had to be beaten out of them.

Though we would like to think that such practices are not common today, in the past decade the child protective services and the juvenile courts have been receiving more and more reports of child abuse. And since 1961, the Children's Bureau of the U.S. Department of Health, Education, and Welfare has been trying to educate the public to the facts of abuse; to alert people to the problem through the news media.

In newspapers, in magazines, and on television, one frequently encounters the term *battered child syndrome*. And although most people know what it means, few can say who is responsible for reporting it. When it is suspected, ignoring it may be easier than taking action, but most school officials feel uneasy about doing nothing.

Those who want something done about child abuse do not know whether it is the duty of the principal, the guidance counselor, or the social worker. They are also uncertain whether those who take action are protected by state law from possible lawsuits.

Having these problems in mind, we decided to attempt to find out what principals and guidance counselors in elementary schools think.

We sent a two-page questionnaire, along with a letter of explanation, to approximately 45 elementary principals and counselors in representative community school districts in a midwest metropolitan area. The questionnaire contained many pertinent questions concerning the role of elementary principals and counselors in the problem of child abuse and the na ture of typical cases they might have encountered. We received 33 responses in return.

Our first question was, "How many cases of child abuse have you encountered?" Twenty-one of the respondents indicated one or more cases, making a combined total of 61: 31 boys and 30 girls. The rest indicated no cases of reported or observed child abuse in the school.

Responses to the question relating to age range showed that 22 were children five to eight years old. Eleven of the children were 9 or 10, and 18 of them were 11 or 12.

In response to "What is the general nature of the abuse?" there were 19 reports of child beating, 14 of cruel punishment, 16 of malnutrition, as well as 3 of neglect, and 2 of no supervision at home either before or after school.

The next question concerned who made the referral. Teachers led with a count of 28. Counselors made 9 referrals; principals, 4. Five of the cases of child abuse were self-referred to a teacher, counselor, or principal, and one case was referred to the school principal by a social worker.

In 13 instances, once a case of child abuse was established, it was reported to the principal for further action. To the counselor, 2 cases were reported; to the social worker, 17; to juvenile law authorities 10; to the superintendent of schools, 5 cases were reported for further action.

Who performed the abuse? The mother in 28 cases; the father in 21. Four children were abused by a stepmother; one, by a stepfather. Six cases involved one or both grandparents.

Answers to the question "What action was taken?" revealed that 27 of the children had a conference with the counselor; a few, with the principal. In 31 cases, a conference was held with the abuser. One parent, who was unable to attend a conference, received a letter. In one case the response indicated that no action was taken, but we could not determine why nothing was done.

What was the result of the action taken? Thirty-three of the abused children remained in the same environment with corrective measures. Ten of the children remained in their environment with protective services. Five children were placed in foster homes, and one in another relative's home. Five were placed in institutions, and two in a private school. In five cases, action brought no results, and the children were not helped.

Our final question asked whether or not legal action was taken. We found that only 11 cases involved some aspect of legal action.

What are the implications of our survey? Limited though it was, we feel that we may draw a few broad conclusions from it. One thing is clear: Elementary school teachers, principals, and counselors have a vital role to play in breaking up the battered child syndrome. When they act, they can help in child-abuse situations; they can even at times eliminate them. ●

What Schools Can Do About CHILD ABUSE

By DAVID G. GIL

Physical abuse of children has received considerable attention and perhaps over-sensationalized publicity in recent years. However, little has been said concerning the roles and responsibilities of educators and schools in dealing with this phenomenon in spite of the fact that about half the children subjected to physical abuse are of school age and are thus in almost daily contact with the schools, our major social institution concerned with the well-being and development of children. Educators consequently may be in a good position to help with the detection and protection of abused children and to aid in reducing and controlling abuse.

Children in our own and many other societies have always been subjected to a wide range of abuse by parents and other caretakers, including teachers and child care personnel, and often indirectly by society as a whole. Such treatment seems to be inherent in the basic inequality of physical makeup and social status between adults and children and in attitudes determined by given cultures which permit or even encourage use of physical force as a legitimate means for rearing and socializing the young.

In centuries past, parents tended to wield absolute power over their offspring's life and death. Many children were abandoned to die of exposure, legally bartered or sold, mutilated to enhance their pity-inciting appeal as beggars, or thrashed by schoolmasters with ferrules, rods, and cat-o'-nine tails. Needless to say, progress has been made concerning the social and legal status and the protection of children. Yet the problem of child abuse continues to be a cause of serious concern in present-day American society.

It was in the early 1940's that professional and public interest was aroused by physicians whose X-rays of young children revealed unexplained multiple fractures of the long bones in conjunction with subdural hematonia (brain damage). Subsequent intensive clinical studies of these strange cases by social workers, pediatricians, and psychiatrists led to the suspicion and eventual confirmation that these injuries were often inflicted by the children's own parents or other persons who took care of them. Physical abuse came to be recognized as a fairly widespread phenomenon which often results in serious, irreversible damage to the physical well-being and emotional development of children and which, at times, is the immediate cause of their death.

Abuse appears in many different forms: minor bruises and cuts, burns, scaldings, fractures and internal injuries, intentional starvation, dismemberment, and severe injuries to the brain and central nervous system. The injuries are inflicted under various circumstances ranging from simple disciplinary measures to premeditated murderous attacks.

As for the phenomenon's underlying causes, many investigators tended to view them as an

SELECTED STATISTICS ON CHILD ABUSE

About 48 percent of the children had been abused by their mothers; over 39 percent by their fathers. However, since many children lived in fatherless homes, the involvement rate in abuse incidents for fathers or father substitutes was higher than for mothers. Over 17 percent of the abuse cases were committed by a male caretaker while the mother was temporarily absent.

37.4 percent of the families had four or more children.

Of the school age children, nearly 80 percent were in grades appropriate for their age.

34.1 percent of the children were psychologically resented and rejected by the abusive parent.

In over 21 percent of the cases, the perpetrators took steps to get help for the child; in 36 percent, other members of the household sought aid; in 16 percent, the school initiated help.

29.01 percent of the victims, 42.7 percent of the mothers, and 45.44 percent of the fathers revealed noticeable deviations in social and behavioral functioning; 15.59 percent of the fathers were known to have criminal records.

At least 14 percent of the mothers and seven percent of the fathers were known to have been abused during childhood themselves.

52.51 percent of the fathers had year-round employment and 11.79 percent were unemployed at the time of the abuse incident.

expression of the abuser's severe personality disorders. Pathological family relationships and environmental strains and stresses—such as those related to life in poverty—are also frequently cited in association with incidents of child abuse. Students of the phenomenon also noted that some children, because of unusual congenital or acquired characteristics, occasionally seemed to provoke abuse attacks against themselves.

Growing public awareness and interest led all the States in the Nation to enact laws during the 1960's requiring or recommending that medical personnel and others report incidents of suspected physical abuse to appropriate local and State authorities.

A major objective of this legislation was to improve mechanisms for locating cases of child abuse and to assure protective services for the victims, their siblings, and their parents. A secondary purpose was to obtain a better understanding of the scope and nature of the phenomenon than was possible when only a few selected cases came to the notice of health, education, welfare, and law-enforcement authorities.

The provisions of reporting legislation vary from State to State, and teachers and school administrators should, therefore, familiarize themselves with legislation in effect in their respective communities. Reporting is mandatory in all States except Alaska, Missouri, New Mexico, North Carolina, Texas, and Wash-

ington; in those States it is left to the discretion of those responsible for reporting. However, all States grant immunity from civil and criminal liability to persons making reports of abuse cases in good faith. The differences between the various State laws are described in a publication of the U.S. Children's Bureau: *The Abused Child, Principles and Suggested Language on Reporting the Physically Abused Child.*

Regardless of whether teachers are among the professions and whether schools are among the institutions specifically mentioned in a State law as being required to report incidents of abuse, they can and should assume a major responsibility in facilitating reporting procedures and in assuring medical and social services for abused children and their families. A good illustration of how this can be done is provided by the Baltimore public schools.

Baltimore school authorities cooperated actively with local health, welfare, and law-enforcement agencies in promoting the enactment of reporting legislation. As a result of their early involvement, educators and school personnel are included in the Maryland statute among the professional groups who are required to report. As soon as the law was enacted, its provisions and procedures for its implementation were inserted in the official manual of the public schools, and all teachers were provided with appropriate guidance and interpretation. As a result, the whole school system became sensitized to the phenomenon

29.49 percent of the children lived in homes without a father or father substitute; 19.42 percent had a step-father at home.

About one-fourth of the abused children were under two years old, one-fourth aged 2-6, one-fourth aged 6-10, and one-fourth over 10 years old.

23.7 percent of the victims required no medical treatment, 58.6 percent no hospitalization. But 21.3 percent required hospitalization for more than a week.

36.1 percent of the abused children were removed from their families; 13.1 percent of the perpetrators were convicted by courts.

Slightly more than half the victims were boys.

37.67 percent of the families earned less than $3,500 a year; 51.85 percent earned less than $4,500; and 3.61 percent earned $10,000 or more; 37.2 percent were receiving public assistance when the abuse took place and nearly 60 percent had previously received assistance.

Injuries were rated as not serious in 53.3 percent of the cases, serious without permanent damage in 36.5 percent, serious with permanent damage in about 4.6 percent, and fatal in 3.4 percent (fatalities may have been somewhat under-reported).

Approximately 60 percent of the children had been abused previously.

Two-thirds were white, except in metropolitan areas where less than 40 percent were white.

---

of child abuse, and during the first year nearly one in every four cases identified in Maryland was reported by the schools.

School authorities could take some or all of the following steps in order to contribute their part in dealing with child abuse in their communities.

The first step must of necessity be self-education. Teachers should be helped to understand the cultural, social, and personality forces that may interact to bring about parents' violent physical attacks against their children. They should learn that such incidents do happen, that they are quite "human" indeed, and that parents who abuse their children are not necessarily "bad" people, qualitatively different from other parents. In many instances abusive parents merely act out aggressive impulses which many other parents, as well as many teachers, may themselves often feel.

Understanding the motivation does not mean acquiescing in the abusive acts and condoning them. Abused children have a right to be protected, and the abusing parents may also require help. The understanding, observant teacher can encourage a child who appears abused and perhaps fearful, introverted, and depressed to talk over his situation, or he may convince the child to talk with a counselor or the school nurse. If such discussions point to the possibility of abuses in the child's home, the school should take appropriate action to assure that the child's home situation is more thoroughly explored and that protective and social services are provided, if needed.

Exploration of the home situation and provision of protective social services may require close cooperation among local school authorities and social, health, and law-enforcement agencies, although in some school systems the school authorities themselves may be equipped to look into their students' home circumstances. The actual division of responsibilities depends, of course, on local arrangements. But in any event, the classroom teacher should become the most important link in the preventive and protective chain, since his daily contacts put him in a strategic position to observe early indications of abuse. His observations can lead to protective intervention before a situation becomes irreversible.

Abused children may not always reveal signs of maltreatment on their bodies or in their behavior. It might, therefore, be indicated for teachers and counseling teachers to learn about all their students' family relationships and disciplinary measures used in their homes and to initiate steps for protection of children whose home circumstances reveal elements of potential abuse.

Many parents who physically abuse their children may, nevertheless, love them as much as other parents love their children. Schools could help such parents toward better understanding of their parental roles through family life education programs. Most abusive incidents occur in the course of disciplining children. Thus parent education programs focused on constructive approaches to discipline and on the emotional forces underlying parent-child relationships could be of definite help.

Abuse is at times "child initiated" because of certain types of deviance in the behavior of some children. Teachers, counselors, and nurses could identify such children and initiate steps to assure appropriate specialized treatment for them before their interaction with their parents leads to serious abuse.

Today's children are tomorrow's parents, and some are tomorrow's child abusers. The schools could play a more consistent part in preparing today's children for parenthood. Many parents who abuse their children are unprepared for the psychological demands of parenthood. High school courses dealing with family life, its responsibilities, and its emotional demands, as well as with violence as an undesirable mode of interpersonal relations, could, perhaps, contribute in a small measure to the emergence of a better prepared generation of parents and thus indirectly reduce the incidence of abuse in the next generation.

Some States still permit the use of physical force by teachers in assuring discipline among their students. Ironically, some of the laws permitting corporal punishment were passed at the same legislative session which enacted legislation requiring the reporting of child abuse. A teacher who uses physical force against a child teaches that child and all children in the classroom that physical force is an appropriate means for human interaction. If such children grow into child abusing parents, they are practicing what they were taught in school. Education has developed constructive approaches to motivate children, to create a challenging learning milieu, and to assure the necessary discipline in the classroom and needs no longer to regress to the destructive approach which is symbolized by corporal punishment.

With the passage in the States of legislation that required child abuse reporting, it became feasible to design the first nationwide study of all legally reported incidents. The study was launched in 1965 by Brandeis University in cooperation with the U.S. Children's Bureau. It has produced systematic information on the number of legally reported incidents of child abuse throughout the United States, the distribution of patterns of these incidents, the characteristics of the children, families, and perpetrators involved, the circumstances surrounding the incidents, and the measures taken by health, welfare, and law-enforcement authorities in dealing with the reported cases. All incidents reported in 1967 were studied, and those reported in 38 representative communities were subjected to a comprehensive investigation and analysis. Selected statistics drawn from the 5,993 cases reported in 1967 appear in the accompanying box.

It should be noted that these legally reported cases may constitute only a part of the total of child abuse incidents. Since abuse incidents tend to occur in the privacy of the home, all may not come to the attention of individuals or institutions who are required to report, and these individuals and institutions may not actually report all the cases known to them. The reporting may also be subject to some bias. It is a well known fact that many physicians in private practice are less ready to report incidents than are those in public hospitals. Consequently, incidents from middle and upper class families may be under-reported to a greater extent than cases from economically deprived families. Other factors, such as differences in administrative procedures, may also influence reporting. The limitations must be kept in mind in reviewing the boxed statistics.

The findings of the nationwide survey of abuse incidents and of a preceding national survey of public knowledge, attitudes, and opinions about physical child abuse suggest that it is a multidimensional phenomenon rather than a uniform one with one set of causal factors. The basic dimension on which all other factors are superimposed is the general culturally determined permissiveness toward the use of a measure of physical force in caretaker-child interaction, and the related absence of clear-cut legal prohibitions and sanctions against this particular form of interpersonal violence. A permissive attitude toward acts of physical violence against children and a tendency to regard the perpetrators of such acts with tolerance were brought out in the opinions expressed by a majority of the respondents in the public opinion survey.

The next dimension of the phenomenon results from specific child-rearing traditions and practices of different social classes and ethnic and nationality groups, and the different attitudes these groups hold toward physical force as an acceptable measure in rearing their children. A vast majority of the nearly 6,000 abusive incidents reported through legal channels during 1967 were the result of disciplinary measures considered more or less "acceptable" to certain groups in society and which did not result in serious injury. A large majority of the families involved in these abuse cases belonged to socioeconomically deprived segments of the population whose income and educational and occupational status tended to be quite low. Moreover, families from ethnic minority groups were over-represented in the cases reported, in relation to their total percentage of the population.

A third dimension of child abuse is determined by the environmental chance circumstances that may transform an "acceptable" disciplinary measure into an "unacceptable" outcome, resulting in relatively severe injury to the child. Fourth, there are many environmental stress factors which may weaken or even temporarily paralyze a person's ability to control his impulses and aggressive and destructive feeling toward physically powerless children. A vast array of environmental strains were precipitating elements in a large proportion of the incidents reported.

The various forms of physical, social, intellectual, and emotional deviance and pathology that may afflict caretakers and/or children in their care constitute the final dimension of child abuse. A higher than "normal" proportion of the abused children, their abusers, and their families revealed a wide range of deviance and pathology in areas of physical, social, intellectual, and emotional functioning. A high rate of deviance in family structure was also reflected in the large proportion of child abuse cases in households headed by women or by stepfathers.

While no claim can be made that the true incidence rate of physical abuse of children has been uncovered by the nationwide survey, it seems clear, nevertheless, that the quantity and quality of abuse as a serious social problem has been exaggerated. Six thousand reported cases per year in a Nation of 200 million, in spite of under-reporting, do not constitute a major social problem—at least in relative terms—tragic as every single incident may be. More-over, it may be assumed that the more serious incidents of child abuse are most likely to be included among the reported incidents, since the severity of an injury may be an important criterion with regard to the selection of cases entering official reporting channels. Yet among the reported incidents, serious injuries and the classical "battered child syndrome" are relatively infrequent occurrences. Even if allowance is made for the gross under-reporting of fatalities, physical abuse cannot be considered a major killer and maimer of children.

The study also demonstrated that legally reported cases of child abuse are over-concentrated among the poor. While it is valid to argue that the poor are more likely to be reported for anything they do or fail to do than are those who are not poor, and that their over-representation may be in part a result of biased reporting, it must not, however, be overlooked that child abuse seems to be one aspect of the style of life associated with the poverty syndrome. The poor are subject to the same psychological conditions that may cause violent behavior toward children as are those in better financial circumstances. In addition, they suffer special environmental stresses and strains associated with socioeconomic deprivation and they have fewer alternatives and escapes for dealing with aggressive impulses toward their children. There is also a tendency among the poor toward more direct, less inhibited expression and discharge of aggressive impulses, a tendency learned apparently through lower class socialization.

Measures aimed at preventing or gradually reducing the incidence of specific social problems can achieve their purpose when they attack the causes of these problems. Attempts to deal with physical abuse of children might, therefore, begin by touching what seems to be the common core of all these incidents in American society—the permissiveness toward the use of physical force in child rearing. Systematic efforts aimed at gradually changing this particular aspect of the prevailing child rearing philosophy and at developing clear-cut cultural prohibitions and legal sanctions against this use of physical force are likely to produce the strongest possible reduction of the incidence and prevalence of physical child abuse.

Another logical route toward reducing child abuse is the elimination of poverty from the

Child Abuse

midst of America's affluent society. No doubt this is only a partial answer to the complex issue of preventing violence toward children, but it is, perhaps, a very vital part of the total answer. Without the elimination of poverty, other preventive efforts may be utterly futile.

Finally, a wide range of social and medical services should be made available in every community to deal with child abuse. Some of these services should be aimed at prevention and amelioration of deviance and pathology, helping thus to strengthen the physical, social, intellectual, and emotional functioning of individuals and family units. Comprehensive family planning programs and availability of therapeutic abortions, where indicated, would probably reduce considerably the number of unwanted children, known to be the frequent victims of severe physical abuse and even of infanticide. Liberalized legislation concerning family planning would also probably help alleviate this aspect of the abuse problem.

Comprehensive neighborhood-based health services financed through tax funds could be aimed not only at the treatment of serious deviance and acute and chronic illness but toward the promotion of maximum physical and mental health for every citizen. Child care facilities with flexible hours should be routinely available to offer mothers opportunities for carefree rest and recreation, thus lifting some of the environmental stress from their lives. Family life education and counseling programs to help adolescents and adults before and after marriage might be offered within the public schools where there is less likelihood that they will be identified in the public mind with deviance-focused agencies.

In addition, every community needs a system of social services geared to assist families and children who cannot live together because of severe relationship strains or other problems. Physically abused children belong frequently to this category, and in such situations the welfare of the child and the family may require permanent or temporary separation.

All these measures might help to reduce the incidence and prevalence of physical abuse of children. However, the services must be based on a constructive and therapeutic—rather than a punitive—philosophy, if they are to serve the ultimate objective: to reduce the general level of violence in the country and to raise the level of human well-being throughout our entire society. ■

Dr. Gil, associate professor, Florence Heller Graduate School for Advanced Studies in Social Welfare, Brandeis University, is director of the Nationwide Epidemiologic Study of Child Abuse, supported by U.S. Children's Bureau grant PR 288-1. For further information on child abuse, contact Dr. Gil at Brandeis University, Waltham, Mass., 02154.

GUIDELINES FOR SCHOOLS

Teachers
Nurses
Counselors
Administrators

TO HELP PROTECT NEGLECTED AND ABUSED CHILDREN

THE ALERT TEACHER

If teachers are alert to the signs and symptoms which point to the possibility of neglect or abuse they can take the first step to bring help to children whose needs are not being met at home. That first step is to invoke the community's child protective services on behalf of the troubled child.

The protective program is charged with responsibility for bringing services to neglected and abused children and their neglecting parents. It is a non-punitive, helping, skilled social service. Its focus is on seeking to stabilize family life, on enhancing parental capacity for good child care and on maintaining family intactness where possible.

CHILDREN IN TROUBLED FAMILIES

Teachers come into frequent contact with children who are physically or emotionally neglected or who are victims of physical or sexual abuse. Such troubled children may be found in families at any economic level or of any social status in the community. This is so because the motivating factors for child neglect or abuse may afflict any family. Common, underlying factors are emotional immaturity of parents, marital friction, alcoholism, drug usage, emotional disturbance or psychosis. These are families with problems, families under stress and, sometimes, families in crisis.

IMPORTANCE OF EARLY CASEFINDING

If children are identified when they show the earliest impact of their families' troubles, help can be made available at a stage when their problems can be more readily resolved. Too often referrals to protective services are not made until the conditions of neglect or abuse become acute and intolerable. Such referrals may come too late to salvage the home.

Here are some of the things to look for:

INDICATORS OF A CHILD'S NEED FOR PROTECTION

THE CHILD'S BEHAVIOR

▶ Is the child aggressive, disruptive, destructive? Such a child may be acting out of need to secure attention. He may be shouting for help. His behavior may reflect a hostile or emotionally destructive climate at home, or he may be imitating destructive parental behavior.

▶ Is the child shy, withdrawn, passive or overly compliant? This child may be as emotionally damaged as the aggressive child. He has internalized his problem; his cry for help is a whisper instead of a shout. He may be inattentive; he may daydream; he may be out of touch with reality.

▶ Is the child an habitual truant — chronically late or tardy? Is he frequently absent for flimsy reasons and lame excuses? This behavior points to problems of adjustment — problems at home, in school, within the child, or in combination.

▶ Does the child come to school much too early? Does he loiter and hang around after school is dismissed? This child may be seeking to escape from home — he may lack normal satisfactions at home. On the other hand, he may be "pushed out" in the morning and has no place to go after school because there is no one to supervise or care for him.

THE CHILD'S APPEARANCE

▶ Is the child inadequately dressed for the weather? Is his clothing torn, tattered or unwashed? Is the child not clean; is he unbathed? Do other children refuse to sit next to him because he smells? These are all signs of physical neglect, a condition not related to poverty. It reflects a breakdown in household management and in concern for the child.

▶ Is the child undernourished? Is he coming to school without breakfast; does he go without lunch? Again, this is often a problem unrelated to poverty.

▶ Is the child always tired? Does he sleep in class? Is he lethargic or listless? Such conditions are symptomatic of parental failure to regulate the child's routines, or of family problems which disrupt family routines.

▶ Is the child in need of medical attention? Does he need glasses or dental work?

▶ Does the child bear bruises, welts and contusions? Is he injured frequently? Does he complain of beatings or other maltreatment? Is there reason to suspect physical or sexual abuse?

PARENTAL ATTITUDES

▶ Are the parents aggressive or abusive when approached about problems concerning their child?

▶ Are they apathetic or unresponsive?

▶ Is parental behavior, as observed by school personnel, or as related by the child, bizarre and strange?

▶ Do the parents show little concern about the child? Do they fail to show interest in what he is doing? Do they fail to participate in school activities or to permit the child to participate?

ROLE OF CHILD PROTECTIVE SERVICES

The presence of one or more of these characteristics should arouse a teacher's concern for the child's welfare. Whether there is true need for protection, however, is a determination which the protective services program will make after it has explored the situation. But, Child Protective Services cannot make such an exploration unless, and until, a person in contact with the child reports the circumstances pointing to the possible need for protection.

Teachers, and other school personnel, who report cases of suspected child neglect or abuse will rarely, if ever, get involved beyond the initial report itself. Protective services will develop the facts in each case and will diagnose the type and quality of service needed to rehabilitate the home and to reduce the neglect. It offers its special brand of social services to help parents become more responsible.

WHY OF NEGLECT AND ABUSE

Neglect and abuse of children is rarely willful or deliberate. It usually results from the inadequacy or incapacity of parents to live up to parental roles. Basically, most parents want to be good parents. It is the function and purpose of child protective services to give help to neglecting parents so that they may become more adequate and their functioning more acceptable.

A SCHOOL RESPONSIBILITY

Because schools are concerned with the whole child, seeking help for the child in trouble is quite compatible with educational objectives. The emotional impact of serious neglect and abuse often sets up blocks which inhibit and create learning disabilities for the child victim.

HOW MAY YOUR SCHOOL HELP?

If you identify a child who needs protection because of neglect or abuse your school should telephone and report the conditions to your local Child Protective program. This service is usually provided by the public state or county services to families and children.

●

A HANDBOOK FOR
SCHOOL STAFF MEMBERS

Identifying the Battered or Molested Child

**Published by the Palo Alto
Unified School District, January 1972**
25 Churchill Avenue, Palo Alto, California 94306
**Based on a report prepared by
Mrs. Nancy B. Greene, Supervising Officer,
Santa Clara County Juvenile Probation Department**

IDENTIFYING THE BATTERED OR MOLESTED CHILD

Physical Factors

1. **Marks and Bruises on the Body:** Some are visible, but some may be hidden from view. This is why a nurse's check is so important. Sometimes these marks and bruises may be hard to identi-

fy—especially if they are made by teeth or unusual instruments. It is particularly meaningful to note when these marks could not possibly be made by or incurred in the situation the child reports; i.e., bite marks on back due to "falling off a bike," whip marks on legs due to "falling while jumping rope," black eyes due to getting in a "fight with my cat," patches of hair missing due to "washing my hair too hard."

A young child was seen in a nursery school to have odd marks, like bites, all over his back. When the mother was questioned she said they were indeed bites and that the child got them at the nursery school. The mother had not previously reported this to the nursery school, and the nursery school reported the situation to the Juvenile Probation Department and denied the charges. The mother then changed her story and said that they might not be bites, and she didn't know what they were. Police pictures were taken of the marks, and these pictures were shown to a group of five dentists who all stated that they were indeed the bite marks of a human adult.

2. **Serious Injuries such as Broken Bones:** Although these are most dramatically evidenced in very young children, an older battered child may often come up with a series of broken arms, fingers, head injuries, etc., or a variety of burns, ranging from minor to fatal, but consistently viewable.

3. **Distended Stomach:** Many battered children are not fed properly and appear to be malnourished. The parents often give excuses such as "he's a finicky eater," "he has a vitamin deficiency," or the "doctor doesn't know what's wrong with her." The truth of the matter is that these children are not fed at home or are fed only on scraps. They often do not come to school with lunch and steal food from other children, or they steal candy which they share to gain friends.

Santa Clara County had a tragic and classic example of this in a fourteen-year-old girl who physically looked about seven, had not attained puberty, and who had been physically mistreated most of her life. She was also being starved to death.

A lack of medical care for injuries can also be a significant factor and should be noted. Many parents will report that their child has "brain damage" and this, in fact, may be true. A neurological report on the child should be requested and obtained whenever possible. It has been found that many children do sustain minimal or severe brain damage through beatings or may be permanently damaged from incidents inflicted in early childhood.

4. **Appearance of Mental Retardation:** Battered and molested children often appear retarded, especially if the maltreatment has gone undetected for a prolonged period of time. This is often an excuse their parents give to questioning people in order to shift the blame away from themselves. Many of these children mature mentally and physically to a dramatic degree when removed from the family home.

5. **Dirty Appearance:** These children are often hygienically uncared for and are forced to wear cast-off clothing. The parents may report that they are clean when they leave for school and "just get dirty on the way." They may also say that the child has "torn up all the good clothes I just got her", implying that the child is mentally retarded or disturbed. It is especially important to note when one child is treated differently from the other children in the family—in the type of clothing, lunches, number of injuries or body cleanliness. Very often only one child in the family is singled out for cruel treatment, and this situation of scapegoating is also something that should be documented.

6. **Cleanliness of the Home:** Battered and molested children do not necessarily come from poor or lower income houses or families. It is just more difficult to detect and document those cases from middle and upper class families because the parents are usually more skillful in their deceit and have more sources available to cover up their pathology. It is not uncommon, however, to find a very clean, tidy lower income home with many children, all well cared for, that also houses one battered and neglected child.

Emotional Factors

1. **Regressive Behavior:** Battered and/or molested children usually show signs of regressive behavior. They may become very childish, cry a lot, suck their thumbs or withdraw into fantasy worlds. An abrupt change in a child's behavior should be documented and investigated. Sometimes these children give the impression of being mentally retarded when, in fact, they are not. The degree of emotional disturbance may be proportionate to the length of severity of trauma. Diagnosis is difficult if the child brings this behavior pattern with him when entering a new school. However, close observation will reveal deterioration as the child moves from grade to grade. School psychological services should be requested.

2. **Acting Out Aggressive Behavior:** Battered and molested children often act out their anger and hostility on others. They may become involved in delinquencies, i.e., petty thefts or trinkets which they give to other children to form friendships. Often they will steal food and money in order to survive.

The sexually molested girl may become sexually promiscuous, and her behavior may become the talk of, not only the school, but the whole neighborhood. Often a molested girl will confide in a special girlfriend or a favorite woman teacher. These confidences may not take the direct form of information about being molested, but may involve such statements as "I'm afraid to go home tonight," "I want you to help me go live with my aunt in Stockton," etc. A wise and interested teacher can build up trust in a child and be standing by when the child holds out a desperate hand.

3. **Poor Peer Relationships or Inability to Make Friends:** Often these children do not have social skills or are too emotionally disturbed to form peer relationships. These relationships are usually frowned upon or forbidden by parents. The parents have a vested interest in keeping them emotionally isolated. The children have such a bad self-image that they cannot believe another human being could be interested in them in any way. Their built in "bad me" concept overshadows their whole existence.

Parents often move or try to move these children from school to school or environment to environment. An example of this was seen in the case of the previously mentioned fourteen-year-old girl who appeared to be age seven. Her mother withdrew her from school, stating she was going to live with relatives out of the county. Unfortunately, the school did not make contact with the "new" school, and the child was being kept at home and being mistreated. There were siblings attending school in the same district who could have provided this information, had they been asked.

4. **Deep-seated Pathological Impact:** The victims of battering and/or child molestation often develop deep-seated psychiatric problems which have an impact on their whole future development. Evidence shows that the majority of men in prison who are classified as psychopathic or sociopathic personalities were beaten children. They have little feeling for others or guilt about their misconduct. The molested girl often becomes a prostitute. She finds it difficult to relate to men on any meaningful level and often fails to protect her own children from the same victimization.

The home life of these victims as adults is usually very unsatisfactory, and their pathology is passed on to their children . . . then to their children's children. Victims of molest are plagued with feeling of insecurity, guilt, bad self image, depression and sexual problems. The victims of battering are filled with feelings of fear, hate, aggression, and an inability to empathize. The molested and battered child almost always needs psychiatric treatment if he is to make any kind of a positive psychological adjustment to life.

SUMMARY

It is hard to believe that such abuse happens in our so-called "enlightened age," and in a society which is essentially child-centered. As we have seen, work is being done on this problem, but there is much more to be done as many people do not recognize child abuse as a major problem for consideration.

All classroom teachers, administrators, and counselors at some time or another will come into contact with an abused child. It is the responsibility of these educators to become involved until we reach a point where misuse of young children is no longer an everyday occurence.

The laws are not clear as to what an abused child is. Therefore, educators need to learn from professionals in medicine, law, and the behavioral sciences what should and should not be done as well as what can and cannot be done.

It is necessary for educators not only to be sensitive to the needs of crippled, meek, fearful, lonesome, and aggressive children, but also to be able to identify and relate to the battered child. This child in particular needs someone to make him feel that he belongs, that he is wanted, that someone cares. He is a child in desperate need.

One of the tragedies of the battered child is that he has often developed characteristics that make him difficult; he is a child who has come to stimulate antipathy in the ones whose help he most needs: who is seemingly unresponsive or antagonistic to friendly and concerned outreach.

It is often said that a child is never so unlovable as when he most needs loving. This is so frequently true of the battered child that the classroom teacher who still reaches through to discern his need, his concealed cries for help, and who thus can begin the long process of his rescue and rehabilitation, meets a great challenge and must call on the sensitivity and empathy that characterize a remarkable and dedicated person. Of such people, there are more than we realize.

STUDY QUESTIONS

1. Do most teachers encounter an abused child in their work?

2. Should all elementary age school children be made aware that there are battered children and that there is help available for them?

3. What responsibilities do teachers and school administrators have in reporting child abuse and protecting children?

4. Why do many teachers look the other way when they suspect child abuse?

5. What procedures do schools usually have for follow-up on child abuse? What should they have?

6. Does the community or public school have the right to interfere in battered child cases? Through what means?

REFERENCES

A. Readings Included in This Text

American Humane Association. *Guidelines for Schools* . The American Humane Association, Denver, 1971.

Gil, David G. "What Schools Can Do About Child Abuse." *American Education,* 5 (1969):2-4.

Greene, Nancy B. *Identifying the Battered or Molested Child.* Palo Alto Unified School District, Palo Alto, 1972.

Leavitt, Jerome E. "The Battered Child." *The Instructor,* 75 (1966):50, 142, 150.

Oettinger, Katherine B. "The Abused Child." *Childhood Education,* 41 (1965): 235-237.

Rochester, Dean E.; Ellis, Mary Ann; and Sciortino, Sam C. "What Can the Schools Do About Child Abuse?" *Today's Education,* 57 (1968):59-60.

B. Suggested Additional Readings

Batinich, M. E. M. "How School Can Aid The Abused Child: Principal's Role Central in Protecting Children." *Chicago School Journal,* 46 (1964):57-62.

Bechtold, M. L. "That Battered Child Could Be Dead Tomorrow." *Instructor,* 77 (1968):20.

Davies, Joann E. and Jorgensen, James D. "Battered, But Not Defeated: The Story of an Abused Child and Positive Casework." *Child Welfare,* 49 (1970):101-104.

Freeman, C. B. "Children's Petition of 1669 and Its Sequel." *British Journal of Educational Studies,* 14 (1966): 216-223.

Giovannoni, Jeanne M., and Billingsley, Andrew. "Child Neglect Among the Poor: A Study of Parental Adequacy in Families of Three Ethnic Groups." *Child Welfare,* 49 (1970):196-204.

Polansky, N. A. *et al.* "Two Modes of Maternal Immaturity and Their Consequences; Neglected or Marginal Care." *Child Welfare,* 49 (1970):312-323.

VII

What Can Be Done for Battered Children?

Throughout the United States there are thousands of children who are getting a poor start in life because of the inability or the failure of their parents to give them proper care and supervision.

So far, we have taken a look at the battered child syndrome with the psychologist, criminologist, social worker, medical worker, and educator. Each of these professionals has given us insights into the causes, problems, and treatment of the battered child and his parents.

The major question now is what can be done for the battered child, the subject of this final chapter. We will now look at the battered and neglected child through the eyes of the abusing parent, the media, the medical profession, social agencies, the law, and the schools.

These concluding articles help us to see what the next steps should be in dealing with the battered child.

*Some social signs of abusive parents
are helpful in efforts . . .*

TOWARD PREVENTION
OF CHILD ABUSE

MARIAN G. MORRIS
Formerly, Director

ROBERT W. GOULD
Social Worker

PATRICIA J. MATTHEWS
Social Worker

*Social Work Department
Children's Hospital of Philadelphia*

THIS PAPER is written on the premise that constructive, preventive intervention in the cycle of violence and punishment is necessary for preventing the physical neglect and abuse of children. Its purpose is to present the consistent social signs which our experience at the Children's Hospital of Philadelphia has led us to believe have implications for early identification of neglectful or abusive parents and for the prevention of further child neglect and abuse. Our observations of the parents suspected of causing the condition for which their children were brought to the hospital have led us to believe that in such cases chronic neglect and brutal punishment have followed down the generations, with gathering force.[1] Thus prevention implies not only protecting the child from future abuse—and possible death—but in somehow breaking the chain which so often leads the once abused and neglected child to neglect or abuse his own child.[2]

Our observations are based on two studies made at the hospital: the most recent, of the case records and followup of 33 severely neglected or battered children from 29 families; and a previous one of 23 infants and children brought to the hospital for serious "failure to thrive."[3] From these observations we have arrived at three groupings of the kinds of parents found in cases of abuse or neglect. We think

that further studies and refinement of results will eventually lead to a larger number of groupings. The three main groupings are: (1) neglecting parents who are readily responsive to treatment by the hospital team; (2) neglecting parents readily responsive to a combination of hospital and community services; (3) unresponsive parents whose children are in acute danger. There is no sharp line between these groups. The criteria for classification are in fact matters of degree and have to do with:

1. The degree to which a parent's personality development permits frustration tolerance without self-disintegration.

2. The soundness of parental motivation, flexibility, and capacity for learning and assuming or resuming the role of promoting child growth and development.

3. The degree of the parent's reality testing capacity.

4. The seriousness of the child's symptoms.

5. The seriousness of the parent's reality situations.

These criteria aid in predicting margins of safety for children, in determining the use of continued hospital team services, and in determining what collaborating community services need to be called upon

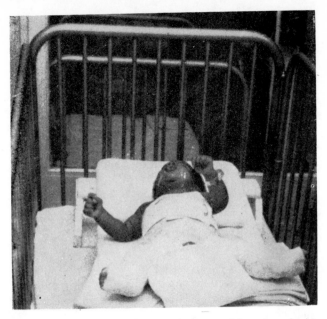

An overfed 3-month-old baby with fractured legs, in a double cast. Parents who batter their children, according to the authors, are expressing parental incapacities in action language.

to protect the child. Our case material points up essential areas of interviewing for purposes of social assessment and case management no matter which classification a parent falls into. These major interviewing areas are concerned with the following questions:

1. What is a parent's own estimate of current life needs as they are filled or threatened by children's needs for care?

2. Did this parent have positive role connections with society before his parenthood?

3. What are this parent's feelings about his own childhood?

4. What are this parent's feelings about his own parents?

5. Has this parent ever identified with the nurturing parent role?

6. How strong is this parent's motivation to be connected to society by a social role? which role? as an adult "child," a worker, a parent?

7. How does this parent respond to a child's everyday needs? as natural and acceptable? as simple interference? as assaultive and oppressive?

8. Does this parent attribute irrational degrees of motivation, responsibility, and judgment to an infant or a young child?

9. Do these parents expect a child to protect *them* instead of their protecting *him?*

10. Does this parent admit any responsibility in the child's neglect and abuse?

11. Is this child held completely responsible for the neglect and abuse?

In finding answers to these questions it becomes possible to gauge margins of safety and the probability of recurrence in order to plan appropriately. They help lead the way through the maze of contradictory statements and lack of real facts which so often surround cases of seriously neglected or battered children.[4]

In our dealings with parents of seriously neglected or abused children brought to our hospital we have used a noncritical, nonpunitive approach not only for purposes of sound data collection on which to base practical plans for protecting children, but also in order to protect parents from further acting out their frustrations on their children.[5] This has been based on our recognition that parents who neglect and batter their children are actually speaking their parental incapacities in action language and are asking to be stopped in behaving as they do.[1] Why else do they bring their children to hospitals and so run a high risk of punishment? We think that parents run this risk because the risk of total, internal, personality disintegration is even more terrifying—a risk they run in continuing the care of their children.

While we have presented the guidelines for interviewing in the form of questions, we cannot stress strongly enough the importance of observation in the diagnostic assessment of the parents' child caring potential, and the disintegrating effects of direct questioning as to how the injury was incurred on parents' ability to cooperate in eliciting information or planning for their child.[1]

What specifically can be observed about parents that is helpful not only in assessing the validity of suspicions that the condition of the child brought to a hospital might have been caused by his parents' brutality or neglect, but also in gauging something of their potential for providing nurturing care to the child? From our experience with the parents of injured and severely neglected children brought to the Children's Hospital, we have been able to identify the following typical reactions and attitudes of nurturing parents and the contrasting reactions and attitudes of neglecting, battering parents.

Typical reactions and attitudes of protective parents to children's injuries:

1. Are voluble and spontaneous in reporting details of a child's illness or injury.

2. Show concern about the degree of the damage.

3. Show concern about the treatment.

4. Show concern about the possibility of residual damage.

5. Exhibit a sense of guilt. The younger the child, the more guilt the parents feel for not protecting him. Guilt and remorse are felt even when the parent has had no part in the child's injury.

6. Ask many questions regarding the prognosis of the child's condition.

7. Have difficulty in detaching from the child on admission.

8. Attempt restitution through frequent visiting, toys, and other gifts, in apology to the child.

9. Ask questions about discharge date.

10. Ask questions regarding followup care.

11. Identify with the child's feelings, both physical and emotional, when he is injured.

12. Are positively related to the child.

Some typical reactions and attitudes of neglecting, battering persons:

1. Do not volunteer information about the child's illness or injury.

2. Are evasive or contradict themselves regarding the circumstances under which the child's condition occurred.

3. Show irritation at being asked about the development of the child's symptoms.

4. Critical of the child and angry with him for being injured.

5. Give no indications of feeling guilt or remorse regarding the child's condition.

6. Show no concern about the injury.

7. Show no concern about the treatment.

8. Show no concern about the prognosis.

9. Often disappear from the hospital during examination or shortly after the child is admitted.

10. Tend not to visit the child in the hospital.

11. Seldom touch the child or look at the child.

12. Do not involve themselves in the child's care in the hospital.

13. Do not inquire about the discharge date.

14. Ask to have child home only when interrogation has frightened them.

15. Do not ask about followup care.

16. Show concern not about the child but about what will happen to themselves and others involved in the child's illness or injury.

17. Maintain that the child has injured himself.

18. Act as though the child's injuries are an assault on them.

19. Fail to respond to the child or respond inappropriately.

20. Give no indication of having any perception of how a child could feel, physically or emotionally.

21. Constantly criticize the child.

22. Never mention any good quality in the child.

23. Show no concept of the rights of others.

24. Are preoccupied with themselves and the concrete things in life.

25. Are often neglectful of their own physical health.

26. Exhibit violent feelings and behavior and in interviewing reveal that this was a pattern in their original family.

27. Reveal in the interviewing that they are concerned about having been abandoned and punished by their own parents and are longing for a mother.

28. Show overwhelming feelings that they and their children are worthless.

The following cases illustrate some of these reactions in varying degrees. The first case could be classified as Group I—a case where in spite of considerable negatives enough positives were present for effective treatment:

Joe Green, 3 months old, was brought to the hospital by his parents at his maternal grandparents' insistence because of severe growth failure. The 22-year-old parents also had an 18-month-old boy, who was thriving well. The Greens vented their anger with violent words on members of the hospital team, but their real anger was at Mrs. Green's mother, who treated them like adolescents but insisted that they be better parents.

The interviewing revealed that Mrs. Green was afraid of her children and mistrusted her ability to care for them. She preferred to work and have her parents care for the babies, though this meant that she and her husband with her two children must live in one room in the grandparents' home and continue in the status of adolescents. Mr. Green worked, brought home the money, and kept out of the family fuss.

Mrs. Green visited Joe constantly. Though she fought any idea that she had any talent for aiding in his growth and development, she gradually engaged herself in Joe's care in the hospital. After the child's release she quit her job and was able to get her parents to let her family have an additional room. She brought Joe to the clinic regularly and he continued to thrive well. The wizened, hungry baby was replaced by a rounded, happy, satisfied, satisfying baby. Mrs. Green had a new look, softer, more composed, and confident. At the clinic she asked many questions and presented her own ideas about Joe's care.

Engagement in Joe's medical care enabled some resolution of the maturational crisis of these young parents. Joe was the epicenter of a family crisis. Now he is just a baby, with a mother who enjoys caring for him and a father who carries financial responsibility. Although maternal deprivation [6, 7] characterized Joe's first 2 months of life, prevention of the full force of the syndrome came early.

The next case, also with both positive and negative factors, comes from our Group II classification—cases requiring long-term conjoint community services for the development of parents' potentials:

Jane Ford, 6 years old, was having three to four epileptic seizures a night, the equivalent of several harsh beatings, when her mother brought her to the hospital. Mrs. Ford had stopped giving the child previously prescribed anticonvulsant pills, although she knew she could have received them free of charge at any time if she would only ask for them.

The interview with the social worker indicated that Mrs. Ford's concerns were not about Jane, but about her own recently deceased father who had died under mysterious, brutal circumstances; about two children she had lost to their father and his mother via a court order; about her finances, her housing, and her job. She was desperate and furious. In addition, she was physically ill although she was working at an outdoor winter job to support her children.

Mrs. Ford was in a panic, but she did not evade responsibility for Jane's condition:

"Nobody has to tell me I am neglecting Jane; I know that. I'm the one who watches her have the fits. I may not know how to be a *mother,* but I know how to give pills. . . .

"I don't remember my mother. I was dragged in and out of boarding houses by my father. Nobody could have cared less about me. I could always depend on my father if I had to. I was tough. I fought them all. But now I know I need help. I know Jane needs pills, but I don't know how to ask for them, and I don't know what *I* need."

The hospital team helped Mrs. Ford to assume consistent, constructive use of medical care for herself and Jane. Later she asked voluntarily for medical care for her older daughter. Assessing her goals in parenthood, she gave up her dangerously overtaxing job, secured medical help for herself, and decided to devote her efforts to caring for her children, even though it meant accepting public assistance and the authority and limitations that go with it.

A followup visit 6 years later revealed that though Mrs. Ford had been hospitalized twice for a serious heart and kidney condition, Jane's seizures were still controlled. All three children were doing well. Mrs. Ford was relatively healthy and proud of her own and her family's progress.

Parents with social signs overweighted in the negative direction are those in our Group III classification—those whose children are in acute danger as long as they are in the home. The cases are grim. For example:

Jack Burt, 3 years old, dead on arrival, with continuous welts around both arms, across his back, a large swelling on his head, old burn scars from chest to lower abdomen. As his stepfather carried him in, a nurses' aide heard the man say, "I don't want any more of this; I won't take any more of this. No more." Depositing the boy's body on an examining table, he walked across the room, saying in casual social tones to the aide, "Don't I know you from somewhere? I'm sure I've met you somewhere before."

The physician's question brought, "I just hit him like I always do when he pees the bed. This time he went and fell on his head."

Review of the hospital records showed that 11 months before, Jack's sister, Rita, age 3 months, had been admitted for a head injury. The history noted, "Infant recently fell out of bed," and "An accidental 'clip' on the chin." These pieces of information had not been recognized in their true meanings.

Although Rita was already damaged, recognition of danger signals and request for careful social assessment and quick, joint medical-social action might have prevented further damage, and might have prevented Jack's torture and subsequent death. After Jack's death, Rita was placed in a foster home by a protective agency. She is now spastic, is apparently retarded, and needs expensive, protracted care.

Though both Mrs. Burt and her mother knew Jack was being "punished" by being placed on a hot gas burner, neither woman had asked for protective placement. Legal charges against the father came with Jack's death.

In another family, protection from permanent physical damage came in time:

Mary O'Toole, 3 years, 8 months, who had not previously been our patient, was presented in our receiving ward by both parents in late evening for a broken leg, multiple body bruises, a pulled-off fingernail, a large swelling on her forehead, all said by her parents to have been caused by clumsy Mary, whose behavior could not be controlled, who got struck by a car, who got her fingers stuck in a curtain rod. This time, according to the parents, she had fallen downstairs.

The O'Tooles asked that we find why Mary bruised so easily, what made her clumsy, and why she was so wild and careless. They showed no appropriate concern about her broken leg, her injuries, or her prognoses.

Behind their bringing the child to the hospital lay an anonymous report to the department of health that they had neglected Mary's twin siblings, aged 2½ months. The community nurse had called on the family and found that the twins were poorly cared for, as were their two other siblings, aged 4 years and 1 year. A friend of Mrs. O'Toole's was in the house at the time and drew the nurse's attention to Mary, who had been sitting quietly in the background, by saying, "Let's tell the nurse; we can trust her."

Both women said Mary had fallen that morning. The nurse advised emergency care since Mary's leg looked bad. Mrs. O'Toole said she would wait until her husband came home from work. The parents brought Mary to the hospital at 8:30 p.m. Her leg had been broken and untreated for at least 10 hours.

On the ward, Mary was quiet but continuously watchful. She ate ravenously, two and three of everything. Both parents evaded all responsibility for Mary's condition and seldom came to see her.

Mary said she had been pushed down the stairs. The O'Tooles are the only parents in our records who have been overheard telling a child not to talk, and Mary is the only child we know who "talked."

Despite this data, it was impossible to convince the protective agency that Mary needed protective care direct from hospital. Later, the protective agency moved all five O'Toole children into protective care.

Children's Reactions

The neglected, battered children brought to a hospital are often too young to tell how they were injured. If old enough, they may be afraid or ashamed to tell. Usually older children have learned to cover up. The signs of their fear of their parents are subtle rather than overt and can easily be overlooked.

Behavioral signs of abuse among infants are even more subtle than among children old enough to speak. There are, however, some noticeable contrasts among the well-nurtured infants and the severely battered or neglected. For example: Nurtured, cared for infants old enough to recognize their parents cry and roll toward them or reach for them. Neglected and battered infants shut their eyes, turn their heads or bodies away, and cry irritably. The more severe the neglect and battering, the more withdrawn or irritable the infant.

Some typical forms of behavior of well-nurtured children in a hospital:

1. Cling to parents when they are brought in.
2. Turn to their parents for assurance.
3. Turn to their parents for comfort during and after examination and treatment.
4. Constantly show by words and action that they want their parents and want to go home.
5. Are reassured by their parents' visits.

Children in this group do not have to have the total situation under inspection at all times for safety's sake. They find safety in their parents.

Some typical forms of behavior of neglected and battered children in a hospital:

1. Cry hopelessly under treatment and examination.
2. Cry very little in general.
3. Do not look to parents for assurance.
4. Show no real expectation of being comforted.
5. Are wary of physical contact initiated by parents or anyone else.
6. Are apprehensive when other children cry and watch them with curiosity.
7. Become apprehensive when adults approach some other crying child.
8. Seem less afraid than other children when admitted to the wards and settle in quickly.

9. Seem to seek safety in sizing up the situation rather than in their parents.
10. Are constantly on the alert for danger.
11. Are constantly asking in words and through their actions what will happen next.
12. Are constantly in search of something: food, favors, things, services.
13. Ask, "When am I going home?" or announce, "I'm *not* going home," rather than crying "I want to go home."
14. Assume a flat "poker face" when discharge home is mentioned or taking place.

In general, cared for children turn to their parents for safety in life. Neglected and battered children endure life as if they are alone in a dangerous world with no real hope of safety.

Some Implications

Because of the repugnance of the idea that parents could be cruel to their own children, parental neglect or abuse often goes unrecognized even after the children's conditions have become serious enough to require hospitalization. The social signs are therefore important aids to diagnosis for preventing further serious damage in children who have already been damaged by their own parents. We think however, that these signs can also be recognized in earlier stages in other settings, in some instances early enough to prevent the extreme deterioration in parent-child relationships that is behind the abusive behavior, or at least in getting services to the child and family before the deteriorated relationship has resulted in serious damage to the child. The signs can be observed by visiting nurses, child welfare workers, doctors and nurses in well-baby clinics, the staff of day-care centers, and others who have normal access to families and children and can set in motion the community services to bring protection to the child who needs it.

But community services must exist and work in a coordinated manner. For example, in extreme cases shelter care is necessary during periods of investigation and decision reaching. It is not safe for a child to remain in a neglecting-battering home during extended periods of investigation, pending court hearings. Neither should the child remain in a hospital ward used for acutely ill children when his physical condition no longer requires it.

Clear lines of accountability and coordination are necessary among the agencies involved. Laws requiring hospitals to report cases to the court should also require notification of child welfare services from the time reportage is thought necessary; otherwise fragmentation of knowledge and effort further endangers children.[8, 9]   Public agencies are in a strategic leadership position for coordinating services and knowledge.

The maturational crisis following childbirth in which the social role of nurturing parenthood is assumed has proved to be a prime intervention period for preventing acute and chronic neglect.[3]   Evidence from the fields of social work, pediatrics, psychology, child psychiatry, and animal experimentation points to the first few months of life as the period when neglect disrupts the integrative capacity of infant perceptual systems.[6, 10]   In this same period, families integrate or disintegrate as parents master or fail to master their parental role tasks.

Old and orthodox methods of providing protective service are not enough.   Creative new uses and new combinations of old services are necessary [1, 2, 11] as well as willingness to communicate and to experience the unpleasant truths in the neglected, battered-child syndrome.   The apparent high incidence of infant, young child neglect and battering suggests need to extend the postnatal period of social public health supervision through the period of greatest infant vulnerability and across social class lines for families showing serious disturbance and difficulty in mastering tasks of parenthood.

Collaborative programs under public health and public child welfare aegis, using current services in new combinations, are in a strategic position for the earliest recognition of neglecting, battering families and for providing immediate and continuing protective services.

Preventing neglect and battering depends in the long run on preventing transmission of the kind of social deprivation which takes children's lives, damages their physical health, and retards their minds [12] and which contributes through those who survive to a rising population of next generation parents who will not be able to nurture children.

[1] Morris, Marian G.; Gould, Robert W.: Role reversal: A concept in dealing with the neglected battered-child syndrome. *In* The neglected battered-child syndrome; role reversal in parents. Child Welfare League of America, New York.   1963.

[2] Ackerman, Nathan W.: Preventive implications of family research. *In* Prevention of mental disorders in children. (Gerald Caplan, ed.). Basic Books, New York.   1961.

[3] Barbero, Giulio J.; Morris, Marian G.; Reford, Margaret T.: Malidentification of mother-baby-father relationships expressed in infant failure to thrive. *In* the neglected battered-child syndrome: role reversal in parents. Child Welfare League of America, New York.   1963.

[4] Elmer, Elizabeth: Identification of abused children. *Children*, September–October 1963.

[5] Griffin, M. E.; Johnson, A. M.; Litin, E. M.: The transmission of supergo defects in the family. *In* A modern introduction to the family   (N. W. Bell and E. W. Vogel, eds.).   Free Press of Glencoe, Glencoe, Ill.   1960

[6] Prugh, D. G.; Harlow, R. G.: Masked deprivation in infants and young children. *In* Deprivation of maternal care—a reassessment of its effects. (WHO Public Health Paper No. 14). Columbia University Press, New York.   1962.

[7] Patton, R. G.; Gardner, L. I.: Growth failure in maternal deprivation. Charles C Thomas, Springfield, Ill.   1963.

[8] U.S. Department of Health, Education, and Welfare, Welfare Administration, Children's Bureau: The abused child: principles and suggested language for legislation on reporting of the physically abused child. 1963.

[9] American Humane Association: Position statement on proposals for mandatory reporting of suspected inflicted injuries on children.   Denver, Colo.   October 1962.

[10] Philbrick, E. B.: Treating parental pathology through child protective services.   Children's Division, American Humane Association, Denver, Colo.   1960.

[11] Riese, H.: Heal the hurt child.   University of Chicago Press, Chicago, Ill.   1962.

[12] Coleman, R. W.; Provence, S.: Environmental retardation (hospitalism) in infants living in families. *Pediatrics*, February 1957.

The Need for Intervention

JEAN RUBIN *is Consultant on Child Abuse, Children's Bureau, Welfare Administration, DHEW. Her paper is based on a presentation made at APWA's 1965 Southwest Regional Conference.*

We are all aware of cases of children who have been unbelievably and tragically harmed by their own families. Newspapers, magazines, and TV have put them very much in the public's mind, and many of us know cases at first hand. Public reaction varies from those who cannot believe it is possible for a mother to harm her own child intentionally, to those who react with such a total revulsion that they are extremely punitive toward the parents. Neither of these attitudes is helpful in working toward a solution to the problem; but since there is a strong public reaction, we should be able to use it to help achieve better programs on behalf of these children and their families.

There is need for special attention to the problems of children abused in their own homes, because these children are in imminent danger of death, permanent crippling, or brain damage. Time is of the essence if they are to be saved. All children who are seriously neglected are also in danger—and will suffer emotionally as well—but

for children abused in their own homes, it may be a life-or-death matter which needs a most immediate remedy. It is our task to see that this remedy is available to every child who needs it, no matter where he lives.

INCIDENCE OF CHILD ABUSE

We have no reliable evidence as to a real rise in the ratio of children who are abused. More cases seem to be coming to the attention of the community, however. We do know that more cases are being recognized as child abuse which previously might have been regarded as accidental. Physicians are increasingly aware of the problem and its true cause, and X-ray techniques have improved to the point where a diagnosis of inflicted injury may be more easily made. In the years ahead, as more research is done, and as the reporting statutes take effect, we will learn more about the incidence of the problem. The Children's Bureau is currently supporting an epidemiologic study of child abuse at Brandeis University, under the direction of David G. Gil. This study will provide much new data on a nationwide basis.

From the statistics we already have, we know that the percentage of physically abused children is small compared with the over-all number of neglected children; but whatever the percentage, the figure is much too large. For example, in Colorado where there is a state-wide protective services program, statistics for 1963 indicate that there were over 5,000 protective service cases. Lack of adequate care accounted for over 3,500 children—and abuse or cruel treatment for 472, which was about 8 or 9 percent of the Colorado total protective service caseload.

CHARACTERISTICS OF THE CHILDREN

We need to increase our knowledge about the characteristics of these children and their parents, but we already have some knowledge from previous and on-going studies. In the majority of cases the children are young—under 4 years of age. The death rate is highest in the very youngest age group, and there is a decrease in the number of cases as age increases. For example, in a survey made by the American Humane Association in 1962, out of 662 cases, 178 of the children died, and over half of those who died were under 2 years of age.

In a Kansas study, out of 85 known cases, 70 percent of the children were under 3. Thirty-two percent of them were under 6 months of age. Fourteen deaths occurred—all of children under 4 years.

There seems to be no socioeconomic pattern of child abuse, since cases occur throughout the population. Parents may be college graduates and professional persons as well as young school dropouts. They come from high-, middle-, and low-income groups, and from various cultural, religious, and racial groups.

PARENTAL HISTORIES

It seems obvious that parents who inflict injury on children reflect disturbed patterns of behavior. Researchers tell us that these adults are usually reacting to their own feelings rather than to specific behavior of the child, although in some cases the attacks may be precipitated by a particular incident. The parental histories frequently reveal physical abuse and neglect during their own childhood. Parents are likely to deny inflicting the injury and offer explanations of accidents as their cause, but their stories are likely to be contradictory. Researchers report that some parents express an unusually high degree of self-justification about their abusive actions. This factor deserves attention and investigation because it is contrary to many of the more popular ideas of the child-beater being an irresponsible, unprincipled, dastardly type of character.

Many attacking parents have a high sense of righteousness about expectations of good behavior from their infants, and a corresponding belief that the correct way of dealing with this is physical attack and punishment. On the other hand, they have at times a high degree of shame and guilt over their behavior.

Another phenomenon which has surprised some researchers has been the degree to which, despite obvious conscious denial and distress, the non-beating spouse has not only condoned but also aided, abetted, or even subtly instigated the actions of the beating parent. Focusing on the marriage problem seems to be a vital factor in dealing with the problem of child-beating in many cases. Uncovering the marital discord is usually an arduous and lengthy task: Both the beating and the non-beating parent tend to keep up a strong façade of "everything is all right in the marriage."

We know that adults who attack children are likely to repeat the incident. In view of the repetitive nature of the injuries, authorities on this subject therefore believe it is dangerous to permit these children to remain or return to their own homes until the homes have been proved to be safe.

It is not always easy, however, to identify the parents who fall into this category, and research efforts are devoted to finding the differential factors which will be helpful in identifying these families. We need this information so that we can determine when it will be safe to permit a child to remain in his home and when he must be removed. It may also help us to identify these families early enough so that help may be given before abuse occurs.

WHAT CAN BE DONE?

Given what we know about the problem, what can be done and what is being done about it? We must keep in mind two basic principles: Parents have the primary responsibility for meeting the needs of their children, and society has an obligation to help parents discharge the responsibility. However, when parents are unable or unwilling to do so, society must undertake to protect children.

Our question is then—at what point, and how shall we intervene? First of all, we must have a way of discovering which children are in need of protection. How do we find out about the children who are in need of assistance?

Some cases of child abuse, particularly of pre-school age, cannot be easily discovered because the children are very young, cannot ask for help, and the harm is done in the privacy of homes where there are no witnesses. Sometimes relatives and neighbors will know about these problems and may bring them to the attention of the community. In other cases, no one knows about the abuse except the parents unless and until a child is brought to a hospital or physician for treatment. The physician's diagnostic skill and expertise may be the only possible means of discovery. It is for this reason that in 1963 the Children's Bureau proposed suggested legislative language for state laws which would require physicians and hospitals to report these cases to an appropriate community authority so that the child in hazard could be identified and thus protected.

Physicians, as well as judges, police chiefs, lawyers, and social workers, were among the expert advisors recommending this legislation. The sole purpose of this recommendation was to protect the child in danger by identifying him so that the protective services of the state could come to his aid. No punitive intent was contemplated by this recommendation.

Although the suggested mandatory reporting legislation is limited to those in the medical profession, it is not intended to prevent or in any way discourage voluntary reporting by others. In many states, however, physicians may need special statutory protection since the physician-patient relationship may deter them from giving information. In order to protect physicians, the recommended bill also provided for immunity from liability in case of any legal or judicial proceeding resulting from the reporting.

The proposed legislation deals only with instances where a physician is *required* to report. He may, of course, like everyone else, also report voluntarily about other cases in which he believes a child to be in danger.

WHO SHOULD RECEIVE REPORTS?

The original Children's Bureau proposal provided that reports should be made to "an appropriate police authority." The police were designated at the time because they are the only agency universally available in every community. However, in view of the current development of protective services, the Children's Bureau now recommends that, where a public welfare agency exists that is authorized and staffed to provide child protective services, it would be the appropriate agency to receive such reports. The choice of agency in any community depends upon what is available, but in each community there should be a single agency designated to receive the reports. There has been confusion and poor administration of programs in communities where more than one agency was given this responsibility.

Although 49 states and the Virgin Islands now have reporting statutes, clearly such laws are but a first step toward providing the needed protection for abused children. Even the best of these laws is useless unless there is proper and adequate follow-up once a report has been made. Therefore, in addition to recommending legislation requiring reporting, the Children's Bureau is also deeply concerned about encouraging the necessary services in a community for the follow-up investigation and service.

After the physician reports, a social investigation is usually necessary in order to determine whether, in fact, the injury was inflicted and whether the home is a dangerous place for the child to remain. In order to encourage persons to make reports, we must be sure that the agency will take prompt, discreet, and helpful action. This requires skilled and tactful workers—with an ability to acquire information for whatever judicial action may become necessary.

PROTECTIVE SERVICES

The Children's Bureau believes that there should be child protective services available as part of a public child welfare program in every community to provide the investigatory services and offer care to children who have been victims of parental abuse. Where such services by the public child welfare agency are authorized by the legislature and adequately financed so that sufficient trained staff is available, there is a ready-made agency to undertake the necessary and difficult task of following up complaints of child abuse.

Previous Children's Bureau legislative guides have recommended that child protective services be a mandatory responsibility of state welfare departments. In some states legislation providing for a protective service program has been part of a legislative package which also includes a reporting statute. In addition, foster care, emergency shelter care, and homemakers are among the useful services which the community should have available to aid these children.

In some communities there has also been an interest in the establishment of a central register of suspected child abuse cases. A central register would make information about these families more readily available during the investigative process. These parents frequently take the children to different physicians or hospitals on different occasions in order to avoid detection. A central register is, therefore, helpful in identifying these cases. Additional legislation may be necessary in some instances to institute such a procedure.

The Children's Bureau hopes that more states and communities will see the need for establishing and strengthening protective services programs, which would, of course, aid neglected as well as abused children. Emphasis has already been given in this direction by the 1962 Public Welfare Amendments which clarified the definition of child welfare services so as to affirm the concept of public child welfare responsibility for child protective services. In addition, there are hopeful signs that the requirements for social services in the AFDC program will also help to detect some of these children at an earlier point.

Even with adequate state legislation, of course, the problems of staffing, financing, and community planning present familiar difficulties. Child welfare agencies must face these problems in developing programs to cope with abused-child cases.

COMMUNITY PLANNING AND EDUCATION

In addition to providing services, there is also a need for community planning and education to implement reporting legislation when it becomes effective. The persons required to report should know exactly what their responsibilities are and what facilities are available to them. The agency

responsible to receive the reports must also have clear guidelines to follow. In order to provide adequate child protective services, definite procedures must be worked out in each community so that the physicians and hospitals, law enforcement officers, social welfare agencies, and the courts are clear about their own functions as part of an over-all plan. This sort of effective planning is as important as the legislation itself, if there is to be effective service on behalf of the abused child.

In addition to concern for adequate legislation, social services, and community planning, the Children's Bureau is also interested in the role of juvenile courts and law enforcement agencies in the protection of abused children. Here we may need some thoughtful consideration of the role of the law and the legal profession. And it is here, too, that it is particularly essential to foster a cooperative working relationship between the social agencies, the courts, and law enforcement agencies. Without planned cooperative effort, there is a possibility of conflict which results in a lack of protection for the abused child.

First, we must be clear about our goal. If protection of the child is our primary aim, will punishment of the parents be helpful or harmful toward that end? If a child is unsafe in his own home, is the community willing to terminate the parents' right to custody and undertake responsibility to provide a substitute home? Are physicians and social workers able to provide facts sufficient to prove danger to the child so that courts may wisely make their decisions? Do our juvenile court laws provide sufficient jurisdictional grounds for action in these cases? Are child welfare workers and court personnel sufficiently knowledgeable to know when they must initiate court action in order to protect the abused child and his siblings? We need to think about answers to these questions.

Usually after a case of child abuse is reported, a police authority or child welfare agency undertakes an investigation, and forms an opinion about the child's probable safety in his own home. The danger, of course, may be so clear that the child has already been removed on an emergency basis or hospitalized for treatment. In either case, decisions must be made about future custody to insure the child's safety. Is the situation one in which injury is likely to reoccur? If the child is to be removed from his parents on either a temporary or permanent basis, the decision must, of course, be a judicial one. Presumably and hopefully, such a case would be taken to a juvenile court for decision, and court services would be readily available so that emergencies could be handled without delay.

JUVENILE COURT ACTIONS

In some communities where effective planning for good liaison between the welfare agency, police, and juvenile courts has not taken place, we have seen a failure to use the juvenile court properly and a lack of understanding between welfare workers and court personnel on the problems involved.

Since juvenile court actions on behalf of a child are not criminal prosecutions against any person, "proof of guilt beyond a reasonable doubt" is not required; but court decisions must be based upon a preponderance of the evidence, and reasonable doubt may be resolved in favor of the child's protection. Therefore, the courts must have available all possible relevant facts if wise decisions are to be made. Physicians and social workers must be prepared to present well-documented evidence, and they may need the assistance of legal counsel to do so. The law *can* intervene on behalf of neglected and abused children, but sufficient evidence is essential to a judicial decision.

Judges may need expert guidance from professional persons about the significance of the medical and social factors in an abused child case. As we acquire more knowledge about parents who abuse their children, we will be better able to inform judges as well as physicians, social workers, and others about the uniqueness of these cases.

A judge's decision about what will be best for a child may also be influenced by the availability of community facilities to care for children if they must be removed from their own homes. If the alternative possibilities are very poor, the judge may hestitate to remove a child from a home even when he suspects that the child may be harmed again. He may therefore be willing to take a greater risk. On the other hand, however, social workers have sometimes delayed too long before taking a case to court, and the child has been harmed again. In these instances, judges have been critical of the ability of social workers to

judge when a child requires the protection of the courts. These are not easy decisions to make, and neither the courts nor social agencies are infallible. There will be less conflict, however, when the courts and the welfare agencies have more knowledge about how to handle these cases and understand each other better.

The person who abuses a child may be committing a crime under state statute and a criminal prosecution may also be contemplated, which further complicates the problem. In most cases it is far more helpful to bring proceedings on behalf of the children in juvenile court than to prosecute a parent in a criminal action. Not only are criminal charges in child abuse cases difficult to prove, since witnesses are generally not present, but punishing the parent does not help to change his behavior, nor do threats of punishment seem to deter him from further acts of abuse.

Since guilt must be proved beyond a reasonable doubt in criminal proceedings, the lack of evidence may make it impossible to obtain a conviction. When such a prosecution fails, therefore, the child may remain in the care of parents who may feel even more justified than before in continuing the abusive treatment. In addition, the publicity which surrounds such trials may also make it more difficult to work with the parents. If we seek to encourage physicians and other persons to report, we will get more cooperation if the end result of the reporting is helpful services to the child and family, rather than criminal prosecutions of the parents.

The parents of these children do present difficult problems, both of diagnosis and treatment. It takes skill and knowledge to be able to predict a child's future safety, and clearly we do not yet know enough about identifying and treating parents who actively harm their own children. The Children's Bureau is encouraging further research to bring us more of the answers to these difficult questions. Some psychiatric studies are now going on, more are needed. Demonstration and research projects on methods of working with these parents and establishing community networks of protective services are also under way.

If we can help the abused child of today, we may be able to prevent some of the problem parents of tomorrow. Far too many parents who abuse their children have histories of childhood neglect and abuse themselves. We must not lose sight of the fact that these parents are also in need of help and understanding, although the current state of psychiatric knowledge may not be sufficient to change them all into the good parents we might wish them to be. Although we may have to accept the fact that there are parents whom we are unable to help now, we must continue to seek to help their children to gain a better life so that they may become adequate parents in the future.

Coping with Child Abuse: One State's Experience

The late
CYRIL H. WINKING

Mr. Winking's paper was presented at APWA's *1967 National Round Table Conference. It is a moving and eloquent testimony to the devotion of this public welfare leader to the goal of protecting children and enabling parents to fulfill their role. The author died suddenly in March before we had an opportunity to let him know that we had selected his paper for publication. We publish it as a tribute to him.*

Illinois is now in its third year of administering a child abuse law. It is a good law because of its precise language and specific directives for implementation. I will summarize the salient features of the law, describe some of our findings, and point up some of the formidable problems faced by child protective agencies in providing comprehensive follow-up services to the abused child and his family.

SINGLE DESIGNATED AGENCY

Among the significant features of the Illinois law is the designation of a single, statewide agency to receive reports from hospitals and physicians—and then to act upon them. I am not conversant with all the state laws on reporting of child abuse, but I do know that a number of them seem to leave this responsibility in "limbo," by stating that reports are to be sent to the "nearest law enforcement or welfare agency." The upshot of such diffusion of responsibility could be that those required to report suspected abuse cases may not know exactly where to turn when confronted by a reportable case. Likewise, it seems to me that diffusion would make it difficult, if not impossible, for the various agencies which could conceivably get involved to know what to do—and how to do it—after receiving a report. In Illinois, the designated agency is the Department of Children and Family Services, whose state-administered child welfare program covers every urban and rural area of the state.

Reports of suspected child abuse may likewise be filed with the local law enforcement agency, but the law requires the reporter to inform the Department when such referral is made. The law is mandatory in terms of the requirement to report to our Department; it is permissive as to similar reports being sent to law enforcement agencies.

AUTHORITATIVE MEDICAL DIAGNOSES

In addition to designating a single state agency to which reports are to be made, the law particularizes in other respects. For example, it defines a child as "any person under 16 years of age." It requires that reports of suspected abuse be filed by physicians, surgeons, dentists, and other practitioners, as well as hospitals. As might be expected, there have been pressures for the Department to support a broadening of the law to require reporting by nurses, teachers, and other persons. We have, thus far, successfully resisted such pressures on the basis that the intent of the law is to secure reports from persons who can make authoritative medical diagnoses and judgments about the causative factors.

I am not implying that persons in these allied fields should not make complaints of hazardous or abusive situations involving children. Indeed they should! As a matter of fact, they *have* been referring such cases to our child welfare offices for many years—because of our Department's broad powers to provide protective services around-the-clock, seven days a week, 365 days a year. But the Abused Child Law has a target audience—doctors and hospitals—and we hope to keep it that way.

IMMUNITY PROVISION

Another key feature of the Illinois law, which is probably the most important in child abuse legislation, is the "immunity" provision which protects the reporter from both civil and criminal liability.

The Illinois law makes it mandatory that the Department of Children and Family Services maintain a central registry of all suspected abuse cases reported. Other states or municipalities are now requiring similar registries. But I believe Illinois was the first state to spell out this responsibility in the Child Abuse Statute.

We have found the registry to be an excellent repository of information on child abuse. It has enabled the Department to engage in studies of the problem. It has been a useful tool in evaluating casework performance in individual protective situations. And, generally, it has been of help in letting us alert the public to the size and complexity of the problem as it exists in a large, highly industrialized state. Hopefully, the registry can be a step toward control of the problem, comparable, in a real sense, to the communicable disease registries used in the public health field.

NOT PUNITIVE IN INTENT

A general characteristic of the Illinois law which I consider highly important is that it is *not punitive* in intent. Rather, it is focused on the discovery of abuse cases, protection of the children involved, and rehabilitation of the family whenever possible. If we are to spare children from death or permanent injury and have a chance to stabilize the family, intervention by the Department at the earliest moment of *suspected* abuse is essential. If the law emphasized punishment of the parents, I am convinced that physicians would be quite leery of reporting "borderline" cases of abuse. Doctors and hospital administrators, reluctant to see parents locked up

on marginal evidence, would be inclined to wait and to report only those cases in which the abuse was indisputable. Obviously, this would mean that a child might be reported only after he had suffered irreparable damage, both physical and mental.

As you can gather, we are pleased with the Illinois law—although admittedly horrified by the cases it has unearthed. More than 1,100 cases have been reported in 29 months, and there is no evidence of any decline in the reporting volume. This indicates that physicians and hospitals are fulfilling their responsibilities. While hospitals account for the largest portion of the reports, we have noticed a slight increase in direct reports from doctors following examination or treatment of children in their offices.

THE VERY YOUNG CHILD

Let me give you a few other highlights of our findings in Illinois. The abused child is, most often, the very young child. One-fourth of the children reported have been less than a year old; 28 percent have been one or two years old. In other words, more than half of the cases involve children less than 3 years of age. More boys than girls are the pitiful victims. *They are beaten, starved, fractured, burned, sexually assaulted, and severely neglected*—in that order.

Most of the abused youngsters come from poor families; their parents have had little or no education. Although our experience in Illinois proves that no particular level of society has a corner on the child abuse "market," there is no question but that the crowded ghettos of our inner cities spawn the conditions which lead to child abuse.

HOPELESSNESS AND DESPAIR

Let me elaborate briefly. I do not think for a minute that an adult becomes a child abuser simply because he is poor or semiliterate. If a man and his wife are poor, and their families before them were poor, and there is no chance for a job anywhere, how does one keep alive the possibility of escaping the ghetto? How does one avoid its contagious air of hopelessness and despair? And when hope flickers and dies, we have all the charged elements that can ignite a violent, abusive episode. When children are beaten or burned, it is frequently because the abuser must vent his uncontrollable rage toward society on someone least able to retaliate—even if it means maiming his own child. In many instances in which children are totally neglected and starved, it is because the parents have simply given up. They are thinking only of themselves and how they can somehow relieve the monotony of their meaningless day to day existence.

Each Case Has Its Own Complex, Contributing Factors

This word picture of the child abuse situation does not hold true in all cases, of course, for sociologists, psychiatrists and professional people in other disciplines have shown that each case has its own complex, contributing factors. But poverty, hunger, disease, lack of opportunity— and the personal frustration that are triggered by all of these—are the very problems that we in public welfare deal with every day and know something about. If we are successful in doing something about them in our lifetime, then it seems to me we have a chance to reduce the incidence of child abuse that we all find so shocking.

I have digressed from our findings in Illinois, so let me return to that subject. In terms of the suspected abuser, our findings are similar to those in other states. Natural parents are most frequently the abusers, with stepfathers and baby-sitters next in line for this dubious distinction.

During the first year of the Illinois law, 53 deaths were reported. In the second year, 28 were reported. We hesitate to attach great significance to this sharp decline in fatalities because of our relatively brief experience with the Abused Child Law. However, we are heartened by the fact that the ratio of deaths to reported child abuse cases has dipped from 11.1 percent during the first year to 8.2 percent for the entire period since the law took effect.

As I have indicated, we are convinced that the reporting process in Illinois has been excellent. This resulted largely from a comprehensive, planned educational program pointed toward the target audience well in advance of the effective date of the legislation. I firmly believe that lack of preparation of the publics involved is one of the greatest impediments that states encounter in implementing their programs successfully.

Follow-Up Counts Most

Yet, reporting is only *phase one* of the job of implementing abused child legislation. The follow-up is what counts most. As I see it, the thrust of most state laws on this subject is directed first toward protection of the child or children involved, and secondly toward strengthening the family. Each report of abuse, therefore, should propel the agency into immediate investigation and provision of needed services that will remedy the abusive situation and prevent recurrence. This is too often where our programs bog down.

There are real, practical reasons why we do not deliver as we should. Let me touch very briefly on the four roadblocks that, from our vantage point in Illinois, appear to be most significant: staff shortages; lack of sufficient skill in dealing with the "sick" abuser; the dearth of temporary care and treatment resources; and the varying philosophies of the social and legal agencies which, of necessity, must interact in abused child cases.

Shortage of staff is perhaps the most serious problem we face in attempting to fulfill our investigatory and service obligations under the Abused Child Law. It is a problem that has reached the acute stage in other welfare services as well. But if we use it as a crutch, an alibi, an excuse to throw in the towel and abdicate our responsibilities, then we abuse the fundamental principles on which the social work profession was founded. In these critical cases of child abuse, it is almost unforgivable that days can go by before an investigation is started. Yet consider the administrator's painful dilemma. Can agencies afford special case loads? Can they deploy scarce staff in disproportionate numbers to this function? Can they give protective service so high a priority that all other services suffer?

Run a Grave Risk

No one, to my knowledge, has all the answers. But we must forge ahead creatively to fashion at least partial answers. These answers include consciously planned differential use of staff, intensified staff development, use of carefully selected and well trained volunteers, streamlined procedures, and use of group methods. If we fail to utilize these and other methods to broaden the base of our action-oriented personnel, we run a grave risk of alienating those whose cooperation we have so earnestly sought: the reporters of suspected abuse. If our follow-up is characterized by unconscionable delays and superficial, once-over-lightly service approaches, doctors and hospital administrators have every right to feel that their action in reporting suspected abuse cases has been futile and meaningless. On the other hand, if we do the very best job we know how under the most trying circumstances, we may emerge with a strong ally to help us extract from our legislatures the funds we need to hire the persons to do the job the way it should be done in every single instance.

But more bodies to do the job is not in itself the solution. Because of the nature of the work involved, *skilled* staff is an absolute necessity. Workers must be perceptive and action-oriented. They must be experts in fact-finding and especially capable of making immediate, delicate decisions. They must have an understanding of the "battering" person, what it is that triggers his violence, and how to help transform his rages— if not into tenderness, at least into elemental human compassion. A tall order, indeed! And beyond all this, the workers must have the intestinal fortitude and personal control to "take it," to give consistently and regularly, and to tolerate tremendous anxieties and frustrations in dealing with the "hardest" of the "hard to reach": the child abuser. A question that bothers me deeply is: How long can an agency rightfully expect a worker to stay on the firing line and still be effective?

SUFFICIENT RESOURCES FOR DIAGNOSIS AND TREATMENT

Even if we had enough skilled workers, however, an essential component in the service spectrum would still be missing: sufficient resources for diagnosis and treatment, whether they be clinical services, home-helps such as day care and homemaker service, or adequate child care facilities for temporary or long term treatment. In so many cases, the skilled worker could make the right judgment at the right time if only he had the tools, the resources. But how does one fight a void?

A problem of another dimension has always been with us, but it is likely to become much more of a problem—especially in view of the recent U.S. Supreme Court decision in the Gault case which will undoubtedly have ramifications for juvenile courts across the nation. I refer to the widening gap between the social agency and the law enforcing bodies. In child abuse cases, it is not merely a matter of the punitive versus the non-punitive approach. Even with our non-punitive law in Illinois, law enforcement agencies have been involved in nearly half the cases, and charges were filed against the abuser in at least one out of five cases. The crucial question seems to be who has the priority of rights—the parent, as abuser, or the helpless, abused child. In too many cases, the abuser is given another chance with the child, a chance that sometimes can become license to hurt, cripple, and even murder.

SOCIAL AGENCIES ARE NOT ALWAYS RIGHT

Lest we appear too self-righteous, however, let us admit publicly and for the record that social agencies are not always right and the courts wrong when there is a conflict about the disposition of a child abuse case. But somehow, both the agencies and the courts must come to an agreement to strengthen the protection of the child. Both must face up to the reality that the parent does not always have to win when there is a conflict between his and the child's rights. I do not believe that taking the parents into court is always the solution to the problem, nor do I believe they should never go to court. My point is that we must bring about a meeting of the legal and social work minds on what constitutes the right decision for the child. If the right decision is *not* made, the child may never again have his day in court.

Looking back at our experiences in Illinois with the Child Abuse Law, I feel a sense of pride at the accomplishments. The law is good, the reporting is remarkably good, and the follow-through on the reports, in terms of investigation and service, is probably as good as we can expect with limited staff and scarce treatment resources. But I cannot help but envision what more money —a lot more money—could do. Not only could it fill in the gaps in the diagnostic and treatment areas, but more important, it would provide us with the means for strengthening and extending our preventive services. Without these services, how else can the vicious circle of the sick begetting the sick be broken?

Mothers Anonymous: the Last Resort

Mrs. J.H. of Redondo Beach, California, is a child-abuser. For four years, she explains, she struggled with an uncontrollable urge to severely punish her daughter. When she tried to obtain counseling, social agencies told her she "didn't fit into the right category" for treatment. One afternoon, she attempted to strangle her child; desperate, she confronted the local child-guidance clinic. If they didn't do something to help her, she threatened, they'd be guilty of her daughter's death. Finally, she was placed in therapy.

Her case is not unusual. Doctors say that child abuse continues to be a major problem in this country. When discovered by authorities, the battered child can receive special care. But, as Mrs. J.H. found, little help is available for the troubled parents. Often, these adults have grown up as abused children themselves, and

they are continuing the child-beating cycle. Encouraged by her therapist, Mrs. J.H. developed an idea. "I decided," she explains, "that if alcoholics could stop drinking by getting together, and gamblers could stop gambling, maybe the same principle would work for abusers, too."

Early in 1970 she started running a series of newspaper ads: "Mothers Anonymous, for moms who blow their cool with their kids—call 379-6896."

More than 200 mothers called her and then joined M.A. Currently two groups meet in a church in Redondo Beach, another in Long Beach, and a fourth at Corona Women's Prison (for women not helped in time). Most abusers find that they can be rehabilitated in a short time: An M.A. psychiatric consultant says that almost all mothers can stop beating their children after

three months with a group. Nevertheless, the mothers continue to attend meetings.

Although a professional counselor attends each meeting, the mothers do most of the talking. "What we have here," says Mrs. J.H., "is not a confrontation group, not sensitivity training, not Freudian analysis. I guess you'd call it laymen's reality therapy. We don't let people just moan about how they were beaten when they were three; we say, 'You're thirty-three now, the problem is to stop doing what you're doing to *your* children.'"

Members call each other whenever they're under stress, and receive instant help. "Want me to come over? Should I take your child for a few days?" In fact, the mothers say that swapping kids is one of their most effective methods of help. It's a quirk of the child-abuse syndrome that often

only one child in a family serves as "whipping boy" (usually the one who reminds the parent of her own faults). When a mother starts losing control, it's urgent that this child be removed temporarily.

M.A. is expanding rapidly, steered by a board of directors composed of three social workers, two M.D.'s, three abusers, and one lawyer. New groups are forming in Santa Monica and Santa Ana, California, with plans for a group in Saint Paul, Minnesota.

M.A. has attracted considerable attention in recent months. Dr. R. E. Helfer, leading authority on child abuse, and author of *The Battered Child,* made a special trip to California to study the group. "It all makes me very proud," says Mrs. J. H., who admits with a smile that being proud is a brand-new wonderful feeling.   —Phyllis Zauner

the ABUSED parent
of the ABUSED child

SIDNEY WASSERMAN

Willful intent in parents to injure their own children is an "unthinkable thought" for most of us. Even physicians, persons who seem to be in a position to judge whether violence has been done to a child, are often unwilling to accept the "reality of willful child abuse," according to a recent survey among physicians in the Washington metropolitan area conducted by a group of psychiatrists.[1] A fifth of the nearly 200 physicians questioned said they rarely or never considered the "battered child syndrome" when seeing an injured child, and a fourth said they would not report a suspected case even if protected by law against legal action by the parents. Apparently, they did not believe the evidence would stand up in court.

To accept as fact that some parents intentionally injure their children is difficult and upsetting. Thus, we all tend, like the physicians studied, to give the parent "the benefit of the doubt." There may be many reasons for our reluctance, but one is certainly this— when we accept willful intent as a fact, we must face our anger at such parents and our desire to protect the child, even if we harm the parent. But we cannot effectively intervene to protect an abused child and prevent abuse from recurring unless we understand what it is like to be a "battering parent."

One of the dangers of using the label "battering parent" is the possibility of increasing bias and prejudice against the parent. Labeling a particular person as a "battering parent" can release us from the responsibility of making our response to and attitude toward his actions sensitive to his needs. The temptation is great to think of him as being far removed from those of us who do not batter our children. In so thinking, we keep intact our image of ourselves as righteous.

How easy it is to deny that within all of us lies a potential for violence and that any of us could be unreachable! What is more repugnant to our rational, "mature" minds than the thought of committing impulsive, violent acts against a helpless child? We tell ourselves that the primitive, untempered instincts responsible for such acts could not erupt in us. But stripped of our defenses against such instincts and placed in a social and psychological climate conducive to violent behavior, any of us could do the "unthinkable." This thought should humble us: perhaps we are not battering parents only because conditions do not lead us to commit "unnatural" acts.

No class monopoly

Writers on social phenomenon, lawyers, social scientists, and others interested in social problems have long recognized that the phenomenon of parents physically abusing their children has been with us since the beginnings of mankind. Only since World War II, however, has much been written on the subject of unexplained, shocking, and traumatic injuries to children. Since then, too, much has been said and written about the legal confusion surrounding the use of authority and sanctions in instances of apparent abuse of children by their parents.

Historically, the helping professions have viewed physical abuse of children by their parents as the result of poverty, life in the slums, ignorance, and the hardships produced by immigration, war, industrialization, and urbanization. No one can deny that these conditions can be a cause of child abuse. Nevertheless, we are finding that the phenomenon can be found anywhere in society. Once we regarded violence against a child as characteristic of parents in the lower socioeconomic classes. Now we are finding that such behavior is not exclusive with any particular social class but that "better" families can more easily conceal the problem than poor ones. In other words, a sociological explanation by itself is inadequate and simplistic.

Through sometimes frustrating and bitter experience, the professions, and particularly that of social work, have come to see that prosecuting the battering parent solves the problems of neither the child nor the parent. Helping the abused child leads us inevitably to the need to help the battering parent and family. As pointed out by Delsordo,[2] Boardman,[3] Nurse,[4] and others in studies of child abuse, practically all cases of abuse involve longstanding, severe interpersonal conflict either between the parents themselves or between one parent and another member of the family.

Because we are dealing with a complex subject involving many social, psychological, medical, and legal elements, we must narrow our scope and take first things first. Nothing precedes understanding who the battering parent is and what he is. Studies point out that battering parents and families, regardless of class, have certain psychological and social characteristics in common; for example, we are learning more all the time about the severe damage to personality these people suffer. Few are psychotic, but all have marked inability to set up a genuine relationship with another human being. Absorbed by their own hurt feelings, they cannot sympathize with the feelings of others. The nonpsychotic battering parent seldom shows remorse for having hurt his child, but he can be very much concerned about the harm a person in authority might inflict on his own person. When facing a person in authority, he cries out: "What are you going to do to me?"

"Done to"

Obviously, something went haywire or was not touched in the humanization process when such persons were growing up. Apparently, they never had the kind of relations with other people that offers incentives for delaying pleasure or gratification or the feeling that it is worthwhile to yield an immediate, antisocial pleasure for the love and acceptance of another. They have been "done to" both socially and psychologically. A battering adult goes about his daily life with the gnawing, unfulfilled feeling of having been unloved or not having been loved as much as he should have been as a child. His life is focused on his own needs, and he cannot tolerate any frustration to the gratification of those needs. What else can he feel but his own hurt, his own hunger for love? He is anesthetized against feeling compassion for others.

This kind of person, according to Reiner and Kaufman,[5] is unaware that he has a buried feeling of "imbedded depression" because he was emotionally or psychologically abandoned by his parent as a child, an act he interpreted as rejection of himself. Unable to understand such a distressing emotional event and not psychologically strong enough to bear it, as a child he buried the feeling of rejection deep within himself and with it the accompanying depression. Because his use of language was not developed, he expressed his feelings by the only means he had—his behavior. Explosive, violent behavior became his means of communicating with those around him. When he was violent, he was unable to feel his hurt, his sense of worthlessness, his depression. Denied a consistent, supportive relationship with an adult, he set up a life pattern of aggression and violence—and is now inflicting on others what was inflicted on him. For him the world is hostile and dangerous; it is a place where one attacks or is attacked.

Studies also suggest that the battering parent feels his parents were punishing him when they rejected him and that he is longing for a mother. He wants to be loved, yet does everything to prevent another from loving him. Instead, he is caught in a cycle of violence and rejection. When speaking of his physical attacks on his child, the battering parent strongly defends his right to act as he has. He seems unable to feel love for and protectiveness toward his child. He can be extremely compulsive in his behavior and make unreasonable demands on his child. Cleanliness, for instance, may be an obsession with some. I have heard of a child being mercilessly beaten for putting chicken bones on a clean tablecloth and of an 18-month-old baby being seated with his buttocks uncovered on a hotplate whenever he soiled himself. Such people are way over their heads when they become parents. How can they give a child what they have never had themselves—security, safety, and love?

The hostility sponge

This description is supported by a growing amount of evidence that when a battering parent becomes

Sidney Wasserman has recently moved to England to become a lecturer at the Undergraduate School of Studies in Applied Social Studies, University of Bradford. For the past 3 years, he has been associate professor at the Smith College School of Social Work. He received both his master's and doctor's degrees in social work from Western Reserve University.

violent, he apparently is releasing his rage on a particular child, selected to act as the "hostility sponge" for that rage. The parent views the child as a competitor, as someone taking and getting what belongs to him. The child is an unconscious symbol of someone or something that once caused him pain—a competitive brother or sister, a distrusted parent, his rejected self. Sometimes the parent is reliving a childhood experience that left him traumatized. Some of these parents talk about being rejected by their own parents in favor of a brother or sister.

In many instances the abused child has been conceived out of wedlock. The parent is now punishing him for being the cause of an unwanted marriage. Sometimes a stepfather is the offender. He beats the child for reminding him of his wife's "badness." Or the mother may beat the child because he reminds her of her "badness" or of that "bad" man, his father, who deserted her when she was pregnant. By beating out the "badness" in the child, the parent beats out his own badness or that of another person who has injured him. In other words, the parent is reacting to his own inner feelings, not to the behavior of the child. The child is the provoker by being what he is—an infant or a child demanding attention. It is this demand that provokes the parent.

The use of the child as a hostility sponge may be absolutely essential to the mental balance of the parent, and, thus, the child is sacrificed to that mental balance. Removing the child from the home without a well thought-out plan to help the parent and the family may only invite the parent to shift his rage to another child. We can easily get caught up in symptom-shifting without getting to the bottom of the problem—the parent's need to be protected from himself.

To really help such a parent, we must break the chains he has inherited. To do that, we must clearly understand that intervention should act as a brake on the parent's behavior and that the injuries he inflicts on the child, injuries that bring the attention of the community to join them, are his way of saying—"Stop me!" The act of rushing a child to a hospital or of beating him in front of neighbors or strangers carries a message to the community— "Please save me from going out of control. Stop me from going out of my mind. Keep me from—killing!"

We are gradually realizing that in such cases we are dealing not only with a seriously disturbed person but also with a disturbed family. Once the existence of abuse is ascertained and the degree of imminent danger determined, the parent and the family must be dealt with whether or not the child is removed from the home. Even in cases where law enforcement has been effective and community services have been well coordinated, problems in helping the battering parent and the family remain.

According to Zalba,[6] battering parents tend to deny their actions, the husband or wife of the battering parent protects the other, or the children are too young to explain to outsiders what has occurred in the home. The parents also tend to deny the existence of personal or family problems and to provoke judges, lawyers, and social workers by making impossible demands on them; or they rage at everyone in authority and, sometimes, physically attack them.

Firmness above all

In reaching out to the battering parent, we must keep in mind an important key to his behavior—his fear of a close relationship. Because he suffered rejection in early life, he wards off human relationships.[5] He has emotionally divorced himself from the significant people in his life. He feels safer with and responds more readily to a relationship that clearly offers authority—firm but not punitive. In other words, the battering parent can often be reached by setting firm limits and controls on his behavior. Whatever he may say, he needs firm control—and wants it. In the early stages of trying to reach the battering parent and family, the social caseworker or other helper must make realistic judgments and decisions for and with the parents and family to gradually help them develop a sense of reality.

To provide this basic treatment requires long-term help from a consistent relationship with one person only. Shifting the parent from one worker to another only stirs up his basic, deep-seated belief that to get close to another human being is to expose one's self to hurt and abandonment. Deep within, he sees himself as the kiss of death in personal relations. He wants to get close to another person, but he thinks that if he does the person will learn to dislike him and will break off the relationship. For a long, indefinite period, the helping person must stand by and support the parent by setting limits and by providing services through community resources. He must not try to get too close to or expect such a person to unload his innermost feelings, especially feelings he is hardly aware of. For such a person, having limits set on explosive, violent behavior provides the kind of protection a good parent would give. The battering parent must be constantly assured that he will not be allowed to get out of control. At the same time, he must be assured that the worker believes that he does not want to hurt his child, that he is capable of change, and that he wants to be a better parent. He needs to learn what the community expects of him and what choices he has. He needs to be helped to understand clearly that consequences will follow his violent act and what those consequences will be.

A long process

In this long and trying process, such a parent will continually test the patience of the helping person and will use every means to provoke rejection to reassure himself that he will not be rejected. For a long time he will reveal only his unlikeable side. When he is reassured, he will make feeble attempts to plant the seeds of a relationship. Reaching out to such a person makes a very great emotional and intellectual demand on the helping person. The battering parent is very perceptive and can immediately sense insincerity. Actually, the helping person must become the "hostility sponge" instead of the child by letting the parent test him, yet he must never let the parent get out of control.

Psychiatrists, psychologists, social caseworkers, and other persons trained for this work have observed that as treatment progresses and a basic trust is established the battering parent gradually faces up to the depression within himself. With extreme caution, he talks about his deep-seated fear that he is a loser and that people always desert him. Only when his need for violence abandons him and he stops expressing himself through it can he talk about his childhood and begin to come to grips with his problems. Though he improves, he continues to try to provoke the helping person, for he is never convinced that he will not be rejected. However, he does move cautiously toward having a relationship with the helping person, gives up or modifies his violent outbursts, and lets himself be guided toward patterning his actions after the standards of the helping person. In time, the pattern becomes a part of him and a new self appears.

To start and set in motion such a long, painstaking process requires a firm commitment by the community to providing excellent service, a goal not easily attained. To obtain qualified staff members and to train persons specifically as workers are expensive and time-consuming. Often efforts to reach the battering parent are obstructed because workers—nurses, social workers, volunteers—come and go frequently on the staffs of agencies. For the battering parent is likely to regard a change in workers as another experience in rejection. The helping person may leave the staff at the most critical moment—just as the parent is testing the worker to find out if rejection will follow his actions. The parent takes the worker's leaving the agency as proof that it never pays to get close to another person. If only a community or agency could insure permanent service for such troubled human beings!

But life affords few opportunities for permanency. We are all only temporary to each other. That is a human condition, and most people accept it. The battering parent cannot. Plans for helping him must include ways to help him accept this truth. We must be ready to test various methods of working with him, always keeping in mind his deep fear of involvement and loss. We must continue to direct efforts to alert the medical, legal, and social work professions, and all groups who might come in contact with the battering person to the need for continuity in helping him. The challenge is not a small one; social workers are finding that cases involving battering parents as well as other hard-to-reach families are making up more and more of their caseloads.

In addition to individual treatment, working with groups of battering parents and their spouses is also proving effective. Many of these parents are isolated from the community. Having an opportunity to socialize in a group of similarly troubled parents tends to lower their resistance to facing and discussing their problems.[6] Working with such families as family groups has also proved effective.[6]

The community must learn

Beyond the abused child, his parents, and his family is the community around them. Battering parents and their families suffer from a not uncommon malaise often called "community exclusion." In various ways, whether economically, politically, psychologically, or socially, these families frequently suffer exclusion. Unfortunately, when such persons vent their rage on their children and the shocked community retaliates immediately, the family's sense of rejection is increased. A cycle of reciprocal aggression is set in motion and, once set in motion, is difficult to halt. The battering parent often succeeds in provoking hospitals, the police, the courts, and social agencies into treating him as his parents once treated him—the opposite of what he needs. Communities must constantly reexamine ways to set up controls and limits while bringing all families into the community life. When a battering parent has only known "community exclusion," he desperately needs "inclusion" to break the cycle.

Finally, we cannot examine our attitude as a community toward the battering parent without examining what it means to be part of a whole—a State, a nation, or the world. Like it or not, we are bound each to the other and our destinies are interwoven. As we try to understand the battering parent, we must look into ourselves to find out what there is in each of us, in our community, our Nation, and the world that the battering parent takes as a sign that what he is doing is permissible.

To answer this question we must face up to the paradoxes in our moral code that condemn violence in one form, permit it in another. Many Americans seem to persistently dismiss from their thoughts and acts a basic truth—there is nothing more precious than human life, or so it seems to me.

The people of the United States have yet to learn how to convert their tendency to violence into compassion and tenderness. We are in danger of losing sight of one of this Nation's major social goals, one on which it was founded, that is, to tap the humanity and creative potential of all citizens and to provide the environment and resources necessary for the individual citizen to realize his creative potential. We possess the potential both for violence and for humaneness, and are capable of acting in brotherhood and with understanding. If this were not so, we would not now be seeking new and different ways of helping our less fortunate citizens. By seeking to tap the humanity and potential for growth of the battering parent and family, we are tapping our own potential for personal, community, national, and international growth. We must ever encourage the tapping of this potential.

[1] Silver, L. B.; Barton, W.; Dublin, C. C.: Child abuse laws—are they enough? *The Journal of the American Medical Association*, January 9, 1967.

[2] Delsordo, J. D.: Protective casework for abused children. *Children*, November–December 1963.

[3] Boardman, H. E.: A project to rescue children from inflicted injuries. *Social Work*, January 1962.

[4] Nurse, S. M.: Familial patterns of parents who abuse their children. *Smith College Studies in Social Work*, October 1964.

[5] Reiner, B. S.; Kaufman, I.: Character disorders in parents of delinquents. Family Service Association of America, New York. 1959.

[6] Zalba, S. R.: The abused child: II. A typology for classification and treatment. *Social Work*, January 1967.

SUMMARY

The battered child has a parent or parents who suffer certain social and psychological traits: (1) some are psychotic, and all have the marked inability to set up a close, genuine relationship with others, (2) some are marked by explosive, violent behavior as a means of communicating with others, (3) most see the world as a hostile environment, (4) many abusing parents view their child as a competitor, (5) some are parents whose child reminds them of a deserted spouse or an unwanted marriage, and (6) many such parents feel more secure with a relationship that offers firm authority.

To help the battered child, he must first be identified and this identification can be done through the discovery of bruises, cuts, burns, scaldings, malnutrition, brain damage, bone lesions, and internal injuries. Perhaps the most conclusive evidence to identify the abused child is the X-ray which not only shows current fractures, but also shows stages of healing from bone injuries previously received.

Educators, physicians, social workers, and others can assume a useful and important role in helping the battered child by recognizing the symptoms and understanding the laws enacted for his protection.

The parents of these children need to be dealt with in a firm authoritative, but not punitive, manner. Treatment should include the services of a social worker and must take place in a community setting that will try to understand and aid them. Every community needs to provide a wide range of social and medical services to help both the parents and children.

Educators, law enforcement agents and others need to refrain from using physical punishment in dealing with behavioral problems. More intelligent methods of dealing with such problems need to be developed in order to teach these and other children that physical force is an inappropriate means for handling human problems.

Identification and protection are bare beginnings. Without effective rehabilitation the child not only remains a warped and tragic being but within him will be perpetuated the seeds of later tragedy—the child abuser.

STUDY QUESTIONS

1. What are guidelines that can be used to identify a battered child?

2. What can you do as an individual to help an abused child? an abusing parent?

3. Which professionals are concerned and working to help abused children and their abusers?

4. Which agencies are concerned and working to help abused children and their abusers?

5. Does the long range picture look good or bad for the battered child?

6. What are the most positive steps that are now being taken to help the abused child?

REFERENCES

A. Readings Included in This Text

Morris, Marion G.; Gould, Robert W.; and Matthews, Patricia J. "Toward Prevention of Child Abuse." *Children*, 2 (1964):55-60.

Rubin, Jean. "The Need for Intervention." *Public Welfare*, 24 (1966):230-235.

Wasserman, Sidney. "The Abused Parent of the Abused Child." *Children*, 14 (1967):175-179.

Winking, Cyril H. "Coping With Child Abuse: One State's Experience." *Public Welfare*, 26 (1968):189-192.

Zauner, Phyllis. "Mothers Anonymous: the Last Resort." *McCall's*, 99 (1972):57.

B. Suggested Additional Readings

Davies, J. R., and Jorgensen, J. D. "Battered, But Not Defeated: The Story of An Abused Child and Positive Casework." *Child Welfare*, 49 (1970):101-104.

Elmer, Elizabeth. "Identification of Abused Children." *Children*, 10 (1963):180-184.

Fulk, Delores Leusby. "The Battered Child." *Nursing Forum*, 3 (1964):10-26.

Gil, David G. "What Schools Can Do About Child Abuse." *American Education*, 5 (1969):2-4.

"Help for Child Beaters." *Newsweek*, 80 (1972):66, 69.

Leavitt, Jerome E. "The Battered Child." *The Instructor*, 75 (1966):50, 142, 150.

Moorehead, C. "Seven-Man Team Helps Parents of Battered Babies." *Times Educational Supplement*, 2897 (1970):12.

Oettinger, Katherine B. "The Abused Child." *Childhood Education*, 41 (1965):235-237.

Sandusky, Anna Lee. "Services to Neglected Children." *Children*, 7 (1960):23-28.

Shaffer, Helen B. "Child Abuse: Search for Remedies." *Editorial Research Reports*, 1 (1965):343-369.

BIBLIOGRAPHY

"The Abused Child, Parents, and the Law," *Rhode Island Medical Journal,* 47 (1964):39-90.

The Abused Child in this Community, a report by the Kent County Department of Social Welfare, Child Protective Services. Grand Rapids, Mich., October 25, 1965.

The Abused Child—Principles and Suggested Language for Legislation on Reporting of the Physically Abused Child. Children's Bureau, U.S. Department of Health, Education, and Welfare. Washington, D.C.: U.S. Government Printing Office, 1963.

Adelson, Lester, "Slaughter of the Innocents—A Study of Forty-Six Homicides in Which the Victims Were Children." *The New England Journal of Medicine 264,* No. 26, 1345-1349, June 29, 1961.

Allen, Anne, and Morton, Arthur. *This Is Your Child: The Story of the National Society for the Prevention of Cruelty to Children.* London: Routledge and K. Paul, Ltd., 1961.

Alverson, Charles E. "Protecting Children: Medical, Legal Drive Aims to Spot, Reduce Cases of Child Abuse." *Wall Street Journal,* 166 (1965):1+.

The American Humane Association. *Child Protective Services.* Denver: Children's Divison, The American Humane Association, P.O. Box 1266, 1967.

The American Humane Association. *Report of National Agencies Workshop in Child Protective Services.* Denver: Children's Division, The American Humane Association, P.O. Box 1266, 1957.

The American Humane Association. *Report of National Agencies Workshop in Child Protective Services, Part Two.* Denver: Children's Division, The American Humane Association, P.O. Box 1266, 1958.

Andrews, John P., "The Battered Baby Syndrome." *Illinois Medical Journal 122,* 494, November, 1962.

Arnold, Mildred. *Termination of Parental Rights.* The American Humane Association. Children's Division, 1961. 14 pp.
"Assaulted Children." *Lancet 1* (1964):543-544.

Auerbach, Mary C., *et al.* "The Abused Child in Washington, D.C. June 1, 1963-November 30, 1964." Master's thesis, Howard University, School of Social Work, June 1965.

Bain, Katherine. "The Physically Abused Child." *Pediatrics 31,* No. 6, 895-897, June 1963.

Bain, Katherine; Milowe, Irvin D.; Wenger, Donald S.; Fairchild, John P.; and Moore, Harley L., Jr. "Child Abuse and Injury." *Military Medicine 130,* No. 8, 747-762, August, 1965. Presented before the 1964 Forensic Sciences Symposium at the Armed Forces Institute of Pathology, Washington, D.C.

Bakwin, Harry. "Multiple Skeletal Lesions in Young Children Due to Traumas," *Journal of Pediatrics 49.* No. 1, 7-16, July 1956.

Bakwin, Harry. "Report of the Meeting of the American Humane Society." *Newsletter* (American Academy of Pediatrics), 13, No. 8, 5 September-October 1962.

Barmeyer, G. H.; Anderson, L. R.; and Cox, W. B. "Traumatic Periostitis in Young Children," *Journal of Pediatrics 38,* No. 2, 184-190, February 1951.

Barta, R. A., Jr., and Smith, Nathan J. "Willful Trauma to Young Children." *Clinical Pediatrics* (Philadelphia) 2 (1963): 545-554.

Batinich, M. E. M. "How School Can Aid The Abused Child: Principal's Role Central in Protecting Children." Chicago School Journal, 46 (1964):57-62.

"The Battered Child." *Newsweek,* 71 (1968):68-69.

"Battered Child Cases." *America,* 110 (1964):559.

"Battered Child Syndrome." *America,* 116 (1967):236.

"Battered Child Syndrome." *Time,* 80 (1962):60.

"The Battered Child Syndrome." *Journal of the Louisiana Medical Society* 115 (1963):322-324.

"Battered Child Syndrome: Child Beating." *Time,* 80 (1962): 60.

"Battering Parent: Battered Child Syndrome." *Time,* 94 (1969): 77.

Bean, Shirley L. "The Parents' Center Project: A Multiservice Approach to the Prevention of Child Abuse." *Child Welfare,* 50 (1971):277-282.

Bechtold, M. L. "That Battered Child Could Be Dead Tomorrow." *Instructor,* 77 (1968):20.

Bechtold, Mary Lee. "Silent Partner to a Parent's Brutality." *School and Community,* 52 (1965):33.

Bilainkin, G. "Children In Peril." *Contemporary Review,* 201 (1962):67-71.

Billingsley, Andrew; Streshingsky, Noami; and Gurgin, Vonnie. "Agency Structure and the Commitment to Service." *Public Welfare,* 24 (1966):246-251.

Blue, M. T. "The Battered Child Syndrome from a Social Work View Point." *Canadian Journal of Public Health,* 56 (1965): 197-198.

Blumberg, Myrna. "When Parents Hit Out." *Twentieth Century* 173 (1964-65):39-44.

Boardman, Helen E. "A Project to Rescue Children from Inflicted Injuries." *Social Work 7,* No. 1, 43-51, January 1962.

Boehm, Bernice. "An Assessment of Family Adequacy in Protective Cases." *Child Welfare,* 41 (1962):11-16.

Boisvert, Maurice J. "Battered Child Syndrome." *Social Casework,* 53 (1972):475-480.

Branigan, Eileen, *et al.* "An Exploratory Study of the Neglected-Battered Child Syndrome." Boston College of Social Work, Boston, 1964. 149 pp.

Braun, Ida G.; Braun, Edgar J.; and Simonds, Charlotte. "The Mistreated Child." *California Medicine* 99 (1963):98-103.

Brown, Marsena, and Pappas, Margaret McCullough. "Eight Children with Suspected Inflicted Injury: A Follow-Up Pilot Study." Master's thesis, University of Southern California, School of Social Work, June 1965.

Bryant, Harold D., *et al.* "Physical Abuse of Children: An Agency Study." *Child Welfare* 42 (1963):125-130.

Buell, Bradley. "Is Prevention Possible?" Presented at National Conference on Social Welfare, 1959.

Buell, Bradley; Beisser, Paul T.; and Wedemeyer, John M. "Reorganizing to Prevent and Control Disordered Behavior." *Mental Hygiene* 42 (1958):155-194.

Butler, Raymon V. "Lend the Client an Ear." *Public Welfare,* 23 (1965):105-107.

Caffey, John. "Traumatic Lesions in Growing Bones other than Fractures and Dislocations–Clinical and Radiological Features; The MacKenzie Davidson Memorial Lecture." *British Journal of Radiology 30,* No. 353, 225-233, May 1957.

Caffey, John. *Journal of Pediatric X-ray Diagnosis.* Chicago: Year Book Publishers, Inc., 2nd ed., 684-687, 1950.

Caffey, John. "Significance of the History in the Diagnosis of Traumatic Injury to Children." *Journal of Pediatrics 67,* No. 5, 1008-1014, November 1965.

Caffey, John. "Infantile Cortical Hyperostosis." *Journal of Pediatrics* 29 (1946):541-559.

Caffey, John. "Multiple Fractures in the Long Bones of Infants Suffering From Chronic Subdural Hematoma." *American Journal of Roentgenology 56,* No. 2, 163-173, August 1946.

Chesser, Eustace. *Cruelty to Children.* New York: Philosophical Library, Inc., 1952. 169 pp.

"Child Abuse: An Anonymous Answer?" *Medical World News,* 12 (1971):6.

"Child Abuse and the Physician's Responsibility." *Postgraduate Medicine* 35 (1964):446.

(Editorial) "The Child Abuse Problem in Iowa. The Extent of the Problem, and a Proposal for Remedying It." *Journal of the Iowa State Medical Society* 53 (1963):692-694.

"Child Abuse: Syndrome in Search of a Cure." *Medical World News 6,* No. 41, 144-151, November 5, 1965.

Child Welfare League of America. "The Neglected Battered Child Syndrome, Role Reversal in Parents." July 1963. Compilation of articles.

"Children In Peril." *Nation,* 214 (1972):293-294.

Children's Bureau, Welfare Administration, U.S. Department of Health, Education, and Welfare. *The Abused Child–Principles and Suggested Language for Legislation on Reporting of the Physically Abused Child.* Washington, D.C. 20402: U.S. Government Printing Office, 1963. 13 pp.

Children's Division, American Humane Association. *Guidelines for Legislation to Protect the Battered Child.* American Humane Association, P.O. Box 1266, Denver, Colo., 1963. 10 pp.

Clarke, A. D. B., and Koluchova, J. "Severe Deprivation in Twins: A Case Study." *Journal of Child Psychology and Psychiatry,* 13 (1972):103-114.

Class, Norris E. "Neglect, Social Deviance and Community Action." *National Probation and Parole Association Journal 6,* No. 1, 17-23, January 1960.

Cochrone, W. "The Battered Child Syndrome." *Canadian Journal Of Public Health,* 65 (1965):193-4.

Coles, Robert. "Terror-Struck Children." *The New Republic,* May 30, 1964 pp. 11-13.

Committee on Infant and Pre-School Child. "Maltreatment of Children: The Physically Abused Child." *Pediatrics 37,* No. 2, pp. 377-382, February 1966.

Connell, John R., Jr. "The Devil's Battered Children: The Increasing Incidence of Willful Injuries to Children." *Journal of the Kansas Medical Society* 64 (1963):385-391.

Cooper, James T. "What Happens in Child Protection." *Canadian Welfare,* 38 (1962):66-69.

Corbett, James T. "A Psychiatrist Reviews the Battered Child Syndrome and Mandatory Reporting Legislation." *Northwest Medicine* 63 (1964):920-922.

"Cruelty to Children." *British Medical Journal* 5372 (1963): 1544-1545.

"Cry Rises From Beaten Babies." (Illustrated) *Life,* 54 (1963): 38-9.

Curphey, Theodore J.; Kade, Harold; Noguchi, Thomas T.; and Moore, Serge M. "The Battered Child Syndrome: Responsibilities of the Pathologist." *California Medicine* 102 (1965): 102-104.

Curtis, George C. "Violence Breeds Violence–Perhaps." *American Journal of Psychiatry* 120 (1963):386-387.

D'Ambrosio, R. "No Language But a Cry." *Good Housekeeping,* 171 (1970):64-67.

David, Lester. "The Shocking Price of Parental Anger." *Good Housekeeping,* 181-186, March 1964.

Davies, Joan. "When the Agency Must Intervene." *Public Welfare,* 23 (1965):102-105.

Davies, Joann E., and Jorgensen, James D. "Battered, But Not Defeated: The Story of an Abused Child and Positive Casework." *Child Welfare,* 49 (1970):101-104.

DeFrancis, Vincent. "Laws for Mandatory Reporting of Child Abuse Cases." *State Government 39,* No. 1, 8-13, Winter 1966.

DeFrancis, Vincent. *Review of Legislation to Protect the Battered Child: A Study of Laws Enacted in 1963.* Denver: Children's Division, American Humane Association, P.O. Box 1266, 1964. 22 pp.

DeFrancis, Vincent. *Child Abuse–Preview of a Nationwide Survey.* Denver: Children's Division, American Humane Association, P.O. Box 1266, 1963. 10 pp.

DeFrancis, Vincent. "Parents Who Abuse Children." *PTA Magazine 58,* No. 3, 16-18, November 1963.

DeFrancis, Vincent. "The Battered Child–A Role for the Juvenile Court, the Legislature, and the Child Welfare Agency." *Juvenile Court Judges Journal 14,* No. 2, June 1963.

DeFrancis, Vincent. *Protective Services and Community Expectations.* Denver: Children's Division, The American Humane Association, 1961.

DeFrancis, Vincent. *Child Protective Services in the United States.* Denver: Children's Division, The American Humane Association, P.O. Box 1266, 1956.

DeFrancis, Vincent. *The Fundamentals of Child Protection.* Children's Division, The American Humane Association, 1955.

Delsordo, James D. "Protective Casework for Abused Children." *Children 10,* No. 6, 213-218, November-December 1963.

Dine, Mark S. "Tranquilizer Poisoning: An Example of Child Abuse." *Pediatrics 36,* No. 5, 782-785, November 1965.

Dodge, Philip R. "Medical Implications of Physical Abuse of Children." *Protecting the Battered Child,* Children's Division. The American Humane Association, pp. 23-25, 1962.

Duncan, Glenn M.; Frazier, S. H.; Litin, E. M.; Johnson, A. M.; and Barron, A. J. "Etiological Factors in First-Degree Murder." *Journal of the American Medical Association 168,* No. 13, 1755-1758, November 29, 1958.

Earl, Howard G. "Ten Thousand Children Battered and Starved." *Today's Health,* September 1965, 24-31.

Eisenstein, Elliot M.; Delta, Basil G.; and Clifford, John H. "Jejunal Hematom: An Unusual Manifestation of the Battered Child Syndrome." *Clinical Pediatrics* 4 (1965):436-440.

Elmer, Elizabeth. "Abused Young Children Seen in Hospitals." *Social Work 5,* No. 4, 98-102, October 1960.

Elmer, Elizabeth. "Identification of Abused Children." *Children 10,* No. 5, 180-184, September-October 1963.

Elmer, Elizabeth. *Fifty Families Study: A Study of Abused and Neglected Children and Their Families* (Report covering period June 1, 1962-September 30, 1964). University of Pittsburgh School of Medicine, Pittsburgh, Pa., June 1965.

Erwin, Donald T. "The Battered Child Syndrome." *Medico-Legal Bulletin,* No. 130, 1-10, February 1964.

Fairburn, A. C. and Hunt, A. C. "Caffey's 'third syndrome'–A Critical Evaluation ('The Battered Baby')," *Medicine, Science and the Law* 4 (1964):123-126.

Feinstein, Howard N., *et al.* "Group Therapy for Mothers with Infanticidal Impulses." *American Journal of Psychiatry* 120 (1964):882-886.

Felder, Samuel. "A Lawyer's View of Child Abuse." *Public Welfare,* 29 (1971):181-188.

Ferguson, William M. "The Reporting of Child Abuse." *Bulletin of the Menninger Clinic 28,* No. 5, 269-270, September 1964.

Ferguson, William M. "Battered Child Syndrome. Attorney General's Opinion Regarding the Reporting of Such Occurrences." *Journal of the Kansas Medical Society* 65 (1964):67-69.

Finberg, Laurence. "A Pediatrician's View of the Abused Child." *Child Welfare 44,* No. 1, 41-43, January 1965.

Fisher, Samuel H. "Skeletal Manifestations of Parent-Induced Trauma in Infants and Children." *Southern Medical Journal* 51 (1958):956-960.

Flato, Charles. "Parents Who Beat Children." *Saturday Evening Post* 235 (1962):30-35.

Fontana, Vincent J. "Which Parents Abuse Children?" *Medical Insight,* 16 (1971):18-21.

Fontana, Vincent J. "The Neglect and Abuse of Children." *New York State Journal of Medicine* 64 (1964):215-224.

Fontana, Vincent J. "An Insidious and Disturbing Medical Entity." *Public Welfare,* 24 (1966):235-239.

Fontana, Vincent J. *The Maltreated Child: the Maltreatment Syndrome in Children.* Springfield, Ill.: Charles C. Thomas, 1964. 67 pp.

Fontana, Vincent J.; Donovan, Denis; and Wong, Raymond J. "The Maltreatment Syndrome in Children." *New England Journal of Medicine 269,* No. 26, 1389-1394, December 26, 1963.

Foster, H. "Battered Child Legal and Professional Immunity." *American Bar Association Journal,* 52 (1966):1071-1073.

Foster, H., and Freed, Doris Jonas. "Battered Child Legislation and Professional Immunity." *American Bar Association Journal* 199 (1967):65-8.

Franklin, Lee R. "An Exception to Use of the Physician-Patient Privilege in Child Abuse Cases." *University of Detroit Law Journal* 42 (1964):88-94.

Freeman, C. B. "Children's Petition of 1669 and Its Sequel." *British Journal of Educational Studies,* 14 (1966):216-223.

Friedman, Morris. "Traumatic Periostitis in Infants and Children." *Journal of the American Medical Association 166,* No. 15, 1840-1845, April 12, 1958.

Fruchtl, Gertrude, and Brodeur, A. E. "The Battered Child, Know Enough to Care–Care Enough to Know." *The Catholic World,* 209 (1969):156-159.

Fulk, Delores Leusby. "The Battered Child." *Nursing Forum* 3 (1964):10-26.

Galdston, Richard. "Observations on Children Who Have Been Physically Abused and Their Parents." *American Journal of Psychiatry 122,* No. 4, 440-443, October 1965.

Gardner, S. W. "Abused Child." *McCall's,* 94 (1967):96-97.

Gil, David G. "Sociocultural Perspective on Physical Child Abuse." *Child Welfare,* 50 (1971):389-395.

Gil, David G. "What Schools Can Do About Child Abuse." *American Education,* 5 (1969):2-4.

Gil, David G. Violence Against Children. Cambridge: Harvard University Press, 1970. 204 pp.

Gil, Thomas D. "The Legal Nature of Neglect." *National Probation and Parole Association Journal 6*, No. 1, 1-16, January 1960.

Giovannoni, J. M. "Parental Mistreatment: Perpetrators and Victims." (Bibliography) *Journal of Marriage and the Family*, 33 (1971):649-57.

Giovannoni, Jeanne M., and Billingsley, Andrew. "Child Neglect Among the Poor: A Study of Parental Adequacy in Families of Three Ethnic Groups." *Child Welfare*, 49 (1970):196-204.

Gordon, Alex. "A Child is Being Beaten." *Physicians Management*, June 1965, pp. 22-34.

Greene, K. "Diagnosing the Battered Child Syndrome." *Maryland State Medical Journal* 14 (1965):83-84.

Greene, Nancy B. *Identifying the Battered or Molested Child.* Palo Alto Unified School District, January 1972.

Greengard, Joseph. "The Battered Child Syndrome." *American Journal of Nursing* 64·(1964):98-100.

Griffiths, D. L., and Moynihan, F. J. "Multiple Epiphysial Injuries in Babies ('Battered Baby' Syndrome)." *British Medical Journal*, No. 5372, 1558-1561, December 21, 1963.

Gwinn, John L.; Lewin, Kenneth W.; and Peterson, Herbert G., Jr. "Roentgenographic Manifestations of Unsuspected Trauma in Infancy." *Journal of the American Medical Association 176*, No. 11, 926-929, June 17, 1961.

Haas, L. "Injured Baby." *British Medical Journal* 5462 (1965):645.

Hammell, Charlotte L. "Preserving Family Life for Our Children." *Child Welfare*, 48 (1966):591-594.

Hancock, Claire. *Children and Neglect...Hazardous Home Conditons.* Bureau of Family Services, Welfare Administration, U.S. Department of Health, Education, and Welfare. Washington, D.C. 20402: U.S. Government Printing Office, 1963. 59 pp.

Harper, Fowler V. "The Physician, the Battered Child, and the Law." *Pediatrics 31*, No. 6, 899-902, June 1963.

Hearing Before Subcommittee No. 3 of the Committee on the District of Columbia, House of Representatives, Eighty-ninth Congress, First Session, on H.R. 3394, H.R. 3411, and H.R. 3814 "To provide for the Mandatory Reporting by Physicians and Institutions in the District of Columbia of Certain Physical Abuse of Children," June 10, 1965. Washington, D.C.: U.S. Government Printing Office, 1965.

Helfer, Ray E. "A Plan for Protection: The Child Abuse Center." *Child Welfare*, 49 (1970):486-494.

Helfer, Ray E., and Kempe, C. Henry. *The Battered Child.* Chicago. University of Chicago Press, 1968.

Helfer, Ray E., and Wheeler, John S. "Child Abuse and the Private Pediatrician." *Feelings*, 14 (1972):1-4.

"Help for Child Beaters." *Newsweek*, 80 (1972):66, 69.

"Helping Physicians Protect Children; Illinois Law to Exempt Physicians from Libel Suits by Parents." *Christian Century*, 82 (1965):516.

Herre, Ernest A. "A Community Mobilizes to Protect Its Children." *Public Welfare*, 23 (1965):93-97.

Hill, Esther P. "Child Neglect, Maltreatment, and Trauma: Three Views." Presented at Training Center in Youth Development, Law-Medicine Institute, Boston University, November 13, 1964.

Holter, Jane C., and Friedman, Stanford B. *Principles of Management in Child Abuse Cases ("Battered Child Syndrome")*, (Mimeographed report covering period December 1963-December 1965). Departments of Medical Social Service, Pediatrics, and Psychiatry, University of Rochester Medical Center, Rochester, N.Y., 1966.

Housden, Leslie George. *The Prevention of Cruelty to Children*, New York: Philosophical Library, Inc., 1956.

Ireland, William H. "A Registry in Child Abuse." *Children*, 13 (1966):113-115.

Jacobziner, Harold. "Rescuing the Battered Child." *American Journal of Nursing* 64 (1964):92-97.

Johnson, Betty, and Morse, Harold A. "Injured Children and their Parents." *Children*, 15 (1968):147-152.

Jones, Henry H., and Davis, Joseph H. "Multiple Traumatic Lesions of the Infant Skeleton." *Stanford Medical Bulletin 15*, No. 3, 259-273, August 1957.

Joyce, W. C.; Haynes, E.; and Gardner, T. G. "Child Molested At Home." *Instructor*, 79 (1970):35.

Kaplan, Morris. "Deaths of Young Studied by City." *New York Times*, May 5, 1962.

Kaufman, Irving. "Discussion of Physical Abuse of Children." Paper read at the National Conference on Social Welfare, sponsored by the Children's Division, American Humane Association, June 1, 1962, New York, N.Y.

Kaufman, Irving. "Psychiatric Implications of Physical Abuse of Children." *Protecting the Battered Child.* Denver: Children's Division. The American Humane Association, P.O. Box 1266, pp. 17-22, 1962.

Kaufman, Irving; Frank, Thomas; Heims, Lora; Herrick, Joan; and Willer, Lee. "Four Types of Defense in Mothers and Fathers of Schizophrenic Children." *American Journal of Orthopsychiatry*, 29 (1959):460-472.

Kelly, Joseph B. "What Protective Services Can Do." *Child Welfare*, 38 (1959):21-25.

Kempe, Henry; Silver, Henry; and Brien, Donough. "Current Pediatric Diagnosis and Treatment." *Lange Medical Publication*, Los Altos, California, pp. 718-722, 1964.

Kempe, C. Henry; Silverman, Frederic N.; Steele, Brandt F.; Droegemueller, William; and Silver, Henry K. "The Battered-Child Syndrome." *Journal of American Medical Association*, 181 (1962):105-112.

Kempe, C. Henry, *et al.* "The Battered-Child Syndrome." *Journal of the American Medical Association 181*, No. 1, 17-24, July 7, 1962.

Koluchova, Clarke J. "Severe Deprivation in Twins: a Case

Study" (with comments by A. D. B.). *Journal of Child Psychology and Psychiatry,* 13 (1972):103-14.

Leavitt, Jerome E. "The Battered Child." *The Instructor,* 75 (1966):50, 142, 150.

Leiken, Sanford L., *et al.* "Clinical Pathological Conference: The Battered Child Syndrome." *Clinical Proceedings of Children's Hospital,* (Washington, D.C.) 19 (1963):301-306.

Lesermann, Sidney. "There's a Murderer in My Waiting Room." *Medical Economics 41,* No. 17, 62-71, August 24, 1964.

"Mandatory Reporting of Injuries Inflicted by Other than Accidental Means Upon Children Under the Age of Eighteen Years." Legislation passed at the January 1964 session of the Rhode Island General Assembly, **Rhode Island Medical Journal,** 47 (1964):398-399.

McCloskey, Kenneth D. "Torts: Parental Liability to a Minor Child for Injuries Caused by Excessive Punishment." *Hastings Law Journal,* 11 (1960):335-340.

McCoid, Allan H. "The Battered Child and Other Assaults Upon the Family: Part One." *Minnesota Law Review 50,* No. 1, 1-58, November 1968.

McCort, James, *et al.* "Visceral Injuries in Battered Children." *Radiology* 82 (1964):424-428.

McHenry, Thomas; Girdany, Bertram R.; and Elmer, Elizabeth. "Unsuspected Trauma With Multiple Skeletal Injuries During Infancy and Childhood." *Pediatrics 31,* No. 6, 903-908, June 1963.

Merrill, Edgar J. "Physical Abuse of Children—An Agency Study." *Protecting the Battered Child.* Denver: Children's Division. The American Humane Association, P.O. Box 1266, pp. 1-15, 1962.

Merrill, Edgar J. "Physical Abuse of Children." Paper read at National Conference on Social Welfare, New York, May 31, 1962 (unpublished).

Miller, Donald S. "Fractures Among Children." *Minnesota Medicine 42,* No. 9, 1209-1213, September 1959; *42,* No. 10, 1414-1415, October 1959.

Miller, Merle K., and Fay, Henry J. "Emergency Child Care Service." *Child Welfare,* 48 (1969):496-499.

Milowe, Irvin D., and Lourie, Reginald S. "The Battered Child Syndrome: Some Unanswered Questions and Some Variations on the Theme." Workshop paper presented at American Orthopsychiatric Association Meeting, March 1964.

Milowe, Irvin D., and Lourie, Reginald S. "The Child's Role in the Battered Child Syndrome." *Journal of Pediatrics 65,* No. 6, 1079-1081, December 1964.

Milowe, Irvin D., and Lourie, Reginald S. *Some Provocative and Controversial Mental Health Problems Posed by the Battered Child Syndrome.* National Institute of Mental Health publication 1245, 70-76, 1964.

Mintz, A. A. "Battered Child Syndrome." *Texas Journal of Medicine* 60 (1964):107-108.

Mitchiner, Myra J. "Providing Preventive and Protective Services to Children in a Public Welfare Agency." *Child Welfare,* 45 (1966):224-227.

Moorehead, C. "Seven-Man Team Helps Parents of Battered Babies." *Times Educational Supplement,* 2897:12, November 27, 1970.

(Editorial) "More on the Battered Child." *New England Journal of Medicine 269,* No. 26, 1436, December 26, 1963.

Morris, Marian G.; Gould, Robert W.; and Matthews, Patricia J. "Toward Prevention of Child Abuse." *Children 11,* No. 2, 55-60, March-April 1964.

Morris, Marian G., and Gould, Robert W. "Role Reversal: A Necessary Concept in Dealing with the 'Battered Child Syndrome'." *American Journal of Orthopsychiatry 33,* No. 2, 298-299, March 1963. Reprinted in *The Neglected Battered Child Syndrome,* New York: Child Welfare League of America, July 1963. 49 pp.

"Mother Confines Three To House for Ten Years." *Life,* 49, No. 9, August 29, 1960, 29-30.

Myren, Richard A., and Swanson, Lynn D. *Police Work with Children.* Children's Bureau, Welfare Administration, U.S. Department of Health, Education, and Welfare. Washington, D.C. 20402: U.S. Government Printing Office, 1962. 106 pp.

The Neglected Battered Child Syndrome. New York: Child Welfare League of America, 1963.

New Jersey. Senate. Child Abuse Study Committee. *Public Hearing Held*: Trenton, New Jersey, March 26, 1971. State House, Trenton, New Jersey 08625.

New York, New York Mayor's Task Force on Child Abuse and Neglect. *Final Report.* Theo Solomon *et al.* 1971. Center for Community Research, 33 W. Goth Street, New York 10023.

Nurse, Shirley M. "Familial Patterns of Parents Who Abuse Their Children." *Smith College Studies in Social Work* 35 (1964):11-25.

Nyden, Paul V. "The Use of Authority." *Public Welfare,* 24 (1966):239-245, 252.

O'Doherty, N. J. "Subdural Haematoma in Battered Babies." *Developmental Medicine and Child Neurology* 6 (1964):192-193.

Oettinger, Katherine B. "The Abused Child." *Childhood Education,* 41 (1965):235-237.

Oettinger, Katherine B. "Protecting Children from Abuse." *Parents 39,* No. 11, 12, November 1964.

Ott, John F. "Neglected or Physically Abused Children," *Journal of the South Carolina Medical Association* 60 (1964):309-315.

Page, Miriam O. "Cohesion, Dignity, and Hope for Multi-problem Families." *Children,* 8 (1961):63-68.

"Parent Accused of Child Beating May Not Claim the Doctor-Patient Privilege to Present Medical Testimony—Opinion No. 63-80 dated September 24, 1963 and signed by William M. Ferguson, Attorney General," *Kansas Law Review 12* (1964): 467-469.

Parker, G. E. "The Battered Child Syndrome." (The Problem in the United States) *Medicine, Science, and the Law* 5 (1965): 160-163.

Paulsen, Monrad G.; Parker, Graham; and Adelman, Lynn. "Child Abuse Reporting Laws—Some Legislative History." *The George Washington Law Review 34*, No. 3, 482-506, March, 1966.

Paulsen, Monrad G. "Legal Framework of Child Protection." *Columbia Law Review 66*, No. 4, April 1966.

Paulsen, Monrad G. "Legal Protections Against Child Abuse." *Children 13*, No. 2, 42-48, March-April 1966.

Paulsen, Monrad G. "Child Abuse Reporting Laws: the Shape of the Legislation." *Columbia Law Review*, 67 (1967):1-49.

Pfundt, Theodore R. "The Problem of the Battered Child." *Postgraduate Medicine* 35 (1964):426-431.

"Physical Abuse of Children." *Suggested State Legislation* (Council of State Governments) 24 (1965):66-68.

(Editorial) "Physicians Required to Report Child Beatings." *Minnesota Medicine* 46 (1963):376.

Platou, Ralph V. "Battering." *Bulletin of the Tulane Medical Faculty* 23 (1964):157-165.

Polansky, N. A., *et al.* "Two Modes of Maternal Immaturity and Their Consequences; Neglected or Marginal Care." *Child Welfare*, 49 (1970):312-323.

Polansky, Norman A.; Borgman, Robert D.; De Saix, Christine; and Sharlin, Shiomo. "Verbal Accessibility in the Treatment of Child Neglect." *Child Welfare*, 50 (1971):349-356.

Polomeque, F. E., *et al.* " 'Battered Child' Syndrome: Unusual Dermatological Manifestation." *Archives of Dermatology* 90 (1964):326-327.

Potts, William E., and Forbis, O. L. "Willful Injury in Childhood—A Distinct Syndrome." *Journal of the Arkansas Medical Society* 59 (1962):266-270.

Protecting the Battered Child. Denver: Children's Division. The American Humane Association, 1962.

Rall, Mary E. "The Casework Process in Work with the Child and the Family in the Child's Own Home." *National Conference of Social Work, Casework Papers, 1954*, 31-43, 1955.

Rein, Martin. *Child Protective Services in Massachusetts.* Waltham: Florence Heller Graduate School for Advanced Studies in Social Welfare, Brandeis University, November 1963. 171 pp.

Reinhart, John B., *et al.* "The Abused Child: Mandatory Reporting Legislation." *Journal of the American Medical Association* 133 (1964):358-362.

Reinitz, Freda G. "Special Registration Project on the Abused Child." *Child Welfare 44*, No. 2, 103-105, February 1965.

Report of National Agencies Workshop in Child Protective Services. Denver: Children's Division, The American Humane Association, 1957.

"The Reporting of Child Abuse," *Bulletin of the Menninger Clinic* 28 (1964):271-272.

Riese, Herta *Heal the Hurt Child.* Chicago: University of Chicago Press, 1962.

Rhymes, Julina P. "Working with Mothers and Babies Who Fail to Thrive." *American Journal of Nursing*, 66 (1966):1972-1976.

Roaf, Robert. "Trauma in Early Childhood." *British Medical Journal*, 1 (1965):1541-1543.

Rochester, Dean E., Ellis, Mary Ann; and Sciortina, Sam C. "What Can the Schools Do About Child Abuse?" *Today's Education*, 57:59-60, 1968.

Rubin, Jean. "The Battered Child." *Wellesley Alumnae Magazine 50*, No. 3, 8-9, March 1966.

Rubin, Jean. "The Need for Intervention." *Public Welfare*, 24 (1966):230-235.

Russell, Patricia. "Subdural Hematomas in Infancy." *Medical Science*, 15 (1964):82-91.

Sandusky, Annie Lee. "Services to Neglected Children." *Children 7*, No. 1, 23-28, January-February 1960.

Sattin, Dana B., and Miller, John K. "The Ecology of Child Abuse Within A Military Community." *American Journal of Orthopsychiatry*, 41 (1971):675-678.

Sauer, L. W. "Problems of Teen-age Parents." *PTA Magazine*, 59 (1964):27-28.

"Saving Battered Children." *Time*, 85 (1965):43.

Schachter, M. "Contribution to the Clinical and Psychological Study of Mistreated Children; Physical and Moral Cruelty." *Giornale di Psichiatriae di Neuropatologia (Ferrara) 80*, No. 3, 311-317, 1952.

Schleyer, F., and Pioch, W. "Fatal Outcome by Crush Syndrome After Continuous Beatings of a Child." *Monatsschrist fur Kinderjeilkunde 105*, No. 10, 392-394, October 1957.

Schloesser, Patricia T. "The Abused Child." *Bulletin of the Menninger Clinic 28*, No. 5, 260-268, September 1964.

Schmidt, Delores M. "The Challenge of Helping the 'Untreatable.' " *Public Welfare*, 23 (1965):98-102.

Schoepfer, Arthur E. "Legal Implications in Connection with Physical Abuse of Children." *Protecting the Battered Child.* Denver: Children's Division. The American Humane Association, P.O. Box 1266, pp. 26-30, 1962.

Schrotel, S. R. "Responsibilities of Physicians in Suspected Cases of Brutality." *Cincinnati Journal of Medicine 42*, No. 10, 406-407, October 1961.

Seminar on the Battered Child Syndrome, Casebook and Proceedings, Sponsored by: Community Mental Health Services, Division of Institutional Management, State Department of Social Welfare, Topeka, Kansas, January 21, 1965.

Shade, Delores A. "Limits to Service in Child Abuse." *American Journal of Nursing*, 69 (1969):1710-1712.

Shaffer, Helen B. "Child Abuse: Search for Remedies," *Editorial Research Reports 1*, No. 18, 343-359, May 12, 1965.

Shaw, Anthony. "The Surgeon and the Battered Child." *Surgery, Gynecology and Obstetrics* 119 (1964):355.

Shaw, Anthony. "How to Help the Battered Child." *RISS* (National Magazine for Residents, Internes, and Senior Students published by *Medical Economics*) 6, No. 12, 71-104, December 1963.

"Shelter: Children's Center Deluged with Child Abuse Cases." *New Yorker*, 45 (1969):21-22.

Sherriff, Hilla. "The Abused Child," *Journal of the South Carolina Medical Association 60*, 191-193, June 1964.

Shepherd, Robert E., Jr. "The Abused Child and the Law." *Virginia Medical Monthly* 93 (1966):3-6.

Shepherd, Robert E., Jr. "The Battered Child and the Law." *Washington and Lee Law Review* 22 (1965):180-195.

Silver, Henry K., and Kempe, C. Henry. "The Problem of Parental Criminal Neglect and Severe Physical Abuse of Children." Paper read at annual meetings of the American Pediatric Society, May 1959. *American Journal of Diseases of Children 98*, No. 4, 528, October 1959.

Silver, Larry B.; Barton, William, and Dublin, Christina C. "Child Abuse Laws—Are They Enough?" *American Medical Association Journal*, 199 (1967):65-68.

Silver, Larry B.; Dublin, Christina C.; and Lourie, Reginald S. "Agency Action and Interaction in Cases of Child Abuse." *Social Casework*, 52 (1971):164-171.

Silverman, F. N. "The Battered Child." *Manitoba Medical Review* 45 (1965):473-477.

Silverman, F. N. "Unrecognized Trauma—A Medical-Social Problem." Presented at Detroit Children's Alumni Association, April 1958.

Silverman, F. N. "The Roentgen Manifestations of Unrecognized Skeletal Trauma in Infants." *American Journal of Roentgenology, Radium Therapy and Nuclear Medicine 69*, No. 3, 413-427, March 1953.

Simons, Betty; Downs, Elinor F.; Hurster, Madeline M.; and Archer, Morton. *Child Abuse: A Perspective on Legislation in Five Middle-Atlantic States, and a Survey of Reported Cases in New York City*. Report by Columbia University School of Public Health and Administrative Medicine, New York, N.Y., February 1966.

Smith, Austin E. "The Beaten Child." *Hygeia* 22 (1944):386.

Snedeker, Lendon. "Traumatization of Children." *New England Journal of Medicine* 267 (1962):572.

Stallones, Renel A.; Corsa, Leslie, Jr. "Childhood Accidents in Two California Counties." *Public Health Reports*, January, 1961.

Standards for Child Protective Service. Child Welfare League of America Committee on Standards for Child Protective Service. New York: Child Welfare League of America, 1960.

Storey, Bruce. "The Battered Child," *Medical Journal of Australia* 2 (1964):789-791.

Stringer, Elizabeth A. "Homemaker Service in Neglect and Abuse: II. A Tool for Case Evaluation." *Children 12*, No. 1, 26-29, January-February 1965.

Sullivan, Eugene, *et al.* "Symposium: Battered Child Syndrome." *Clinical Proceedings of Children's Hospital* (Washington, D.C.) 20 (1964):229-239.

Swanson, Lynn D. "Role of Police in the Protection of Children From Neglect and Abuse." *Federal Probation 25*, No. 1, 43-48, March 1961.

Ten Bensel, Robert W., and Raile, R. B. "The Battered Child Syndrome." *Minnesota Medicine* 46 (1963):977-982.

Teng, Ching-tseng; Singleton, Edward B.; and Daeschner, C. W., Jr. "Skeletal Injuries of the Battered Child." *American Journal of Orthopedics* 6 (1964):202-207.

Tenhave, Ralph. "A Preventive Approach to Problems of Child Abuse and Neglect." *Michigan Medicine 64*, No. 9, 645-649, September 1965.

"Their Prison Was Home." *Newsweek*, 56, No. 6, August 8, 1960, 43.

Thomas, Mason P., Jr. "Child Abuse Cases—A Complex Problem." *State Government*, October 1965.

Tocchio, O. J. "Procedural Problems Inhibiting Effective County and Community-Wide Resolution of Battered Child Problems." *Police*, 14 (1970):16-21.

Toland, Marjorie. "Abuse of Children—Whose Responsibility?" *Connecticut Medicine* 28 (1964):438-442.

U.S. Children's Bureau. *The Child Abuse Reporting Laws: A Tabular View*. Washington, D.C., Superintendent of Documents, 1967.

U.S. House. Committee on the District of Columbia. Subcommittee No. 3. Reporting physical abuse of children; hearing. June 10, 1965, on H.R. 3394, 3411, and 3814, to provide for the mandatory reporting by physicians and institutions in the District of Columbia of certain physical abuses of children. (89th Congress, 1st session).

U.S. Senate Committee of Labor and Public Welfare. Subcommittee on Children and Youth. *Rights of Children: 1972:* Hearing: part 1, January 25, 1972.

Vaughn, M. "Hungry Children Scavenge in Portsmouth Dustbins." 2911 (1971):3.

Walton, Cynthia. "The Battered Baby Syndrome." *New Statesman*, 72 (1966):348.

Wasserman, Sidney. "The Abused Parent of the Abused Child." *Children*, 14 (1967):175-179.

"Welfare of Children." *British Medical Journal* 5360 (1963): 761-762.

"When They're Angry." *Newsweek*, 59 (1962):74.

Whitehorn, K. "C and A." *Spectator,* 206 (1961):775-6.

"Willful Injuries to Children." *What's New* (Abbott Laboratories), No. 228, Summer 1962.

Wilson, J. B., Jr. "The Battered Child Act—A Summary and Analysis," Res Gestae (Indiana State Bar Association Journal) *9,* No. 6, 9-10, June 1965.

Wilson, Thelma Garrett. *Ventura Ventures Into Child Protective Services.* Denver: Children's Division, The American Humane Association.

Winking, Cyril H. "Coping With Child Abuse: One State's Experience." *Public Welfare,* 26 (1968):189-192.

Woolley, Paul V., Jr. "The Pediatrician and the Young Child Subjected to Repeated Physical Abuse." *Journal of Pediatrics* 62 (1963):628-630.

Woolley, Paul V., Jr. and Evans, W. A., Jr. "Significance of Skeletal Lesions in Infants Resembling Those of Traumatic Origin." *Journal of the American Medical Association 158,* No. 7, 539-543, June 18, 1955.

Wurfel, L. J., *et al.* "Radiographic Features of the Battered Child Syndrome." *Journal of the College of Radiologists of Australia* 9 (1965):220-223.

Young, Leontine. *Wednesday's Children: A Study of Child Neglect and Abuse.* New York: McGraw Hill, 1964. 193 pp.

Zalba, S. R. "Battered Children." *Science Digest,* 70 (1971): 8-13.

Zauner, Phyllis. "Mothers Anonymous: the Last Resort." *McCall's,* 99 (1972):57.

Ziering, William. "The Battered Baby Syndrome." *Journal of Pediatrics* 65 (1964):321-322.

INDEX

ACKNOWLEDGEMENTS

We wish to acknowledge permission to reprint the materials contained in this collection from the following sources.

"10,000 Children Battered and Starved. " Howard G. Earl. *Today's Health*, September 1965.

"The Battered-Child Syndrome." C. Henry Kempe, Frederic N. Silverman, Brandt F. Steele, William Droegemueller, and Henry K. Silver. *Journal of the American Medical Association*, July 7, 1962.

"Unsuspected Trauma with Multiple Skeletal Injuries During Infancy and Childhood." Thomas McHenry, Bertram R. Girdany, and Elizabeth Elmer. *Pediatrics*, June 1963.

"Injured Children and their Parents." Betty Johnson and Harold A. Morse. *Children*, July-August 1968.

"Identification of Abused Children." Elizabeth Elmer. *Children*, September-October 1963.

"Hazards in Determining Child Abuse." Elizabeth Elmer. *Child Welfare*, January 1966.

"Emergency Child Care Service: The Evaluation of a Project." Merle K. Miller and Henry J. Fay. *Child Welfare*, October 1969.

"Preserving Family Life for Children." Charlotte L. Hammell. *Child Welfare*, December 1969.

"Protective Casework for Abused Children." James D. Delsordo. *Children*, November-December 1963.

"Observations on Children Who Have Been Physically Abused and Their Parents." Richard Galdston. *The American Journal of Psychiatry*, October 1965.

"The Parents' Center Project: A Multiservice Approach to the Prevention of Child Abuse." Shirley L. Bean. *Child Welfare*, May 1971.

"Group Therapy for Mothers with Infanticidal Impulses." Howard M. Feinstein, Norman Paul, and Pattison Esmiol. *The American Journal of Psychiatry*, March 1964.

"Verbal Accessibility in the Treatment of Child Neglect." Norman A. Polansky, Robert D. Borgman, Christine De Saix, and Shlomo Sharlin. *Child Welfare*, June 1971.

"Violence Breeds Violence — Perhaps?" George C. Curtis. *The American Journal of Psychiatry*, October 1963.

"A Lawyer's View of Child Abuse." Samuel Felder. *Public Welfare*, Spring 1971.

"The Physician, The Battered Child, and The Law." Fowler V. Harper. *Pediatrics*, June 1963.

"Legal Protections Against Child Abuse." Monrad G. Paulsen. *Children*, March-April 1966.

"Child Abuse Laws — Are They Enough?" Larry B. Silver, William Barton, and Christina C. Dublin. *The Journal of the American Medical Association*, January 9, 1967.

"Laws for Mandatory Reporting of Child Abuse Cases." Vincent De Francis. *State Government*, Winter 1966.

"Role of the Police in the Protection of Children From Neglect and Abuse." Lynn D. Swanson. *Federal Probation*, March 1961.

"Procedural Problems Inhibiting Effective County and Community-Wide Resolution of Battered Child Problems." O. J. Tocchio. *Police*, May-June 1970. Charles C. Thomas, publisher, Springfield, Illinois.

"The Use of Authority." Paul V. Nyden. *Public Welfare*, July 1966. The American Public Welfare Association.

"Cohesion, Dignity, and Hope for Multiproblem Families." Miriam O. Page. *Children*, March-April 1961.

"The Battered-Child Syndrome." Maurice J. Boisvert. *Social Casework*, October 1972. The Family Service Association of America.

"Agency Structure and the Commitment to Service." Andrew Billingsley, Naomi Streshinsky, and Vonnie Gurgin. *Public Welfare*, July 1966.

"Services to Neglected Children." Annie Lee Sandusky. *Children*, January-February 1960.

"Homemaker Service in Neglect and Abuse: A Tool for Case Evaluation." Elizabeth Stringer. *Children*, January-February 1965.

"Providing Preventive and Protective Services to Children in a Public Welfare Agency." Myra J. Mitchiner. *Child Welfare*, April 1966.

"A Sociocultural Perspective on Physical Child Abuse." David G. Gil. *Child Welfare*, July 1971.

"Child Neglect Among the Poor: A Study of Parental Adequacy in Families of Three Ethnic Groups." Jeanne M. Giovannoni and Andrew Billingsley. *Child Welfare*, April 1970.

"The Physically Abused Child." Katherine Bain. *Pediatrics*, June 1963.

"An Insidious and Disturbing Medical Entity." Vincent J. Fontana. *Public Welfare*, July 1966.

"Trauma in Childhood." Robert Roaf. *British Medical Journal*, June 12, 1965.

"Which Parents Abuse Children?" Vincent J. Fontana. *Medical Insight*, October 1971.

"Child Abuse and the Private Pediatrician." Ray E. Helfer and John S. Wheeler. *Feelings and their Medical Significance*, May-June 1972. Ross Laboratories, publisher.

"The Battered Child." Jerome E. Leavitt. *The Instructor*, March 1966. The Instructor Publications, Inc.

"The Abused Child." Katherine B. Oettinger. *Childhood Education*, January 1965. The Association for Childhood Development Education International, 3615 Wisconsin Avenue, N.W.,Washington, D.C.

"What Can the Schools Do About Child Abuse." Dean E. Rochester with Mary Ann Ellis and Sam C. Sciortino. *Today's Education*, September 1968.

"What Schools Can Do About Child Abuse." David G. Gil. *American Education*, April 1969.

Guidelines for Schools / Teachers, Nurses, Counselors, Administrators / To Help Protect Neglected and Abused Children. The American Humane Association, 1971.

Identifying the Battered or Molested Child. Nancy B. Greene, Supervising Probation Officer, Santa Clara County. Palo Alto Unified School District, January 1972.

"Toward Prevention of Child Abuse." Marian G. Morris, Robert W. Gould, and Patricia J. Matthews. *Children*, March-April 1964.

"The Need for Intervention." Jean Rubin. *Public Welfare*, July 1966.

"Coping with Child Abuse: One State's Experience." Cyril H. Winking. *Public Welfare*, July 1968.

"Mothers Anonymous: the Last Resort." Phyllis Zauner. *McCall's*, January 1972.

"The Abused Parent of the Abused Child." Sidney Wasserman. *Children*, September-October 1967.